Frontiers of Evolutionary Economics

Frontiers of Evolutionary Economics

Competition, Self-Organization and Innovation Policy

Edited by
John Foster

Professor of Economics and Head of the School of Economics,
The University of Queensland,
Brisbane, Australia

and

J. Stanley Metcalfe

Stanley Jevons Professor of Economics
and Co-Director,
ESRC Centre for Research on Innovation and Competition,
University of Manchester, UK

Edward Elgar
Cheltenham, UK • Northampton, MA, USA

Published by
Edward Elgar Publishing Limited
Glensanda House
Montpellier Parade
Cheltenham
Glos GL50 1UA
UK

Edward Elgar Publishing, Inc.
136 West Street
Suite 202
Northampton
Massachusetts 01060
USA

A catalogue record for this book
is available from the British Library

Library of Congress Cataloguing in Publication Data
Frontiers of evolutionary economics : competition, self-organization, and innovation policy / edited by John Foster and J. Stanley Metcalfe.
Based on papers and commentaries from a workshop held at the University of Queensland in Brisbane, Australia, in July 1999.
Includes index.
1. Evolutionary economics. 2. Rational expectations (Economic theory) 3. Economic development. I. Foster, John, 1947–. II. Metcalfe, J. S. (J. Stanley)

HB97.3 .F76 2001
330—dc21

00–046640

ISBN 1 8 4064 525 3

Typeset by Manton Typesetters, Louth, Lincolnshire, UK.
Printed and bound in Great Britain by MPG Books Ltd, Bodmin, Cornwall.

Contents

Contributors

Professor Peter M. Allen, Director of the ESRC Sustainable Complex Systems Network (NEXSUS), Director of the Complex Systems Management Centre, School of Management, Cranfield University, Bedford, UK.

Dr Kevin Bryant, Director, Science and Technology Analysis Section, Department of Industry, Science and Resources (ISR), Canberra, Australia.

Dr Uwe Cantner, Department of Economics, University of Augsburg, Augsburg, Germany.

Professor Robert Delorme, Université de Versailles and CEPREMAP, Paris, France.

Professor Kurt Dopfer, Department of Economics, University of St Gallen, St Gallen, Switzerland.

Professor John Foster, Head, Department of Economics, The University of Queensland, Brisbane, Australia.

Professor John M. Gowdy, Department of Economics, School of Humanities & Social Sciences, Rensselaer Polytechnic Institute, New York, USA.

Professor Horst Hanusch, School of Economics, University of Augsburg, Augsburg, Germany.

Dr Steve Keen, Department of Economics & Finance, University of Western Sydney–Macarthur, New South Wales, Australia.

Dr Francisco Louçã, Instituto Superior de Economia e Gest,,o da Universidade Tècnica de Lisboa, Lisbon, Portugal.

Professor J. Stanley Metcalfe, Stanley Jevons Professor of Economics and Co-Director of the ESRC Centre for Research on Innovation and Competition and the School of Economic Studies, University of Manchester, UK.

Bryan Morgan, Department of Banking and Finance, University of Southern Queensland, Toowoomba, Australia.

Professor Richard R. Nelson, George Blumenthal Professor of International and Public Affairs, Business and Law, Department of Economics, Columbia University, USA.

Dr John Nightingale, School of Economic Studies, University of New England, Armidale, Australia.

Professor Bart Nooteboom, Faculty of Management and Organization, Erasmus University, Rotterdam, The Netherlands.

Dr Pavel Pelikan, IUI, Stockholm, Sweden.

Dr Jason Potts, School of Economics, The University of Queensland, Brisbane, Australia.

Dr Paolo Ramazzotti, Department of Economics, University of Macerata, Macerata, Italy.

Professor Paolo Saviotti, Director, Institut National de la Recherche Agronomique (INRA-SERD), Université Pierre Mendès-France, Grenoble, France.

Dr Drew Wollin, School of Management, The University of Queensland, Brisbane, Australia.

Preface

Modern evolutionary economics is now roughly two decades old and, in 1999, we decided that it was time to reflect upon what has been achieved and to explore the new directions that research in this field is likely to take in the new millennium. To this end, we decided to organize an intensive international workshop to evaluate 'work in progress' and to highlight the 'frontier' issues that now confront evolutionary economists. We invited a group of very distinguished evolutionary economists to join us at the University of Queensland in Brisbane, Australia, in July 1999. The workshop was designed to be highly interactive: some participants presented full papers and others responded with challenging and insightful commentaries that facilitated the extended group discussions that followed. This book is the product of these deliberations.

Unlike many books that come under the label of 'evolutionary economics', this one devotes very little space to critiques of 'neoclassical economics'. Instead, evolutionary economics itself is subjected to scrutiny and is found to be deficient in a number of respects. However, its critics are invariably constructive, offering a range of insightful suggestions as to the shape and direction of future research. A key development that can be discerned in the book is a shift in focus away from a traditional concern with selection mechanisms towards a preoccupation with the manner in which novelty and variety provide fuel for such mechanisms. This has drawn many evolutionary economists into the modern complexity science literature that attempts to provide an understanding of how and why 'complex adaptive systems' engage in processes of self-organization. The goal is to provide an integrated analysis of both selection and self-organization that is uniquely economic in orientation. What this means, in practice, is that considerations pertaining to the nature of human knowledge and the unique character of economic organization must be taken into account in an explicit manner.

The book commences with our own brief overview of many of the key achievements, dilemmas and challenges in evolutionary economics at the present time. Part I of the book, which deals with theoretical perspectives, begins with a chapter in which Richard Nelson, one of the seminal contributors to the modern evolutionary approach in economics, expresses the view that it is time to seek more formal ways of dealing with institutional change, in addition to technological change, if we are to obtain a full understanding of economic evolution. In his commentary, John Gowdy argues that a shift of focus towards institutions may be highly problematic because it leads to questions that cannot be formalized in the context of an individual or a firm as the answers often lie in the field of cultural anthropology. In Chapter 3, Bart Nooteboom follows up these comments by stressing the importance of social constructions, such as language, in the generation of the novelty and variety that give rise to the routines that are subject to selection in the Nelsonian approach. It is argued that, to understand such processes, learning must not be separated from selection but, rather, it is necessary to understand how they interact to generate new novelty. Paolo Ramazzotti raises a number of difficulties with Nooteboom's 'exploitation–exploration' cycle theory of learning and selection sequences that arise because of the openness of systems and their resultant complexity.

The issue of complexity is the theme of Chapter 4, where Robert Delorme asks whether we can theorize in the presence of complexity. Different forms of complexity and associated definitions of 'rationality' are proposed. It is made clear that questions concerning the nature of knowledge are fundamental not only in evolutionary economics but also in the discipline as a whole. In his commentary, Drew Wollin warms to this theme and, sharing Delorme's enthusiasm for the systemic insights of Herbert Simon, argues that simple theorizing is possible in the presence of complexity provided that we are careful to adopt an appropriate methodology. One of the ways in which complexity has been dealt with in the natural sciences has been through the distinction between organized and disorganized complexity. The former is derived from processes of self-organization that may be the outcome of selection or can be viewed as a distinctive, but compatible, part of the evolutionary story. In Chapter 5, Pavel Pelikan argues that it is essential in considering economic evolution that selection and self-organization are dealt with together, and he suggests an analytical framework suited to this task. Bryan Morgan, although generally sympathetic to this theme, argues that there is too much emphasis on the use of a Darwinian selection mechanism analogy in Pelikan's approach, arguing that it is necessary, in the economic domain, to acknowledge the importance of human intentionality. Like Wollin, he argues that thinking in terms of 'complex adaptive systems' provides a more useful way of approaching economic selection and self-organization in this regard.

In Chapter 6, Kurt Dopfer raises a key question concerning theorizing: to what extent does it interface with historical experience and, therefore, be rendered useful in empirical endeavours? He reminds us that the problematic nature of abstract, timeless theories in this regard is not confined to neoclassical economics – evolutionary economics also contains theories that deal only with outcomes and not historical processes. Dopfer offers a 'histonomic' approach to theorizing that allows, explicitly, for historical context. It is an approach that is drawn from the complexity perspective of self-organization theory, focusing upon the manner in which both development and discontinuous transitions occur in historical sequences. In his commentary, Jason Potts further stresses the fact that the histonomic approach relates to complex systems and he goes on to argue that the analysis of spatial hyperstructures, using, for example, a graph theoretic approach, can provide a formal theoretical framework in which historical context dependence can be dealt with.

In Part II of the book, we deal with empirical perspectives. In evolutionary modelling, replicator dynamics have come to be the preferred vehicle for simulating economic selection mechanisms. Paolo Saviotti has been one of the pioneers in this field and, in Chapter 7, he examines how qualitative change in a multisectoral system can be incorporated in the replicator dynamic approach. This is an important development because it deals with the generation of the new variety that fuels competitive selection and, thus, allows self-organization to gain expression in an empirical model of economic evolution. In Chapter 8, Uwe Cantner and Horst Hanusch continue on this empirical theme by considering how we can measure heterogeneity and its dynamics. This has constituted a decade-long research programme. Extensive empirical insights have been gained and explicit links have been forged with evolutionary theory. Attention is focused upon total factor productivity at different levels of aggregation and examples are provided of empirical studies of evolutionary change that have been undertaken. In his commentary, John Nightingale provides a careful critique in which he raises both methodological and measurement issues. His comments concerning the pitfalls and difficulties in this kind of research highlight the pioneering nature of Cantner and Hanusch's research programme.

In Chapter 9, Francisco Louçã moves on from questions on how to deal with variety and heterogeneity in the empirical domain to look at the measurement of complexity in a more general sense. He discusses how complexity leads to the presence of non-linear dynamic features in time-series data with attendant difficulties for conventional statistical methods. It is pointed out that, although we cannot predict how such series will behave if non-linearities are present, it remains possible to understand the structure of historical flows and identify critical points, that is, transitions. Louçã sees this as bringing back history into economics and, in this respect, his approach is very compatible with that of Dopfer in Chapter 6. In his commentary, Steve Keen is generally supportive and adds some historical and methodological weight to the arguments made. He points out that many economists, in largely rejecting non-linear dynamic perspectives on modelling, because of the interpretative and predictive difficulties that they raise, are falling well behind natural scientists, with important implications for the scientific status of economics.

In Chapter 10, we are introduced to a modelling approach that deals explicitly with emergence and evolution, building on the view that organizational structures in the economy are complex adaptive systems. Peter Allen has been at the forefront of this type of modelling for two decades. For much of that time, evolutionary economists did not pay enough attention to his path-breaking work simply because it did not focus upon the operation of selection mechanisms but, rather, entailed a broader conception of the dynamics of complex systems. In this chapter, he reviews his carefully developed approach to evolutionary modelling and considers how knowledge and learning can be dealt with in his analytical structure. This chapter is important because it brings together many of the theoretical and empirical issues discussed throughout this book in a coherent modelling approach that is designed to address important policy questions. The commentator in this chapter is Kevin Bryant, an experienced policy analyst, who provides a wide-ranging evaluation of Allen's approach and finds it very congenial. However, he confirms that the complex adaptive systems approach was much less familiar to him, compared to Nelsonian evolutionary economics prior to the workshop, and thus is still at the 'frontier' in the policy arena. In Chapter 11, Bryant goes on to evaluate the usefulness of evolutionary economics, more generally in formulating innovation policy. It is striking just how well suited evolutionary economics is to this task which, in a sense, is not surprising given that it was a preoccupation with the determinants and effects of innovation that stimulated modern evolutionary economic ideas in the first place.

Finally, having introduced the contributors to the book and its main themes, it remains for us to acknowledge the contributions of those who made this book, and the associated workshop, possible. First of all, we would like to thank Amy Lindley for all her organizational efforts, both in making the workshop a success and in coordinating the book project. Thanks are also due to Kevin Bryant for his strong support from the beginning of the project – we hope that it will make a lasting contribution to Australian technology and innovation policy. We would also like to thank the following organizations for their material support, without which this book would not have been written: the Australian Department of Industry, Science and Resources; Queensland Treasury; Research Services, University of Queensland; School of Economics, University of Queensland. The contribution of the Economic and Social Research Council of the UK is also acknowledged gratefully, through their support of the Centre for Innovation and Competition at the University of Manchester.

J.F.
J.S.M.

1. Modern evolutionary economic perspectives: an overview

John Foster and J. Stanley Metcalfe

INTRODUCTION

Over the past two decades, evolutionary approaches to economics have become increasingly popular. Prior to 1980, evolutionary economics tended to be identified with American institutionalism which, in turn, was derived from the writings of the German Historical School in the latter part of the nineteenth century. Thorstein Veblen set out an 'evolutionary economic' agenda for institutionalists in his famous article of 1898, where he asked, 'Why is economics not an evolutionary science?' As the twentieth century unfolded, American institutionalism became a mixture of political economy, cultural anthropology and, of course, the study of institutions. It became difficult to discern any evolutionary principles that could offer an alternative analytical framework to the neoclassical principles that came to underpin most of economic analysis in the twentieth century. However, there have been economists in all schools of thought who have attempted to think of the economic system as the product of an evolutionary process (see Hogdson, 1993), therefore modern evolutionary economists have tended to draw widely in their quest for evolutionary principles. In particular, the contributions of Joseph Schumpeter and, more recently, Austrians such as Friedrich von Hayek, have exerted a considerable influence.

The birth of modern evolutionary economics can be traced back to the beginning of the 1980s. In 1981, Kenneth Boulding published a remarkable little book appropriately titled *Evolutionary Economics*. This was quickly followed by Richard Nelson and Sidney Winter's *An Evolutionary Theory of Economic Change* in 1982. Such was the sparse and disconnected nature of the literature in this field at that time that the authors of these books do not cite each other's work. In both, evolutionary analogies, drawn from biology, are employed: it is argued that selection mechanisms bring to the fore techniques, organizational routines and products that are best adapted to their respective environmental contexts. In both books, biological analogy is only viewed as the starting point of a new research programme. Questions are posed as to how selection principles operate in specifically economic contexts and, crucially, how the variety upon which selection works comes into being. By the late 1980s, a remarkable surge in interest in evolutionary economics was underway, spawning a voluminous literature in the 1990s. Articles on evolutionary economics began to be published on a regular basis in major academic journals and the new *Journal of Evolutionary Economics* increased its impact, as measured by citations, steadily throughout the decade.

It is not the purpose in this volume to review the modern literature on evolutionary economics in any systematic way. We have a more forward-looking objective: to identify the research agendas of prominent evolutionary economists at the present time in order to discern the direction that their research is likely to take in the course of the next decade. To assist in the achievement of this objective, experts have written evaluations of these agendas throughout the volume and, in the concluding chapter, a broad assessment is made of some of the policy challenges and opportunities that an evolutionary economic perspective will offer in the next decade. Before moving on to the contributions themselves, we would like to provide a summary assessment of the direction that evolutionary economics is taking and what will be the likely priorities in the coming years.

THE 'NEW' EVOLUTIONARY ECONOMICS

Selection mechanisms are clearly important in evolutionary economic processes. In the 1990s, there was increasing discussion and debate concerning the appropriate units of selection in different contexts and how these units of selection come into being. This, inevitably, made evolutionary economists think more carefully about the kinds of systems they have to deal with. Using the terminology that emerged in the 1990s, economic structures, such as firms, can be viewed as 'complex adaptive systems' with self-organizational features. Because such systems contain forward-looking agents and have both endogenous and adaptive capabilities, the outcomes of selection mechanisms become less clear cut, even in principle. Peter Allen was one of the first to argue that it is necessary to deal with *both* self-organizational development and selection, before a complete analytical treatment of economic evolution can be achieved.

Complexity is a daunting prospect for anyone in search of tractable analytical principles, as the literature on cybernetics and 'systems thinking' generally in the 1950s and 1960s will testify. However, in the natural sciences, advances in non-equilibrium thermodynamics by, for example, Ilya Prigogine demonstrated that complex systems that are dissipative can have orderly features that are self-organizational in character and, when we move from the physiochemical to the biological level of inquiry, evolutionary features associated with selection mechanisms. Thus the new 'complexity science' offered the possibility that analytical principles could also be discovered in social science contexts. However, this was not a matter of analogy, since both self-organization and selection operate differently in different kinds of systems. A homology is necessary that captures the unique way that economic systems operate and how they interface with social and natural systems (see Foster, 1997). This requires the evolutionary economist to understand the key social and psychological dispositions that result in economic coordination and competition, drawing not only upon modern literature but also on the classic contributions of, for example, Joseph Schumpeter and Herbert Simon.

The 'old' evolutionary economics eschewed the use of abstract theoretical principles, preferring a kind of inductive, interdisciplinary empiricism that was alien to conventional economists. The 'new' evolutionary economics attempts to embrace conventional scientific goals, but their achievement is approached differently: simple analytical principles are sought that can be used to understand temporal and spatial patterns in complex realities. This contrasts with the prevailing tendency in conventional economics to apply complex dynamical mathematics in contrived unrealistic states of simplicity. Thus there has been an emphasis in evolutionary economic modelling upon simulating complex dynamics using simple rules embodied in algorithmic structures. The observation of recurring patterns in such simulations then provides a basis for understanding actual processes and outcomes.

Our ability to apply a range of algorithmic tools in building evolutionary models has expanded enormously under the stimulus provided by large expansions in computing power. Cellular automata, neural nets and genetic algorithms are all devices that can be used to simulate the behaviour of agents in response to environmentally conditioned interactions with other agents. They provide natural bridges with advanced research in physics and biology and they pose intriguing problems when applied in economic settings. Their application raises age-old questions concerning methodological individualism versus holism, and free will versus determinism. On these matters, we are in favour of sophisticated methodological individualism in which the 'parts' are important, although not all of the outcomes can be reduced to their individual properties. Interactions, most obviously, are not properties of individual agents, nor are institutional rules. Similarly, we favour creativity as a key element in economic evolution, realizing, however, that creative efforts can be constrained by many factors. Echoing Richard Langlois' perspective, agents are not cybernetic reactors: economic and social agents are not passive recipients of messages emanating from the environment to which they mutually adjust their behaviour (Langlois, 1983). This suggests that algorithmic modelling is only part, albeit an important part, of the overall approach to self-organization in evolutionary processes.

Self-organizing behaviour can be viewed as pattern formation that arises from the interactions (typically local in domain) between the component elements of a system. The pattern is not necessarily repeated in the individual components, each of which may behave differently; it is an aggregate, emergent property of component interactions. This way of thinking about the economic and social world is naturally systemic, distinguishing that which is inside from that which is outside and breaking the inside down into components, connections and consequences. This is (or at least was) familiar territory for social scientists at least since David Hume and the Scottish enlightenment. Adam Smith's division of labour, the significance of the unintentional consequences of individual or collective behaviours, the primacy of institutions which create interactions and provide coordination are good examples of phenomena familiar in the treatment of complex adaptive systems.

Evolving systems change according to particular kinds of process, and two processes take pride of place: selection and development. All evolutionary models are based at least on the first and all the more sophisticated evolutionary models necessarily combine the two. Such evolutionary systems are characterized by three important properties: they are naturally dynamic – evolutionary theory is naturally 'growth' theory; they may involve selection and development at a multiplicity of distinct, interdependent levels; they give rise to the possibility of positive, reinforcing feedback behaviours, with all that implies for path dependency and history proper.

KNOWLEDGE AND INFORMATION

In this section we elaborate upon the point that the distinctive, complex, evolutionary property of economic and social systems is that they are knowledge based and that the primary interactions within them are exchanges of information. Information flow dominates energy flow in the economic context. The former is an active, creative domain, while the latter is passive. Because of this, economic systems are necessarily restless. As Alfred Marshall and, much more recently, Karl Popper (1985) recognized, economic and human activity changes knowledge both directly and indirectly and every change in knowledge opens up the conditions for changes in activity and, thus, further changes in knowledge *ad infinitum*. Economic systems are open, they are necessarily restless, the clock can never be turned back (Foster, 1993) and these features are uniquely associated with economic organization in the capitalist system. From a self-organization perspective, knowledge-based systems are autocatalytic: knowledge feeds on itself to generate more knowledge in quite unpredictable ways. Thus the crucial attribute of economic agents is not a rational search for efficiency but rather the imaginative construction of future, alternative economic worlds (Loasby, 1999). It is vastly more productive to ask how ignorance is overcome than to postulate perfect foresight as the basis for economic reasoning.

One immediate casualty of this perspective is equilibrium-based reasoning, whether or not it is based on Olympian notions of rationality. Restless systems are coordinated, but know no equilibria. A second consequence is a clear acceptance of the inherently unpredictable nature of imaginative, creative processes. A predictive theory of novelty is simply a contradiction in terms – this is the bargain we make as evolutionists in betting our theoretical chips on the question of why and how the world changes. This is the deep consequence of the link between self-organization and Marshall's economics in Foster (1993), and one that Hayek, Schumpeter and other Austrian economists highlight from a different perspective. A third consequence is the loss of any robust foundations for the normative appraisal of system pathologies (Brian Loasby's imaginative term). Restless systems have about them a sense of unease, of hopes dashed, of capital and skills devalued and expectations falsified for better or worse. Life is not entirely comfortable, however wealthy one might be. There is creation and there is destruction in both the economic and social domains, and the beliefs so engendered play a key role in the evolution of the system. This line of thought raises some very interesting questions about the role of public policy in evolving economies to which we shall return below. Can there be and do we need evolutionary concepts of economic and social welfare?

We can develop these general themes in three broad stages: (a) the interdependence between selection and development in evolutionary processes, (b) the division of labour as the key element in the process of knowledge accumulation, and (c) positive feedback processes as a definitive element in the economic processes which create restless capitalism.

EVOLUTION, SELECTION AND DEVELOPMENT

The central evolutionary issue is not being but becoming: why is it that the world changes in the way it does with respect to rate and direction? For the economist or economic historian, the development of evolutionary thinking in relation to economic activity has provided a powerful set of ideas to make sense of innovation (social, technical and organizational) and its relation to economic growth, structural change and competitive processes. These ideas emphasize the role of interaction and coordination processes in the economy, whether they be markets or innovation systems, and they dispense entirely with the concept of equilibrium as an organizing principle, if by the latter is meant a state of rest or a moving position in which all elements in the economy maintain their relative positions. There are no states of rest, nor are there stable attractors that form the reference positions for dynamic processes of convergence. All is flux. However, flux arises within the ambit of particular institutions that facilitate interaction and coordination – markets are prominent examples. Capitalism in equilibrium is a contradiction in terms. Here we need to distinguish two-stage from three-stage models of evolution (Figure 1.1).

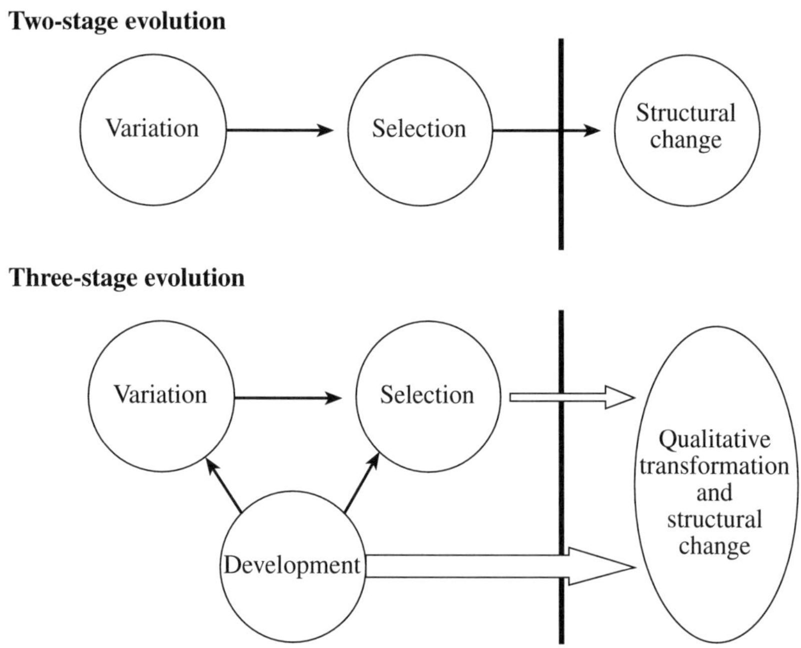

Figure 1.1 Models of evolution

The Two-stage Scheme

In traditional evolutionary theory a two-step framework is often used to spell out the main elements in the approach. This starts from the idea of variety in the characteristics of a population of selection units and combines this with a process of selection which evaluates the characteristics to create a 'fitness' score, from which follows a pattern of change in the relative importance of the selection units – the fitter than average increasing in relative importance, and conversely for the less fit than average. In this approach the characteristics of the selection units are exogenously given, although their selective significance is a product of interaction with other units in a specified environment. (In an economic model the behavioural characteristics of firms can be given, although the associated economic characteristics are contingent on the mode of interaction.)

Several aspects of this two-stage scheme are worth noting. First, fitness is not an attribute of any particular selective unit, it is a derived consequence of interaction within a given environmental context. No question of tautology arises in this respect. Second, notions of fitness, adaptation, unit of selection and selection environment form a unity: one cannot have one without the other. Third, fitness is a dynamic concept that is associated with the growth rates of competing units of selection. In a nutshell, evolutionary explanations are explanations of differential fitness and they are inherently dynamic.

It is not surprising that students of innovation and of technology more generally have found this a congenial framework within which to work. Innovations in products, organizations and methods of production generate variety, market processes evaluate that variety and translate it into differential profitability and the competitive dynamic translates profitability into differential growth (Nelson and Winter, 1982; Dosi *et al.*, 1988; Saviotti, 1996; Metcalfe, 1998). From this follow patterns of structural change which are a defining, emergent feature of modern capitalism. Such economies are never in states of steady growth; and the more we disaggregate, the greater the evidence we find for diversity of growth experience; conversely, the more we aggregate the more we hide, by averaging away, this essentially evolutionary phenomenon. We can measure and observe patterns at the macro level but our understanding necessarily flows from the interactions between varieties of micro behaviour.

There are many ways to formulate this evolutionary story. One is to develop the analysis in ecological terms, focusing on the competitive interactions and summarizing them in terms of Lotka-Volterra processes (Saviotti, 1996). A second, virtually equivalent, method is to follow the Fisherian route and think of the units of selection as statistical populations such that the moments (strictly speaking the cumulants) of the joint distributions of *given* characteristics evolve according to rules which are conditional upon the competitive process of market interactions (Nelson and Winter, 1982; Metcalfe, 1998). It is this route which leads us to the economics of replicator dynamic processes.

The principal insight behind replicator dynamics is that the rate of change in the structure of a population depends upon the distribution of the characteristics of selective units around the population means for those characteristics. Even though individual behaviours are given, there is change at the population level. Any number of selective characteristics can be incorporated, in principle. The tendency to focus upon productive efficiency as a single illustrative characteristic is just that – illustrative.

Replicator dynamics in market processes have a number of novel attributes, several of which we can take *seriatim*.

- The population averages for each selective characteristic change over time as a consequence of the selective process, with the rate and direction of change depending on the measured variety in the population. More precisely, how these averages change depends on the variance in the characteristics and the covariances with all the other characteristics. This is an example of Fisher's Principle (Metcalfe, 1998), or, more accurately, the cumulant theorem.
- Whether or not individual characteristics are based on optimizing behaviour, the evolution of the population as a whole reflects an optimizing principle. The pattern of structural change that flows from the replicator dynamic maximizes the rate of change of average population characteristics, relative to any other possible pattern of structural change in that population.
- Competitive selection works with the current characteristics of the population, not with their possible future characteristics; in this sense, it is myopic. However, what those current selective characteristics are may well depend on the memory of past events and upon expectations held with respect to future events. Past and future are gathered together in the present selective moment. Of course, those characteristics reflect purposeful behaviour. Purpose is not an argument against economic and social evolution; indeed, quite the contrary.
- Replicator dynamics allows us to deal with processes without using equilibrium attractors as devices to postulate convergence to 'long-run' positions. *Pace* the latter, the adjustment processes are neither *ad hoc* nor are they limited in value by the existence of multiple equilibrium or equilibria which are themselves subject to change over time at rates which preclude convergence. A given population may have an attractor if the set of selective characteristics and the environment are held constant so that evolution runs its course. However, the method is not limited to this special case.

All of the above propositions do depend upon the existence of some form of market coordination and they reflect a duality between agents and markets which is consonant with market reasoning. Firms determine product qualities and production methods, and set supply prices for outputs and inputs. Consumers evaluate product offerings and set demand prices. Market institutions disseminate this information to suppliers and consumers and, thus, facilitate market coordination. Market institutions are not, however, exogenous, they are the result of decisions made by agents in relation to matters such as standards and rules of exchange. The more effective are institutional rules at ensuring widespread dissemination of the relevant information, the less is the scope for consumers and suppliers to post independent demand and supply prices. In the limit of a 'perfect' market, all transactions for goods of the same quality are consummated at identical prices.

Before moving on to wider matters, some comment is necessary on the demise of the representative agent in the above, since this has become an important analytic device in mainstream economics. Since evolution depends on variety in behaviour, the idea of uniform agents is ruled out from the beginning. Instead, we work with a distribution of behaviours, each of which has equivalent status. Of course, we can define statistically a notion of representativeness. However, such representative behaviour is not the property of any individual agent (Horan, 1995), nor can it be determined *a priori*; rather, it is a consequence of the evolutionary process.

One intriguing aspect of evolution is that it consumes its own fuel. Processes of competitive selection necessarily destroy (or rather absorb) the very variety on which evolution depends. Unless this variety is replenished, evolution will come to an end. At this point we have reached the limits of the two-stage scheme and need now to move to a three-stage scheme: variety, selection and regeneration of variety. This requires a serious treatment of developmental processes in terms of the origins of variety and the endogenous recreation of variety. By developmental processes we mean processes which revise, add to or subtract from the distinctive units of selection in a population. In economic terms, we see these as innovative processes allied more or less closely with processes for creating new business units in the relevant populations.

The Three-stage Scheme

No one should pretend that the study of economic development processes is straightforward. There are good grounds for believing that the innovation 'black box' will always remain partially closed. To reinforce what was said above, a predictive theory of novelty is not in our grasp. Consequently, while the 'learning economy' is a useful metaphor, it must not be at the expense of a proper understanding of the unpredictable role of creativity and imagination in human affairs. None the less, a great deal remains to be said.

One way forward is to treat innovation processes as akin to random mutation or copy-error processes. This is the traditional Darwinian scheme – chance and necessity, random variation combined with deterministic selection. Of course, variety cannot be completely random, for randomized processes drift, they do not evolve according to selection. Randomness must remain at the margin.

In the economic and social sphere, the random hypothesis hardly seems adequate. Random processes are too slow to explain the observed rates of economic and social development; the range of combinatorial possibilities arising from the interconnection of established ideas is simply too vast to contemplate. Much more credence can be placed on the idea that there are non-random aspects of development processes. The rate of economic progress that we observe reflects guided variation within conceptual schemes that channel explorative, creative enquiry in particular directions. In so doing they create some opportunities and rule out others. This is the substantial grain of truth behind the notions of technological paradigms, design configurations, focusing devices and technological heuristics that evolutionary economic students of innovation processes employ. Within these non-random constraints, randomness can be given a proper place (Allen, 1988). Of course, all variation is, in effect, blind variation, since it necessarily deals in the unknowable consequences of a present decision: it is, in George Shackle's terms, the imagined deemed possible (Loasby, 1999).

To a substantial degree the innovation process is endogenous to the economic system so that development and selection are subject to mutual interaction. The distribution of profitability influences the distribution of R&D in an industry, the relative size of different firms sharply affects the pay-off from innovation, and, most fundamentally, the experience gained in R&D in production and in market activity is an important determinant of the differential innovative performance of firms. Indeed, the accumulation of practically useful knowledge is perhaps the most important kind of joint production in economics. Presented in this light, a compelling case can be made for the endogeneity of evolutionary innovation processes such that the development of variety and the selection of variety become inseparable processes.

In taking this idea further, more needs to be said concerning the production of knowledge and the division of labour.

KNOWLEDGE AND THE DIVISION OF LABOUR

In recent theoretical and empirical work on innovation, the idea of innovation systems has justifiably occupied a position of prominence (Freeman, 1987; Nelson, 1993; Carlsson, 1995; Edquist, 1996). These ideas hark back, of course, to Adam Smith and his powerful insight that the production of knowledge reflects a division of labour in which special importance attaches to 'philosophers and men of speculation'. In modern innovation systems this is reflected in an increasingly roundabout process of producing practically useful knowledge in which there is specialization of institution, specialization of discipline and the combination of an increasingly wide range of knowledge types to the solution of practical problems. In terms of the insights of Richardson (1972), we observe increasing complementarity and increasing dissimilarity of the relevant knowledge bases leading to the 'mode-2' production of knowledge (Gibbons *et al.*, 1994). Knowledge generation and application systems raise several interesting avenues for exploration.

At one level, they invite systems thinking, the analysis of phenomena in terms of components and connections and the outcomes of the associated interactions. Potts (2000) has argued persuasively for a graph theoretic understanding of these problems, and there are obvious connections to be made with more traditional systems literatures on autopoiesis and autogenesis (Zeleny, 1996; Csanyi, 1996).

Seen in this light, innovative systems may be defined at various levels at which the national is only one possibility. More importantly, the relevant evolutionary issues imply a dynamic perspective. How do systemic attributes influence the selection of inventive ideas, how do they influence the translation of invention into innovation? How do innovation systems emerge as a consequence of higher-order development processes, how do they grow, how do they decline? How fluid are the relations between component elements? A systems approach with its potential for distinguishing between changes in components and changes in connections seems a natural way forward. Selection and development apply within components of the system just as they do in relation to the connectivity between components in the system. The fact that innovation systems may be depicted as networks, just as markets are, can reinforce the point that innovation systems and market systems interpenetrate one another. This helps us locate an interest in user–supplier interactions (Lundvall, 1988) and an interest in the coevolution of industries within their institutional framework (Nelson and Sampat, 1999).

Two further points are worth making to develop this systems approach to the division of labour in knowledge production. One is the significance of distinguishing between different kinds of knowledge, each with their institutional set-up in relation to accumulation and dissemination. That science is fundamentally different from engineering, that technology is not merely applied science, that much scientific work is not purely motivated but undertaken with practical objectives in mind (Stokes, 1996) are points well established in the relevant literatures. Clearly, the codified/tacit dimension is only part of the relevant set of distinctions. There are multiple knowledge-generating systems and how they connect and when is a natural systemic question.

The second is the importance of not being too beguiled by formal (science, technology) knowledge in the innovation process. Here we want to press for the significance of less formal business knowledge of market demand and organization. These kinds of knowledge are conjecture-based, like all knowledge, and are subject to refutation or conformation on a trial and error basis, but they do not constitute formal, theoretical knowledge. They should be given full weight in any evolutionary account of knowledge and its relation to development processes. In turn, this suggests that the knowledge of consumers/users needs to be given more weight in our study of innovation. *Pace* Joseph Schumpeter, there are obvious dangers in giving the consumer/user too low a weight in the study of innovation.

A wider picture begins to emerge with regard to the interaction and interdependence of development and selection which Bart Nooteboom has analysed in his treatment of the learning economy in this volume. It is also a picture in which Pavel Pelikan's concerns with entrepreneurship can be given full reign, something which is impossible if one believes the economy is best understood as a 'marvellous mechanical clock' (Nooteboom, 1999; Pelikan, 1999). This seems to take us towards general evolutionary economic principles where the innovative and market interdependence of different sectors is made the subject of wider coordination processes (Metcalfe, 1999). This is a line of argument begun by Adam Smith and developed most persuasively by Allyn Young (1928).

POSITIVE FEEDBACK AND RESTLESS CAPITALISM

The reader will have noted already an 'Austrian' undercurrent to the discussion thus far. The division of labour in knowledge production maps readily into the Hayekian emphasis on the distributed, localized, idiosyncractic, personal nature of knowledge. Equally, it emphasizes the complementarity between the highly disaggregated, dispersed nature of uncoordinated plans to innovate and the order-imposing nature of market processes that resolve differential innovative behaviour into patterns of economic change. The market system links economic rewards to variety and gives the latter a basis for economic change, while creating the incentives to regenerate variety. Every position is open to challenge in capitalism – property rights, the patent system notwithstanding, are inherently insecure (Hayek, 1988). This partly explains the restless nature of capitalism, but only partly. Of equal importance is the endogenous nature of knowledge accumulation, the most powerful source of dynamic increasing returns. Capitalism is restless because it contains within itself the institutional framework and incentive structures to generate variation and to have market coordination turn variety into differential growth and structural change. Thus the coupling of development and selection may be represented as the following schema:

(Economic variety + market coordination) → Differential growth → structural change → differential accumulation of knowledge → renewed economic variety.

It is the growth of knowledge and the application of knowledge, in the context of the day-to-day conduct of economic activity, that gives capitalism its dynamic bias. From this follows Allyn Young's insistence that changes within sectors induce changes in other sectors such that 'Every important advance in the organization of production … alters the conditions of industrial activity and initiates responses elsewhere in the industrial structure which in turn have a further unsettling effect' (Young, 1928, p. 533). This is reciprocal dependence of innovation processes in a pattern of interaction in which cause shades, imperceptibly, into effect.

What Young saw so clearly was that increasing returns create a reciprocal dependence in rates of technical progress within and between activities. This is not only a matter of what the modern student would label 'spillovers', but rather a question of the fruits of innovation in one sector raising per capita incomes and this influencing output growth and the accumulation of knowledge in other sectors. In situations of complementary processes of increasing returns, we see immediately a growth process characterized by mutualism, the logical equivalent of autocatalysis (Ulanowicz, 1996). A higher rate of innovation in A results in a higher rate of innovation in B and, via however many intermediary steps, this has a positive feedback effect on the rate of innovation in A. Thus innovation becomes self-reinforcing, it is growth enhancing. Figure 1.2 is a simple-minded way to illustrate this point.

On the axes we depict the productivity growth rates in each industry, the outcome of internal selection and developmental processes. The schedules *A–A* and *B–B* capture the reciprocal interaction of innovation rates as reflected in productivity growth. Their positions reflect the within-sector innovation dynamics, and the slopes the degree of positive interdependence between sectors. The economy is coordinated at point *a*. Compare this with point *b*, the productivity pattern that would emerge with no dynamic increasing returns. The difference between these two points – 'the Young effect' – is a measure of the stimulus to growth provided by the autocatalytic consequences of increasing returns.

While this is the merest sketch of an argument (Metcalfe, 1999), it serves to illustrate a crucial point: capitalist market economies are economies in which one thing leads to another. The accumulation of knowledge allied with increasing returns makes innovation an endogenous evolutionary process. Economic evolution is open ended; we have no way of knowing where it will lead. However, viewing systems as complex and adaptive, and thus capable of self-organization, provides a most promising way to capture the nature of

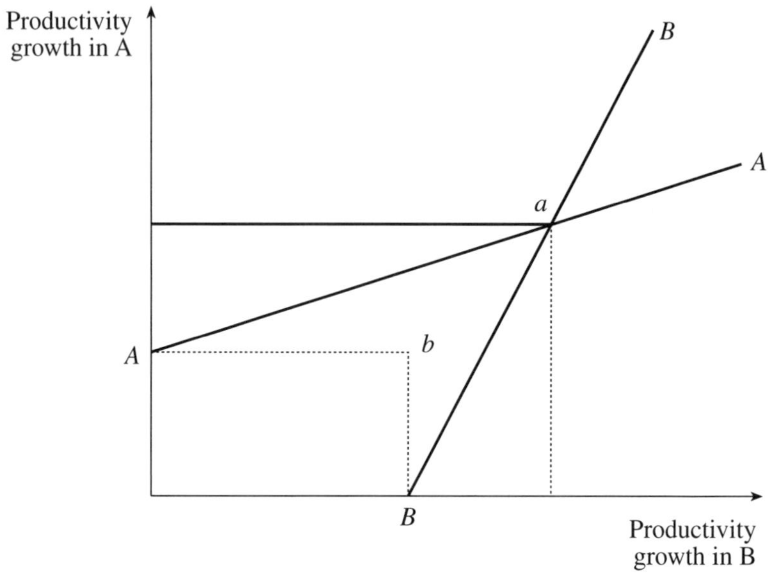

Figure 1.2 The self-reinforcing dynamics of innovation

these dynamic processes. As Foster (2000) points out, self-organization is not a physiochemical analogy but a general principle in systems that process energy, matter and information. Economic self-organization is not the same as biological self-organization, despite the fact that they have common properties. Thus evolutionary economic principles must embrace both *economic* self-organization and *economic* competitive selection, if a unified and versatile analytical framework is to be constructed. The contributors to this volume, in their distinctive but complementary ways, have all made important advances towards this goal. Their insights will, undoubtedly, be pivotal in stimulating further progress towards a new kind of analytical and empirical economics that can improve our understanding of the processes of economic development, growth and decline that we observe at all levels of inquiry.

REFERENCES

Allen, P. (1988), 'Evolution, Innovation and Economics', in G. Dosi *et al.*, *Technical Change and Economic Theory*, London: Pinter.

Carlsson, B. (1995), *Technological Systems and Industrial Dynamics*, Boston: Kluwer.

Csanyi, V. (1996), 'Organization, Function and Creativity in Biological and Social Systems', in E. Khalil and K. Boulding (eds), *Evolution, Order and Complexity*, London: Routledge.

Dosi, G. *et al.* (1988), *Technical Change and Economic Theory*, London: Pinter.
Edquist, C. (1996), *Systems of Innovation*, London: Pinter.
Foster, J. (1993), 'Economics and the self-organization approach: Alfred Marshall revisited', *Economic Journal*, **103**, 975–91.
Foster, J. (1997), 'The analytical foundations of evolutionary economics: from biological analogy to economic self-organisation', *Structural Change and Economic Dynamics*, **8**, 427–51.
Foster, J. (2000), 'Competitive selection, self-organisation and Joseph A. Schumpeter', *Journal of Evolutionary Economics*, **10**(3).
Freeman, C. (1987), *Technology Policy and Economic Performance*, London: Pinter.
Gibbons, M., C. Limoges, H. Nowotny, S. Schwartzman, P. Scott and M. Trow (1994), *The New Production of Knowledge*, London: Sage.
Hayek, F.A. (1988), *The Fatal Conceit*, London: Routledge.
Hodgson, G. (1993), *Economics and Evolution: Bringing Life Back to Economics*, Cambridge: Polity Press.
Horan, B.L. (1995), 'The statistical character of evolutionary theory', *Philosophy of Science*, **61**, 76–95.
Langlois, R.N. (1983), 'Systems Theory, Knowledge and the Social Sciences', in F. Machlup and U. Mansfield (eds), *The Study of Information*, New York: Wiley.
Loasby, B. (1999), *Knowledge, Institutions and Evolution in Economics*, London: Routledge.
Lundvall, B. (1988), 'Innovation as an Interactive Process: From User–Producer Interaction to the National System of Innovation', in G. Dosi *et al.*, *Technical Change and Economic Theory*, London: Pinter.
Metcalfe, J.S. (1998), Evolutionary Economics and Creative Destruction, London: Routledge.
Metcalfe, J.S. (1999), 'Restless Capitalism: Increasing Returns and Growth in Enterprise Economics', *CRIC*, University of Manchester.
Nelson, R. (1993), *National Systems of Innovation*, Oxford: Oxford University Press.
Nelson, R. and B.N. Sampat (1999), 'Making Sense of Institutions as a Factor Shaping Economic Progress', mimeo, Columbia University.
Nelson, R. and S. Winter (1982), *An Evolutionary Theory of Economic Change*, Harvard: Belknap.
Nooteboom, B. (1999), 'From Evolution to Language and Learning', mimeo, Netherlands Institute for Advanced Studies.
Pelikan, P. (1999), 'Institutions for the Selection of Entrepreneurs', Working Paper 510, IUI, Stockholm.
Popper, K. (1985), *A World of Propensities*, Bristol: Thoemmes.
Potts, J. (2000), *The New Evolutionary Macroeconomies: Complexity Competence and Adaptive Behaviour*, Cheltenham, UK and Northampton, MA, USA: Edward Elgar.
Richardson, G.B. (1972), 'The organization of industry', *Economic Journal*, **82**.
Saviotti, P. (1996), *Technological Evolution, Variety and the Economy*, Cheltenham, UK and Brookfield, US: Edward Elgar.
Stokes, D. (1996), *Pasteur's Quadrant*, Washington DC: Brookings Institute.
Ulanowicz, R. (1996), 'The Propensities of Evolving Systems', in E. Khalil and K. Boulding (eds), *Evolution, Order and Complexity*, London: Routledge.
Veblen, T.B. (1898), 'Why is economics not an evolutionary science?', *Quarterly Journal of Economics*, **12**, 373–426.
Young, A. (1928), 'Increasing returns and economic progress', *Economic Journal*, **38**, 527–42.

Zeleny, M. (1996), 'On the Social Nature of Autopoietic Systems', in E. Khalil and K. Boulding (eds), *Evolution, Order and Complexity*, London: Routledge.

PART I

Theoretical Perspectives

2. The coevolution of technology and institutions as the driver of economic growth

Richard R. Nelson

INTRODUCTION

In several recent papers I have put forth the perspective that technology and institutions should be understood as coevolving, and that this coevolutionary process should be seen as the principal driving force behind economic growth. That proposition should not seem controversial, or novel, to readers of this book. However, my objective is to build institutions and the relationships between institutions and technological advance into an explicitly evolutionary theory of economic growth. I believe and hope that in so doing I can help sharpen our understanding of the key processes involved. But the proof of that pudding obviously is in the eating.

As you may know, the economists who have been active in the development of evolutionary growth theory over the last 20 years were motivated in large part by their perception that neoclassical economic growth theory, while assigning technological change a large role in economic growth, was totally inadequate as an abstract characterization of economic growth fuelled by technological change. In particular, that theory repressed the fact that efforts to advance technology were to a considerable extent 'blind', and hence that episodes where technological advance was rapid and cumulative almost always involved a number of competing efforts and actors, with *ex post* selection rather than forward-looking planning determining the winners and losers.

The language of evolutionary theory has long appealed to empirical scholars of technological advance. The broad notion that technological advance proceeds through an evolutionary process has been developed independently by scholars of technological advance operating in a variety of different disciplines. (See, for example, sociologists like Constant and Bijker, technological historians like Vincenti, Basalla, Petroski and Mokyr, as well as economists interested in modelling like Winter and myself, Metcalfe, Saviotti, Dosi, Soete, Silverberg.)

Sophisticated empirical scholars of technological advance have always understood that the rate and character of technological advance were influenced by the institutional structures supporting it, and that institutions also strongly conditioned whether and how effectively new technology was accepted and absorbed into the economic system. These themes are clear, for example, in David Landes' magisterial *Unbound Prometheus*, and in Christopher Freeman's *The Economics of Industrial Innovation*. And recently, of course, the notion of a national or a sectoral innovation system, which clearly is an institutional concept, has played a significant role in theorizing about technological advance.

However, it seems fair to say that, by and large evolutionary economists writing about technological change, and economists who have been stressing the role of institutions in economic development, have had very little interchange. The principal purpose of this book is to foment and facilitate such interchange.

INSTITUTIONAL ANALYSIS AND EVOLUTIONARY ECONOMIC THEORY: THE HISTORICAL CONNECTIONS

I want to begin my argument by proposing that, before modern neoclassical theory gained its present preponderant position in economics, much of economic analysis was both evolutionary and institutional. Thus Adam Smith's analysis was concerned with how 'the division of labor is limited by the extent of the market' and, in particular, his famous pinmaking example, certainly fits the mould of what I would call evolutionary theorizing about economic change. Indeed, his analysis is very much one about the coevolution of physical technologies and the organization of work, with the latter, I would argue, very much a notion about 'institutions'. In many other places in *The Wealth of Nations*, Smith is expressly concerned with the broader institutional structure of nations, in a way that certainly is consonant with the perspectives of modern institutional economics. Marx of course was both an evolutionary theorist and an institutional theorist. If you consider the broad scan of his writing, so too was Marshall. Thus evolutionary growth theorizing that encompasses institutions in an essential way has a long and honourable tradition in economics.

As neoclassical economic theory became dominant in economics, and increasingly narrowed its intellectual scope, both the institutional and the evolutionary strands of economic analysis became 'counter-cultures'. In some cases, they were intertwined; they certainly were in Veblen and in Hayek. However, there was a tendency for the dissonant strains of institutional economic theorizing, and evolutionary economic theorizing, to take their own separate paths. Thus, in the United States, Commons helped to define the American institutional school. However, his analysis was not very evolutionary. Nor was the perspective of Coase who, later, had a major shaping influence on 'the new institutional economics'. On the other hand, Schumpeter, whose work arguably has provided the starting point for modern evolutionary economics, is seldom footnoted by self-professed institutionalists, despite the fact that he was very much concerned with economic institutions. And Schumpeter's institutional orientation was ignored, as well, in the early writings of the evolutionary economists who cited him as their inspiration.

Thus what has been called the 'new institutional economics', and the new evolutionary economics, have different immediate sources. And their focal orientations have been different. The orientation of institutional economics is towards the set of factors that mould and define human interaction, both within organizations and between them. In contrast, much of modern evolutionary economic theorizing is focused on the processes of technological advance.

However, in my view at least, recent developments have seen the two strands coming together again, as Geoffrey Hodgson and Richard Langlois have long argued should be the case. Thus Douglass North, perhaps today's best known economic 'institutionalist', has gradually adopted an evolutionary perspective regarding the way institutions form and change. And many of the scholars who did the early work on the new evolutionary economics have recently become focused on such subjects as 'national innovation systems', which is an institutional concept par excellence.

There certainly are strong natural affinities, in the form of common core assumptions and perceptions, between institutional economists, at least those in the school of North, and modern evolutionary economists. There also are very strong reasons more generally why they should join forces.

The two camps share a central behavioural premise that human action and interaction needs to be understood as largely the result of shared habits of action and thought. In both there is a deep-cutting rejection of 'maximization' as a process characterization of what humans do. There also is a rejection of the notion that, while humans do not go through actual maximizing calculations, they behave 'as if' they did, and, therefore, that behaviour can be predicted by an analyst who calculates the best possible behaviour for humans operating in a particular context. There is a related rejection of the notion that analysts in fact can do such a calculation, except in the context of a quite simple model, which almost surely misses possibly essential aspects of the actual context. Thus, for scholars in both camps, patterns of action need to be understood in behavioural terms, with improvements over time being explained as occurring through processes of individual and collective learning. For evolutionary theorists, this exactly defines the nature of an evolutionary process.

Scholars in both camps increasingly share a central interest in understanding the determinants of economic performance, and how economic performance differs across nations and over time. Modern evolutionary theorists focus centrally on what they tend to call 'technologies'. For evolutionary theorists, a country's level of technological competence is seen as the basic factor constraining its productivity, with technological advance the central driving force behind economic growth. As noted, increasingly, evolutionary economists are coming to see 'institutions' as moulding the technologies used by a society, and technological change itself. However, institutions have not as yet been incorporated into their formal analysis.

On the other hand, institutional economists tend to focus precisely on these institutions. Many would be happy to admit that the influence of a country's institutions on its ability to master and advance technology is a central way that institutions affect economic performance. However, institutionalists have yet to include technology and technological change explicitly in their formulation.

The arguments for a marriage, I think, are strong. Below I map out what a marriage might look like.

ROUTINES AS A UNIFYING CONCEPT

For this readership I do not need to present an elaborate argument that 'routines', or an equivalent concept, play a central role in modern economic evolutionary theory. As Winter and I have developed the concept, the carrying out of a routine is 'programmatic' in nature and, like a programme, tends largely to be carried out automatically. Like a computer program, our routine concept admits choice within a limited range of alternatives, but channelled choice.

Thus the routines built into a business firm, or another kind of organization that undertakes economic activity, largely determine what it does under the particular circumstances it faces. The performance of that firm or organization will be determined by the routines it possesses and the routines possessed by other firms and economic units with which the firm interacts, including competitors, suppliers and customers. At any given period of time, many of the routines are largely common to firms in the same line of business, but some are not, and these latter, therefore, provide the stuff that determines how firms do relative to their competitors. The distribution of routines in an economy at any time determines overall economic performance. Under evolutionary economic theory, economic growth is caused by changes in the distribution of operative routines, associated both with the creation of superior new routines and with the increasingly widespread use of superior routines and the abandonment of inferior ones. The latter can occur through the relative expansion of organizations that do well, or the adoption of better techniques by organizations that had been using less good ones, or both.

As noted, most of the writing by evolutionary economists has focused on 'physical' technologies as routines. However, the notion of a routine fits very well with the conceptualization of institutional economists. Indeed, if one defines institutions as widely employed 'social' technologies, in the sense I will develop shortly, it is natural to take institutions on board as a component of an evolutionary theory of economic growth.

However, before focusing on that matter, it is useful to reflect a little on some important characteristics of productive routines. A routine involves a collection of procedures which, taken together, result in a predictable and specifiable outcome. Complex routines can almost always be analytically broken down into a collection of subroutines. Thus the routine for making a cake involves subroutines like pour, mix and bake. These operations will often require particular inputs, like flour and sugar, and a stove. And, in turn, virtually all complex routines are linked with other routines that must be effected in order to make them possible, or to enable them to create value. Thus a cake-making routine presupposes that the necessary ingredients and equipment are at hand, and the acquisition of these at some prior date requires its own 'shopping' routines. And still further back in the chain of activity, the inputs themselves needed to be produced, in a form that met the requirements of cake makers.

The aspect of productive routines that I want to highlight here is that, while the operation of a particular routine by a competent individual or organization generally involves certain idiosyncratic elements, at its core almost always are elements that are broadly similar to what other competent parties would do in the same context. By and large, thc ingredients and the equipment used by reasonably skilled bakers are basically the same as those used by other skilled cake makers. And the broad outline of the steps can generally be recognized by someone skilled in the art as being roughly those described in *The Joy of Cooking*, or some comparable reference.

There are two basic reasons why productive routines tend to be widely used by those who are skilled in the art. The first is that great cake recipes, or effective ways of organizing bakeries, or producing steel or semiconductors, tend to be the result of the cumulative contributions of many parties, often operating over many generations. This is a central reason why they are as effective as they are. To deviate from them in significant ways is risky and, while the pay-offs may be considerable, there is also a major chance of failure.

The second reason is that particular routines tend to be a part of systems of routines. This systemic aspect forces a certain basic commonality of ways of doing particular things. The needed inputs tend to be available, routinely, for widely known and used routines. If help is needed, it is generally easy to get help from someone who already knows a lot about what is needed, and can explain the particulars in common language, if the routine involved is widely known and practised. In contrast, idiosyncratic routines tend to lack good fit with complementary routines, and may require their users to build their own support systems.

SOCIAL TECHNOLOGIES AND INSTITUTIONS

In an earlier paper where Bhaven Sampat and I developed many of these notions, we proposed that, if one reflects on the matter, the programme built into a routine generally involves two different aspects: a recipe that is anonymous regarding any division of labour, and a division of labour plus a mode of coordination. We proposed that the former is what scholars often have in mind when they think of 'physical technologies'. The latter we called a 'social technology', and we proposed that social technologies are what many scholars have in mind when they use the term 'institutions'.

Widely employed social technologies certainly are defined by 'the rules of the game', the concept of institutions employed by many scholars, for example Douglass North. Social technologies also can be viewed as widely employed 'modes of governance', which is Williamson's notion of what institutions are about. And in the language of transaction costs, which is widely employed in the institutional literature, generally used 'social technologies' provide low transaction cost ways of getting something done. As this discussion indicates, the concept of social technology is broad enough to encompass both ways of structuring activity within particular organizations – that is, the M form of organization as a social technology – and ways of transacting across organizational borders. Thus markets define and are defined by 'social technologies'. So too are widely used procedures for collective choice and action.

This formulation naturally induces one to see prevailing institutions not so much as do some analysts, as 'constraints' on behaviour, but rather as defining the effective ways to get things done when human cooperation is needed. To view institutions as 'constraints' on behaviour is analogous to seeing prevailing physical technologies as 'constraints on behaviour'. A social technology (an institution) or a physical technology is like a paved road across a swamp. To say that the location of the prevailing road is a constraint on getting across is basically to miss the point. Without a road, getting across would be impossible, or at least much harder.

INSTITUTIONS IN AN EVOLUTIONARY THEORY OF ECONOMIC GROWTH

The question of how institutions fit into a theory of economic growth of course depends not only on what one means by institutions, but also on the other aspects of that theory. I suggest that the concept of institutions as social technologies fits into evolutionary theories of economic growth very nicely.

Technological Advance as the Driving Force

While these days almost all scholars studying economic growth see technological advance as a large part of the story, it seems fair to say that evolutionary theorists put special weight on technological advance. The reason is that, while neoclassical theory sees economic actors as facing a spacious choice set, including possible actions that they have never taken before, within which they can choose with confidence and competence, evolutionary theory sees economic actors as at any time bound by the limited range of routines they have mastered. Each of these has only a small range of choice. Further, the learning of new routines by actors is a time consuming, costly and risky thing. Thus, while neoclassical growth theory sees considerable economic growth as possible simply by 'moving along the production function', in evolutionary theory there are no easy ways to come to master new things.

Put more positively, from the perspective of evolutionary theory, the economic growth we have experienced needs to be understood as the result of the progressive introduction of new technologies which were associated with increasingly higher levels of worker productivity, and the ability to produce new or improved goods and services. As a broad trend, they were also progressively using capital. (Elsewhere I have developed the varied reasons for the capital-using nature of technological change.) Rising human capital intensity has also been a handmaiden to that process, being associated both with the changing inputs that have generated technological advance and with the changing skill requirements of new technologies.

Within this formulation, new 'institutions' and social technologies come into the picture as changes in the modes of interaction – new modes of organizing work, new kinds of markets, new laws, new forms of collective action – that are called for as the new technologies are brought into economic use. In turn, the institutional structure at any time has a profound effect on, and reflects, the technologies that are in use, and which are being developed.

I believe that the concept of institutions as social technologies, the routines language for describing them and the theory sketched above of the way institutions and institutional change are bound up with the advance of physical technologies in the process of economic growth becomes more powerful, the closer the analysis gets to describing actual social technologies in action. Thus I turn now to two particular important developments in the history of experienced modern economic growth: the rise of mass production industry in the United States in the late nineteenth century and the rise of the first science-based industry – synthetic dyestuffs – in Germany at about the same time. Given space constraints, the discussion must be very sketchy, but I hope to provide enough detail so that one can see our proposed conceptualization in action.

The Rise of Mass Production

As Alfred Chandler and other business historians tell the story, during the last part of the nineteenth century and the first half of the twentieth, manufacturing industry in the United States experienced rapid productivity growth, associated with the bringing into operation of methods of production – new technologies or routines – that came to be called 'mass production'. These methods were accompanied by growing scale of plants and firms, rising capital intensity of production and the development of professional management, often with education beyond the secondary level. However, these latter increases in 'physical and human capital per worker', and in the scale of output, should not be considered as an independent source of growth, in the sense of growth accounting; they were productive only because they were needed by the new technologies.

At the same time, it would be a conceptual mistake to try to calculate how much productivity increase the new technologies would have allowed, had physical and human capital per worker, and the scale of output, remained constant. The new production routines involved new physical technologies which incorporated higher levels of physical and human capital per worker than the older routines they replaced. To operate the new routines efficiently required much larger scales of output than previously.

And they also involved new 'social technologies'. Chandler's great studies are largely about the new modes of organizing business that were required to take advantage of the new opportunities for 'scale and scope'. The scale of the new firms exceeded that which owner-managers plus their relatives and close friends could deal with, in terms either of governance or of finance. The growing importance of hired professional management, and the diminished willingness of the original family owners to provide all the financial capital, called for the development of new financial institutions and associated markets. The need for professional managers also pulled business schools into being. More generally, the new industrial organization profoundly reshaped shared beliefs of the way the economy worked, and came to define the concept of modern capitalism.

The development of mass production proceeded especially rapidly in the United States, in part at least because of the large size of the American market, but also because the associated new institutions grew up rapidly in the new world. In general Europe lagged. On the other hand, the rise of new institutions to support science based industry occurred first in Europe.

Synthetic Dyestuffs

I turn now to consider another example: the rise of the first science-based industry, in Germany, that occurred over roughly the same time period as did the rise of mass production in the US.

The basic story has been told by several scholars, but the account I draw most from here is that contained in the thesis by Peter Murmann (Murmann, 1998). Murmann's account is presented in standard language. The account presented here is 'semi-formal' in the sense that it makes explicit use of the concept of routines, and the physical and social technologies involved in routines.

Several new routines play the key roles in the story. The first is a new 'physical technology' for creating new dyestuffs, with university-trained chemists as the key inputs. This new physical technology came into existence in the late 1860s and early 1870s as a result of improved scientific understanding of the structure of organic compounds. The second key element in the story was the development of the 'social technology' for organizing chemists to work in a coordinated way for their employer – the invention of the modern industrial research laboratory. The third element in our story is another social technology, the system of training young chemists in the understandings and research methods of organic chemistry. This social technology was university-based, and funded by national governments. Finally, there are new markets with their own particular rules and norms. One links the firms interested in hiring chemists with the supply of chemists. Another market links dyestuff firms with users of the new dyestuffs.

Several different kinds of 'institutionalized' organizations play key roles in our theoretical story. First, there are chemical products firms, of two types. The old type does not possess an industrial research laboratory, and achieves new dyestuffs slowly through processes that involve only small levels of investment. The other kind of firms, the 'new' type, invests in industrial research laboratories and, because of those investments, achieves new dyestuffs at a much faster rate than do old firms. There are two other kinds of organization in this story as well. One is national chemical products industry associations, who lobby government for support of university training. The other is national universities which train young chemists. National political processes and government funding agencies are also part of our story, but they will be treated implicitly rather than explicitly.

As noted, this account also involves specification of certain 'institutionalized' markets, and the recognition that these markets differ somewhat from nation to nation. In particular, chemists have a national identity, and the firms do also. German chemists (we will assume that these all are trained in German universities) require a significantly higher salary to work in a British firm than in a German one, and British-trained scientists require more to work in Germany than in Britain. (Alternatively, the best of the national graduates would rather work in a national firm.) This means that, other things being equal, it advantages national firms if their national universities are training as many chemists as they want to hire.

There also are national markets for dyestuffs. The British market is significantly larger than the German market throughout the period under analysis. Other things being equal, British firms have an advantage selling in the British market, and German firms in the German market. However, the advantage of national firms can be offset if a foreign firm is offering a richer menu of dyestuffs. Under our specification, if a foreign firm does more R&D than a national firm, it can take away the latter's market, at least partially.

There are several key dynamic processes, and factors influencing them, in our story. To a first approximation, the profits of a firm, gross of its R&D spending, are an increasing function of the level of its technology, defined in terms of the quality of the dyestuffs it offers, and the volume of its sales. This first approximation, however, needs to be modified by two factors. One is that the profits of a firm that does R&D depend on whether the chemists it hires are national or not. The other is that, for a given level of the other variables, British firms earn somewhat more reflecting their advantaged location regarding the market. R&D is funded out of profits, but not all firms invest in R&D. Firms can spend nothing on R&D (as do 'old-style' firms), or they can invest a fraction of their profits in R&D (as do 'new-style' firms). Initially, all firms are 'profitable enough' to be able to afford a small-scale R&D facility. Some (the 'new-style' firms) choose to do so, and others do not. If the profits of a new-style firm grow, the firm spends more on R&D.

Second, given the availability of the new R&D technology, it is profitable to invest in R&D and, given the competition from 'new-style firms', firms that do not do R&D lose money. This is so in both Germany and the UK. In both countries a certain fraction of firms starts to invest in R&D when the new technology arrives. These profitable firms expand, and the unprofitable ones contract. As firms that do R&D expand, their demand for trained chemists grows too. National firms hire nationally trained chemists first, and then (at higher cost) foreign-trained chemists.

The supply of chemists to industry provided by universities is a function of the funding those universities receive from government. For a variety of reasons, the supply of German chemists initially is much greater than the supply of British chemists. This initial cost advantage to German firms that do R&D is sufficient to compensate for the disadvantage regarding the location of the product market. Over time, the political strength of the national industry association, and the amount of money it can induce government to make available to national universities, is proportional to the size of that part of the national industry that undertakes organized research.

Start the dynamics just before the advent of the new scientific understanding that creates a new technique for creating new dyestuffs. There are more (and bigger) British firms than German firms in this initial condition, reflecting their closeness to the large part of the market. No firm has an industrial research laboratory. The supply of chemists being trained at German universities is more than sufficient to meet the limited demands of German firms, and British firms, for chemists.

Now along comes the new scientific technique for creating new dyestuffs. Some British firms and some German firms start doing industrial R&D on a small scale. They do well, and grow. The demand for university-trained chemists grows. Since most of the existing supply of chemists, and the augmentations to that supply, are German trained, German firms are able to hire them at a lower price than can British firms. The German firms who invest in R&D do well, on average, relative to British firms, and their German competitors who have not invested in R&D. They grow and, as they do, their R&D grows. The effectiveness of German university lobbying for government support of the training of chemists increases as the German industry grows. You can run out the rest of the scenario.

PROMISE AND CHALLENGES

I believe that the conception of institutions as defining or shaping social technologies is coherent, broad enough to be useful in analysis of economic growth and well tailored to fit with other aspects of evolutionary economic theory. In my view at least, the advance of physical technologies continues to play the leading role in the story of economic growth. Social technologies enter the story largely in terms of how they enable the implementation or development of physical technologies.

On the other hand, without appropriate institutions in place, or coming into place, the physical technologies that drove economic progress would not have appeared in the way they did, or had the impact they did. This is the meaning of my proposition that technologies and institutions coevolve, and together drive economic growth.

For this group at least, these propositions certainly are not novel. However, I believe there is something to be gained by developing them and working them through in the form of semi-formal or formal models. And that is the next item on my agenda.

Commentary: institutions, macroevolution and economic selection

John M. Gowdy

INTRODUCTION

Richard Nelson has surveyed the many strands of institutional economics and discussed the difficulty of integrating institutions into a coherent theory of the determinants of economic performance. It seems that to really make headway using an institutional framework to enrich economic analysis we have to walk a fine line between either vapid generalizations or, to use Nelson's words, the lean logic of stripped-down neoclassical theory. Georgescu-Roegen said there were only three successful institutional economists, Marx, Veblen and Schumpeter. And, in his usual combative style, he said the only thing modern institutionalists have adopted from Veblen is 'an aggressive scorn for theory' (Georgescu-Roegen, 1971, p. 321). Nevertheless, it is clear that many of the recent policy failures in areas ranging from natural resource management to economic development have resulted from a failure to take institutions into account.

This contribution draws on the fields of anthropology and evolutionary biology to complement some of the ideas in Nelson's paper. Anthropologists have always been concerned with whole societies and with the connections between culture, economy and environment. They are now making important contributions to the study of institutions in industrial societies, partly out of necessity as the traditional cultures they studied in the past rapidly disappear (Douglas, 1986; Nash, 1994). The connection between biology and economics is also deep, with an exchange of ideas between the two disciplines going back at least to Charles Darwin. The topics discussed briefly below draw heavily on recent advances in evolutionary biology, archaeology and cultural anthropology. They represent only a few of the questions raised by Nelson and show the endless possibilities for extending economic analysis beyond the sterile framework of optimization by 'strongly rational' producers and consumers.

ARE INSTITUTIONS EFFICIENT?

Nelson refers to Douglass North's (1990) observation that societies possessing efficient institutions are very lucky. North was referring, of course, to present-day institutions, but his observation is reinforced by a growing body of evidence from past societies. We can take solace or despair from the fact that many complex societies in the past were at least as dysfunctional as our own.

A lively topic in recent years, relating to the debate about environmental and social sustainability, has been the archaeology of Pacific island cultures. The islands of the Pacific were settled from about 2500 years ago by ancestors of present-day Polynesians. Over the next 2000 years these remarkable voyagers colonized thousands of islands, each with its own unique flora, fauna and geographical features. The history of how different cultures developed on these isolated islands is perhaps the closest thing social scientists have to a controlled experiment for human cultures.

The best-known example of an ancient Pacific culture is Easter Island, a culture that has come to symbolize how environmental mismanagement, spurred by dysfunctional social institutions, can result in the collapse of a complex society (Tainter, 1988). Easter Islanders developed a complex religion based on the worship of the huge stone figures called *moai* for which the island is now famous. The construction of these stone heads required the extensive use of logs as skids to move them from quarries to places of prominence around the island. The use of forest resources to support the *moai* cult eventually resulted in complete deforestation of the island. This in turn caused soil erosion, the loss of timber for boats, and a variety of other detrimental consequences that eventually wreaked havoc on the people of Easter Island. The end result was population collapse, and social disintegration into cannibalism and internecine warfare (Bahn and Flenley, 1992; Erickson and Gowdy, 2000). Information about the specific institutional behaviour that drove Easter Islanders to economic and social collapse is of course sketchy. There is an obvious lesson, however, for those who think that human institutions are necessarily rational and adaptive, and that technology will keep pace with a shrinking physical resource base.

A number of other Pacific island cultures apparently followed the same pattern of initial colonization, a period of prosperity, increasing pressure on local resources and eventual collapse (Kirch, 1997). One of the most interesting cases, however, is the island of Tikopia, whose culture did not collapse but rather developed a set of institutions that ensured environmental and social sustainability (McDaniel and Gowdy, 2000). The island was settled about 900 BC and, at first, the people of Tikopia seemed to be headed down the same path of overshoot and collapse followed by other Pacific island people. They practised slash-and-burn agriculture, overhunted native species, driving many of them to extinction, and experienced steady population growth. About 100 BC this pattern changed dramatically. Over the next few centuries, slash-and-burn agriculture was replaced by a kind of permanent arbor-culture of fruit trees, aroids, yams and other plants. Pigs were eliminated from the island, probably because they were incompatible with the multistorey arboriculture. The population levelled off at about 1000 people and remained steady until European contact (Kirch, 1997).

What happened on Tikopia that gave rise to a society that balanced human social and biological needs with long-term biological and physical reality? Oral tradition indicates that Tikopia developed institutions that maintained social and environmental sustainability. One of the most striking institutional changes was the adoption of cultural beliefs that supported zero population growth (Firth, 1967). Evidence from real human societies, as opposed to outcomes from purely deductive mathematical models, suggests two simple but clear lessons. First, institutions, like individuals, may not be efficient or rational. Second, the evolution of economies cannot be understood without understanding the institutional structures which guide them.

SELECTION, INSTITUTIONS AND ECONOMIC EFFICIENCY

The debate over selection processes in economics has a long history. In the 1950s a number of economists used the metaphor of natural selection to justify neoclassical theory. Alchian (1950), in a pioneering article, tried to preserve the essence of neoclassical theory using a Darwinian metaphor and doing away with assumptions like perfect knowledge and profit maximization. The suggested approach embodies the principles of biological evolution and natural selection by interpreting the economic system as an adoptive mechanism which chooses among exploratory actions generated by the adaptive pursuit of 'success' or 'profits'.

Alchian argues that this approach is more complete than standard economic theory because it allows for uncertainty and incomplete information. Firms need only have 'positive profits' not 'maximum profits', to survive. Uncertainty arises from (a) imperfect foresight and (b) human inability to solve complex problems. One idea in Alchian's paper is perhaps more provocative than he realized. He says that success 'does not require proper motivation but it may rather be the result of fortuitous circumstances'. He goes on to use probability distributions to show that firms can exist for decades just by chance, making entirely random decisions. So, just because a firm exists, this does not mean that it is superior in the sense of its managers having better judgment. This is similar to the claim of the advocates of 'punctuated equilibria' in biology that not all current characteristics of a species may represent optimal adaptation.

The best known advocate of the survival-of-the-fittest argument in economics is Milton Friedman (1953): 'The process of "natural selection" thus helps to validate the hypothesis [of profit maximization] – or, rather, given natural selection, acceptance of the hypothesis can be based largely on the judgment that it summarizes approximately the conditions for survival.' A telling criticism of Friedman was made by Sidney Winter (1964), who pointed out that, for 'natural selection' to weed out the less efficient firms, some sustaining feature must be passed from generation to generation (see Hodgson, 1994). There is nothing in Friedman's explanation to ensure that some 'efficient' trait is passed on. Nelson and Winter (1982) take up this idea and argue that 'routines' are the gene equivalents that are passed on from generation to generation. Winter (1964) also argues that the evolutionary process itself changes the environment in which evolution takes place.

The economic view of evolutionary change can be enriched by drawing on recent controversies in evolutionary biology. As in economics, there is a debate in biology between traditionalists who argue that change is gradual, continuous and takes place only at the micro level, and those who believe in hierarchical explanations of evolutionary change. The two main features of the traditional view of evolution by natural selection are that (a) point mutation with structural genes is the source of variability in organisms, and (b) evolutionary change is determined by natural selection working on small variations in phenotype; those organisms that best fit their environment survive (Lewin, 1980). The first feature implies that the pace of evolution is slow and the second implies that the morphology of an organism is determined by the forces of adaptation. This view of evolution as smooth and gradual change was challenged in the 1970s by the idea of punctuated equilibria, which claimed that biological evolution is characterized by long periods of stasis interrupted by periods of rapid change. When Eldredge and Gould (1972) first put forward the idea it was not really a new theory but rather a new interpretation of palaeontological data. As Gould and Eldredge (1986) point out, this finding is not inconsistent with traditional explanations of evolution. Ernst Mayr's theory of speciation driven by the isolation of small populations from a parent stock, for example, could yield a pattern of punctuated equilibrium. Sewall Wright's theory of adaptive landscapes also produces rapid change, in the time frame of geology, within the neo-Darwinian framework. So the idea that the pace of evolutionary change might be rapid need only modify, not overturn, traditional theory. The really radical implication of punctuated equilibrium relates to the claim that natural selection is the only mode of evolutionary change. Gould and Eldredge state that it is the notion of hierarchical selection that really embodies the radical content of punctuated equilibrium because it challenges the notion that what now exists must be present because it has won the struggle for survival. Their arguments are immediately relevant to the implicit assumption of traditional economists that the exiting array of firms and techniques in the economic world is solely the result of the competitive drive towards efficiency.

Gould and Vrba (1982) make a distinction between 'sorting' and 'selection'. Sorting is a general term that simply means differential survival rates. Some species survive while others do not for a number of reasons, including Darwinian selection due to competitive pressure. Selection implies a cause for survival (efficiency) while sorting is a broader term merely indicating an outcome. Gould and Vrba argue further that the term 'adaptation' is too broad to describe the reality of natural selection. They propose to narrow the meaning of the word 'adaptation' to features built by selection for their current role and the use of the term 'exaptation' to refer to features that now enhance fitness but were not built by natural selection for their current use. They argue that the standard view of evolution confuses current utility with reasons for origin. They suggest that the emphasis on adaptation to the exclusion of all other concerns has led researchers to overlook vital aspects of evolutionary change including higher selection processes.

An evolutionary approach to economic change should include a complete and explicit analysis of all sorting mechanisms, that is, all the possible reasons for economic survival, not just efficiency in production. Three possible hierarchies are rationalization, exaptation and macroevolution (Gowdy, 1992). Rationalization refers to the process of weeding out of inefficient firms and techniques, eloquently (and obsessively) described by neoclassical theory. At this level survival depends on the internal decisions of the firm in choosing the most economically efficient techniques of production. A firm may also gain a survival advantage because of exaptation. Some firms find themselves in a better position than their competitors to take advantage of innovations arising in other industries. Such firms have characteristics (exaptations) which enable them (unexpectedly) to take advantage of innovations arising in other industries. In such cases, the move from one technical recipe (or routine or even institution) to another is due not to gradual adaptation but rather to historical accident, by being in the right place at the right time. Other aspects of exaptation include complementarity, historical lock-in (Arthur, 1989; David, 1985) and increasing returns (Arthur, 1994). Eldredge (1997) has used concepts from palaeontology to describe the evolution of the cornet, a musical instrument whose design has evolved not on the basis of conventional notions of efficiency but because of a variety of social and institutional pressures.

At the top of this simple hierarchy is a sorting process which depends on random occurrences in the form of macro shocks which affect the whole economy. There may exist evolutionary processes that involve whole industries, groups of industries or even entire countries. Insofar as economic evolution results from processes other than 'microefficiency', that is, the optimal allocation of resources to be used in a specific production function, it calls into question the use of microeconomic concepts to describe macroeconomic phenomena (Eldredge, 1986, 1997, Foster, 1997). In economics as in biology there are modes of evolutionary change other than through gradual improvement in efficiency.

MICROFOUNDATIONS, INSTITUTIONS AND MACROEVOLUTION

In the decades following the Second World War the innovations in macroeconomic theory of the 1930s were gradually eroded to the point where, today, macro theories not based on micro foundations are virtually eliminated from mainstream economics. Many models of economic change are based more on mathematical tractability than on economic content. Again the controversies in economics and evolutionary biology are remarkably similar, and since the micro/macro controversy in biology is further advanced, economists can gain important insights from the biology debates.

A consensus seems to have emerged in biology that evolution is a hierarchical process with many modes of evolutionary change. A great biologist generally unsympathetic with the punctuated equilibrium position, Francisco Ayala (1998, p. 128) writes:

> Now, I pose the third question raised earlier: can macroevolutionary theory be derived from microevolutionary knowledge? The answer can only be 'no.' If macroevolutionary theory were deducible from microevolutionary principles, it would be possible to decide between competing macroevolutionary models simply by examining the logical implications of microevolutionary theory. But the theory of population genetics is compatible with both, punctualism and gradualism; and, hence, logically it entails neither … Hence, macroevolution and microevolution are decoupled in the sense (which is epistemologically most important) that macroevolution is an autonomous field of study that must develop and test its own theories.

Spurred in part by these parallel controversies in evolutionary biology, a growing number of economists argue that the Walrasian microfoundation approach to macroeconomics, which insists that the neoclassical theory of the firm should be the basis for a theory of macroeconomics, is inadequate and arbitrary (Foster, 1987; Gowdy, 1994; Colander, 1996). Others have called for a 'post Walrasian' macroeconomics which explicitly recognizes uncertainty and the role of institutions in economic life. Challenging the microfoundations position, and the argument that striving towards efficiency at the firm level is the sole mechanism driving economic change, is a central theme which links contemporary evolutionary theory and economic theory.

The microfoundations position in economics has the same problem that ultra-Darwinism has in biology; it is not that it is wrong, but that it is incomplete. It is a description of only part of economic reality, namely, market exchange and optimal allocation of fixed collections of goods or inputs. Taken in context, neoclassical theory is an indispensable tool for the analysis of market outcomes. However, there are many reasons why a particular product, firm or market arrangement might exist, and not all of these reasons are based on narrow economic optimization.

Competition and Cooperation

At the heart of economic theory, since Adam Smith at least, is the idea of perfection through competition. Evidently this idea, from the writings of Thomas Malthus, spurred Charles Darwin to develop the theory of evolution through natural selection. In the hands of Herbert Spencer the idea of evolution through competition became synonymous with progress, a viewed echoed in the application of evolutionary concepts by neoclassical economists. The philosopher of biology Eliot Sober points out, however, that the most familiar textbook examples of evolution do not involve competition for scarce resources. The cases of industrial melanism in moths and evolving insect immunity to DDT, for example, do not involve competition in this sense. According to Sober (1981, p. 100, quoted in Hodgson, 1993a, p. 30), 'Competition is a special case, not a defining characteristic of evolution.' The same could be said about economic competition and economic evolution.

Getting away from a near-exclusive focus on competition among individuals can help economists break away from the assumption of methodological individualism that underlies the microfoundation approach. Hodgson (1995, p. xxi) writes:

> In recent decades, and especially since the 1960s, there has been an increasing tendency for mainstream economists to attempt to explain all economic phenomena in terms of the utility-maximizing individuals which are supposed to make up the system. This 'methodological individualism' has acted to undermine Keynesian macroeconomics with its primary focus on aggregates at the systemic level. As argued elsewhere recognition of the shared problems of complexity in both biology and economics may lead economists to place less faith in methodological individualism and to recognize the legitimacy of levels and units of analysis above the individual (Sober, 1981; Hodgson 1993b). This would involve the reinstatement of aggregative macroeconomics as an autonomous level of analysis.

This leads to another relevant controversy in biology, the role of group selection in evolutionary change.

Group Selection

A heated controversy in biology is whether Darwinian selection can work at levels above the individual. Ultra-reductionists such as Dawkins (1976) argue that the only relevant unit of selection is the gene. A growing number of researchers say that selection can occur at levels above that of individual species (Wynne-Edwards, 1991; Wilson, 1997). Boehm (1997) argues that, among hunter-gatherers, societies with egalitarian institutions had a selective advantage (see the readings in Gowdy, 1998). So, not only biological characteristics of humans are important in our evolution, but also institutions. In economics, selection may take place at the level of product groups, industries or even countries. This is certainly a fruitful area for empirical research that can pave the way for a separate macroeconomics.

CONCLUDING COMMENTS

Obsession with the behaviour of individual firms and individual consumers has led to short-sighted, ineffective and even perverse macroeconomic policies. The overwhelming focus in economics is still on efficiency in allocation rather than distribution, scale or social and environmental impacts. Insights from biology can give us a deeper understanding of economic reality, including its social and environmental context. These insights can lead to public policies which take into account the deeper understanding of reality provided by evolutionary theory.

The perspective provided by evolutionary biology leads us to question polices based on an understanding of only one portion of reality, the market economy. The economic concept of value needs to be expanded to include more levels of hierarchy than the behaviour of atomistic agents and their aggregations, and mechanisms of change in addition to efficiency-driven competition. The greatest policy challenge economists face is to construct a valuation system which will take into account the various differences and contradictions in valuation across hierarchies of space and time.

REFERENCES

Alchian, A.A. (1950), 'Uncertainty, evolution and economic theory', *Journal of Political Economy* , **58**, 211–22.

Arthur, B. (1989), 'Competing technologies, increasing returns, and lock-in by historical events', *Economic Journal*, **99**, 116–31.
Arthur, B. (1994), *Increasing Returns and Path Dependence in the Economy,* Ann Arbor: University of Michigan Press.
Ayala, F. (1998), 'Beyond Darwinism? The Challenge of Macroevolution to the Synthetic Theory of Evolution', in *Philosophy of Biology*, New York: Prometheus Books, Amherst.
Bahn, P. and J. Flenley (1992), *Easter Island, Earth Island*, London and New York: Thames & Hudson.
Boehm, C. (1997), 'Impact of the human egalitarian syndrome on Darwinian selection mechanisms', *The American Naturalist*, 150 (Supplement), S100–S121.
Colander, D. (1996), 'Overview', in D. Colander (ed.), *Beyond Microfoundations*, New York: Cambridge University Press.
David, P. (1985), 'Clio and the economics of QWERTY', *American Economic Review Proceedings*, **75**, 332–7.
Dawkins, R. (1976), *The Selfish Gene*, New York: Oxford University Press.
Douglas, M. (1986), *How Institutions Think*, Syracuse: Syracuse University Press.
Eldredge, N. (1986), 'Information, economics and evolution', *Annual Review of Ecological Systems*, **17**, 351–69.
Eldredge, N. (1997), 'Evolution in the marketplace', *Structural Change and Economic Dynamics*, **8**(4), 385–98.
Eldredge, N. and S.J. Gould (1972), 'Punctuated Equilibria: An Alternative to Phyletic Gradualism', in T.J.M. Scopf (ed.), *Models in Paleobiology*, San Francisco: Freeman, Cooper.
Erickson, J. and J. Gowdy (2000), 'Resource use, institutions and sustainability: a tale of two Pacific island cultures', *Land Economics*, **76**(3), 345–54.
Firth, R. (1967), *The Work of the Gods in Tikopia*, London: The Athlone Press.
Foster, J. (1987), *Evolutionary Macroeconomics*, London: Unwin & Hyman.
Foster, J. (1997), 'The analytical foundations of evolutionary economics: from biological analogy to economic self-organization', *Structural Change and Economic Dynamics*, **8**(4), 427–52.
Friedman, M. (1953), 'The methodology of positive economics', in *Essays in Positive Economics*, Chicago: University of Chicago Press.
Georgescu-Roegen, N. (1971), *The Entropy Law and the Economic Process*, Cambridge, MA: Harvard University Press.
Gould, S.J. and N. Eldredge (1986), 'Punctuated equilibrium at the third stage', *Systematic Zoology*, **35**, 143–8.
Gould, S.J. and E. Vrba (1982), 'Exaptation – a missing term in the science of form', *Paleobiology*, **8**, 4–15.
Gowdy, J. (1992), 'Higher selection processes in evolutionary economic change', *Evolutionary Economics*, **2**, 1–16.
Gowdy, J. (1994), *Coevolutionary Economics: The Economy, Society and the Environment*, Boston: Kluwer Academic Press.
Gowdy, J. (ed.) (1998), *Limited Wants, Unlimited Means: A Reader on Hunter–Gatherer Economics and the Environment*, Washington, DC: Island Press.
Hodgson, G. (1993a), *Economics and Evolution*, Ann Arbor: University of Michigan Press.
Hodgson, G. (1993b), 'Why the problem of reductionism in biology has implications for economics', *World Futures,* **37**, 69–90; reprinted in G. Hodgson (ed.) (1995), *Economics and Biology*, Aldershot, UK and Brookfield, US: Edward Elgar.

Hodgson, G. (1994), 'Optimization and evolution: Winter's criticism of Friedman revisited', *Cambridge Journal of Economics*, **18**, 413–30.

Hodgson, G. (ed.) (1995), *Economics and Biology*, Aldershot, UK and Brookfield, US: Edward Elgar.

Kirch, P. (1997), 'Microcosmic histories: island perspectives on "global change"', *American Anthropologist*, **99,** 30–42.

Lewin, R. (1980), 'Evolutionary theory under fire', *Science*, **210**, 883–7.

McDaniel,C. and J. Gowdy (2000), *Paradise for Sale: Markets, Society and Ecosystem Destruction*, Berkeley: University of California Press.

Nash, J. (1994), 'Global integration and subsistence insecurity', *American Anthropologist*, **96**, 7–30.

Nelson, R. and S. Winter (1982), *An Evolutionary Theory of Economic Change*, Cambridge, MA: Harvard University Press.

North, D. (1990), *Institutions, Institutional Change and Economic Performance*, Cambridge: Cambridge University Press.

Sober, E. (1981), 'Holism, Individualism and the Units of Selection', in R.N. Giere and P.D. Asquith (eds), *Philosophy of Science Association 1982*, **1**, Philosophy of Science Association, East Lansing, MI; reprinted in G. Hodgson (ed.) (1995), *Economics and Biology*, Aldershot, UK and Brookfield, US: Edward Elgar.

Tainter, J. (1988), *The Collapse of Complex Societies*, New York: Cambridge University Press.

Wilson, D.S. (1997), 'Human groups as units of selection', *Science*, **276**, 1816–17.

Winter, S. (1964), 'Economic natural selection and the theory of the firm', *Yale Economic Essays*, **4**, 225–72.

Wynne-Edwards, V.C. (1991), 'Ecology denies neo-Darwinism', *The Ecologist*, **21**.

3. From evolution to language and learning

Bart Nooteboom

INTRODUCTION

Evolutionary theory is based on the well-known explanatory trinity of variety generation, selection and retention. In biology variety is due to migration, genes working out differently in different contexts (Rose, 1997), Mendelian novel combinations of existing genes (in the case of sexual reproduction) and random mutations yielding novel genes. Characteristics adopted in life are not incorporated in the genome (evolution is not Lamarckian). Thus evolutionary theory does not offer much concerning the creation of new variety. In economic systems, on the other hand, new variety is evidently created by learning, which is transmitted in imitation, teaching and training. Yet evolutionary economists tend to emphasize selection from a pre-existing variety of life forms and to neglect the generation of variety. This happens even in as recent a work as Metcalfe (1998). The justification of this approach is that it is interesting to view the market as a selection process, and the effects of selection on the population level of markets and industries are important in their own right. Generation of variety is not denied but left aside for the sake of focus in research.

Nelson and Winter (1982) did allow for adaptation of organizational routines, which they took as the equivalent of genes. Here adaptation is not random, but based on search induced by failure, and consists of novel combinations of elements from old routines. However, adaptation remains separate from selection: generation of variety and selection are separate processes, and occur in succession (Vromen, 1995). While this is understandable for practical reasons of tractability, for the purpose of model building it is ultimately unsatisfactory.

There are two fundamental reasons why it is unsatisfactory. One is that, as Veblen had already indicated, the selection environment includes institutions, which are themselves subject to selection (Hodgson, 1993) and therefore cannot be taken as given exogenously. What is more, institutions are to some extent modified or even created by the units they are supposed to select. By innovation, rhetoric and political action, firms to some extent create the conditions of selection. The second reason is that adaptation by learning is forward looking. It is based on experience acquired in the selection process, which provides the basis for inference concerning future possibilities and conditions; strategic opportunities and threats. This does not mean that foresight is perfect, and indeed innovation entails a great deal of trial and error, but it is not random and it is informed. These two arguments will be developed in more detail in later sections. When the two issues are combined, we see that learning and innovation yield both anticipation and creation of future selection conditions. In other words, selection and adaptation are mutually dependent, and adequate theory must be developed to account for this. If both the selection environment and the creation of novelty are endogenous and mutually dependent, what remains of the selection process, and hence of the central notion of phylogenetic evolution? Does the evolutionary perspective still make fundamental sense, or has it outlived its usefulness, and should we move from evolution to self-organization (Foster, 1997, 2000)? Foster proposed that Schumpeter can be seen as an exemplary evolutionary *economist*, in that he may have been the only one who grasped the notion of an endogenous selection environment that is so characteristic of socioeconomic as opposed to biological evolution. This would make sense of his talk of evolution while rejecting biological analogies, and his use of such a non-evolutionary term as 'creative destruction'.

People operate on the basis of reasoning and mutually influence and constrain each other in language. Why should this be like biological evolution at all? I propose that, in order to understand markets, industries and innovation properly, we should build in theory of knowledge, learning and language. This paper aims to contribute to that process. I leave it to the reader to decide whether this extends evolutionary theory or yields a fundamentally different perspective on self-organization.

First I engage in some preliminaries: my view on knowledge and learning, institutions and language. Then I offer a stage theory of learning and innovation that extends the life cycle theory of innovation.

LEARNING

For knowledge I take a social constructivist, interactionist view. The term 'knowledge' here is a broad one, and denotes any mental activity, including perception and value judgments. People perceive, interpret and evaluate the world according to mental categories (or frames or mental models) which they have developed in interaction with their social and physical environment. This entails that perception, interpretation and evaluation are path-dependent and idiosyncratic to a greater or lesser extent. Different people see the world differently to the extent that they have developed in different social and physical surroundings and have not interacted with each other. In other words, past experience determines 'absorptive capacity' (Cohen and Levinthal, 1990). In social science this approach is linked with the views of G.H. Mead ('symbolic interactionism'). In developmental psychology it is linked, up to a point, with the work of Piaget and, more fully, with the work of Vygotsky (1962). In cognitive science it is linked with the emerging, non-mainstream view of 'situated action' (as opposed to the mainstream 'computational–representational' view: see Shanon, 1988, 1990,1993; Hendriks-Jansen, 1996). In economics it is linked with the notion of subjectivism in the Austrian school: different people not only have different preferences, but 'different minds think different things'. The crux of this view is, as proposed by Piaget and Vygotsky, that intelligence is internalized action and speech, and that both knowledge and meaning are context dependent. This context dependence links with the Austrian view, and particularly Hayek's, that a variety of knowledge is distributed across heterogeneous contexts. Categories develop from interaction, and this is how competition, or markets more generally, constitute a Hayekian discovery process.

Summing up, the term 'constructivist' indicates that intelligence is internalized action. The term 'social' or 'interactionist' indicates that, since one cannot 'climb down from one's mind' to assess whether one's knowledge is properly 'hooked on to the world', the variety of perception and understanding offered by other people is the only source one has for correcting one's errors.

As discussed in Nooteboom (1992a) an implication of this view for the theory of the firm is that in order to achieve a specific joint goal, the categories of thought of the people involved must be aligned to some extent. Different people have a greater or lesser 'cognitive distance' between them (Nooteboom 1999a). This yields the notion of the firm as a 'focusing device', to reduce cognitive distance, that is, achieve a sufficient alignment of mental categories to understand each other, utilize complementary capabilities and achieve a shared goal. Organizations develop their own specialized semiotic systems: language, symbols, metaphors, myths, rituals. This is what we call organizational culture. This differs between organizations to the extent that they have accumulated different experiences, in different industries, technologies and markets. This connects with the idea, in the organization literature, that the crux of the firm is to serve as a 'sensemaking system' (Weick, 1979, 1995), a 'system of shared meaning' (Smircich, 1983) or 'interpretation system' (Choo, 1998). I propose that this yields a more fundamental reason for firms to exist than the reduction of transaction costs, although transaction costs are also part of the story. One interpretation of entrepreneurship, which links with Schumpeter's notion of the entrepreneur as a charismatic figure, is that it is his central task to achieve this: to align perceptions, understandings and goals (cf. Witt, 1998). Note that alignment of cognitive categories need not entail identity. As discussed in Nooteboom (1999a), there is a trade-off between cognitive distance, needed for variety and novelty of cognition, and cognitive proximity, needed for mutual understanding. In fact, different people in a firm will to a greater or lesser extent introduce elements of novelty from their outside lives and experience, and this is a source of both error and innovation.

A second implication is that by the need to achieve a focus, there is a risk of myopia: relevant threats and opportunities to the firm are not perceived. To compensate for this, people, and firms, need complementary sources of outside intelligence, to utilize 'external economy of cognitive scope' (Nooteboom 1992a). Here again the trade-off arises between cognitive distance, for the sake of novelty, and cognitive proximity, for the sake of understanding and utilization of complementarity. This perspective is well suited to the prevalent idea in the literature on innovation systems that innovation derives primarily from interaction between firms (Lundvall, 1985,1988,1993).

The present theory yields a prediction that is opposite to classical transaction cost economics: with increasing uncertainty, in terms of volatility of technology and markets, firms should not integrate activities more, as transaction cost theory prescribes, but less, because the need to utilize outside complementary cognition is greater. Here the prediction is that firms will engage less in mergers and acquisitions and more in intensive alliances at some cognitive distance, but with sufficient durability and intensity to achieve mutual understanding and cooperation. Boundaries of the firm are determined, in part, by the need for cognitive proximity, next to reduction of transaction costs. One might incorporate this into transaction cost theory in terms of cognitive or dynamic transaction costs, but note the reversal of predictions indicated.

In the literature on organizational learning a distinction is made between first- and second-order learning (Hedberg *et al.*, 1976; Fiol and Lyles, 1985) or, equivalently, between 'single loop and double loop' learning (Argyris and Schön, 1978). The first is learning to do existing things better (more efficiently) and the second is learning to do new things. This is linked with the notion of 'parametric' change (Langlois and Robertson, 1995) as opposed to 'architectural' change (Henderson and Clark, 1990). Also related to this, March (1991) and Holland (1975) distinguished between 'exploitation' and 'exploration'. In order to survive in the short term, that is in the present selection environment, firms need to exploit their present resources (or competencies or abilities) efficiently, and to survive in the long term firms need to develop novel competencies, to anticipate or create future selection environments. This combination of exploitation and exploration is the main challenge for management, but it is a paradoxical task. To a greater or lesser extent, depending on the type of product, market, technologies and types of knowledge involved, exploitation requires fixity of standards and tightness of coordination, while exploration requires a loosening of structural ties and conditions. This chapter aims to contribute to the solution of this paradox.

Exploration entails discovery, which is subject to radical uncertainty, in the sense of Knight (1921). In other words, it goes beyond risk, which is associated with a known, closed set of possible alternatives, to which one can attach a probability distribution. The set of options to choose from is open, and often options are discovered or created after, not prior to, action. Options are often options to discover further options. This requires a logic or heuristic of 'abduction' (Peirce, 1957; Holland *et al.*, 1989): how do we explore options that are unknown? How do we arrive at new hypotheses that have some chance of viability? Of all the novel ways of doing things that we can think of, which should we try, and how do we find out what other, as yet unknown, options there are?

Like Nelson and Winter (1982) we might be tempted by this uncertainty to consider searching blind. And, indeed, one way to proceed would be to engage in random novel combinations, and doubtless some of this is going on. But we are thinking animals that make inferences about the future on the basis of our experience with the past. Consider, for example, the famous scenario planning by Shell oil company. It develops contingency plans on the basis of the analysis of alternative policies under different possible futures. Robustness of elements of policy under different possible futures provides a reasonable guess for contingency plans. However, while we can think of many logically possible future worlds, we not only lack knowledge on their likelihood, but we have no way of knowing whether we have thought of all possible futures, and we cannot be certain that the futures we have thought of contain the actual future. In particular, the future is difficult to predict because actions will have unforeseeable consequences, and there will be strategic reactions to our actions from others. We are playing games whose participants, strategies and pay-offs are revealed only as the game is played, and then shift in the process. The future will be different from any of the ones imagined, but nevertheless one may have developed a platform for viable strategies, with capabilities in place to execute them. Thus discovery goes beyond search among existing options, to include the creation of new options. We need to solve the problem of abduction: how can we make steps into the unknown, in exploration, while preserving existing resources in such a way that exploitation is maintained? How do we set about creation with a minimum of destruction? What is the optimal process of discovery? We need a heuristic to move from present competence to novel competence, while surviving in the process.

INSTITUTIONS

North (1990) defined institutions as rules of the game that constrain behaviour, and thereby reduce transaction costs. In his view organizations are not institutions but players confronted with institutions. Sociologists entertain a much wider notion of institutions, as not only regulating but also constituting behaviour, as not only constraining but also enabling behaviour. In the sociological view, institutions are associated with rules that relate to roles, relative to social contexts, and thereby shape expectations and make behaviour predictable.

I take the sociological view and define institutions as sets of rules that regulate and constitute behaviour. Laws and regulations are institutions, but also language, basic categories of thought and norms and values. It is useful to distinguish between the noun 'institution', which indicates a set of rules, and the adjective 'institutionalized', which indicates the extent to which something is subject to rules (without itself being a set of rules). This allows for degrees of institutionalization. Thus a road is not an institution but is institutionalized by the rules of traffic. Science is not itself an institution but is institutionalized to the extent that it is subject to durable regulation, standards of legitimacy and excellence, procedures of evaluation. The labour market in the Netherlands, say, is more institutionalized than in the United States. Methodology, on the other hand, is an institution, if we see methodology as regulative and constitutive of science, since it consists of a set of rules on how to conduct and legitimize science.

The term 'rule' is not perfect. It may emphasize constraints too much, suggest too much that rules consist only of sanctions in the form of physical punishment or financial penalty, while what we have in mind is a much broader notion of 'enabling constraints' in social interaction. Enablers always entail limitations in some respect. To help and guide behaviour in one direction directs attention away from alternatives. Penalties for deviance from 'rules' may also be social (lack of recognition, legitimation, acceptance), psychological (loneliness), cognitive (lack of learning by interaction) or more generally loss of identity. This brings us close to the Veblenian notion of institutions as settled, shared habits of thought. We are thus looking for a term that captures the following connotations: shared, habitual, guiding, constraining, enabling, psychologically constitutive, socially constitutive, enduring but not emprisoning, allowing for personal interpretation and deviance. A crucial question is how the socially constitutive and regulative can be combined with personal idiosyncrasy and variety of interpretation, and freedom of choice.

I propose language as the paradigm example of an institution. It demonstrates very well how an institution enables and constrains behaviour, while it is also subject to shifts on the basis of that behaviour. For this, we may employ de Saussure's distinction between the intersubjective order ('langue') and personal creative language use ('parole'). I note that, after making this distinction, de Saussure focused on 'langue', to the neglect of 'parole', while here we are interested precisely in the latter: the sources of change in idiosyncratic practice. The combination of the two allows for rigorous rules of scientific meaning as well as poetic licence. The issue of exploitation and exploration is closely connected with this tension between individual and community. Exploitation requires coordination ('langue'), which ties individuals down to a greater or lesser extent; exploration arises from individual deviance ('parole') as a source of innovation (Nooteboom, 1992a, 1992b).

Perhaps the term 'routine' is a good candidate to replace the notion of a 'rule' to characterize institutions: it seems to carry all the desired connotations. But it may cause confusion with the use of that term by Nelson and Winter (1982) for organizational procedures as units of selection. Concerning organizations, that fits well with what I mean here, and perhaps with what Nelson and Winter meant, but we want a more general concept, beyond organizational routines. So, for lack of a better word, and to avoid confusion, I stick to the term 'rules'.

Since institutions include language and shared categories of perception and thought, a further elucidation of institutions requires a theory of knowledge and language. As with knowledge, in contrast to the dominant representational–computational theory of knowledge, I assume a 'situated action', social constructivist theory of language. 'Situated action' indicates that meanings and categories are dependent on context and open, subject to shifting across contexts. One cannot specify necessary and sufficient conditions for proper reference, independent of context. Different members of a class often have 'family resemblance' (Wittgenstein, 1976) without having any characteristic shared by all. Characterization of membership is a temporary 'default' (Johnson-Laird, 1983) which is subject to revision.

I admitted that my view of knowledge is sociological in the sense that it entails that interaction with other people is essential for one's knowledge. However, this does not imply that people lose their individuality, initiative and responsibility. What is proposed here surrenders both the methodological individualism of economics and the methodological collectivism of (some) sociology, and adopts what might be called 'methodological interactionism'. It is important to note that the fact that institutions are internalized from social interaction does allow for differentiation between individuals and for a certain amount of autonomy and free will. This is relevant, because the issue has been raised (Hodgson, 1993) whether social selectionism can be consistent with intentionality and free will. This connects with the tension between liberalism and communitarianism. Liberalists take an unacceptable, solipsistic view of individuals, while communitarians tend towards an authoritarian subjection of individuals to the dictates of the dominant opinion. However, one can very well maintain that people 'make sense' and construct categories, and thereby develop their identity, in interaction with others in a social community, and yet allow for that identity to become individualized, so that the individual can exercise more or less independent views, choice and ethical judgment.

SELECTION

The debate on the endogeneity of the selection environment is connected, I propose, to the debate between the view of 'positioning' versus the view of 'strategic choice', in the management and organization literature. The positioning view assumes a given selection environment, exogenous to firms, in the form of 'market structure', in which they have to position themselves. According to the view of strategic choice the selection environment is endogenous: it can be influenced or transformed by entrepreneurial, innovative action.

Porter (1980, 1985) was instrumental in introducing the industrial organization perspective from economics into strategic management, in the 'positioning' view. This perspective entails the 'structure–conduct–performance' view, according to which market structure determines conduct, and conduct determines performance. The underlying assumption, as generally in mainstream economics, is that technology and demand are given, and that firms find themselves in an established field of competitive forces, in which they should find an appropriate niche. This perspective has been criticized from the 'competence' perspective for its neglect of 'strategic choice' and entrepreneurial abilities to transcend competition for existing scarce resources by the creation of novel resources, and to distinguish a firm from its competitors by means of firm-specific competencies. The difference between these perspectives is sometimes exaggerated. Nevertheless, the notion of strategic intent and the scope for entrepreneurial shifts of technology and preferences to alter the field of competitive forces yields a useful shift of perspective. This also has sometimes been exaggerated. Of course a firm cannot create any environment and any competencies it likes. It will need to make entrepreneurial use of niches of technological and institutional opportunity, and will need to overcome internal and external obstacles to change.

The bias towards exogenous market and industry structure, with studies that explain conduct and performance as a result of industrial structure and properties of technology, still prevails in much neo-Schumpeterian and evolutionary innovation research. Such researchers typically devise sector taxonomies and derive conditions for conduct and performance from them (Pavitt, 1984; Malerba and Orsenigo, 1995).

Apart from the fact that innovations change market conditions and political action influences the making of laws, we should recognize that many of the institutions that govern technological development are not objectively given but are to a greater or lesser extent socially constructed. They form a 'negotiated order' (Bijker *et al.*, 1987; Latour, 1987; Latour and Woolgar, 1979). Technology and its evaluation often have a shared cognitive bias.

An illustration of this is the study by Garud and Rappa (1996) of the development of hearing aids by using implants in the cochlea, in the inner ear. There were two rival systems: a single-channel and a multiple-channel device. The first carried less risk than the second, but the second yielded a greater and easier improvement of hearing. The problem was that objective, independent measures of these dimensions of performance were not available, and the balancing between them was subjective. The same ideas that informed the choice of device also informed the methodologies for selecting between them, so that there were rival evaluation methods. The rival methods were championed by rival commercial interest groups, and the stakes were high. The single-channel group argued that the obvious choice was to begin with the low-risk device, and step up to the other after its risks were clearer and could be reduced. The multiple-channel group argued that this would not reduce risk but add to it in the process of taking out one device and replacing it with the other. No objective experience was available to back up either claim.

We need to achieve a synthesis of entrepreneurial action that creates new conditions and competencies, and conditions from the environment in terms of other firms and institutions, which enable and constrain such actions, in patterns of cooperation, competition and negotiation.

In evolutionary theory, the question lingers what we should take as the unit of selection in markets. According to Nelson and Winter (1982) it is organizational routines; according to Metcalfe (1998) it is business units. In the organizational literature, next to a market selection mechanism outside the firm, a selection mechanism within the firm has been postulated: internally generated ideas are subjected to a sometimes erratic mechanism of selection in organizational bureaucracies (Burgelman 1996). I am tempted to see the indeterminacy of the unit of selection as another indication that, in human affairs, evolutionary theory is simply not adequate. What would be the unit of selection in language; in speech, scientific articles and storytelling? The question does not seem to make sense. But let us nevertheless try to stay as close to evolutionary theory as possible.

Classical Darwinism was non-hierarchical, that is, focused on evolution on a single level of life forms. There selection and sorting go together. Gould and Eldredge recognized that there may be a hierarchy of several levels (genes within the organism; species of organisms) and then selection and sorting may separate and take place on different levels: sorting on one level may be due to selection at another. Species sorting may be due to selection from its individuals, and then is thoroughly Darwinian. It may also be due to species selection, on the basis of group characteristics affecting the fitness of the species, which is controversial. Such characteristics may, or may not, take the form of emergent characteristics that arise by non-additivity and interaction among lower-level traits, affecting differential birth rate, for example (Gould 1989).

'Punctuated equilibrium' theory, initiated by Eldredge and Gould (1972), seeks to explain the stylized fact that, in the development of many species, there have been prolonged periods of stasis, punctuated by change that is abrupt in terms of geological time. The explanation of stasis is not yet satisfactory, but it is attributed to external constraints on variety such as inherent limitations of geometry, physics and chemistry, and to internal factors such as the elimination of deviants in the population. Punctuation is attributed to 'allopatric speciation': small populations isolated at peripheries of parental ranges, develop into separate species. I will propose a cycle of development that yields something like that.

An example of geometric constraint on forms of life lies in the geometry of spheres and circles. For example, metabolism (consumption of nutrients and waste production) can be proportional to content, while assimilation of food and excretion of waste are proportional to surface, as in a cell. Then beyond a certain size the life form will starve or poison itself. In animals, heat exchange with the environment also operates through the surface, while heat production is proportional to content. Therefore, when there is a large difference between internal and external temperature, as is the case for warm-blooded animals in polar climates, or not so warm-blooded animals in hot climates, these animals need to be large and bulbous, or to have thick furs or skins: consider whales, polar bears, walruses, elephants and hippopotami. However, animals that in strenuous exertion produce a lot of heat in hot climates, such as panthers, cougars and the like, need to be thin and slim.

In both biological and economic evolution group selection is controversial. The problem is that any trait that is conducive to group survival is transmitted through the individual, who is better off to free-ride or prey on other people's commitment to the group, and this would favour the proliferation of genes of opportunism. Only commitment to next of kin might survive the logic of selection. But in socioeconomics transmission may be social rather than individual, as indicated in my theory of language. Furthermore, the interests of the individual may be tied to the interest of the group. This may be due to the focusing and creation of shared meanings and categories that I proposed as the crux of the firm. In fact, this is part of the reason why this *is* the crucial function of the firm. Here opportunism may be limited by default, on the basis of routines: certain 'opportunities for opportunism' are not perceived. This is how trustworthiness may go beyond calculative self-interest (Nooteboom 1996, 1999a). Alternatively, the inclination to utilize opportunities for opportunism may be contained by ethical categories of norms and values, or reputation mechanisms. And, to the extent that people still seek and attempt to utilize such opportunities, we try to contain them with the incentive mechanisms with which the economic literature abounds.

Thus there may be no need to choose any single unit of selection: ideas, routines, teams, divisions, business units and entire firms may all qualify.

THE CYCLE THEORY OF INNOVATION

In the organizational and economic literatures there is a stream of thought that suggests that innovation proceeds according to a 'cycle' with two stages: an initial stage of volatility, with the creation of Schumpeterian 'novel combinations', and a later stage of consolidation, with 'dominant designs' (Abernathy, 1978; Abernathy and Utterback, 1978; Abernathy and Clark, 1985) and efficient production systems that employ economies of scale and routinization. The cycle is generally held to imply a shift from product to process innovations, as product forms settle down and competitive pressure shifts to efficient production.

Note that standardization and utilization of scale economies do not necessarily imply 'Fordist' production. Standards can allow for a wide scope of differentiated production and still be standards, requiring a certain amount of control and coordination. Take, for example, the consultancy firm Arthur Andersen, which is proposed as a paradigm example of a flexible firm. Its consultants are highly autonomous, employing their individual knowledge, skill and creativity to provide custom-made advice. But, even there, attempts are made to safeguard professional standards and consistent quality. Scale is exploited by requiring consultants to contribute their experience to a common pool, and to work together, which requires a certain amount of standardization of definitions and procedures. Almost any type of efficient production will require some amount, no matter how limited, of routinization and standardization, of actions, output, skill, knowledge or information (Mintzberg, 1983).

The life cycle theory of innovation has been complemented by the product life cycle theory of internationalization (Vernon, 1966). According to this theory, the consolidated innovation, which originated in countries with advanced technology and demand, is 'generalized', that is, carried to less developed countries with lower wages, in order to further extend the market and fight the competition with a further decrease in costs.

The life cycle theory of innovation suggests that the first, volatile stage of novel combinations requires decentralized, disintegrated organizational forms such as industrial districts of small, independent firms (Piore and Sabel, 1983), or firms with a decentralized 'organic' structure, while the stage of consolidation requires a more integrated, bureaucratic structure. In other words, the degree of organizational integration depends on the stage in the innovation cycle. This connects with a long tradition in the organizational literature to propose that stable, predictable environments require integrated, 'mechanistic'; bureaucratic forms of organization, while volatile, unpredictable environments require disintegrated, 'organic' forms of organization (Burns and Stalker, 1961, Emery and Trist, 1965; Thompson, 1967; Lawrence and Lorsch, 1967).

The cycle theory has met with empirical contradictions. Among other things, often process innovation precedes rather than follows product innovation. But my main objection to the cycle, perhaps related to the empirical anomalies, is that this cycle is not really a cycle. A genuine cycle leads back to the beginning. Like evolutionary theory, existing theory tells us how exogenously generated novel variety settles down. The origins of novelty remain a mystery, and that is precisely what we would like to understand. How does the discovery process work?

A HEURISTIC OF DISCOVERY

Thomas Kuhn (1970) proposed that a certain amount of conservatism in theory is rational: counter to what Popper was supposed to have prescribed, it is not rational to drop any investment, including investment in theory, whenever the first indication ('falsifier') arises to prove that it is not perfect. In fact, scientists engage in solving puzzles within the purview of 'normal science', within its dominant 'paradigm', until the cumulative weight of anomalies becomes 'excessive', and then novelty generally comes from outside. In fact, Popper agreed that a certain amount of theoretical tenacity is rational, because 'otherwise we will never find out where the real strengths of our theories lie' (Popper, 1976, p. 52).

Expanding on these insights, Nooteboom (1992a, 1999b) proposed that, like crime, discovery is guided by motive, opportunity and means. One needs an accumulation of unsatisfactory performance to generate motive, to overcome one's own inertia or that of others in an organization. In markets, one also needs an opportunity of demand and/or technology. And one needs insights into what novel elements to obtain from what source and how to incorporate them in present competence. I propose that one can obtain such conditions only by moving one's present competencies across a variety of contexts ('generalization'), adapting them to local conditions ('differentiation'), seeking interaction with novel conditions and people, to adopt elements of novelty from them ('reciprocation'). That is how we obtain motive, opportunity and means for change.

Generalization often needs to be preceded by 'consolidation', to find out what precisely it is that one is transferring to novel contexts, and to do so efficiently. This often requires the codification of knowledge that at first was tacit. Transfer to novel contexts often requires standardization for the sake of division of labour and coordination. The need for this depends on how systemic the activity or technology involved is. Novel combinations produced by grafting elements from outside practice yield syncretic structures that induce pressure for more radical 'architectural' innovations. I will specify this in more detail later.

This, I propose, is how a Hayekian discovery process in markets works. The basic principle is an alternation of variety of form and variety of context: variety of form is reduced and replaced by variety of context that generates novel variety of form.

In language we find this in the 'hermeneutic circle' (Gadamer, 1977). Whereas, in the earlier analytic tradition, going back to Frege (1892), sentence meaning is a grammatical function of the given, context-independent meanings of component words, here the meanings of words shift as they are applied in different sentences, in different discourses. This aligns with the interactionist, 'situated action' theory of knowledge and language.

Meanings depend on context and shift as they are applied in different contexts. This is further developed in Jacobson's (1987) theory of poetics. Words have 'paradigmatic' repertoires of meaning, from which selections are made, guided by the context of discourse in which words are used, and substituted into the 'syntagmatic' structure of sentences. But on the occasion of their proximity in a sentence, or by similarity of sound or rhythm, through a mechanism of metaphor, in which one concept is suddenly seen in the light of another, suggestions arise for words to lend each other novel meanings. When these are adopted in the speech community, they yield novel elements of paradigmatic repertoires. Thus meanings shift in their use, in the dynamics of Saussurian 'parole'. This is illustrated in Figure 3.1.

I propose that learning proceeds similarly: by applying knowledge in novel contexts we encounter unexpected rival or complementary elements of knowledge that provide the material for novel combinations. For technology novel context entails a new area of application and, for products, it entails a novel market or market segment. This cycle is illustrated in Figure 3.2.

Note that the cycle is proposed as a heuristic: that is, a rule that generally tends to contribute to the goal of preserving exploitation while conducting

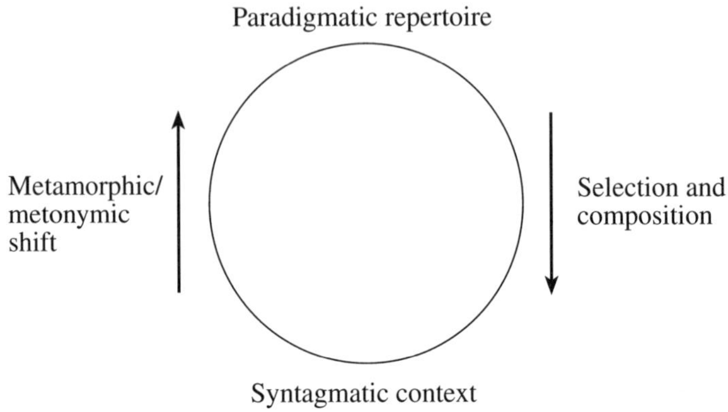

Figure 3.1 Hermeneutic circle

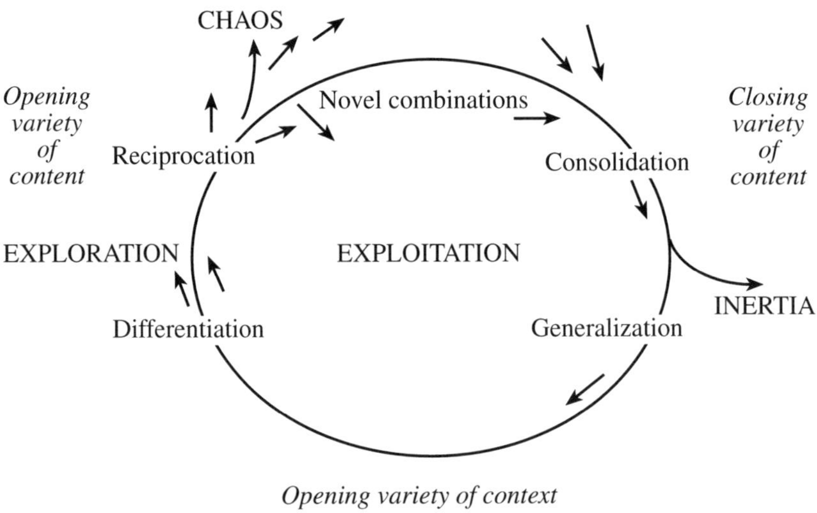

Figure 3.2 Cycle of exploitation and exploration

exploitation. It is not proposed as an inexorable march of logic that is necessary, uniform and universal. It is not necessary: innovation can occur on the basis of purely random trial and error. That, however, is likely to be associated with excessive waste and failure. Here we might preserve a principle of selection on a higher level: firms survive to the extent that they manage this process of discovery. The cycle is not inexorable: development may get stalled. In particular, after consolidation development may get stuck in inertia. In markets, however, this is vulnerable to new entry of entrepreneurs, unless they are barred from entry. In the stage of radical innovation, novel combinations may get lost in a chaos of competing systems that fail to lead to any dominant design. The game of rivalry may have no equilibrium. In the stage of consolidation, the importance of fixed standards for the sake of efficient production and generalization depends on the type of product, technology, knowledge and market. There are many contingencies, and some will be discussed later.

Consider product change in more detail. As products are offered in novel markets, one has an opportunity to find out where their limitations lie, in lack of fit with newly discovered characteristics of demand. This yields motive and opportunity for 'differentiation'. A trade-off is involved here between the opportunity in terms of a higher profit margin for tailor-made products and the possible opportunity cost of loss of economy of scale. This trade-off depends on the type of product, technology and market. Next, one may find out how in those respects in which one's own product fails the competing product or comparable products perform better. This yields the means of 'reciprocation'. This is logically equivalent to metaphor in language: one practice is seen in the light of another. Alternatively, one may find novel opportunities in local supply of labour, materials or technology to improve the product or its process of production. A famous example is how Henry Ford's idea of an assembly line in car manufacturing was inspired by the procedure, at a mail-order company, in which boxes on a conveyor belt passed successive stations, to be filled according to order slips.

Syncretic add-ons of outside elements, in reciprocation, labour under one or more of the following problems. Complexity of *ad hoc* add-ons increases architectural complexity ('spaghetti'), which yields problems of coordination and decreasing returns from further add-ons. Duplication of parts in different places of the architecture forgoes opportunities for economy of scale. Above all, initial success of novel elements can be achieved only in niches where they fit into established structures that constitute the local selection environment. Such a structure may be the architecture of the practice itself, or of structures of use, or superordinate structures of distribution channels, legal acceptance, vested interests and so on. This explains why often novelty first emerges in niches other than the ones where they are later most successful. From an evolutionary perspective, we might see this as the 'allopatric speciation' that yields punctuated equilibrium, along the lines proposed by Gould.

As success emerges in the niche, pressures arise for more radical architectural changes, again in the product itself or its structures of use, or the superordinate architectures, to allow the novelty to fully realize its potential. Here the niche which served for the incubation of novelty is expanded, and novelty creates its own selection environment. Such more radical architectural innovation, on different levels of structure, creates confusion, creative destruction and a great deal of uncertainty. This is where a novel 'technical trajectory' or 'technoeconomic paradigm' may arise (Dosi, 1982, 1984; Dosi *et al.*, 1988; Freeman and Perez, 1989). Such architectural change is not random: one hint for change is to design architecture such that novel elements that were proven useful in the preceding stage of reciprocation can better realize their potential. But multiple interests are at stake, and strategic interaction can have unpredictable outcomes. Here we are back at the beginning of the cycle: a process of consolidation is needed. Completion of the cycle explains among other things that, while process innovation may follow product innovation, the reverse can equally be the case.

Note that the cycle appears to solve the problem of exploitation and exploration, at least in part. By applying current competencies in novel contexts we preserve exploitation, needed to survive in the process of discovery, while at the same time contributing to exploration: the accumulation of motives, opportunities and means for change. A criterion for search is to look for novel contexts that are sufficiently close to maintain exploitation and sufficiently distant to offer significant novelty. This connects with the trade-off between cognitive distance and proximity discussed before.

Nooteboom (1999b) employed the notion of scripts to develop a hierarchy of innovations and institutions, on the basis of a hierarchy of structures. A script is an architecture of nodes that represent component activities in more or less rule-guided behaviour. Substitutions into nodes represent alternative ways to perform component activities. Scripts may denote mental concepts or procedures (Abelson, 1976; Shank and Abelson, 1977), organizational routines, primary processes of production and distribution, and industry supply chains. Component activities in an (organizational) script are based on (cognitive) subscripts, and (organizational) scripts substitute their output into superscripts (supply chains). Parametric innovation with respect to a given script entails a novel substitution into a given node; a minor architectural innovation is a reversal of orders of nodes or the creation of alternative branches for different contexts. A more radical architectural innovation is the complete reconfiguration of nodes reconstituted from different parallel scripts.

A CYCLE OF INTEGRATION AND DISINTEGRATION

As in the classical innovation cycle, the extended cycle is associated with integration and disintegration of organizational forms, that is with the strengthening and loosening of linkages of coordination. Generally, after a movement of integration in the process of consolidation and generalization, there is a movement of disintegration, first gradual and later more radical, in the stages of differentiation and reciprocation. This can take several forms: decentralization within the integrated firm, increased autonomy for subsidiaries, outsourcing, management buy-outs, spin-offs, sell-offs, novel entry of independent firms and the formation of industrial districts. These predictions are in line with empirical research which has found that innovation is associated with greater 'complexity' (which here would be called 'variety') and organic structures (here associated with 'disintegration', that is, decentralization) (Hage, 1998). The cycle of (dis)integration is illustrated in Figure 3.3.

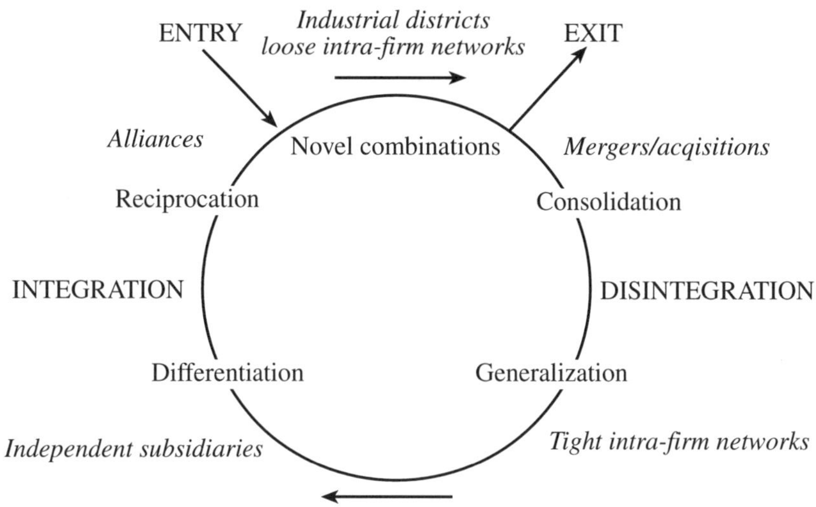

Figure 3.3 Cycle of integration and disintegration

One way to interpret disintegration is to see it as a loosening of connections to reduce group selection on the firm level, and to create novel potential for variety, and opportunities for novel combinations.

In the cycle of innovation, how, more precisely, do the stages connect with (dis)integration? Taking into account the role of distance, novel combinations are promoted by a constellation of separate, relatively small, weakly connected, spatially proximate units in complementary activities ('industrial districts' or autonomous units in large firms). In such constellations, a number of requirements are satisfied. Sufficient cognitive proximity is needed to be able to understand each other, and trust is needed to do without complex, detailed, costly, constraining contracts, and to contain risks of spill-over. They are achieved on the basis of shared norms and values of conduct, an efficient reputation mechanism, the 'shadow of the future' from expected dealings with each other in the future, shared routines. Sufficient cognitive distance is achieved by variety in activity and experience. There is sufficient spatial proximity to allow for frequent and varied contacts, and for intensive interaction in partial joint production, needed for the transfer of tacit, procedural knowledge, which is characteristic of the early stages of innovation. Here competition is not on price but on novelty.

Opportunity is also related to the absence of disadvantages of disintegrated structures that arise at other stages of development. Small, independent units are not so good at orchestrating many parts of a system to innovate in tune (Teece, 1986, 1988; Chesbrough and Teece, 1996), but, since we are dealing here with radical innovations, in 'novel combinations', which break up existing systems, that presents no obstacle. Tacit, procedural knowledge has the disadvantage of lacking the basis for formalized procedures with documented communication that is needed for large scale production, with specialization in different departments. But at the early stage of innovation both the opportunity and the need for large-scale are absent: no opportunity because the market is still small; no need because, owing to initial monopoly, pressure from competition is weak.

Large, integrated firms can survive or indeed create the discontinuities of novel combinations by means of decentralization of highly autonomous divisions or even individual 'intrapreneurs'. This is discussed in more detail in a later section. But there are limits to the variety that can be created and sustained in a large firm. How can one foresee the kinds of variety that might become relevant? In the extreme case, to create that variety the large firm would have to engage in practically everything, allowing for any combinations, and what then remains of the notion of an organization? It seems necessary also to maintain a readiness to mop up successful small innovators, in order to tap into a variety of independent firms that would be hard to reproduce within the firm. And, to benefit from their advantages of integration, large firms must also maintain a capability for systemic alignment, with strong ties, in the later stages of consolidation and in the stage of generalization. In this way it is conceivable that a large firm combines the best of two worlds. While it is not easy to perform this balancing act, it is conceivable, and indeed appears to be achieved by firms such as 3M and INTEL. However, an illustration of how difficult this is is given by the recent federalization of IBM, which was instituted to compete with more flexible, specialized and independent firms.

In the stage of consolidation, with the search for a dominant design, it is important that there is flexibility to try out various combinations and forms, and that misfits are efficiently weeded out. Here also lies the strength of the variety and idiosyncrasy of small, independent units, and the fact that misfits cannot be kept alive by cross-subsidization from successful products in a portfolio. Here we run into a second restriction on the mimicry of industrial districts by large firms: the efficiency of the elimination of failures becomes doubtful owing to the possibility of propping them up with cross-subsidization. In that sense they are not efficient from a societal perspective, but that of course still leaves the possibility for their existence. Depending on the selection environment of markets and institutions, such practices are not necessarily weeded out.

Examples of small firms running ahead in commercialization are semiconductors and computer-aided design (Rothwell and Zegveld, 1985), microcomputers (Langlois and Robertson, 1995) and self-service retailing (Nooteboom, 1984).

In the stage of generalization, after consolidation, integrated structures are better at large-volume production and distribution of novel products in wider world markets. A dominant design has emerged. Tacit, procedural knowledge has been developed into declarative, documented knowledge, which allows for transfer across larger distances. Standards allow for disintegration while maintaining fit across interfaces in chains of production. At the same time, increase of scale is feasible with the growth of demand, and is necessary to reduce costs due to increasing competition, as patents wear out and imitation increases. Competition has shifted from novelty to price. This favours larger production units, integrated distribution channels, spreading of risks, access to finance and the umbrella of a brand name, on the basis of penetration into extended markets. This favours a larger, more international and more integrated firm. Integrated structures are also better at the development of more coherent systems of connecting technologies, distribution systems, industry structures, supporting infrastructure, technical and commercial standards, yielding the configuration of a novel technoeconomic paradigm (Freeman and Perez, 1989).

Next, as generalization turns into differentiation and reciprocation, comparative advantage shifts again to greater variety, in more autonomous divisions, subsidiaries or independent firms, to give room for the generation of variety by reciprocation, in preparation for the next round of more fundamental innovation. Differentiation of products and processes also contributes to an escape from pure price competition between identical products that developed from generalization. Small firms, or independent units within large firms, are better at product differentiation in niche markets, where they do not run into disadvantages of small scale and can benefit from flexibility and proximity to customers.

CONTINGENCIES

It was noted before that the cycles of discovery and (dis)integration are not offered as inexorable, necessary and uniform. A complete discussion of contingencies that affect the cycles is beyond this chapter, and I can consider only a few. The speed of the cycle, for example, depends on what level we are investigating: individual, firm, industry or technoeconomic paradigm. Higher-level cycles contain many iterations of cycles on lower levels. On the level of idea formation by individuals, the cycle can be quite fast: it can turn around in an hour or a day. Product cycles vary enormously. In financial services and some fashion goods the cycle can be a year; in cars, computers and machine tools two to four years; in major construction projects five to seven years; in pharmaceuticals and telecom infrastructure ten to fifteen years (Quinn, 1992).

The key question is not only how long the cycle is, but whether there is a mismatch between the cycle for the product and the cycle for production. Generally, production systems have long cycles if they are embodied in large sunk investments in the form of dedicated hardware (such as factories), and short cycles when they entail craft production with tools that can easily be replaced or professional work on the basis of knowledge or skill that can easily be updated.

If the cycle of the production system is long, owing to a large fixed sunk cost in hardware, and the product cycle is short, there may be a problem. This problem can be solved at least to some extent if novel products can be made by novel assemblies of components, according to an enduring technology of assembly, or if the production system has the flexibility to adapt product forms in small batches, because it is programmable.

According to the study of technological discontinuities in the cement industry by Tushman and Anderson (1986), it took 13 years to move from the Rotary kiln to the Edison long kiln (1896–1909) and 60 years to move to the Dundee kiln with process control. In the airline industry it took 22 years to move from the generation of the Boeing 247, Douglas DC-2 and DC-3 (with the DC-3 as the dominant design, in 1937) to the era of the jet aircraft, with the Boeing 707 (1959), and then ten years to the wide-body jets, with the Boeing 747 (1969). In the minicomputer industry it took only two years to move from transistors to integrated circuits (in 1964), and seven years to move to semiconductor memories. The speed of movement to integrated circuits derived from the strong pressure to eliminate the constraints that limited the realization of the potential of semiconductors imposed by the assembly of different components of different materials.

The duration and prominence of different stages within the cycle can also vary considerably. This depends, for example, on the intensity of competition and its pressure for change. It also depends on how important product differentiation and economy of scale are, and on what type economy of scale it is. Product differentiation depends on the type of product and customer. In fashions in prosperous countries product differentiation is essential. Engineering economy of scale is crucial in process industries. Economy of scale in the use of information technology has declined enormously with the advent of microcomputers and user-friendly software. In some markets there is enormous economy of scale in marketing, in brand name, advertising and distribution.

When product differentiation is crucial, and economy of scale is limited or absent, and no major discontinuities in production technology occur, industrial districts can last for long periods of time. This is to be expected in fashion goods, where automation is difficult in some activities involved, such as cutting and assembling clothes, which yields a limit to economy of scale, while product differentiation and speedy response are crucial. On the other hand, when economy of scale is crucial and the product is hardly differentiable, large, tightly integrated companies can persist for a long time.

Illustrations of the longevity of industrial districts are found in abundance in Italy (Malerba, 1993): in fashion, shoes and furniture. These satisfy the conditions, great importance of differentiation and low production economies of scale. As indicated by Malerba, a problem may be that information technology may to some extent be destroying competence, because for effective use it cannot be simply attached to existing production but requires its redesign. It may require a change of production scripts. Another consideration is that, as indicated above, there can be large effects of scale in marketing, in distribution and brand name. The prediction would be that in fashion-oriented industrial districts there is, or will be, a tendency for the emergence of central, and perhaps dominant, parties that provide this marketing. This is confirmed by the case of Benetton. Here the economies of scale in marketing and brand name are combined with economy of scale in the provision of the ICT (Information and Communication Technology) network which coordinates flexible, differentiated production with speedy and efficient response to shifts in fashion.

Some markets have a dual structure: a large segment for standardized products and small niche markets for specialized, differentiated products. Examples are clothing and shoes. For the first segment one would expect more integrated, and for the latter more disintegrated, structures. And this is indeed what is found.

FIRM STRATEGY

We have seen that exploration and exploitation can be reconciled along the cycle of discovery: one can explore while maintaining exploitation. But if exploitation requires an integrated organizational structure and exploration a disintegrated one, how are organizations to be structured if they need to combine exploitation and exploration?

Often the growth path of new small firms coincides with part of the discovery cycle. In the literature on the growth of the firm a well-known hurdle arises when the innovating entrepreneur has to delegate responsibility, systematize and formalize the organization after the innovation proves its worth. In the terms of Witt (1998): it will have to shift from 'cognitive leadership' to 'governance' (and back again). Contrary to what Witt claims, cognitive leadership does not always yield better performance than governance. It performs worse in the systematization, rationalization and increase of scale associated with the stage of generalization. Takeovers, alliances, spin-offs and break-ups of firms help to overcome such problems of transition between the stages of the discovery process.

Volberda (1998) identified several ways to solve the paradox of exploitation and exploration. One is separation in place: one part of an organization engages in exploitation, another in exploration. There is horizontal and vertical separation. In horizontal separation one division or department, typically R&D, preferably in collaboration with marketing, engages in exploration, and another, typically production, engages in exploitation. The problem here is, of course, how to govern the interface. There is the perennial frustration of marketing that production is 'not willing' or 'not competent' to deliver what market opportunities call for, and the equally perennial frustration of production people that marketing people are too dense to appreciate what is technically feasible and cost effective. Vertical separation can go two ways. Management yields scope for exploration in the firm, by allowing people who interact with the market, and with sources of technology, labour and inputs, to utilize the opportunities they meet, and management tries to maintain sufficient coherence to prevent waste of duplication and mismatch. Alternatively, management lays claim to choices of direction and content, and coordinates staff in the execution of their vision.

This theme has been dealt with by many organizational scholars (for example, Thompson, 1967). In economics it was discussed by Aoki (1986), who made a distinction between a horizontal and a vertical 'information structure'. In the vertical structure management coordinates workshops but is incapable of adequate monitoring of emerging events in markets and technologies. In the horizontal structure production decisions are coordinated among semi-autonomous shops, who can better respond on the spot to emerging events. Aoki proposed that the former is typically American (the 'A firm') and the latter typically Japanese (the 'J firm'). In the A firm there are clear job specifications and standard operating procedures. Problem solving is relegated to supervisors, repairmen and engineers. In the J firm, duties are not specified in detail and workers rotate across jobs so that they become familiar with a wide range of activities, as a basis for horizontal coordination. Decentralization is also carried across the boundaries of the firm to suppliers, who are given more scope for initiative. The weak spot of this arrangement is that, in spite of rotation, the insight needed for effective coordination may be too limited. And they may have divergent strategic orientations that are at odds with the firm's focus on core competencies or activities.

Separation can also take place between different organizations, and then we might call it the strategy of specialization. A firm focuses on a specific stage, of efficient exploitation or of exploration, and connects with other firms that offer complementary stages. It continually shifts its portfolio of activities, phasing them in and out as they enter and leave the stage in which it specializes. A prominent example is the pharmaceutical industry, where the large pharmaceutical companies provide efficient production, marketing and distribution, and biotechnology firms explore the novel product forms. Another example is industrial districts. Some firms are specialists in R&D or other forms of experimentation with novel combinations; some specialize in consolidation and production, some in large-scale and distant marketing, distribution and exports; some in incremental improvements and differentiation. One may also accept that organizations are formed only temporarily, as the need arises. This is what one sees in building consortia, for example

Another separation is separation in time: exploitation occurs at one time, and exploration at another. This yields the 'oscillating' (Burns and Stalker, 1961) mode, with a to-and-fro between loose and open to tight and homogeneous, and back again. This is very difficult to achieve. Organizational change requires restructuring of organizational scripts, involving a redistribution of people across tasks and a reconstitution of tasks, goals, motives, perspectives and shared meanings. In industrial districts it takes entry and exit of firms and the building of new network relations. Such developments tend to take a long time, especially if they require a change of the 'deep structure' of organizational culture, such as basic categories of perception, interpretation and evaluation (Schein, 1985). Restructuring of systems of production, supply and distribution also takes a long time. Increasingly, the problem of inertia lies in organizational culture and distribution systems rather than production technology. Furthermore, how does one operate this when different products or technologies are in different stages of development? Nonaka and Takeuchi (1995) recommend a 'hypertext' organization, by analogy with windows processing on computers. This is like a flexible form of matrix organization: cross-functional and cross-departmental groups are formed *ad hoc*, according to the opportunity at hand, like opening windows on the computer. A firm may have a basic structure oriented towards either exploitation or exploration, and form temporary task forces for the other task.

One may also try to escape from the cycle by acting as an orchestrator of activities of other companies. ICT increasingly yields the opportunities for this. Quinn (1992) gives the example of a company in custom-made ASICS

(Application Specific Integrated Circuits). They interface with clients directly by means of ICT, to determine functional specifications. They then employ their own specialized software to convert this into photo masks, which are sent by ICT to a company in Japan for etching, next to a company in Korea for dicing and mounting, then to Malaysia for assembly, from where the chip is flown directly to the customer. A similar example in sports shoes is Nike. Another example is Benetton: it also performs the task of orchestration, by means of ICT, of a decentralized network of individual producers and retailers. A new industrial revolution?

Let us reconsider the need for standardization for the sake of efficient production, and the resulting need for integration. Perhaps it is useful to see the present revolution in the organization of firms in terms of the disappearance of standards and integration. Then the cycle of innovation might collapse. Can we do without standardization and durable organizational structure? Can exploration be instant and continuous? Can we do without integration, and retain continuing disintegration? Bennis (1969) already predicted the death of bureaucracy, because all environments become turbulent, permitting only 'organic', disintegrated structures (quoted in Buchanan and Boddy, 1992, p. 35).

From the analysis it follows that this is conceivable when efficient production (exploitation) does not require standardization, scaling up and division of labour, and when the product requires customized differentiation from the very beginning. This is approximated most closely in professional services, such as accountancy and consultancy.

But even there the paradox of exploitation and reciprocation appears, though in a more limited fashion. As we already noted in the discussion of Arthur Andersen, even there professional standards must be set and kept, and consistent quality must be guaranteed across different locations of a multinational customer. And measures must be taken so that different consultants make use of each other's experience in order not to reinvent wheels all the time. This requires incentive systems for consultants to volunteer their experience to a common pool, which requires in turn that they be judged and promoted at least in part on the basis of such contributions, weighted by their usefulness and measured by the extent that colleagues make successful use of them. But such a common pool would require a certain minimal amount of standardization of concepts and procedures in a thesaurus.

In the previous section discussed was the strategy of orchestration to escape the cycle. However, rather than refuting the cycle of innovation, this shows how the orchestrator conducts exploration by flexibly exploiting the productive competencies of different companies, in shifting configurations, and thereby tries to escape the need and the dangers of inertia. The risk of inertia due to standardized, more or less fixed, systems for efficient production is hived off to other players. But, even here, the focal, orchestrating firm must be careful to both maintain and develop its core competence of orchestration.

When standards are not embodied in hardware that represents a large sunk cost (such as cables and switches in telecommunication systems), but in software (as in communication by radio), and it is possible at low cost to translate between different standards by slotting in translation software, there would seem to be no need for any dominant design. Competing, differentiated standards may remain differentiated from the start, in continuing differentiation and reciprocation. However, that would imply that the competing standards would not be appropriable, and how then do firms obtain the reward for their investment and risk taking? This conundrum is in fact with us: some firms freely distribute their system via the Internet. One explanation is that in doing so they quickly obtain a large user base, which gives information on usage and preferences, down to individual users, which gives a basis for adding further added-value services geared to individual preferences. It is, so to speak, not the technical system but the customer base that becomes the core competence.

An example is the famous case of American Hospital Supplies (AHS). They started with dedicated hardware in the form of terminals which captured customers. This captivity was broken by new intermediaries who provided an interface for linkage with other suppliers. But AHS had meanwhile added services, partly based on their accumulated knowledge of client wishes and procedures, and thereby created continuing customer captivity.

Does this invalidate the cycle of innovation? Perhaps it does. But the logic underlying the cycle still helps to analyse the conditions for such instant exploration.

CONCLUSION

Evolutionary theory has the merits of shifting attention away from efficient, equilibrium outcomes to underlying dynamic processes; it yields a much needed focus on the diversity of firms; and it opens up insight into the importance of population dynamics. However, it offers no explanation for the origins of novelty; the institutional selection environment is subject to social construction and negotiation; it is affected by innovation and communicative or political influence by way of the units that it is supposed to select; and there are processes of learning which generate novelty and variety. The selection environment not only selects novelty but also supports its generation. Thus we need to turn to theories of knowledge, learning and language. This chapter has focused on learning, and in particular on the relation between first- and second-order learning; between exploitation and exploration.

It indicated a way to combine the two, which entails an extension of the life cycle theory of innovation and the product cycle theory of internationalization. After novel combinations, consolidation in dominant designs and efficient production, and generalization to novel markets (for products) or applications (for technologies), there are stages of differentiation and reciprocation. These yield exploration during exploitation, and provide the incentives, material and insight for promising novel combinations, at which point we are again at the beginning of the cycle. However, with the aid of ICT, standardization and stable organizational integration can be mitigated, limited or perhaps avoided altogether in a growing number of industries, especially industries with a high proportion of added value in services.

REFERENCES

Abelson, R.P. (1976), 'Script Processing in Attitude Formation and Decision Making', in J.S. Carroll and J.W. Payne (eds), *Cognition and Social Behavior*, Hillsdale, NJ: Erlbaum.

Abernathy, W.J. (1978), *The Productivity Dilemma: Roadblock to Innovation in the Automobile Industry*, Baltimore: Johns Hopkins University Press.

Abernathy, W.J. and K.B. Clark (1985), 'Innovation: Mapping the winds of creative destruction', *Research Policy*, **14**, 3–22.

Abernathy, W.J. and J.M. Utterback (1978), 'Patterns of industrial innovation', *Technology Review*, **81**, June/July, 41–7.

Aoki, M. (1986), 'Horizontal vs. vertical information structure of the firm', *American Economic Review*, **76**(5), 971–83.

Argyris, C. and D. Schön (1978), *Organizational Learning*, Reading, MA: Addison-Wesley.

Bennis, W.G. (1969), *Organizational Development: Its Nature, Origins and Prospects*, Reading, MA: Addison-Wesley.

Bijker, W.E., T.P. Hughes and T.J. Pinch (1987), *The Social Construction of Technological Systems*, Cambridge, MA: MIT Press.

Buchanan, D. and D. Boddy (1992), *The Expertise of the Change Agent*, New York: Prentice-Hall.

Burgelman, R.A. (1996), 'Intraorganizational Ecology of Strategy Making and Organizational Adaptation', in J.R. Meindl, C. Stubbart and J.F. Porac (eds), *Cognition within and between Organizations*, London: Sage; first published in 1991, in *Organization Science*, **2**(3).

Burns, T. and G.M. Stalker (1961), *The Management of Innovation*, London: Tavistock.

Chesbrough, H.W. and D.J. Teece (1996), 'When is Virtual Virtuous? Organizing for Innovation', *Harvard Business Review*, Jan.–Feb., 65–73.

Choo, C.W. (1998), *The Knowing Organization*, Oxford: Oxford University Press.

Cohen, W.M. and D.A. Levinthal (1990), 'Absorptive capacity: A new perspective on learning and innovation', *Administrative Science Quarterly*, **35**, 128–52.

Dosi, G. (1982), 'Technological paradigms and technological trajectories: a suggested interpretation of the determinants and directions of technical change', *Research Policy*, **11**.

Dosi, G. (1984), *Technical Change and Industrial Transformation*, London: Macmillan.
Dosi, G., C. Freeman, R. Nelson, G. Silverberg and L. Soete (eds) (1988), *Technical Change and Economic Theory*, London: Pinter.
Eldredge, N. and S.Y. Gould (1972), 'Punctuated equilibria: an alternative to phyletic gradualism', in T.Y.M. Schopf (ed.), *Models in paleobiology*, San Francisco: Freeman, Cooper and Co., 82–115.
Emery, F.E. and E.L. Trist (1965), 'Causal texture of organizational environments', *Human Relations*, Feb., 21–32.
Fiol, C.M. and M.A. Lyles (1985), 'Organizational learning', *Academy of Management Review*, **10**(4), 803–13.
Foster, J. (1997), 'The analytical foundations of evolutionary economics: from biological analogy to economic self-organization', *Structural Change and Economic Dynamics*, **8**, 427–51.
Foster, J. (2000), 'Competitive selection, self-organization and Joseph A. Schumpeter', *Journal of Evolutionary Economics*, **10**(3).
Freeman, C. and C. Perez (1989), 'Structural crises of adjustment, business cycles and investment behaviour', in G. Dosi (ed.), *Technical Change and Economic Theory*, London: Francis Pinter.
Frege, G. (1892), 'On Sense and reference' (in German), *Zeitschrift fur Philosophie und Philosophische Kritik*, **100**, 25–50.
Gadamer, H.G. (1977), *Philosophical Hermeneutics*, ed. David E. Linge, Berkeley: University of California Press.
Garud, R. and A. Rappa (1996), 'A socio-cognitive model of technology evolution: The case of cochlear implants', in J.R. Meindl, C. Stubbart and J.F. Porac (eds), *Cognition within and between Organizations*, London: Sage; first published in 1994, in *Organization Science*, **5**(3).
Gould, S.J. (1989), 'Punctuated equilibrium in fact and theory', *Journal of Social Biological Structure*, **12**, 117–36.
Hage, J. (ed.) (1998), *Organizational Innovation*, Aldershot: Dartmouth/Ashgate.
Hedberg, B.L.T., P.C. Nystrom and W.H. Starbuck (1976), 'Camping on seesaws: Prescriptions for a self-designing organization', *Administrative Science Quarterly*, **21**, 41–65.
Henderson, R.M. and K.B. Clark (1990), 'Architectural innovation: The reconstruction of existing product technologies and the failure of established firms', *Administrative Science Quarterly*, **35**, 9–30.
Hendriks-Jansen, H. (1996), *Catching Ourselves in the Act; Situated Activity, Interactive Emergence, Evolution and Human Thought*, Cambridge, MA: MIT Press.
Hodgson, G.M. (1993), *Economics and Evolution: Bringing Life Back to Economics*, Cambridge: Polity Press.
Holland, J.H. (1975), *Adaptation in Natural and Artificial Systems*, Ann Arbor: University of Michigan Press.
Holland, J.H., K.J. Holyoak, R.E. Nisbett and P.R. Thagard (1989), *Induction; Processes of Inference, Learning and Discovery*, Cambridge, MA: MIT Press.
Jacobson, R. (1987), *Language in Literature*, ed. K. Pomorska and S. Rudy, Cambridge, MA: Harvard University Press.
Johnson-Laird, P.N. (1983), *Mental Models*, Cambridge: Cambridge University Press.
Knight, F. (1921), *Risk, Uncertainty and Profit*, Boston, MA: Houghton Mifflin.
Kuhn, T.S. (1970), *The Structure of Scientific Revolutions*, 2nd edn, Chicago: University of Chicago Press.

Langlois, R.N. and P.L. Robertson (1995), *Firms, Markets and Economic Change*, London: Routledge.

Latour, B. (1987), *Science in Action*, Cambridge, MA: Harvard University Press.

Latour, B. and S. Woolgar (1979), *Laboratory Life*, Beverley Hills, CA: Sage.

Lawrence, P. and J. Lorsch (1967), *Organization and Environment*, Boston, MA: Harvard Business School.

Lundvall, B.A. (1985), *Product Innovation and User–producer Interaction*, Aalborg: Aalborg University Press.

Lundvall, B.A. (1988), 'Innovation as an interactive process – from user–producer interaction to national systems of innovation', in G. Dosi, C. Freeman, R. Nelson, G. Silverberg and L. Soete (eds), *Technical Change and Economic Theory*, London: Pinter.

Lundvall, B.A. (1993), 'User–producer relationships, national systems of innovation and internationalization', in D. Foray and C. Freeman (eds), *Technology and the Wealth of Nations*, London: Pinter.

Malerba, F. (1993), 'The national system of innovation: Italy', in R.R. Nelson (ed.), *National Innovation Systems*, Oxford and New York: Oxford University Press.

Malerba, F. and L. Orsenigo (1995), 'Schumpeterian patterns of innovation', *Cambridge Journal of Economics*, **19**, 47–65.

March, J. (1991), 'Exploration and exploitation in organizational learning', *Organization Science*, **2**(1).

Metcalfe, J.S. (1998), *Evolutionary Economics and Creative Destruction*, London: Routledge.

Mintzberg, H. (1983), *Structure in Fives: Designing Effective Organizations*, Englewood Cliffs, NJ: Prentice-Hall.

Nelson, R.R. and S. Winter (1982), *An Evolutionary Theory of Economic Change*, Cambridge: Cambridge University Press.

Nonaka, I. and H. Takeuchi (1995), *The Knowledge Creating Company*, Oxford: Oxford University Press.

Nooteboom, B. (1984), 'Innovation, Life Cycle and the Share of Independents: Cases from Retailing', *International Small Business Journal*, **3**(1), 21–33.

Nooteboom, B. (1992a), 'Towards a dynamic theory of transactions', *Journal of Evolutionary Economics*, **2,** 281–99.

Nooteboom, B. (1992b), 'Agent, Context and Innovation: a Saussurian View of Markets', in W. Blaas and J. Foster (eds), *Mixed Economies in Europe: An Evolutionary Perspective on their Emergence, Transition and Regulation*, Aldershot, UK and Brookfield, US: Edward Elgar.

Nooteboom, B. (1996), 'Trust, opportunism and governance: A process and control model', *Organization Studies*, **17**(6), 985–1010.

Nooteboom, B. (1999a), *Inter-firm Alliances; Analysis and Design*, London: Routledge.

Nooteboom, B. (1999b), 'Learning, innovation and industrial organisation', *Cambridge Journal of Economics*, **23,** 127–50.

North, D.C. (1990), *Institutions, Institutional Change and Economic Performance*, Cambridge: Cambridge University Press.

Pavitt, K. (1984), 'Sectoral patterns of technical change: Towards a taxonomy and a theory', *Research Policy*, **13,** 343–73.

Peirce, C.S. (1957), *Essays in the Philosophy of Science*, Indianapolis: Bobbs-Merrill.

Piore, M. and C. Sabel (1983), 'Italian small business development: Lessons for US industrial policy', in J. Zysman and L. Tyson (eds), *American Industry in Interna-*

tional Competition: Government Policies and Corporate Strategies, Ithaca: Cornell University Press.
Popper, K.R. (1976), 'Normal Science and its Dangers', in I. Lakatos and A. Musgrave (eds), *Criticism and the Growth of Knowledge*, Cambridge: Cambridge University Press.
Porter, M.A. (1980), *Competitive Strategy*, New York: Free Press.
Porter, M.A. (1985), *Competitive Advantage*, New York: Free Press.
Quinn, J.B. (1992), *Intelligent Enterprise*, New York: Free Press.
Rose, S. (1997), *Lifelines; Biology, Freedom, Determinism*, London: Penguin.
Rothwell, R. and W. Zegveld (1985), *Innovation and the Small and Medium Sized Firm*, London: Francis Pinter.
Schein, E.H. (1985), *Organizational Culture and Leadership*, San Francisco: Jossey-Bass.
Shank, R. and R. Abelson (1977), *Scripts, Plans, Goals and Understanding*, Hillsdale: Lawrence Erlbaum.
Shanon, B. (1988), 'Semantic representation of meaning: A critique', *Psychological Bulletin*, **104**(1), 70–83.
Shanon, B. (1990), 'What is context?', *Journal for the Theory of Social Behaviour*, **20**(2), 157–66.
Shanon, B. (1993), *The Representational and the Presentational*, New York: Harvester/Wheatsheaf.
Teece, D.J. (1986), 'Profiting from technological innovation: Implications for integration, collaboration, licensing and public policy', *Research Policy*, **15,** 285–305.
Teece, D.J. (1988), 'Technological Change and the Nature of the Firm', in G. Dosi, C. Freeman, R. Nelson, G. Silverberg and L. Soete (eds), *Technical Change and Economic Theory*, London: Pinter.
Thompson, J.D. (1967), *Organizations in Action*, New York: McGraw-Hill.
Tushman, M.L. and P. Anderson (1986), 'Technological discontinuities and organizational environments', *Administrative Science Quarterly*, **31,** 439–65.
Vernon, R. (1966), 'International investment and international trade in the product cycle', *Quarterly Journal of Economics*, **80**.
Volberda, H.W. (1998), *Building the Flexible Firm*, Oxford: Oxford University Press.
Vromen, J.J. (1995), *Economic Evolution*, London: Routledge.
Vygotsky, L.S. (1962), *Thought and Language*, ed. and trans. E. Hanfmann and G. Varkar, Cambridge, MA: MIT Press.
Weick, K.F. (1995), *Sensemaking in organisations*, Thousand Oaks CA: Sage.
Weick, K.F. (1997), *The Social psychology of organising*, Reading MA: Addison-Wesley.
Witt, U. (ed.) (1992), *Evolutionary Economics*, Aldershot, UK and Brookfield, US: Edward Elgar.
Witt, U. (1998), 'Do Entrepreneurs Need Firms?', Workshop 'Recent developments in Austrian economics', Max-Planck-Institut zur Erforschung von Wirtschaftssystemen, 7–8 August, Jena.
Wittgenstein, L. (1976), *Philosophical Investigations*, Oxford: Basil Blackwell.

Commentary: from evolution to language and learning

Paolo Ramazzotti

INTRODUCTION

The chapter is very dense and full of interesting insights. Its attempt to link industrial performance to the learning process is undoubtedly intriguing, especially because, in doing so, it tries to connect not only different strands of thought but also theories defined at different degrees of abstraction.

The key tenet of the chapter is that variety generation and selection are not independent processes. Selection makes sense only within a given industrial context. As the latter changes, so does the former. The industrial context, in turn, is determined by novelty, which is introduced through variety generation and refined through evolving selection.

As for variety generation, an explanation of how it occurs requires an account of how novelty may be conceived of, thus a theory of knowledge. It also requires an explanation of what causes firms to seek novelty. The exploration–exploitation cycle is deemed to account for the latter issue, while the learning process requires a discussion of its own.

Bart Nooteboom very clearly states that what he envisages is not an iron rule, rather a heuristic, subject to a great many contingencies. My impression is that, although the heuristic is worth elaborating upon, it suffers less from lack of empirical qualifications than from a range of very strong theoretical and methodological restrictions.

I will try to point out the above-mentioned restrictions by discussing the exploitation–exploration process first and the learning process subsequently. I will then draw some concluding remarks.

THE EXPLOITATION–EXPLORATION CYCLE AND SURVIVAL

Let us look at how exploration and discovery occur. Bart Nooteboom points to motive, opportunity and means, but he also argues that some enforcement is required: 'we might preserve a principle of selection on a higher level: firms survive to the extent that they manage this process of discovery'.

Two notions of selection are under discussion here. 'Selection' as such relates to a specific industrial context and, presumably, to a specific product. Instead, what is termed the 'principle of selection' relates to future market conditions, thus to those niches and industries that will result tomorrow from the variety generated today. The principle of selection therefore transcends existing industrial contexts. It presumably acts upon firms.

The 'principle' is strictly related to the exploration–exploitation cycle: the cycle is claimed to be possible only insofar as the principle exists. This raises two issues. First, although variety generation and selection appear to be interdependent, the principle of selection underlying the cycle remains an unexplained a priori statement. Second, should firms not comply with the exploration–exploitation cycle, how should we qualify such a principle?

Let us focus on the second issue. Compliance with the exploration–exploitation cycle is neither necessary nor sufficient for the survival of a firm. It is not necessary for a variety of reasons. First, even in industries where radical innovations occur, a firm need not be an innovator itself: it may wait for competitors to identify novelty and then buy them out. In itself this may appear as just a different way to comply with the requirements of the cycle. This is true when a firm waits until it can pick the winning innovation amongst the many available and exploit it by itself. However, a buy-out may be due to reasons other than the exploitation of the innovation. It may actually aim at preventing it. Such a case would occur if exploitation on the part of the innovator precluded another firm from recovering its sunk costs.

Second, compliance with the cycle is not necessary because a firm may compensate for not innovating by resorting to political lobbying and government subsidies. One might object that subsidies exist precisely because some selection occurs, whereby unsubsidized firms cannot survive unless they comply with the cycle. The obverse may apply, however. If firms can manage to be eventually subsidized, motive – one of the requirements for discovery – may well falter throughout an industry, thereby reducing the pressure of competition.

Third, a firm may compensate for not innovating by resorting to cross-subsidization (internal finance). Much like access to government subsidies, cross-subsidization acts upon motive but its origin lies less in public policy than in industrial organization.

Our considerations may be extended to external finance. Some firms may have easier access to financial intermediaries or to the stock market, possibly because they are larger or because of long-standing relations established in the past. This, obviously, has nothing to do with the nature of a given product but it has much to do with who may survive. The difference with cross-subsidization is that, here, selection involves not only 'manufacturing' (albeit in a broad sense) but 'manufacturing plus finance'.

This leads us to the final reason why firms may not comply with the exploration–exploitation cycle, thereby precluding its very existence. Inertia may occur because of the lack of motive. In turn, motive may be absent precisely because survival is possible anyway.

While compliance with the cycle is unnecessary for the survival of a firm, it is also insufficient. A firm may be bought out no matter how involved it is in discovery and exploitation. Its acquisition will generally depend on financial – as opposed to industrial – capacity.

THE MULTIDIMENSIONALITY OF COMPETITION

As mentioned earlier, the above cases are not meant to be a qualification of the list of contingencies that Bart Nooteboom himself provides. The aim is to show that the notion of an exploration–exploitation cycle is hard to grasp on more conceptual grounds. Consider cross-subsidization again. It may allow a firm to survive despite its failure to meet the requirements set by the selection environment. It may also allow long-term investment to be carried out, thereby fostering discovery and the cycle. Whatever the case, however, cross-subsidization implies that firms may not be on an equal standing: multi-product firms have access to cross-subsidization, whereas single-product firms do not. Thus, while all firms apparently compete on equal grounds as far as the price and quality of a product – at a given time – are concerned, the multi-product firm may displace its single-product competitor by resorting to the advantages of cross-subsidization. Similar considerations apply to the other cases outlined above. As a result, selection turns out to be a rather ambiguous concept when referring to single products.

Let us now turn to the 'principle of selection' and focus on the firm as a possible unit of selection. Here the question is how selection operates. Does it cause bankruptcy? Or should we take into account takeovers, mergers, the end of a trade mark or a change in management? What appears to be clear cut when we think of a single-product small firm turns out to be much less intuitive when product differentiation, horizontal and vertical integration, and industry–finance relations are taken into account.

The fact is that competition transcends the boundaries of a product-related industry, or of any single unit of selection for that matter: it is multidimensional.[1] Firms need to take this into account, so their strategies tend to be multidimensional as well. This is what makes productive, financial and/or ownership integration so important.[2]

An applied economist would be more than willing to acknowledge the existence of these problems. They relate to a common empirical issue: the identification of the relevant environment. The issue is not just empirical, however.[3] What emerges from the above discussion is the openness of any economic structure.[4] Each firm has specific relations with its external environment. They may be either intra- or inter-industrial relations. They may be associated with ownership or with other forms of productive or financial integration. As a result, some products may 'survive' – that is, they may remain on the market – precisely because product-related novelty is not the only way that firms make profits. For instance, a firm may be relatively more profitable because it manages to pay lower interest rates or lower wages or because the region it is based in is provided with more infrastructures (or with a higher rate of infrastructure creation) than others. What all this leads to is that the depiction of the boundaries of a given object of inquiry implies an assessment of the specific historical and geographical context.

The open-system character of the economy does not entail that, since boundaries cannot be depicted univocally, no economic inquiry may be carried out.[5] It does suggest, however, that focus on firms as mere manufacturers may be misleading, for two reasons. First, owing to the multidimensionality of competition, manufacturing firms do not just act on the commodity market: they do not merely make goods that they will eventually sell. As mentioned above, they also obtain finance from internal or external sources, they hire workers, they take advantage of public goods, and so on. As a result, profitability (and variety generation) may be pursued in all these environments.

The second reason is that competition transcends manufacturing. In a monetary economy, such as the one we live in, profits are assessed in terms of money. They may or may not be related to real profits. In a world of uncertainty, where shifts of funds from one asset/country to another may lead to abrupt changes in interest rates and relative prices, speculation is a typical case where money profits may be made independently of any real activity. What is more, since speculation may lead to persistent changes in relative prices – as is the case with devaluations – it may well forsake previous efforts at variety generation in manufacturing.

Openness implies that profits may be pursued in a wide range of ways. A proper unit of selection would have to take all of them into account. However, as the range gets wider, interdependence rises. If selection is to mean that, eventually, some firms disappear or some agents lose all their money, that is fine. What this means in terms of economic theory is less clear.

MONEY AND TECHNOLOGY

The notion of a monetary economy is not just a qualification of whatever analysis is carried out in real terms. Money would be irrelevant in a world where production does not require money in order to begin. This might occur in an economy where each individual uses his or her resources to produce goods that he or she will either consume directly or sell on the market. Alternatively, it would occur where production does not occur over time. This is not the case in a modern (capitalist) economy, where production is carried out through a very specific division of labour: firms pay workers to carry out a range of tasks. Output ensues only after these money incomes have been paid out. Only when output is sold do firms get back the money they anticipated. This was a key point in Keynes, who referred to it as the financial motive. It is also a Marxian theme: Marx referred to it as the *M-C-M′* process, where *M* is the money required to begin the production process, *C* are the commodities arising from the process and *M′* is the money resulting from selling the commodities. Finally, it is a Schumpeterian theme: economic development is possible only if the banking system provides entrepreneurs with the money they need to introduce their innovations.

Money would also be irrelevant in a world where there is no reason to forsake investment. This would occur in a world where information is perfect, rationality is substantive and time is reversible.[6] Under these circumstances uncertainty would not exist and there would be no point in withholding investment while holding money. Transactions would only require debits and credits to be registered. Indeed, since money bears no income, it would be pointless to hold it rather than holding other assets. Again, this is not the case in the world we live in.

The above considerations point to the non-neutrality of money: the behaviour of economic agents will be affected both by how much money is available to carry out production and by the interest rate relative to other rates of return. This is a common theme in macroeconomic theory, where non-neutrality refers to the effect that monetary variables have on the overall level of output. It is discussed less in other fields of economic inquiry. Indeed, it is part of conventional wisdom that money may be relevant only at the aggregate level, in that it affects aggregate demand but not the way firms interact.

It is important to point to the fact that monetary variables may also affect the technological features of the production process.[7] First, insofar as rates of return on financial assets make investment not worthwhile, firms do not invest, thus they do not upgrade capacity. Second, when investment is not carried out and demand is slack, there is no incentive to improve the quality of output and production processes.[8] Third, interest rates affect the time range of investment decisions. The higher the rate is, the shorter the time span required for the investment to be profitable. This suggests that, whatever the investment rate, when interest rates are high, time-demanding R&D projects may be forsaken and short-run cost cutting may turn out to be the most profitable strategy.[9]

All this qualifies the previous statement whereby competition (and profitability) transcend manufacturing. It also helps to understand the nature of the learning process that occurs in the business community. This is the subject of what follows.

DIFFERING BODIES OF KNOWLEDGE AND CHANGE

Up to this point I have discussed selection and variety generation. Let us now turn to the learning process which underlies the latter. B. Nooteboom defines knowledge as the way people see the world and stresses that it depends on interaction with a given social and physical environment. Following this definition, let us focus on its application to the business community. People who do business are also involved in other forms of social and physical interaction. The discovery process within this specific environment, however, is determined and bounded by profitability. Thus firms search for novelty, not for the sake of knowledge, but to identify new and better ways to raise profits.

The profit motive may be difficult to define in rigorous terms, since it involves the nature of the goal (maximum profits, constant profits and so on), a time range (such as long-term v. short-term profitability), uncertainty, and so on. It is none the less distinct from other motives, such as social welfare or moral values: in general, there is no reason for knowledge creation – the way people come to see the world – to coincide with discovery in the business community: most people read Shakespeare or listen to Bach for reasons other than the profits such activities may eventually lead to.

Knowledge in general – the way people see the world – and business-related knowledge are not independent, however. Their interaction may be synergistic but it may also lead to conflicting outcomes. Consider industrial pollution: it results from a business activity and it often increases economic welfare, but it contrasts with the way a great many people (want to) see the world. It is a common theme in welfare analysis that externalities may lead to a divergence between economic and general welfare. This is just another way of stating that distinct bodies of knowledge may be mutually inconsistent.

Following Coase, many scholars believe that this kind of divergence may be coped with by resorting to the market, that is, the price-based allocation mechanism. The problem is that they believe that prices are determined in real terms, rather than in money terms. The above considerations on the monetary nature of capitalism suggest that this belief is misleading.

The profit motive is also distinct from the strictly economic welfare that other members of society pursue. Since (money) profits may not be related to the real allocation of resources, the conventionally assumed convergence between the goals of firms and those of consumers and/or workers need not exist. Indeed, social conflict suggests that their goals may clash. Thus firms, consumers and workers presumably perceive, interpret and evaluate their economic environment quite differently: their knowledge systems differ and may even be inconsistent.

Institutions, defined as 'rules that regulate and constitute behaviour', reflect the bodies of knowledge that exist at any given time. Thus, just as the latter may be mutually inconsistent, the same may occur with institutions: business institutions may conflict with religious, political or other types of institutions. Even within the business community institutional conflicts may arise: this is what lobbying is mostly about.

What all this leads to is that learning processes occur both within and outside the business environment. Change also results from their interaction. In Vernon's 1966 article, the life cycle of a product could be smoothly depicted on a logistic curve because firms learned and gradually adapted to market conditions. What is being suggested here is that market conditions, however defined, are only part of the learning process. Countervailing knowledge arises which may either interfere with the smoothness of a life cycle or even preclude it. It may arise within the business environment, as when consumer associations or trade unions act counter to what firms do. It may also come from other environments, as when political and religious groups act counter to the ethics of capitalism.

A CASE OF CONFLICTING KNOWLEDGE SYSTEMS

It may be worthwhile to consider an example in order to stress the relevance of the above issues. I will refer to Italy's economic performance over the 1970s and 1980s.[10] My concern, obviously, is less to discuss Italy's economy than to provide an empirically plausible thought experiment.

During the 1970s high domestic and imported inflation led to trade deficits which were offset from time to time by competitive devaluations. The qualitative and quantitative variability of demand forced firms to introduce new production techniques but this did not prevent them from relying on the key role that exchange rate policy played in their profitability. This led to a vicious circle: inflation caused devaluations which, in turn, accentuated inflation. Furthermore, relying on devaluations, firms did not seek product or price-related novelties which would increase competitiveness.

A conflict arose between the goals pursued by firms and those of the monetary authorities: the (short-run) profitability of single firms was incompatible with (long-run) price stability. A change in monetary policy was therefore called for and, in 1979, Italy joined the European Monetary System. As a result, depreciation of the lira was no longer possible and the only way to adjust the balance of payments deficit was through high interest rates. The expected result was that, since Italian firms could not rely on competitive devaluations any more, they would eventually upgrade their productive capacity in order to cut costs, thereby achieving competitiveness and curbing inflation.

From the perspective of this discussion, what emerges is the coexistence of at least two distinct knowledge systems. Since firms pursue profits, it is to that end that they direct their learning processes: given the circumstances outlined above, it was not profitable for them to pursue long-term competitiveness through discovery processes, so they did not seek that kind of knowledge. Only a different kind of agent, with different priorities (such as the industrial system's overall competitiveness and price stability) and a correspondingly different knowledge system, could try to avoid the perceived consequences of this (procedurally) rational myopia of firms. What ensued was an institutional conflict. The change in exchange rate policy (one of the rules that regulated the central bank's policy) was aimed at changing the learning processes of firms and to induce them to upgrade their technologies.

MONETARY POLICY AND THE (PROCEDURAL) RATIONALITY OF FIRMS

Contrary to expectations, the actual outcome of the new monetary and exchange rate policy on the behaviour of firms was twofold. First, owing to high interest rates, short-termism prevailed: firms could not afford to wait for long-term gains from investment in variety generation. Profits were reaped through cost cutting, while investment in technology was checked. Second, investment in financial assets turned out to be more profitable than investment in manufacturing.

The upswing in the international business cycle allowed demand not to fall while employment dropped and profit margins rose, but competitiveness did not improve. As a result, the outflow due to high interest rates on foreign debt was not offset by a trade surplus. When the downswing in the business cycle arrived, the balance of payments suffered a high deficit, which eventually led to the 1992 devaluation.

A few inferences may be drawn. Before 1979, firms disregarded qualitative innovations because it was less costly to rely on competitive devaluations. Following 1979, firms disregarded qualitative innovations because cost cutting and financial diversification were more effective in terms of short-run profitability.

The second inference is that some institutional set-ups dominate others. 'Making money' dominates the pursuit of real profits. This is why firms shifted from manufacturing to finance, even though it precluded their technological upgrading and long-term real competitiveness.

The third inference is that the central bank got it wrong. They believed firms could behave in only one way, that is, react to changes in relative prices by upgrading their technology and achieving long-term competitiveness in order to be profitable. Competitiveness and profitability, however, are distinct concepts: the former is just one of the possible ways to achieve the latter.

CONCLUDING REMARKS

B. Nooteboom's chapter raises a range of theoretical issues. Each one of them would obviously require a more detailed treatment. I have tried to focus on the key features of his analysis. I have argued that the exploration–exploitation cycle is neither necessary nor sufficient because competition is a multidimensional process associated with the open-system character of the economy in general and of firms in particular. The indeterminateness of the range of possible actions makes it difficult to isolate a unit of selection; it also makes the notion of selection lose its intuitive appeal.

The openness of economic structures and systems suggests that we should not restrict our analysis to real allocation unless very specific circumstances justify such a decision. In general, the monetary nature of capitalist economies implies that firms may pursue (money) profits through a variety of strategies, some of which have nothing to do with the production of goods and services. Furthermore, money may affect technology in a variety of ways. Thus innovation in manufacturing may be the most promising of strategies under some circumstances; a range of other possible actions, which may even cross industries, may be appropriate in other cases.

The above depicted features of the economy affect the way economic and social groups view the world they live in. Countervailing knowledge is likely to arise within and outside the economic environment, leading to social and economic conflicts. Learning processes are hardly restricted to specific environments, such as the market. Interaction among different types of knowledge is less likely to lead to predictable patterns of industrial evolution than to discontinuities in the economy as a whole. Obviously, this is not to deny that such patterns may exist, provided very specific conditions hold. The aim of the discussion was precisely to stress the relevance of these conditions.

NOTES

1. Saviotti and Metcalfe note: 'As in the natural sciences one can recognise a hierarchy of levels at which selection mechanisms operate' (P.P. Saviotti and J.S. Metcalfe, 'Present Development and Trends in Evolutionary Economics', in *ead.*(eds), *Evolutionary Theories of Economic and Technological Change. Present Status and Future Prospects*, Chur: Harwood Academic Publishers, 1991, p. 14). I would add that the tiers of the hierarchy are interdependent.
2. It is interesting to note that, in this perspective, a risk-spreading firm may prefer to diversify its strategic tools rather than focus on a single one, such as product innovation.
3. D. Foray and P. Garrouste, 'The Pertinent Levels of Analysis in Industrial Economics', in G.M. Hodgson and E. Screpanti (eds), *Rethinking Economics – Markets, Technology and Economic Evolution*, Aldershot: Edward Elgar, 1991.
4. K.W. Kapp 'The Open-System Character of the Economy and its Implications', in K. Dopfer (ed.), *Economics in the Future: Towards a New Paradigm*, London: Macmillan, 1976.
5. The issue is discussed in N. Georgescu-Roegen, 'Process in Farming Versus Process in Manufacturing: A Problem of Balanced Development', in *Energy and Economic Myths. Institutional and Analytical Economic Essays*, New York: Pergamon Press, 1976.
6. S.C. Dow, 'Methodology and the Analysis of a Monetary Economy', in *Money and the Economic Process*, Aldershot: Edward Elgar, 1993.
7. Technology is referred to in a broad sense, including techniques and equipment as well as the organization of labour.
8. N. Kaldor, *Causes of the Slow Rate of Economic Growth of the United Kingdom*, Cambridge: Cambridge University Press, 1966.
9. '(A)n economy that places an excessive importance on a quick payback will gradually slip into uncompetitiveness because of neglect of strategic investments that cannot pass the test of a high rate of return'. (M. Perelman, 1986, *The Pathology of the US Economy: The Costs of a Low-Wage System*, London: Macmillan, 124).
10. I discussed these issues in 'Monetary Policy and Industrial Structure: The Italian Experience', a paper presented at the 1997 EAEPE Conference in Athens.

4. Theorizing complexity

Robert Delorme

INTRODUCTION

This chapter addresses the issue of theorizing complexity in its own right. The need for it originates from several sources. It seems to be especially relevant to evolutionary economics. Evolutionary theorizing in economics seems to be divided into two perspectives. One places the emphasis on equilibrium (Krugman, 2000). The other gives a general priority to process (Nelson, 1995). The complexity of the subject matter of economics appears to be used by the proponents of both perspectives as a central reason for justifying their respective choices. This chapter addresses the open-ended, process-oriented perspective and the role played by complexity in it. In his survey, Richard Nelson evokes abundantly a double role of complexity, first as a property of the subject matter of economic change, second as a property of evolutionary theory. In Nelson's words, complex theorizing is the price 'worth paying to buy the better ability to devise and work with a theory that rings right' and to make the intellectual bet 'that evolutionary theory opens up a productive research program, to use Lakatos' idea' (ibid., p. 85).

It is worth comparing this statement with Alan Kirman's observation that economics has got locked into a particular paradigm or standard model but 'what is now happening, in what can loosely be described as complexity theory or the theory of complex adaptive systems, seems likely to have an important impact on the development of economic theory' (Kirman, 1997, p. 102). To Kirman, the analysis of chaotically evolving economies indicates a movement in formal theory departing from the features incorporated in the current economic paradigm. But his view of non-mainstream economics is rather negative:

> However, various other currents [than marginal reasoning] have persisted in economics, although they have been regarded as being outside the mainstream frequently as a result of their lack of rigour. A particular example of this is the so-called 'evolutionary school' of economics, which is typically regarded as having flourished since Schumpeter, although one can find much earlier traces of this sort of reasoning in the work of previous economists. The idea of an economy as an

> open, adapting and evolving system has always been present, but the failure of this point of view to generate any firm propositions about what one might expect to observe and at the same time its failure to construct any sort of axiomatic theoretical framework led to its marginalization. (Ibid, p. 103)

These phrases express by and large a rather widely shared opinion in economic academia. If evolutionary theory is to become a scientific research programme in Lakatos' sense, it seems necessary both to be fruitful and to rely on a systematic theoretical framework. Can the recourse to complexity help in this respect? One may wonder whether complexity does not resemble what Daniel Friedman says about bounded rationality: a Rorschach inkblot for economists. To a majority it is an opportunity to put aside standard formal models in favour of complex computational models 'or simple verbal models or no models at all' (Friedman, 1998, p. 366). To some other economists it is an empirical challenge to study the processes which unfold in the economy.

But complexity is also a theoretical challenge. Indeed, it is a notion in search of a theory. The volume on *The Economy as an Evolving Complex System II* (Arthur *et al.*, 1997) illustrates the uncertainties surrounding complexity, notably on the question of 'what counts as a problem and as a solution' which the editors evoke in their introduction. Then there arises inevitably the question of the generality of the particular notions of complexity used in various studies. A plurality of forms, and relativity, characterize complexity, as will be shown here.

The contention of this chapter is to present in summary a theory of complexity elaborated as a solution to a problem encountered in empirical research on the evolution of public expenditure in France and in international comparison. The central insight is that complexity is a property of both the world and the process of enquiry into the world. This fundamental duality is hierarchized: the process of enquiry comes first. And four meanings of complexity emerge from this reasoning as will be shown later. This contrasts sharply with the common practice which consists of regarding complexity only as a property of observed or designed objects independently of the observer or designer.

We elaborate a behavioural setting through a self-referential extension of Herbert Simon's distinction between substantive and procedural rationality and through working out a conception of a situated satisficing derived from the standard of performance in a given field of activity. In our field, this standard pertains to abiding by rules of scientific practice.

After drawing some necessary distinctions in the next section, we show in subsequent sections how a *second order complexity* can be a *satisficing* solution to an empirically based theorizing problem and how it may have a more general bearing as a commitment to an open, but controlled, mode of knowing.

DRAWING DISTINCTIONS

General Theory and Local Theory

Reflecting on evolutionary economic theorizing without further qualification leads inevitably to differentiating between a general level and a local level of theory. It is broadly analogous to the distinction introduced by Lakatos between a hard core and a periphery in scientific research programmes. We are addressing the issue primarily at the general or hard-core level. One may reasonably claim that, if evolutionary theorizing in economics is to become a progressive research programme, it will have to be both fruitful and cumulative at the local level, and systematized enough at the general level and in the articulation between the two levels. I study below to what extent complexity has to do with this challenge to economic evolutionary theory. My argumentation is derived from my own experience on a local theorizing issue: the problem of the evolution of public expenditure in the long run in France and other industrial countries. Time-series and cross-section analyses, notably the comparison between France and Germany, led to the identification of characteristic configurations of the relationships between the state and the economic sphere. These morphological formations vary over time and across countries and do not appear to be satisfactorily tractable with available analytical tools. They are thus undecomposable for the purpose at hand. This was the basis for attempting to theorize complexity. Complexity takes on varied forms, as will be suggested below, yet there are traits common to all complexity as such. In this sense, this experience may have a general bearing and be relevant for evolutionary theorizing whenever complexity plays a role in it. However, we attempt to show that all forms of complexity do not have the same implications, which necessitates drawing further distinctions.

Several Steps in Complexity

Examination of the references to complexity in the literature suggests quite disparate contexts and meanings attached to this word. They can be ordered according to the consequences they entail for research, going from the merely casual to the most profound. This ordering does not entail any idea of degrees of complexity, an issue which is not tackled here.

In a first step we find the idea of an important difficulty in knowing or acting upon a phenomenon, without further qualification. It is the common sense of a kind of casual complexity. Then comes the idea of complexity considered as a property of an object, of a subject matter. An example of this is choaos theory in non-linear dynamics. In a third step, object-based complexity is deemed to have consequences for the method of theorizing, whereas in the previous case there was no explicit integration of necessary changes of method. Such a kind of complexity is labelled 'essential complexity' by F.A. Hayek (1967, 1989). Hayek borrows from Weaver (1948) the notion of organized complexity and regards it as a characteristic of social phenomena, notably in the economic domain. It reduces the scope for prediction to mere pattern prediction. A similar notion of complexity pervades Nelson's survey (Nelson, 1995) since the complexity of the subject matter of economic change becomes in his view reflected in the style of theorizing appropriate to it: evolutionary theory is itself complex. Considering our interest in drawing differences in complexity, it seems appropriate to call this kind of complexity 'reflexive', to the extent that it is explicitly reflected in method, and to restrict 'essential' complexity to a more profound, 'essential' change in theorizing.[1] Indeed, a change of paradigm is called for. Examples of such claims can be found in the programmes initiated by T. Veblen, J.M. Keynes, W. Eucken and H.A. Simon, and in the French theory of regulation (Delorme, 2000).

Further steps are less familiar. They are self-referential complexity, second-order complexity and meta complexity, and are introduced in the next sections. They arise in a bottom-up way as consequences of essential complexity. Indeed, the motivation for exploring these steps came from a special difficulty encountered in the research on state–economy relationships evoked above. It was felt that none of the available theories could make it possible to come to grips with the undecomposability problem in a satisfactory way. This absence of a satisfactory theory adds another degree of complexity to the complexity coming from undecomposability as such, that is, from the substance of the subject matter, at a first order of investigation. This additional complexity is the complexity in dealing with a complex matter: it is a second-order complexity.

The Relativity of Complexity

W.R. Ashby, one of the founders of the first cybernetics, takes complexity as the quantity of information required to describe a system, and compares the complexity of the brain of a sheep to a butcher and to a neurophysiologist. To a butcher, the brain is simple since it is easy to distinguish it from other 'meats'. To the neurophysiologist, the brain 'as a feltwork of fibers and a soup of enzymes is certainly complex; and equally the transmission of a detailed description of it would require much time' (Ashby, 1973, p. 1). Here complexity becomes purely relative to a given observer. This method rejects the attempt to measure an absolute, or intrinsic, complexity. It conceives complexity as 'something in the eye of the beholder' (ibid.). Although one may discuss attributing complexity exclusively to the observer's interest, the interest of this example is to point to three components: the actor's purpose, the field of activity and the object, given an efficient actor and a state of knowledge in a field of activity. In Ashby's example, the discriminating component is the field of activity. Different fields entail different depictions. Thus complexity derives from the standard of satisfactory performance in a given field of activity.

We have no space to discuss Ashby's definition. We can nevertheless mention that 'to describe a system' is vague. There is no consideration of what constitutes a satisfactory description. Indeed, an implicit assumption is present, according to which it is always possible to achieve a satisfactory description. If we admit that there exist cases in which it is very difficult to achieve a satisfactory description, we can hardly avoid considering the conditions required for a satisfactory description and the ways available or not in order to fulfil them. In other words, it becomes necessary to take explicitly into account the observer's behaviour. And the observer's behaviour is connected to her or his level of aspiration. Indeed, as we will suggest later, it is difficult to separate knowledge from action as soon as the observer is given an active role. This is what the theorizing of complexity sketched here proposes.

We can extend Ashby's example to the case of a butcher and a neurobiologist working on the same sheep brain. To a butcher, the main purpose is to prepare and display the brain in a way which is attractive to the customers. This is routine work. To a neurobiologist, if the purpose is to explain and understand the creation and circulation of information and knowledge in the brain, it is a hypercomplex task. Thus complexity is really in the actor's mind and know-how. It depends both on pure knowledge and on a capacity to act satisfactorily, given a goal, on a given object in a given activity. If we take a given activity, like economics, with a given goal, say prediction, the difficulty varies according to the object. But to define such an exclusively object-based complexity, it is necessary to retain a unique purpose. And this unique purpose of prediction is itself the outcome of a purposeful agreement within a community. Hence it would seem difficult to deny that purpose remains the primary factor of complexity.

A Plurality of Forms of Complexity with an Invariant Property

A consequence of the relativity of complexity is that it can take different forms according to the respective purposes and domains of activity. But in all cases we find irreducibility as an invariant property of complexity. The undecomposability of an object or a system is such a form. It lies in the impossibility of reducing or decomposing the object to a satisfactory level. The deterministic unpredictability of chaos theory is another example. Irreducibility is also present in probabilistic unpredictability represented by radical uncertainty. Another instance is uncompressibility in algorithmic information theory. This plurality suggests that there is a priori no reason to favour one form of complexity in the study of complex phenomena. The relevant notion of complexity depends on the purpose, the field of activity and the object. A whole situation or context – not only an object – is at stake here. This justifies our examining the links between the complexity of objects and of situations.

From Complex Objects to Complex Situations

Defining complexity as irreducibility is helpful at this stage. However, it will be qualified and complemented in a later section. Here it helps to differentiate complexity from non-complexity. Non-complexity is related to reducibility or achieving a satisfactory solution. This can be done either easily and rapidly, and so defines simplicity, or it is more difficult and requires more time, and so defines complication.

An object is cognitively complex if the knowledge an observer has of it remains insufficient with respect to the observer's purpose. It is a level of ignorance irreducible to a lower level associated with a given goal of knowledge. Physicist J-M. Lévy-Leblond notes that physical science is confronted with such a situation (the reality of nature is irreducibly complex) and yet it is possible to describe and predict the orbits of planets and to perform satisfactorily a number of operations because there exist methods or techniques of treatment allowing it (Lévy-Leblond, 1991). This suggests that it is the combination of the characteristics of an object (perceived as complex or not) with a technique of treatment of it (available or not) which defines whether a situation is complex or not. In this sense the three dimensions of the relativity of complexity make it difficult to maintain a separation between knowledge and action.

Diverse configurations may arise, from simplicity to complexity of a situation. The complexity of an object does not entail the complexity of the situation when a satisfactory technique of treatment is available. Thus the problem can be solved and the situation is only complicated. In economics, all theories which detect an essential complexity and consider that the methods designed by them are satisfactory end in a non-complex situation according to the distinction we introduce. What makes this distinction interesting appears when no satisfactory technique of treatment is available. Then the situation created is complex. This is what we experienced on the state–economy relationships. The central question lies, naturally, in what is meant by 'satisfactory'. At this point an explicit behavioural setting is required.

A Behavioural Setting

What to do or how to behave are questions which arise naturally in a complex situation. H.A. Simon's distinction between substantive and procedural rationality offers a useful insight. Simon defines these notions in the following way: 'Behavior is substantively rational when it is appropriate to the achievement of given goals within the limits imposed by given conditions and constraints [...]. Behavior is procedurally rational when it is the outcome of appropriate deliberation. Its procedural rationality depends on the process that generated it' (Simon, 1976, pp. 130–1). Procedural rationality may be expected in situations that are not 'sufficiently simple as to be transparent to [the] mind'. Thus 'we must expect that the mind will use such imperfect information as it has, will simplify and represent the situation as it can, and will make such calculations as are within its powers' (ibid., p. 144). Using the correct available algorithm is the usual way to operate in substantive rationality. There is no interference between the decision maker and the way to solve a problem. No such thing is, by definition, available when radical uncertainty, ignorance or complexity prevail. In this case, decision embodies deliberation, search and the forms of representation the decision maker considers to be appropriate. A solution is then constructed through a heuristic process in which it is reasonable to retain 'an alternative that meets or exceeds specified criteria, but that is not guaranteed to be either unique or in any sense the best', which defines *satisficing*, a term introduced by Simon in 1956. A situation is satisficing when it is adequate to some aspiration level or, in short, good enough. This is the essence of procedural rationality.

Let us assume that the observer is facing the same problem as the Simonian decision maker. This assumption introduces self-reference, a thing Simon seems to have constantly avoided. It necessitates distinguishing an object level, at which complexity emerges, and a meta level at which designing a satisficing technique of treatment may be envisaged. It is at the meta level that the complexity of dealing with a complex situation, or second-order complexity, appears. We discuss this in the next section.

SECOND-ORDER COMPLEXITY

Satisficing has no determinate substantive contents, and it may lead to subjectivism. Thus it needs to be controlled by submitting it to an external constraint. This constraint cannot but be related to the environment of the research process. Here the relevant environment is scientific practice. The constraint consists of making compatible the three dimensions around which our argumentation has revolved until now: scientific practice, inclusion of complexity and operationality. They define an aspiration level for which it is reasonable to consider that a wide agreement on the following global injunction may be obtained: *do science, embody complexity* and *be operational.* A theory will be appropriate if it meets these three constraints. Let us explore how it can be done.

Scientific Practice

Definition

Viewed from a basic, practical level, what distinguishes doing science from other cognitive or intellectual operations may be learnt from a commonly accepted definition of science. There seems to be a wide consensus on the combination of three elements. Doing science is to search for some explanation of some reality and systematically put it to the test (Granger, 1990). It seems reasonable to consider that this definition is the common reference to all scientific activity. It is the shared vision from which the divide between conceptions of science arises. This divide comes from the various ways of conceiving explanation, reality and testing.

Explanation is taken here, at this stage, in a broad, generic sense. It refers to the operation of producing knowledge. It can be causal explanation in a strict sense, but it can also be prediction, representation or understanding. For the purpose at hand, the main differentiation is between the goals of causal explanation and prediction of mainstream economics and the emphasis on representation common to most heterodox views.

The next divide occurs about what is considered as reality. The subject matter of science bears on the real world, but here there is a profound separation between two positions. One is ontological realism, which attempts to know the nature of reality, to discover its laws, thus viewing it as objective, independent from the mind, the goal being to produce statements that will be scientific because they depict a reality independently from the observer's eye. According to another conception one would consider that the true reality is beyond reach and that we know it only through our experience of phenomena. This is phenomenological realism. Instead of being discovered, laws and other statements are invented. Scientific practice aims more at diminishing our ignorance than at establishing truths. It is a fallibilistic standpoint with which complexity fits well.

This brings us to the third feature, namely, testing. This is the key and most difficult question in economic science, for it lacks a final arbiter. The situation is incomparably better in natural science, where experimentation and controlled observation provide criteria for empirical validation. Insofar as we are interested in empirico-theoretic science, not in formal science, a final arbiter rests on controlled protocols of empirical validation. It is not indulging in catastrophism to acknowledge that standard economics is in a disastrous state in this regard. Exceptions can be found in simple, transparent enough problems such as those for which substantive rationality is relevant, at a micro level, or those which are simple enough at the macroeconomic level, thus enabling reasonably reliable prediction. This difficult state of affairs is widely admitted in the literature on economic methodology. Until now one must say that its influence on the way most economists work still has been almost nil. The greatest part of economic theory consists mainly of conversation at a formal and abstract level. As a consequence, a final arbiter is avoided.

How to put scientific knowledge to the test?

There are two other features that are closely linked to scientific practice. They pertain to the manner in which reasoning is conducted and is communicated. It needs a language. As any other language, it is made with signs, symbols and rules. The first feature has to do with the requirement contained in the triplet of communicability, systematicity and cumulativeness of science. Communication is the basis for diminishing confusion and establishing systematicity thanks to which some progress and cumulative knowledge may be envisaged. These notions point to the importance of the way scientific knowledge is represented and communicated. This is the second feature.

At this stage it is necessary to emphasize a feature to which still only a little attention seems to be paid in scientific practice. Every science embodies its statements and results in signs. Semiotics, the science of signs, comprises three fields of investigating languages (Carnap), also termed portions of semiotics (Morris) or levels of communication (Weaver, 1949). Syntax (Carnap), also called syntactics (Morris) or the technical level (Weaver), pertains to the relations of signs to one another independently of the relations of signs to objects or to interpreters. Semantics deals with the signification of signs understood as the relation of signs to the objects which they denote. Pragmatics designates the relation of signs to their interpreters, thus dealing with the origin, the uses and the effects of signs (Morris, 1971). Scientific practice may be expressed as covering necessarily these three fields, and symbolized by a triangle whose summits are these fields.

Within the economic discipline, perspectives can be differentiated according to the relative weights they give to these levels. The formal orientation focuses on syntax, while most dissident perspectives emphasize the other summits of the triangle. The ideal is a balance. The standard perspective in economics gives a priority to syntax. Thus, in the case of radical uncertainty or complexity, it is no surprise that primacy will be given to the method over the object of enquiry, that is, to syntax over semantics. Exclusion of radical uncertainty, because it cannot be captured with the analytical toolkit, illustrates this point clearly. The tools are thus taken for granted and applied to situations which are made to adapt to them thanks to *ad hoc* assumptions. A different approach is to start from problematic situations and empirical facts and try to adjust the method and syntax applied to them, thus putting the bulk of adjustment on the pragmatic and syntactic levels. Yet this procedure does not mean that facts can be taken a priori as granted. They are inevitably arbitrary in a first step. However, we would find it difficult to express our experience of reality without relying on facts. Thus it seems reasonable to admit that some adaptation of the facts is inevitable. Of course, it does not mean that observation will be modified in order to fit the observer's own preferences! Adjusting facts means making them relevant to the question addressed. In the research mentioned above, we found that it was impossible to address public spending in the long run independently from public finance. And we discovered that it would be quite difficult to investigate public finance over time and in international comparison independently of the other forms, both quantitative and qualitative, of interaction between the state and the economy. Thus the facts investigated were initially public spending, then public finance, then quantitative and qualitative dimensions of the public sector (Delorme, 1984).

One would expect that in any empirical science consistency prevails not only in the manner the signs are used, in the way they are relevant and in the way they combine in syntax, but also in the overall consistency of the semiotic triangle. It is difficult here not to think of the discrepancy which exists in economics between professed and actual method. It is the price paid to preserve formalism. It illustrates how excessive formalism may constrain scientific practice either by preventing the study of empirical situations that do not fit with syntax or by asking the public at large, first, to accept that economics relies mainly on syntax and must be programmatic for the time being and, second, to believe that it will have empirically relevant results in an ever-postponed unknown future. The alternative approach also has its own price: the weakness of its syntax, the evasiveness or the absence of a body of founding logical principles. Here we face once again the continuing debate over the trade-offs of 'well-derived' versus 'empirically-relevant' theories.

Complexity

The choice made in the trade-off discussed above is driven by the condition that it be consistent with complexity. It led to recursiveness. How can we ensure that a procedure is consistent with complexity? How does it compare with the analytical perspective? A condensed way to answer these questions consists in concentrating on the logical bases of each perspective. The contention is that complexity may be related to a set of founding principles which have the same status as those of the analytical perspective. This may answer a criticism often made of what may be called 'heterodoxy', namely that 'heterodoxy' has no chain of basic principles ensuring its internal consistency in a way comparable to 'orthodoxy'. Hence the presumed superiority of 'orthodoxy'. That this seems to be no longer true, at least for complexity, can be shown through a comparison of axioms of classical logic with the progressively emerging axioms of complexity. They are naturally much less codified, communicated and known than the analytical axioms. It may thus make them appear quite abstract and strange. Yet, if we reflect on the rationale of the axioms which form the basis of analytical theorizing, we will see that they are not more obvious than the complex ones. It is habituation which makes them look familiar and self-evident to the point where we never refer to them explicitly, as if they were the unsaid basic consensus to be preserved from questioning.

Let it be clear at this stage that we do not contend that what may be called the analytical perspective pertains to only one system of logic. There is a plurality of logics. However, it can hardly be denied that the debate within the economic discipline revolves mainly around the issue of consistency grounded in a set of axioms whose ultimate basis is found in classical logic. The lack of such a consistency is still the main criticism opposed to 'heterodox' views. It is the reason why such criticism has to be taken seriously. Yet we must acknowledge that the concern for establishing basic principles for complexity is recent and has consequently still not led to a well-established and stabilized system of axioms. The presentation made below derives from our own enquiry and from the generalization of its results. It does not contradict Le Moigne's presentation of basic principles, though it differs from it (Le Moigne, 1990). In presenting what appears as basic principles, we stick to a heuristic strategy enabling the comparison with the axioms of analytical modelling envisaged here.

The classical axioms of analytical modelling

The reality to be modelled is perceived through three axioms. A and B stand for propositions or entities.

- Identity: A is A.
- Non contradiction: A cannot be simultaneously A and not-A.
- Excluded middle: there does not exist B such that B is simultaneously A and not-A.

Basic principles of complex modelling

The phenomena to be modelled are perceived through four principles.

1. Relationship: the basic phenomenon is a relationship between A and B, B being different from A.
2. Identity: for a given relationship, A is A.
3. Non-negation: given principle 2, A cannot be simultaneously A and not-A.
4. Included middle: given A and not-A, there exists C such that C is simultaneously A and not-A.

Operationality

Until now we have remained at the logical and methodological levels. The next task is to combine what has been stated about scientific practice and about complexity in an operational way, enabling us to apply these results to actual cases and to compare them with alternative theoretical perspectives. The satisficing principle has been fulfilled until now. But we still need to submit complexity to the test of its adequacy to the problem. In this sense complexity becomes controlled complexity. For such an operational control it seems necessary to rely on the three rules of consistency, communicability and relevance.

Consistency

Consistency is concerned with avoiding the discrepancy between professed and actual method and an imbalance between the three elements of the semiotic triangle. Although it is difficult to define substantively a balance between these elements, it can be defined procedurally as mutually adjusting semantics and syntax up to the point where the actually practised pragmatics meets the declared pragmatics – that is, the professed method. It may be summarized as preach what you can do, do what you preach. In the study of a phenomenon perceived as complex, for which there exists no available substantive theory or model, empirical investigation comes together with abduction and the attempt at theorizing. Hence the priority given to the object of study and to the semantics over the syntax in the first step.

Communicability

It may look trivial to insist on *communicability* as a rule, yet it conditions potential systematicity and cumulativeness. Above all it is a precondition for mutual criticism and the real exercise of control within and outside the scientific community. It implies transparency and voluntary exposure to criticism. It runs opposite to the immunization so often denounced by methodologists in economics (Caldwell, 1991). Even if it may look too idealistic to believe in the elimination of immunization, the least that can be done is to eliminate hidden immunization. This requires that, when immunization is introduced, it be made explicit. One finds here an illustration that the proof of the pudding is sometimes more in the making than in the eating. A way to foster transparency is the comparison between theories for a given problem, in a meliorative strategy. It implies that statements should be designed in a way that makes comparison possible.

Relevance

In line with the fallibilistic stance of the complex perspective, relevance amounts to reducing ignorance and arbitrariness in theorizing. Emphasizing the reduction of arbitrariness seems fruitful because of its generality and of its capacity to be used as a criterion for comparison and for assessment. We express this in the following proposition:

- There is no non-arbitrary way of reasoning. There is no non-arbitrary ultimate foundation.
- There are degrees of arbitrariness. They can be identified through comparison.
- The aim is to reduce the degree of arbitrariness for a given problem.

Second-order, Anchored Complexity

These conditions constitute the outcome of a process of reasoning developed at the meta level. This outcome translates into a generating principle at the object level. This generating principle is informed and constrained by the meta level. It is literally anchored to it. These conditions may be named 'anchored complexity'. It provides a solution to the problem of the unifying principle mentioned above: anchored complexity is a leading thread satisfying the conditions enumerated. The plurality of methods intrinsic to complexity is bounded by what is admissible for anchored complexity. Moreover, anchored complexity reduces *ipso facto* the degree of arbitrariness in comparison to the analytical approach, since it takes into account complexity.

Finally, anchored complexity may be considered as a generating principle whose product stimulated its own production. This sentence simply describes the recursive loop between an initial enquiry leading to an observed phenomenon transformed into an empirically based conjecture (characteristic configuration of the interaction between the state and the economy) and later into a theoretical notion (mode of interaction between the state and the economy: MISE), having been informed by anchored complexity (symbolized as ACX in Figure 4.1).

It seems reasonable to think at this point that the above development is adequate to the purpose at hand and is thus a satisficing solution. However, it

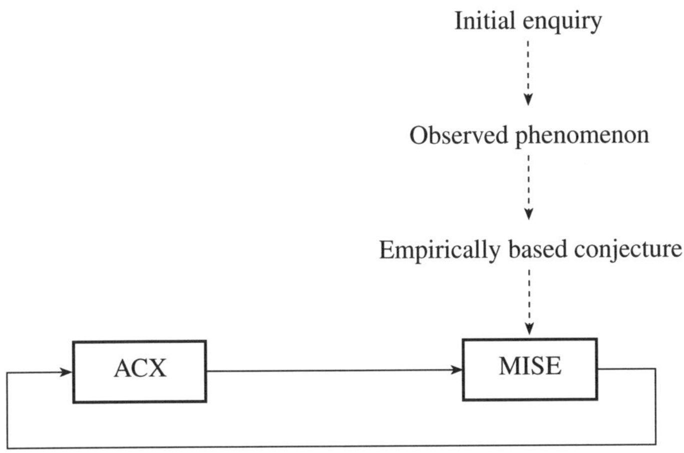

Figure 4.1 *Research on the case in point as a recursive loop*

must be acknowledged that there is no external universal criterion to assess whether it is true or false. The only way is to expose it to criticism, but here what is exposed to criticism is more accurate, more specified, more operational than what was available at the beginning.

GENERALITY

Second-order complexity was designed in order to conceive a solution to a specific problem. Can it be extended? To what degree? We attempt to answer these questions in this section. For this it proved necessary to work out several notions. They are the notions of chain of reasoning, of irreducibility, of non-separability and of asymmetry and meta complexity which are successively considered below.

A Chain of Reasoning

The arguments which have been incorporated in the previous section provide an array that is consistent and that offers a complete chain of reasoning. The central difference occurs with the principle of included middle, which departs from its equivalent, the axiom of the excluded middle. Indeed, this axiom is central to analytical reasoning, and the included middle is central to the complex way of reasoning. Putting together the pieces that would have to be introduced in a fully developed argument makes possible a comparison of the analytical and the complex perspectives (Table 4.1).

Table 4.1 The analytical and complex scientific perspectives compared

		ANALYSIS	COMPLEXITY
1	General definition of scientific practice	Common to both perspectives: some kind of explanation of reality, systematically put to the test	
2	Conception of scientific knowledge	Positivism	Constructivism and fallibilism
3	Mode of reasoning	Analytical	Systemic
4	Position on reality	Objective character of reality	Constructed character of reality
5	Main purpose of scientific practice	Prediction	Active representation
6	Logical core	Axioms of classical logic (notably excluded middle)	Principles of complex logic (notably included middle)
7	Methodological stance	Deduction, induction Disjunction Discovery Universal norm	Abduction Conjunction Design, invention Satisficing
8	Method	Taken as granted: 'the scientific method'	Adjusted according to anchored complexity: built-in controlled pluralism
9	Theoretical perspective and theorizing	$x, y, z, \ldots$	$a, b, c, \ldots$
10	End product (statements on the real world, policy prescriptions)	$x', y', z', \ldots$	$a', b', c', \ldots$

The construction proposed here obeys a hierarchy covering ten levels. The first level is the one for which a divide occurs between the standard approach and the approach of complexity. We assume that the dictionary definition of scientific practice is considered relevant by proponents of both perspectives. The divide occurs about the conception of scientific knowledge and unfolds downwards until the end product layer.

The terms mentioned in each column indicate the primary focus of each perspective at each level. They do not describe all the ingredients. We simply contend that the terms retained here form the respective starting points, on which other features are dependent, in each approach. Considering the previous developments, the items in Table 4.1 do not seem to require further explanation, given the scope of this contribution. The exception to this concerns the main purpose of scientific practice in the complex perspective at level 5. A common trait of complex reasoning is its representation of a reality that is itself perceived primarily through a process of construction. Representation is then active, not passive. In passive representation, knowledge is viewed as reflecting a world with intrinsic predefined properties, leaving the scientist with the task of uncovering some hidden truth 'already there'. In active representation, design and invention play an important part.

Let us come back to the world view issue. Having a world view cannot be abolished. It is commonly understood in the economic discipline as pertaining to a set of basic statements, shared by a scientific community, on how the economy functions. Neoclassical, Keynesian, Post-Keynesian, Austrian and Marxian world views, among others, illustrate this definition. The divide in the discipline is usually thought of in terms of these world views. The conception presented here is different. We have attempted to show that introducing complexity displaces the issue from a matter of substantive preferences shared by respective communities to a matter of cognitive procedure. We introduced the conception of scientific knowledge as a basic criterion of choice independently of any preference on the substance of how the economy performs. Indeed, it is only at level 9 that particular theoretical perspectives come into the picture. On the one hand, one may find at this level the theoretical perspectives mentioned at the beginning of this chapter, together with the particular theorizing derived from them (x,y,z...) and end statements (x',y',z'...). On the other hand, the MISE may appear as a, together with other theoretical notions and end statements likely to be developed along complex lines (b,c, b',c',...). The end statements will logically differ from one approach to another.

In view of the confusion and of the limitations attached to the substantive world views in the case of complexity, we think that the cognitive conception developed here clarifies the issue and is more general.

The complex and the analytical perspectives are not symmetrical. At first sight, one might consider that the analytical perspective is warranted whenever we are in no-complexity. However, the analytical approach cannot accommodate complexity, while the complex approach can accommodate the situations pertaining to the analytical approach. One finds the same asymmetry between substantive and procedural rationality: the former excludes consideration of the latter, whereas the reverse is not true since procedural search allows by definition for the possibility of constructing situations locally relevant for substantive rationality (Delorme, 1998).

Thus complexity subsumes analysis. The situations relevant for analysis appear as particular cases. Whereas the trademark of analysis is exclusivism, complexity does not exclude a priori the analytical method. It excludes only analytical exclusivism. It subsumes the analytical approach thanks to its greater generality and relevance. It allows for the local relevance of analytical and positivist methods provided their relevance is established on every specific subject matter under consideration. This asymmetry supports the case for considering that the complex perspective offers a more general methodological stance than the analytical one. However, complexity does not reduce to methodology. We have attempted to show how designing a research strategy and putting it to work as anchored complexity makes sense. The analytical perspective can no longer base its strength on the absence of an alternative perspective which would meet similar standards of consistency and of operationality.

An Irreducible Cognitive Gap

A provisional definition

Let D^i be the degree of difficulty in performing a task *i* or in solving a problem *i* and $\overline{D}$ be the degree of difficulty associated with a norm of validation or of performance in the activity or discipline in which *i* takes place. It is the difficulty of achieving a good enough, satisfactory or valid solution or outcome. Difficulty pertains to knowledge and action. The higher the difficulty is, the higher is the level (amount and quality) of knowledge required for performing satisfactorily the task. Complexity, defined as an irreducible lack of knowledge, depends on the norm of validation and on the level of difficulty D^i. It can be symbolized as:

$$CX = f(D^i, \overline{D})$$

D^i appears in our research on the state–economy relationships when one makes attempts at applying 'normal', analytic standards to the objects uncovered. It emerges primarily as undecomposability and ultimately as unavailability of a method or technique making it possible simultaneously to meet established standards in the economics discipline (it looks descriptive, non-explanatory; it is not derived from a theoretical specification; it is even not framed in the hypothesis testing way) and to integrate the hard facts that are observed. D^i and $\overline{D}$ are not measurable. This is not too bad, since we are interested in definitions, and especially in making sense of the difference between D^i and $\overline{D}$. D^i greater than $\overline{D}$ means that the difficulty of solving a problem remains higher than the level of difficulty associated with a norm or standard of knowledge in a community, which amounts to what is considered valid or acceptable by the community. Although this may look surprising, it is a way to introduce a kind of cognitive irreducibility which will appear helpful later on. In order to clarify this way of defining irreducibility, we will have to come back again to differentiating between a complex object and a complex situation.

Ignorance is unsufficient knowledge compared to a required level or a norm. It can be expressed by $D^i - \overline{D} > 0$, which means that the level of difficulty D^i is irreducibly larger than the level of difficulty attached to the norm: the norm cannot be achieved because of this lack of knowledge. Conversely, reducibility corresponds to the case in which available knowledge is larger than or equal to what is required. Complexity corresponds to the former. It is a degree of ignorance that is irreducible to a degree compatible with a norm of valid knowledge in a given activity or discipline. A further reflection on second-order complexity will show that this definition is incomplete. It is, however, sufficient for the purpose at hand now. The latter case is reducibility. It may be called non-complexity. Two cases may occur. First, when D^i is inferior to $\overline{D}$, it is simplicity. Complication is the second case. It means that a satisfactory solution can be achieved whatever time and effort are needed to reach it: $D^i \leq \overline{D}$.

This can be summarized in the following way, with D^i and $\overline{D} > 0$.

Reducibility: $D^i - \overline{D} \leq 0$: simplicity $D^i - \overline{D} < 0$
complication $D^i - \overline{D} \leq 0$
Irreducibility: $D^i - \overline{D} > 0$: complexity

This is a way to define complexity and non-complexity and to distinguish complexity from complication. However, this definition is provisional. It will be rendered more precise thanks to the distinctions between logical levels and between generating mechanism and outcome.

Different logical levels

The solution that we designed as second-order complexity was grounded in a self-referential use of the behavioural notions of procedural and substantive rationality systematised by H.A. Simon. We had to develop a procedure in order to obtain a satisficing outcome. This procedure belongs to a level of reasoning logically superior to the level at which the objects of inquiry are primarily considered, that is, the object level. The level of this self-referential procedure is the meta level. We named anchored complexity the particular solution that we obtained. Anchored complexity is the outcome (O) of this procedure at the meta level. The mechanism from which this outcome originates may be called a generative mechanism (GM).

The pair (GM,O) provides a fundamental representation for the working of complexity. Notice that I do not say 'the working *on* complexity', as if the source of the working, the observer, were contemplating complexity from a separate, exterior standpoint. Indeed, a reasonable way of working is *with* complexity, meaning that the observer is part of the complex system, a thing Heinz von Foerster has repeatedly illustrated (1988, 1992). The pairs (*procedure, substance*), (*meta, object*), (*observer, observed*) may thus be considered to be to a large extent special instances of (GM,O) which takes in this way a status of generative complex pair. This property has rather far-reaching consequences that we will consider later.

At this point, it may be worth summarizing our pathway to a solution. It started with establishing the legitimacy so to speak of our object of investigation (the MISE) on grounds of observation, empirical investigation, comparison and of robustness and resistance of this object to different ways of addressing the issue. In the absence of a method enabling us to theorize satisfactorily on this object according to the available theoretical systems playing the role of norms of validation, we attempted to conceive a generating mechanism abiding by a set of scientific rules of which the MISE would appear a theoretical outcome. The chain of complex reasoning which was exposed constitutes the generating mechanism which was sought. Indeed it is a case of second-order complexity. It provides a method validating the initial object of enquiry and a solution to the complex situation which was created.

The MISE is an outcome at the object level. It is generated by an empirical, comparative, contrastive investigation (Lawson, 1997) also developed at the object level. This result was obtained in a bottom-up way. Once it is obtained it can also be viewed the other way around, in that the MISE is also the factor from which the generating mechanism was built. It remains to assess whether this is specific to this particular case study or can be extended. The latter will prove to be the case after an additional step in the reasoning is made. For the moment, the two-way relationship mentioned above means that it is recursive or circular. This particular recursive loop operates at the object level. The generative mechanism at this level is reappraised as an outcome at the meta level. It is generated at this level by the chain of complex reasoning. Its generative mechanism is scientific practice and fallibilism. This meta level is itself the object level of a meta-meta level, and so on. For the issue at stake, we stop when a satisficing outcome is achieved. Given that our goal was to provide a scientific theoretical status to the MISE, we were able to stop after considering two consecutive loops, at the meta and object levels.

It is worth noticing an apparent paradox here. Having a solution means having achieved reducibility. And reducibility is non-complexity. So how can it be consistent with continuing to refer to second-order complexity? There is indeed no contradiction once the double level of complexity – meta and object – is aknowledged. Reduction is performed at the meta level only. Complexity remains at the object level. It must be added that it is a solution at the meta level. But there is no reason to believe that it is the best solution. It is only satisficing. The possibility that it may be modified, improved or replaced cannot be ruled out. Hence potential recursion must be allowed at the meta level. It is symbolized by broken lines in Figure 4.2.

Irreducibility is not eliminated at the object level, but a way of dealing with it is defined at the meta level. Second-order complexity is the conjunc-

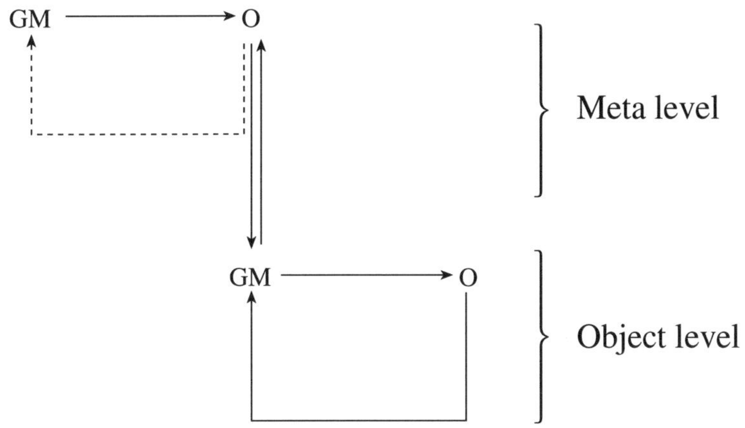

Figure 4.2 Second-order complexity

tion of these two levels. These levels are not separated, although they are distinct. In the same way, GM and O are not separated, at each level. Reducibility (meta level) and irreducibility (object level) are not separated. Second-order complexity is the irreducibility (at a meta-meta level) of the (reducibility, irreducibility) pair.

It must also be kept in mind that object-based complexity, or first-order complexity, implies the existence of second-order complexity only if a complex situation is created. And it will be shown that second-order complexity does not necessarily entail first-order complexity. There is no necessary general implication between these notions of complexity.

Second-order complexity defined

We are now in a position to define complexity more precisely than at the beginning of this chapter. We will base it on the distinctions between object and meta levels, and GM and O, respectively. For the sake of simplicity, let us drop the *i* superscript of D^i and replace GM with *p*, standing for procedure, and replace O with *s*, standing for substance. Let us also symbolize the meta level with *m* and the object level with *o* subscripts. This avoids a possible confusion between O for outcome (in GM,O) and *o* for object level (in *m*, *o*). Replacing GM with *p* and O with *s* should not be a source of confusion since *p* and *s* (procedure and substance) are particular instances of GM and O. Here *p* is a method of treatment (validation, reduction) and *s* is the object. We start by expressing complexity at the object level and then at the meta level, and finally at both the meta and the object levels.

With *D* standing for a degree of difficulty and the bar (–) representing a standard or norm of validation, we now have to consider $D_o^s, D_o^p, \overline{D}_o^s, \overline{D}_o^p$, at the object level, and $D_m^s, D_m^p, \overline{D}_m^s, \overline{D}_m^p$ at the meta level.

Object level
Reducibility: $D_o^s - \overline{D}_o^s \leq 0$

$$\begin{cases} \text{simplicity } D_o^s < \overline{D}_o^s \\ \text{complication } D_o^s \leq \overline{D}_o^s \end{cases}$$

Irreducibility: $D_o^s - \overline{D}_o^s > 0$ with two cases:
(1) there exists p such that $D_o^p = \overline{D}_o^p$;
(2) there is no p such that condition (1) is met: $D_o^p > \overline{D}_o^p$.
In case (1) the object is complex but the situation is not complex; in case (2) the object and the situation are complex.

Meta level Given a complex situation (case (2) of irreducibility above) the problem is to find at the meta level D_m^p such that $D_m^p = \overline{D}_m^p$; that is, D_m^p such that the meta object is reducible: $D_m^s = \overline{D}_m^s$.

This is meta complication. D_m^s is produced by D_m^p. It is anchored complexity in our case. It is satisficing. It is the outcome of the operation 'produce a satisficing generating mechanism' ($D_m^s = \overline{D}_m^s$). It is itself produced by a complex chain of reasoning D_m^p. This chain is satisficing ($D_m^p = \overline{D}_m^p$). In turn, D_m^p is produced by a meta-meta mechanism, and so on (see Figure 4.3).

The requirement about $\overline{D}_m^s$ was to reduce the degree of arbitrariness through comparison with the available theories. The norm $\overline{D}_m^p$ was to abide by scientific practice. Both norms were defined in the second section of this chapter.

Synthesis The object level problem becomes the object or the substance of the meta level. The object level problem is:

$$(D_o^p > \overline{D}_o^p, D_o^s > \overline{D}_o^s)$$

Irreducibility affects both the procedure and the substance: the situation is complex.

In carrying the issue up to the meta level, we seek a procedure D_m^p whose outcome D_m^s makes it possible to have a satisficing procedure D_o^p at the object level. This entails that D_m^p must itself be satisficing at its own, proper level:

$$D_m^p = \overline{D}_m^p$$

Its outcome is also satisficing:

$$D_m^s = \overline{D}_m^s$$

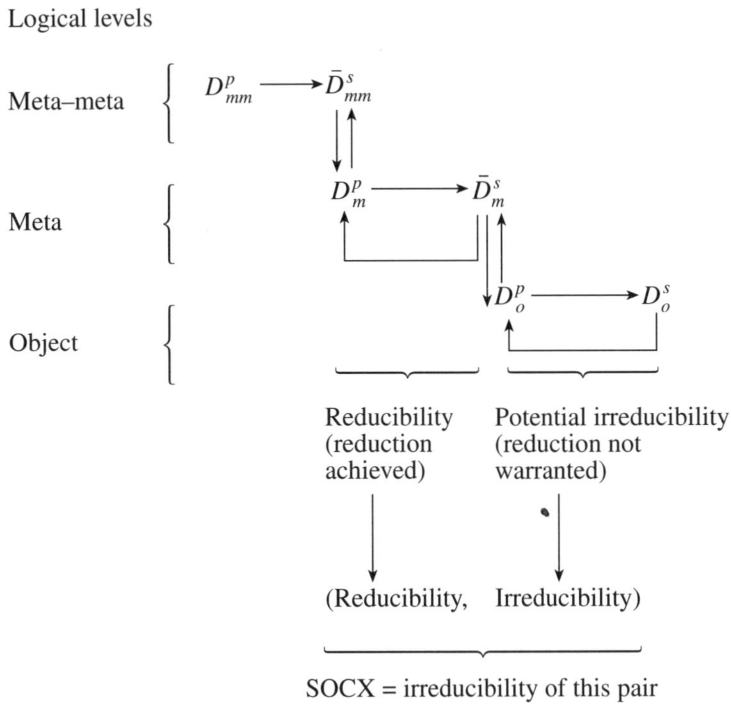

Figure 4.3 Second-order complexity (SOCX) defined

$\overline{D}_m^s$ informs D_o^p the procedure at the object level, but $\overline{D}_m^s$ must not be equated with D_0^p. In our case, $\overline{D}_m^s$ is anchored complexity. It constrains D_o^p to the extent that D_o^p must be compatible with it. D_o^p is no longer restricted to being a generating mechanism produced by analytical reasoning. $\overline{D}_m^s$ does not eliminate irreducibility at the object level, but it enlarges the scope of potentially valid techniques of treatment.

We thus have at the object level:

$$(D_o^p \geq \overline{D}_o^p, D_o^s \geq \overline{D}_o^s$$

If total equality is achieved, it means that simplicity or complication are obtained. If $D_o^s > \overline{D}_o^s$, we still have a complex object, but the situation is not necessarily complex. It is complex only if $D_o^p > \overline{D}_o^p$. This is synthesized in Figure 4.3.

Since the potential irreducibility of the object *s* at the object level cannot be eliminated, the kind and level of difficulty that may arise cannot be known in advance. It can either be solvable through a satisficing procedure $\overline{D}_o^p$ available at the object level or it cannot. In the latter case, the situation is complex and necessitates reactivating a meta-level reasoning. Starting from the object level, the situation can be summarized as follows.

If reducibility: reduction to $\overline{D}_o^s$ is achieved by means of a satisfactory first-order technique of treatment. Then D_o^p is neutralized and does not require to be reactivated.
If irreducibility: D_o^p is activated, it is informed by $\overline{D}_m^s$, which is itself informed by D_m^p, and so on.

Essential Non-separability

Second-order complexity appears as an outcome of cognitive irreducibility. In order to come to grips with it, we had to work out a way of reducing irreducibility. We did this through the distinction between meta and object levels. However, this does not eliminate irreducibility. Indeed, SOCX is based on the explicit recognition of the couple (reducibility, irreducibility). SOCX cannot be reduced to one of these terms. It is both of them simultaneously. We already came across such a paradoxical notion when we considered the subject or observer and the object (or observed world) couple. A similar paradox may arise in the notion of effective complexity and its measure, presented by M. Gell-Mann (Gell-Mann, 1994), since complexity appears in a region which is neither total order nor total disorder but in between. This intermediate situation may be considered in strictly quantitative terms: it is a degree of order or a degree of disorder. But we do not know how to measure it. The conception proposed here avoids this shortcoming of the quantitative definition. Complexity is irreducibly order and disorder. And we have worked out an operational way that we hope will make sense of it.

Non-separability defined

It can be claimed that this dualistic conception offers a new definition of irreducibility. The irreducibility of an entity containing a number of components is the minimum variety below which it is impossible to further reduce without losing or changing the defining character of the entity. The pair (order, disorder) illustrates this definition: it is impossible to reduce to less than these two components – either to order or to disorder – without losing the very notion of complexity.

The same can be said by stating that it is impossible to reduce the entity under consideration to unity, to one single characteristic. The most that can be done is reduction to two components, A and B:

$$CX = (A, B)$$

Moreover, the relationship between A and B is particular: one component cannot be considered without considering the other. This is non-separability. Whenever non-separability vanishes, complexity disappears. This is also illustrated by the (order, disorder) pair. We cannot have both complexity and order alone or disorder alone. Complexity is order-and-disorder. Order alone or disorder alone pertain to non-complexity. This illustration operates at the object level. Second-order complexity illustrates a meta-level non-separability from the start when the (subject, object) pair was emphasized. It is only in non-complexity that the observed object can be analysed as if the observing subject were neutralized and considered given. It was also demonstrated above that the essence of second-order complexity lies in the apparently strange combination of reducibility (meta) and irreducibility (object level) which opens the way to stating that complexity thus understood is both an obstacle and a solution. These paradoxical or contradictory couples would hardly make sense in the absence of non-separability. Complexity vanishes when separability appears. Non-separability is at the root of cognitive irreducibility. It is thus constitutive of complexity. Non-separability starts with two components. It makes it possible to consider that the dualistic representation (A,B) is a basic, general representation of complexity.

A brief typology of non-separability

The relationship between the two components of essential non-separability is varied. Indeed, we came across three kinds of relationships. First is paradoxical non-separability, grounded in paradox. The included middle, being both A and non-A, is an instance of it. Other paradoxical pairs are (order, disorder), (reducibility, irreducibility), (obstacle, solution). A second kind is cognitive or epistemic non-separability, which is ubiquitous to the extent that complexity always entails making explicit the relationship between subject and object, thus underlying the non-separability of the pair (subject, object). The third kind is hierarchized or generative non-separability, which represents occurrences in which one component is the outcome of the other in the sense that it could not exist without the other operating. The latter operates as a condition of possibility of the former either explicitly or implicitly. Instances are the pairs (generating mechanism, outcome), (procedural rationality, substantive rationality), (meta level, object level).

One could argue that the (subject, object) pair is both epistemic and generative since it is also (meta, object). We prefer to maintain the distinction which avoids the risk of considering that the real (object) is generated by the subject, although there seems to be some grounds for the claim that reality and the subject are not totally separated. Prigogine and Stengers, commenting on a debate between Einstein and Tagore, express it nicely: 'Whatever we call reality, it is revealed to us only through the active construction in which we participate' (Prigogine and Stengers, 1984, p. 293).

Things would be made easier if we could reduce this diversity of non-separability to one representative pair. Such a pair should encompass both the meta and object levels. If we take generality as an additional criterion it seems that the (GM,O) pair is the most satisfactory: it is meta first, it leaves open the object level, including the (order, disorder) occurrence and is thus compatible with all the cases mentioned above. This (GM,O) pair framed our reasoning about second-order complexity.

Indeed, there are at least two reasons why the (order, disorder) pair is of the (GM,O) type. First, if the pair (order, disorder) is considered at the object level, it is necessarily viewed from a meta (GM) level. The (GM,O) structure is thus more general than the (order, disorder) one. Second, the pair (order, disorder) translates into the pair (reducibility, irreducibility) in the framing developed here. Then disorder denotes the irreducibility of the (reducibility, irreducibility) pair and order denotes reducibility at the meta level from which something is said about the (reducibility, irreducibility) pair. In this case order operates as a generating mechanism and disorder as an outcome.

Three additional remarks need to be made at this point. This way of conceiving complexity extends and systematizes J. Von Neumann's intuition about complexity:

> '(...) complication' on its lower levels is probably degenerative, that is ... every automaton that can produce other automata will only be able to produce less complicated ones. There is, however, a certain minimum level where this degenerative characteristic ceases to be universal. At this point, automata which can reproduce themselves, or even construct higher entities, become possible. This fact, that complication, as well as organization, below a certain minimum level is degenerative, and beyond that level can become self-supporting and even increasing, will clearly play an important role in any future theory of the subject. (Von Neumann, 1961, p. 318)

Our conception also provides a grounding for associating recursion with complexity, and thus complements Von Foerster and Simon's insights about self-reference (Von Foerster, 1988, 1992) and behavioural rationality (Simon, 1976), respectively. Finally, it introduces a hierarchy in the definition of complexity: there can be no outcome without a condition of possibility for its being explicitly dealt with. This hierarchical essential non-separability has a rather far-reaching consequence. It creates an asymmetry which provides a strong case for generalizing second-order complexity from a solution of a particular problem to a mode of knowing.

Asymmetry and Meta Complexity

We wish to show how non-separability provides an argument in favour of generalizing complexity as a mode of knowing. Yet this is not the sole argument. There exist several others. We consider these first and will come back to the non-separability argument at the end.

Generalizing is related to asymmetry. The reason is that it is possible to model complexity and non-complexity with a complex model, whereas it is not possible to model complexity with a non-complex model. In the latter case, only non-complex features can be modelled. It may be satisfactory in some cases, but not in all.

We came across this asymmetry in the previous section when we compared the analytical and complex chains of reasoning and found that they were complementary rather than mutually exclusive provided it is reckoned that complexity subsumes analytical non-complexity. The consequence is the need to attribute a priority to complexity over non-complexity. This whole argument can be developed in an equivalent manner in terms of cognitively open and closed systems. A system is cognitively closed if its constituent variables and relations are known or knowable according to available methods. It is open if not all them are known or knowable. This distinction, expressed in quasi-similar terms, is at the root of transcendental or critical realism, as exposed by R. Bhaskar and T. Lawson. It is the basis for the advocacy of openness of approach in social science by these authors (Delorme, 1999a).

Another argument comes from what resembles a principle of increasing cognitive gap to which we alluded at the beginning of this chapter. Put simply, it says that the more collective knowledge increases, the more specialization must increase, then the more relative ignorance extends, which is a way of saying that the more complexity also enlarges. Given this trend the rationale for giving priority to consideration of complexity becomes compelling.

Finally, a clear-cut argument seems to arise from our presentation of complexity as non-separability. Under the (GM,O) configuration, non-separability is hierarchically asymmetric. If the starting point is O, there is no way compelling us to take GM into consideration, whereas the reverse is not true. The same occurs for (procedural rationality, substantive rationality – PR, SR) and (meta, object). The terms contained in these pairs are not on an equal footing: the order in which they are mutually considered is not indifferent and going from the more general, left-hand side term to the less general, right-hand side term, is superior to doing the opposite whenever the non-complex character of the object of inquiry – which would allow us to focus only on O, SR or object, respectively – is not warranted. Staying at the level of O, SR or object may even induce ignorance of GM, PR or meta, or, at the least, induce us to consider that their inclusion is not required.

This is a way to reject stepwise reasoning starting from non-complexity when non-complexity is not totally established. In all cases in which we are not sure, it is therefore superior to start from the GM standpoint. This argument can even be pushed a little further owing to the open-ended nature of this asymmetry. Let us admit that in scientific practice the world is not always complex. Indeed, it is complex and non-complex. This first-order or object-level property can be identified better by means of a sorting mechanism. This sorting mechanism is necessarily meta. We showed how second-order complexity can be such a sorting mechanism. Thus, although the world is not always complex, it is superior to act as if it were always complex by the means of second-order complexity. This establishes second-order complexity as a starting point. Moreover, the cognitive behavioural grounding of second-order complexity gives it a status of a mode of knowing and of action: enquire about both the non-complex and the complex from the complex instead of enquiring from the non-complex.

Thus we obtain several pairs: (GM, O), (procedural rationality, substantive rationality), (meta level, object level), (subject, object) or (observer, observed). Their components are ordered in such a way that, if the right-hand side term can be considered independently of the left-hand side term, complexity vanishes and the situation is non-complex. The reverse case defines complexity. Moreover, every pair can appear either at a meta or at an object level, including the (meta, object) pair. This pair is an object for a meta-meta level. The double loop structure is constitutive of complexity.

CONCLUSION

In the theory developed here we have exploited the idea that complexity is fundamentally a property of the relation between an actor and an object. Purposefulness is central to it. Thus complexity is both a property attributed to an object by an actor and a property of the process of enquiry itself. In the former sense, it can be viewed as a property of the world. In the latter sense, complexity has three other meanings. It is a relative ignorance or equivalently the amount of information required to describe satisfactorily an object. It is also a satisficing technique of treatment when it is considered at a second-order, meta level, in a bottom-up procedure. Finally, this meaning can be extended to a mode of knowing and action, in a kind of top-down procedure.

Meta complexity is this mode of knowing and action. It is the most general notion and tells us that it is better to behave at the start as if the world were always complex, because of the asymmetry between complexity and analysis. Meta complexity relies on the commitment to situated satisficing, it compels both rendering explicit the convention on a satisficing practice and transparency of scientific practice. It entails a systemic view of the world and notably the economy. This view accepts classical analysis as being locally relevant, in non-complex situations. The only constraint is transparency of scientific practice. This leaves open the substance of enquiry. At a local theory level it does not entail any particular content of theorizing; it constrains only the procedure. At a general theory level it is compatible with viewing the economy as a complex evolving system. But, to repeat, it emphasizes transparency of complete scientific practice, not limited to syntax or speculation. It is the constraint which informs an otherwise open practice oriented towards empirical validation. It provides a systematized generative principle to a diversity of local theories or outcomes and makes it possible to replace a current floating and ambiguous eclecticism with a more controlled one. In this way it might provide evolutionary theory with an opportunity to become more systematized while retaining its commitment to an open-ended perception of economic life.

NOTE

1. Reflexivity in the former case is limited to method and brings a methodologically reflexive complexity. A more profound form is reflexivity affecting the observer and opening the way to self-referentiality. This reflexivity is introduced later in a behavioural setting underlying second-order complexity.

REFERENCES

Arthur, W.B., S.N. Durlauf and D.A. Lane (eds) (1997), *The Economy as an Evolving Complex System II*, Reading, MA: Addison-Wesley.

Ashby, W.R. (1973), 'Some peculiarities of complex systems', *Cybernetic Medicine*, **9**, 1–8.

Caldwell, B.J. (1991), 'Clarifying Popper', *Journal of Economic Literature*, March, 1–33.

Delorme, R. (1984), 'A New View on the Economic Theory of the State. A Case Study of France', *Journal of Economic Issues*, September, 715–44; reprinted in M.R. Tool and W.J. Samuels (eds) (1988), *State, Society and Corporate Power*, New Brunswick: Transaction Publishers.

Delorme, R. (1998), 'From First Order to Second Order Complexity in Economic Theorizing', mimeo, Paris, CEPREMAP.

Delorme, R. (1999), 'A propos du réalisme critique en économie', *Economie appliquée*, **1**, 63–92.

Delorme, R. (2000), 'Ordnungstheorie and the Theory of Regulation Compared from the Standpoint of Complexity', in A. Labrousse and J-D. Weisz (eds), *Institutional Economics in France and Germany*, Berlin: Springer Verlag.

Friedman, D. (1998), 'Review of A. Rubinstein: modeling bounded rationality', *Southern Economic Journal*, **65**(2), 366–8.

Gell-Mann, M. (1994), *The Quark and the Jaguar: Adventures in the Simple and the Complex*, New York: W.H. Freeman.
Granger, G.G. (1990), *Epistémologie*, Paris: Encyclopaedia Universalis.
Hayek, F.A. (1967), 'The Theory of Complex Phenomena' in F.A. Hayek, *Studies in Philosophy, Politics and Economics*, Chicago: University of Chicago Press.
Hayek, F.A. (1989), 'The pretence of knowledge', *The American Economic Review*, **79**(6), 3–7.
Kirman, A.P. (1997), 'The evolution of economic theory', in A. d'Autume and J. Cartelier (eds), *Is Economics Becoming a Hard Science*?, Cheltenham, UK and Lyme, US: Edward Elgar.
Krugman, P. (2000), 'What Economists Can Learn from Evolutionary Theorists – and vice versa', in J. Groenewegen and J. Vromen (eds), *Institutions and the Evolution of Capitalism*, Cheltenham, UK and Lyme, US: Edward Elgar.
Lawson, T. (1997), *Economics and Reality*, London: Routledge.
Le Moigne, J.L. (1990) *La modélisation des systèmes complexes*, Paris: Dunod.
Lévy-Leblond, J-M. (1991), 'La physique, une science sans complexe?', in F. Fogelman-Soulie (ed.), *Les théories de la complexité. Autour de l'œuvre d'H. Atlan*, Paris: Seuil.
Morris, C. (1971), *Writings on the General Theory of Signs*, The Hague: Mouton.
Nelson, R. (1995), 'Recent evolutionary theorizing about economic change', *Journal of Economic Literature*, March, 48–90.
Prigogine, I. and I. Stengers (1984), *Order out of Chaos. Man's New Dialogue with Nature*, New York: Bantam Books.
Simon, H.A. (1976), 'From Substantive to Procedural Rationality' in S. Latsis (ed.), *Method and Appraisal in Economics*, Cambridge: Cambridge University Press.
Von Foerster, H. (1988), 'La construction d'une réalité', in P. Watzlawick (ed.), *L'invention de la réalité. Contributions au constructivisme*, Paris: Seuil; edn of *Die Erfundene Wirklichkeit. Wie wissen wir, was wir zu wissen glauben? Beiträge zum Konstruktivismus*, Munich: R. Piper Co. Verlag.
Von Foerster, H. (1992), 'Ethics and second order cybernetics', *Cybernetics and Human Knowing*, **1**(1), 9–19.
Von Neumann, J. (1961), *John Von Neumann Collected Works*, Volume V, ed. A.H. Taub, Oxford: Pergamon Press.
Weaver, W. (1948), 'Science and complexity', *American Scientist*, **36**, 536–44.
Weaver, W. (1949), 'Recent Contributions to the Mathematical Theory of Communication' in C.E. Shannon and W. Weaver, *The Mathematical Theory of Communication*, Urbana: University of Illinois Press.

Commentary: simplicity in theories of complexity – defining, knowing and doing

Drew Wollin

INTRODUCTION

Complexity theory is a relatively new field in the social sciences, but there is little unity or integration of the different approaches. It is more a loose collection of themes and ideas, leading to a lack of clarity and complex explanations. We argue that complexity theory may be more integrated than it seems: simplifying complexity.

Delorme suggests that complexity has four possible meanings: complexity as a property of an object or system, system complexity as being relative to an observer's purpose, complexity as a limit to cognition, and complexity as a mode of knowing. The first and second are concerned with defining complexity, the third and the fourth with the epistemology or knowing of complexity, and the second and third with decision making or doing in complex systems. As a response to Delorme, we follow his broad themes in approaching complexity: defining, knowing (epistemology) and doing (decision making), the three parts of his paper.

The first part considers whether complexity can be defined simply, through consideration of the common dictionary meanings of the words used in complexity theory. Complexity is concerned with systems where some aspects are inherently unknowable (as opposed to random). Complex systems are partly explainable and predictable, in that they commonly behave in a dominant or average manner. However, they may also behave in non-average or non-ergodic ways. Following the paradoxical naming of deterministic chaos (predictable randomness), we suggest a play on the words 'simple' and 'complex', to delineate the different forms of behaviour in complex systems, with complex adaptive systems as the most general and encompassing.

In the second part, we examine the epistemology of complexity, how we know what we know about complexity. We give an overview of the constructs of scientific or transcendental realism, as it offers a philosophical means of dealing with systems that have aspects that are either unknowable or unobservable. It assumes that generative mechanisms exist in the real domain that under contingent conditions may act in the actual domain, which may be observed in the empirical domain. As such, theory is simplified or compressed description that is fallible, believed a true representation of reality with the possibility of its being in error.

The third part is about doing or decision making with complex systems. Imperfect knowledge is not a new problem in decision making, a point recognized with bounded rationality. However, complexity theory suggests a further limit, that of inherently unknowable aspects of complex systems and inevitable limits to reductionism. There can be no theories of everything. However, we argue that Simon's multi-level architecture of order offers a means of dealing with such systems. While there may be disorder at one level, there may be order at a more fundamental level. Decision making is contrasted with science, in that the former is concerned with the best available information and theory as 'fit for purpose', with the onus on user.

DEFINING COMPLEXITY SIMPLY?

Can complexity be defined simply? Consideration of the ordinary meanings of some of the words suggests it can and enables us to identify some of the more defining characteristics of complex systems. Let us consider some word definitions from the *Webster Dictionary* (1999): *Complexity*: 'a group of obviously related units of which the degree and nature of the relationship is imperfectly known', *Random*: 'lacking a definite plan, purpose, or pattern' or 'without definite aim, direction, rule, or method'. Complex systems are not random, although they may appear to be random. The missing information is either not known or, more particularly, not knowable. Not knowable is not the same thing as random.

Not knowable reflects the concept of irreducibility or non-separability that Delorme raises. A complex system ceases to be a complex system when broken into its many component parts. The peculiar characteristics of a complex system do not exist with the parts in isolation. From basic systems theory, the dictum of emergence helps: the whole is more than the sum of the parts. Emergent properties are 'the properties of the whole and are meaningful only at the level of the whole' (Checkland and Scholes, 1990, p. 309). The parts of a bicycle when appropriately assembled constitute a mode of transport, an emergent property, but not assembled are just parts. However, a bicycle is a simple system, with *simple* being defined as 'readily understood'.

An inherent characteristic of complex systems is their emergent properties. Like a simple system, the emergent properties do not exist with the unconnected parts. Returning to the earlier definition of a complex system, the connections or relationships between the parts are imperfectly known. Thus it is not possible to know or understand a complex system just by examining its parts. Emergence is the flip side to irreducibility. Put in terms of evolution, the dictionary definition of *emergent* is the 'appearance of new characters and qualities at complex levels of organisation (as the cell or organism) which cannot be predicted solely from the study of less complex levels (as the atom or molecule)'.

Studying or describing a complex system becomes a tough order when it has aspects that are inherently unknown or unknowable, and with emergent properties that can only be observed at the level of the system itself, not at the level of its parts. Back to the dictionary again, to see if definitions shed much light. *Analysis*: 'the separation of a whole into its component parts'. Not a good sign. Analysis works for simple systems that are decomposable or reducible, but have limited application for complex systems. What about *synthesis*, the antithesis of analysis: 'the composition or combination of parts or elements so as to form a whole' or 'the combining of often diverse conceptions into a coherent whole'? The concept of synthesis gives insight into how to create both complex (irreducible) and simple (reducible) systems, which is a start. Perhaps we need to think more about how we synthesize theory.

A traditional approach to the analysis of complex systems has been to treat some aspects as random, then assume they do not matter. More definitions: *stochastic* 'random: involving a random variable (a *stochastic* process)' or 'involving chance or probability'. *Probable*: 'supported by evidence strong enough to establish presumption but not proof'. Interesting? Probabilistic analysis gives an understanding of the dominant or average system behaviour, provided the outliers, the noise, the things we treat as random or unknown, do not affect the overall outcome (too much). Probabilistic analysis thus allows us to describe imperfectly or approximately the dominant behaviour of some complex systems, by ignoring the unexplainable variations or noise, provided the noise does not affect the system outcomes. Effectively, the system is being treated as reducible and analysable in the earlier sense. Given the widespread use of probabilistic analysis in science and engineering, this imprecise understanding is good enough for many practical and research purposes. Such use is an example of Simon's 'satisficing' that Delorme discusses. Satisficing is common and accepted practice in science whenever probabilistic analysis is used.

What about complex systems where the unknown or unknowable aspects cannot be ignored? One of the defining features of complex systems is path dependence, their sensitivity to small differences, such as in starting conditions or system parameters, or to small disturbances, as popularized by the butterfly effect (Gleick, 1988, pp. 22–3). The outcomes of complex systems can be determined by these small changes, whereas in simpler systems their effects are averaged away by countless similar disturbances to be reduced to background noise ('non-ergodic' systems: Arthur, 1989, p. 117). However, this sensitivity is not to suggest that every small disturbance has a dramatic effect on system behaviour; rather, the effects of only a few are amplified through positive feedback to determine outcomes. Put in the words of the earlier metaphor, while the flap of a butterfly's wing may cause a hurricane in a far-removed place, thankfully, not every flap of every butterfly's wings has such an effect; otherwise, it would be chaos in the popular meaning of the word.

A tantalizing prospect is that the ability to explain the occasional non-average behaviour of a complex system should also explain when it does behave in an average or predictable manner. Similarly, Delorme suggests, 'complexity subsumes analysis'. If we can explain complex behaviour, we can explain simple behaviour. The reverse is not possible. Analysis alone cannot explain complex systems, but that is not to say that analysis has no role, as noted earlier.

The idea of occasional non-average behaviour highlights the point that the complex systems are *partially irreducible*, rather than perfectly irreducible. We have some understanding of how the system works and it is partially predictable. Complexity scholars tend to overstate the degree of instability in complex systems. Complex systems, by definition, are partially explainable and partially predictable. Conventional analysis techniques can be used for many practical purposes, where the system can be approximated as reducible. Other techniques are needed to examine the system when this approximation is not possible.

If a system was perfectly irreducible, we could not know anything of the parts of the system, or even the existence of the whole system. Perfectly irreducible systems are not knowable at any level or form. Simon (1962, 1996) described the phenomenon of partially irreducible as 'partially-decomposable'. The description or knowledge of a complex system requires that it be either partially or completely decomposable. A perfectly irreducible system would seem to be similar or even the same as a random system. The concept of random needs to be revisited in social science, but that is beyond our current purpose.

In this section, we have discussed a number of features of complex systems, path dependence, emergence, partial irreducibility and non-average behaviour, among others. In the next section, we would like to suggest a relatively straightforward schema for relating these different characteristics that can be used to integrate several of the theories of complexity.

Word Plays: Simple and Complex

The term 'deterministic chaos' is a play on words, in that it is a paradox or an oxymoron. It implies predictable randomness, an inherent contradiction. Deterministic chaos is about simple systems that have apparently random behaviour, but are predictable in principle but not practice (Hilborn, 1994; Ruelle, 1990). In this spirit, it is possible to tabulate the different categories that can be generated from the permutations of the terms 'complex' or 'simple', as shown in Table 4A.1. While this schema seems to border on the obvious or trivial, it has reasonable explanatory power. The schema may form the basis of an adjunct taxonomy of theories of change, beyond those proposed in organization theory (Van de Ven and Poole, 1995) and evolutionary economics (Hodgson, 1993). The complex behaviour of adaptive complex systems is the most general case, with the others being special cases of it. Again, 'complexity subsumes analysis', as Delorme suggests.

Table 4A.1 Permutations of the terms 'complex' or 'simple' to the behaviour of systems

Permutations of the terms simple and complex	Name(s) of category
Simple behaviour in simple systems	Deterministic order (linear systems)
Complex behaviour in simple systems	Deterministic chaos (non-linear dynamics)
Simple behaviour in non-adaptive complex systems	Indeterministic order (self-ordering systems)
Complex behaviour in adaptive complex systems	Indeterministic order (complex adaptive systems)
Random behaviour	Indeterministic chaos (truly random)

At its heart, complexity theory seeks to identify patterns in complex systems. Identifying and describing patterns is one of the most basic tasks in science. Complex systems, in that they can only ever be imperfectly known, pose a significant problem for traditional approaches to knowing and theorizing.

KNOWING AND THEORIZING COMPLEX SYSTEMS

The basis of knowing, epistemology, of complex systems is an underexplored area, which Delorme begins to consider. In this section, we explore an epistemology for complexity, primarily through the approach of scientific or transcendental realism. We continue with some definitions – *epistemology*: how we know what we know, or the 'nature and grounds of knowledge especially with reference to its limits and validity'; *ontology*: the nature of reality, or the 'nature and relations of being'.

Transcendental Realism as the Basis of Knowing Complex Systems

We will briefly consider the tenets of scientific or transcendental realism (Bhaskar, 1978) and how they relate to complexity.[1] Delorme mentions Bhaskar's scientific realism, but does not elaborate. Transcendental realism seems to be a useful epistemological approach in understanding or theorizing about complexity, as it specifically acknowledges the difficulty of studying the unobservable and the unknowable. 'Unobservables' (Godfrey and Hill, 1995) are not a problem unique to complexity, rather a problem across many social science disciplines.

We do not argue for epistemological exclusivity, but rather for pluralism. Different epistemological positions offer alternative ways of viewing social phenomena. Each has something to contribute. None is perfect. All are fallible. Each emphasizes different epistemological issues. Scholars need to know the assumptions underlying the epistemology they use, together with rival or alternative positions of enquiry. Pluralism in epistemology is essential in studying complexity. Inherent to complexity itself, there are no perfect answers or ways of knowing.

Transcendental realism (Bhaskar, 1978; Tsoukas, 1989) is a relatively new epistemology emerging from sociology, but one finding application across many disciplines. Like all epistemologies, it has a number of central assumptions. First is the ontological assumption that the world consists of *real structures* that are independent of our knowledge or perception of them, hence the term 'realism' in the name. The world is considered in terms of a socially constructed reality, but from the perspective of shared rather than individual realities, and not the absolute reality of naive realism or empiricism.

Second, it is assumed that these structures and 'generative mechanisms' (causal powers) are independent of the events they generate (Tsoukas, 1989, p. 552). Hence the use of the adjective *transcendental* defined as 'transcending experience but not human knowledge'; in other words, real but more than just the sense experience.

A third assumption is that there are three domains of reality: the real, actual and empirical, shown in Table 4A.2. Generative mechanisms exist in the real domain and under contingent conditions cause observable events. The events exist in the actual domain in that they exist independently of a researcher taking notice of them. The events are observable even if the researcher did not notice or experience them. Experiences exist in the empirical domain in that the researcher notices and experiences the events (ibid., p. 553).

Table 4A.2 Ontological assumptions of transcendental realism

	Real domain	Actual domain	Empirical domain
Mechanisms	✓		
Events	✓	✓	
Experiences	✓	✓	✓

Source: Adapted from Tsoukas (1989) and Bhaskar (1978, p. 13).

Generative mechanisms exist even when conditions are not conducive to generating observable events. A generative mechanism still acts even though the expected outcome is not observable because of the occurrence of countervailing forces or the simultaneous operation of other mechanisms (Tsoukas, 1989, p. 552). Descriptions of generative mechanisms are better considered as 'tendencies' (Bhaskar, 1978, p. 20) that may or may not manifest themselves in the empirical domain, rather than iron-clad causal laws (Tsoukas 1989, p. 558).

Fourth, it is assumed that descriptions of the generative mechanisms constructed by the observer are real, but fallible or capable of being mistaken, the philosophical position of 'fallibility' (Hunt, 1991, p. 100). Transcendental realism rejects the notion of 'imagined models' of transcendental idealism (Bhaskar, 1978, p. 15) or the 'convenient fictions' of instrumentalism (Chalmers, 1982, p. 146) by arguing that the structures and associated generative mechanisms are real. Dogmatic scepticism, that nothing is knowable for certain, is similarly rejected.

Working within this framework of assumptions, the task of the researcher is to identify, describe and test the structures, the generative mechanisms and the contingent factors responsible for observed events (Tsoukas, 1989, p. 556). The initial step in the process is the experience by the researcher of events arising from generative events and contingent conditions. The researcher then develops theory to describe the real generative mechanisms and thus explain (rather than predict) the events and the conditions under which they occur. The final step in transcendental realism is that the model or theory (the claims to knowledge) be empirically tested to determine correspondence between it and the real structures and generative mechanisms (Bhaskar, 1978, p. 15).

In describing complex systems, the practical difficulties of empirically observing all possible manifestations or outcomes of a generative mechanism are addressed. Working within transcendental realism, it is valid to postulate theory, in terms of describing generative mechanisms, for which empirical observations of every possible permutation were not possible, *provided* the theory is also able to explain why observations were not possible. The theory should cover the generative mechanisms, the necessary conditions under which events will be caused, and other mechanisms or combinations of conditions that will countervail or otherwise inhibit the operation of the focal generative mechanism in the expected way. The idea of generative mechanisms operating under contingent conditions overcomes some of the problems of accommodating unobservable constructs and events (Godfrey and Hill, 1995).

DOING: DECISION MAKING IN COMPLEX SYSTEMS

Cognitive limits to decision making have been much theorized, going back to the seminal work of Simon on bounded rationality, as Delorme notes. Complexity adds another dimension to bounded rationality by denying reductionism in terms of chains of causality from the whole to its parts. Some aspects of complex systems are inherently unknowable. However, while complexity theory further constrains decision making, it also enables it, through ideas such as partial irreducibility. Of greatest utility is Simon's concept of a multi-level architecture of order, in our view essential to dealing with complex systems, but largely unrecognized by present-day complexity writers.

Multi-level Architecture of Order

In his seminal paper on the architecture of complexity, Simon argues that the inherent redundancy, partial decomposability or partial irreducibility of a complex system may be resolved through a nested, multi-level hierarchy of ordering. Order at one level is dependent on order or rules at a more fundamental level, that in turn are dependent on even more fundamental order (Wollin, 1999). This multi-level ordering forms the basis of radical evolutionary theory that suggests that evolution may occur at any level in the genetic hierarchy: genes, chromosomes, individuals and species (Allen and Starr, 1982; Vrba and Eldredge, 1984; Vrba and Gould, 1986; Salthe, 1985). The concept of emergence suggests a multi-level system where the whole is more than its parts through the interactions between its parts. For a complex system, each part may in turn be a whole at a different level, which in turn has parts, *ad infinitum*.

Complexity as Relative to Purpose, Theory as Fit for Purpose

Complexity is relative. The necessary level of detail of explanation is relative to the purpose at hand. As Delorme notes, the level of detail or complexity needed in working with a brain is vastly different depending on the purpose of the observer, be they a neurologist or a butcher. It is not necessary to know the inner workings of a video recorder to know how to use it, although a greater level of knowledge is needed to repair it, and an even greater level to design it. At any particular level, rules existing at the focal and more fundamental levels will be apparent, but rules at more marginal levels appear superfluous and can largely be ignored. 'When defining complexity it is always necessary to specify a level of detail up to which the system is described, with finer detail being ignored. Physicists call that "coarse graining"' (Gell-Mann, 1994, p. 29). Parsimony or 'Ockham's razor' appear parallel concepts (Hoffmann *et al.* 1997).

Scholars confuse the roles of science and practice (decision making). Science is an inevitably unending search for knowledge. Practice is more pragmatic and resource constrained, requiring decisions on the best available information at the time. For practice, theory must be 'fit for purpose', with the onus on the user, not the theorist, rather than integrated or exact. The knowledge of turbulence in fluid dynamics is an example. Air turbulence is a complex system that has been studied for centuries. Turbulence was described by Feynman, a Noble Laureate physicist, as 'the most important unsolved problem of classical physics' (Moin and Kim, 1997, p. 62). However, this lack of knowledge of turbulence within the science of physics does not stop practice. Aeroplanes are designed without perfect or exact theory. When faced with limited analysis techniques, designers devise their own simplifications, such as scale modelling in wind tunnels or numerical approximations on computers. As such, practice may move ahead of science, especially with the development of artefacts, like aeroplanes, that are new to nature: Simon's (1996) 'sciences of the artificial'. Engineering is more than applied science, but is the practice of management or economics more than applied social science?

Practice relies on making decisions on the best available information, recognizing that a complex system can never be known perfectly. Even with unlimited processing capacity, complex systems cannot be predicted perfectly. Practice must exist with approximations and their attendant fallibility.

Complexity: Simultaneous Opposites

A useful heuristic device for working within complex systems is the idea of simultaneous opposites. This notion is captured in the naming of deterministic chaos. It is possible to generate a series of couplets of simultaneous opposites along the many dimensions of complex social systems, as shown in Table 4A.3. A multi-level architecture of order is a means of dealing with these simultaneous opposites. What may be stable at one level may be unstable at a less fundamental level. Usually, the instability at a more marginal level is not

Table 4A.3 Dealing with complexity through couplets of simultaneous opposites

Order–disorder	Stability–instability	Equilibrium–discontinuity
Constrain–enable	Structure–action	Competition–cooperation
Predictable–uncertain	Group–individual	Tight coupling–loose coupling
Analysis–synthesis	Reductionism–holism	Reducible–irreducible

propagated to a more fundamental level, but in exceptional circumstances it may be, leading to non-average outcomes (Wollin, 1999). Such a multi-level system may be simultaneously stable and unstable. Usually, it is stable (partial equilibrium), but prone to discontinuous change (bounded disorder), leading to a new form of order, or disintegration (disorder) in response to an environmental disturbance.

CONCLUSIONS

We can draw a number of conclusions from our response to Delorme. Complexity is a fascinating area of enquiry that allows us to move beyond the limited techniques of analysis in social science, just as it has done in the physical and natural sciences. However, complexity theory suffers by not having a more unified or integrated approach. Using common word definitions, we have argued that the ideas behind complexity are relatively simple and provide a means of categorizing many of the different approaches to complexity theory. There is simplicity in theories of complexity.

Is complexity a new mode of knowing, as Delorme suggests? Dealing with unknowables or unobservables is not a new problem. Transcendental or scientific realism seems to provide a robust philosophical base for theorizing in complexity, rather than a new one being required.

For practice or decision making in complex systems, complexity theory both constrains and enables. In furthering bounded rationality, complexity suggests inevitable unknowables. However, through partial irreducibility, complexity offers a means of simplifying complex systems, albeit with complexity relative to purpose. Complexity does not displace analysis, where analysis is adequate and fit for purpose. Following Simon, we argue that a multi-level architecture of order is a means of dealing with partial irreducibility. Although neglected by most writers on complexity, it is essential for understanding complex social systems and provides a means of resolving many of the paradoxes or simultaneous opposites.

NOTE

1. Bhaskar uses the adjectives 'scientific' and 'transcendental' interchangeably, but we will use the latter as it is less ambiguous.

REFERENCES

Allen, T.F.H. and T.B. Starr (1982), *Hierarchy: Perspectives for Ecological Complexity*, Chicago: University of Chicago Press.

Arthur, W.B. (1989) 'Competing technologies, increasing returns and lock-in by historical events', *The Economic Journal*, **99**, 116–31.

Bhaskar, R. (1978), *A Realist Theory of Science*, Brighton: The Harvester Press.

Chalmers, A.F. (1982), *What is this Thing called Science?*, St Lucia, Australia: University of Queensland Press.

Checkland, P. and J. Scholes (1990), *Soft Systems Methodology in Action*, Chichester: John Wiley & Sons.

Gell-Mann, M. (1994), *The Quark and the Jaguar: Adventures in the Simple and the Complex*, New York: W.H. Freeman.

Gleick, J. (1988), *Chaos: Making a new science*, London: Cardinal.

Godfrey, P.C. and C.W.L. Hill (1995), 'The problem of unobservables in strategic management research', *Strategic Management Journal*, **16**, 519–33.

Hilborn, R.C. (1994) *Chaos and Nonlinear Dynamics: An Introduction for Scientists and Engineers*, New York: Oxford University Press.

Hodgson, G.M. (1993), 'Theories of economic evolution: A preliminary taxonomy', *The Manchester School of Economics and Social Studies*, **61**(2), 125–43.

Hoffmann, R., B. Carpenter and V. Minkin (1997), 'Ockham's razor and chemistry', *HYLE: An International Journal for the Philosophy of Chemistry*, **3**, 3–28.

Hunt, S. (1991), *Modern Marketing Theory: Critical Issues in the Philosophy of Marketing Science*, Cincinnati, Ohio: South-West Publishing Co.

Moin, P. and J. Kim (1997), 'Tackling turbulence with super computers', *Scientific American*, **276**(1), 62–8.

Ruelle, D. (1990), 'Deterministic chaos: The science and the fiction', *Proceedings of the Royal Society of London*, **A427** 241–8.

Salthe, S.N. (1985), *Evolving Hierarchical Systems: Their Structure and Representation*, New York: Columbia University Press.

Simon, H.A. (1962), 'The architecture of complex systems', *Proceedings of the American Philosophical Society*, **106**, 467–82; reprinted in H.A. Simon (1996), *The sciences of the artificial*, 3rd edn, Cambridge, MA: MIT Press.

Simon, H.A. (1996), *The Sciences of the Artificial*, 3rd edn, Cambridge, MA: MIT Press.

Tsoukas, H. (1989), 'The validity of idiographic research explanations', *Academy of Management Review*, **14**(4), 551–61.

Van de Ven, A.H. and M.S. Poole (1995), 'Explaining development and change in organisations', *Academy of Management Review*, **20**(3), 510–40.

Vrba, E.S. and N. Eldredge (1984), 'Individuals, hierarchies and processes: towards a more complete evolutionary theory', *Palaeobiology*, **10**(2), 146–71.

Vrba, E.S. and S.J. Gould (1986), 'The hierarchical expansion of sorting and selection: sorting and selection cannot be equated', *Palaeobiology*, **12**(2), 217–8.

Wollin, A.S. (1999), 'Punctuated-equilibrium: Reconciling the theory of revolutionary and incremental change', *Systems Research and Behavioural Science*, **16**(4), 359–67.

5. Self-organizing and Darwinian selection in economic and biological evolutions: an enquiry into the sources of organizing information

Pavel Pelikan

INTRODUCTION

Evolutionary economics has so far paid more attention to selection among already formed (organized) entities than to their origins. Thus analysis of market selection of firms usually begins by assuming all the firms involved initially given; similarly, the game-theoretical studies of selection of strategies assume some bearer(s) of each of the strategies also as initially given. Without neglecting selection, this paper extends evolutionary analysis by enquiring into the origins of the entities that are being selected, and in particular into the origins of economic organizations.

Economic organizations will be defined broadly as sets of interconnected economic agents which together perform a certain function, or functions, including firms, markets, and governments, as well as national and supranational economies. As explained in the next section, such a broad definition is a logical consequence of the Darwinian evolutionary view. While economists often limit the definition of organizations to purposeful entities pursuing objectives of their organizers – which would include, among the above examples, only firms and governments – the Darwinian view cannot be so categoric. Which entities have, and which have not, 'purposes' or 'objectives' is in this view a subtle question: its answer depends more upon the perspective of an observer than upon empirical properties of the world itself. Agents may thus form an organization which an observer can see to pursue certain objectives of its own, more or less different from the objectives which can be ascribed to any of its agents.

But economic organizations will not be the only organizations considered. To follow the fruitful habit of evolutionary economics to learn from evolutionary biology, references will also be made to the forming of biological organizations, such as proteins, cells, brains, organisms and societies of organisms. Similarities and differences between biological and economic organizing will be important sources of insight.[1]

As a rarely conducted enquiry may be suspected of lacking interest, let me mention two reasons why the enquiry into the origins of economic organizations is well above any such suspicion. First, as already noted by Alchian (1950), selection is always limited to the set of actually tried alternatives. Thus, if we wish to study selection of economic organizations in order to find out what they are or can be, we also need to learn about how they can possibly form. Second, more generally, even if our ultimate interest is in how economic organizations function and perform, to learn about their origins is important because much of their functioning and performance is a straightforward consequence of their form. This learning is important not only in the search for primary causes in pure theory, but perhaps even more so in the search for performance-improving policies. As is well known in the practice of redressing both firms and economies in crisis, acting upon their forming and reforming can have much stronger and more definitive impact on their performance than intervening in their functioning without changing their form.[2]

The main concern of the present enquiry can be expressed by two questions: how do economic organizations arise from individual actions, and why, among otherwise comparable organizations, do some become significantly more successful (in terms of given success criteria) than others?

To search for the answers, the enquiry will develop a special perspective which concentrates on the demand for, and supply of, organizing information ('o-information'). This will be defined as the information which guides given agents towards the forming of a certain organization, rather than others, and which thus becomes expressed by the organization actually formed. From this perspective, to ask about the origins of successful economic organizations is to ask about the sources of the o-information for their forming.[3]

This perspective has two important advantages. First, it facilitates exchanges between evolutionary economics and evolutionary biology. To view both the evolution of species and that of economic organizations as ways of producing o-information helps to establish a clear connection between the two and to identify their similarities and differences. A particularly interesting part of these exchanges is the application of Darwinian ideas in economics, which the perspective saves from the well-known difficulties with the terms 'genes' and 'replication'.[4] Namely, it allows Darwinism to be neatly divided into a general explanation of how o-information can be produced by a blind trial-and-error search, and the particular biochemical example of such production during the evolution of species. Genes thus appear as biochemical examples of carriers and memories of o-information, and replication as a biochemical example of the way its memories can be preserved over long periods of time. While effort is still needed to identify the corresponding carriers and memories in economic organizations, this appears to be a more fruitful endeavour than looking there for direct analogues to genes and replication.[5]

Second, this perspective throws light on the origins of organizations which possess more complex features than what could have possibly be formed by Darwinian trial-and-error search alone.[6] As has been pointed out many times, such organizations imply the existence of another organizing principle, able to complement or replace the Darwinian search. Two main hypotheses have been advanced about what this principle might be: Lamarckian evolution, and self-organization or self-organizing.[7] But it has not yet been fully explained in clear operational terms how these principles work, or how they may relate to the Darwinian search. The perspective on o-information will make it possible to explain self-organizing clearly and to show that the cases of evolution that some authors denote as Lamarckian can be explained with more precision as cases of Darwinian search complemented and constrained by a special form of self-organizing.[8]

But addressing not very usual questions from a not very usual perspective also has a disadvantage. This is the need for extensive preliminary clarifications, for which I found it necessary to make frequent excursions outside economics, in particular into biology and information theory. Emphatically, the purpose of these excursions is not to look for superficial analogies, but only to clarify certain general principles which have important implications for economics, but have so far been much better understood in other disciplines. I am aware of the inconvenience caused to the readers unused to interdisciplinary references; I hope that in spite of it, they will eventually find these excursions worth making.

The enquiry is organized as follows. Three sections clarify the key terms used: 'organization', 'information', 'organizing information'. The section 'Information, Energy and Scarce Resources' explains how organizing information is related to energy in biology and to scarce resources in economics. As existing literature does not explain self-organizing with sufficient clarity for the present purposes, 'Self-organizing' and 'Energy and Resources in Self-organizing' suggest an explanation of my own. The more familiar Darwinian trial-and-error search is then interpreted in compatible terms in the section 'Darwinian Trial-and-error Search'. The section 'Multi-level Organizing' examines how self-organizing and Darwinian search can combine and complement each other, including their possible combinations across different organizational levels. To conclude, the section 'Particularities of Human Economic Organizing' points out the main particularities of human economic organizing by which it differs the most from the organizing that the usual classification of sciences assigns to the realm of biology.

ORGANIZATIONS

As already noted, an organization is defined here as a set of interconnected agents that together perform a certain function (or functions). (In the language of system theories, an organization may thus also be referred to as an 'organized and functioning system'.)

The interconnections form a network of channels which provide for exchanges (transactions) of resources (including information and energy) among specified agents within specified limits. They can be exemplified by chemical bonds and mechanical forces in organisms, and by property rights and employment contracts in economies.

The channels to which an agent is connected determine its access – in terms of both possibilities (rights) and obligations (physical or institutional) – to such exchanges, and thus imply its role within the organization.

The roles implied by the network of channels are distinguished from properties of the agents that assume them. This distinction is essential in organizations formed of heterogeneous agents, where the outcome of a role may strongly depend upon which particular agent has been assigned to (selected for) it. The performance of such an organization thus depends on both how its network is designed and how the roles within this network are assigned. This distinction will prove to be of particular importance in the study of economic organizations, whose human agents are significantly more heterogeneous than the chemical agents of biological organizations.[9]

In the perspective on o-information, the central notions are the set of constituent agents from which an organization is formed ('a-set') and the set of all the alternative organizations into which these agents might possibly be interconnected ('possible o-set'). In general, only a subset of this set consists of organizations which can be said to function ('functioning o-subset') and only a subset of this subset consists of organizations which are successful, in the sense that their functioning meets certain absolute or relative performance criteria ('successful o-subset').

It remains to be clarified why such a broad definition of organizations, which does not refer to any purposes or objectives that they might be intended to pursue, is a logical consequence of the Darwinian evolutionary view. One of the greatest achievement of this view is precisely a plausible explanation of how living organisms could have formed and evolved by causal natural processes, without any purposeful organizer. As opposed to the now discredited vitalism and teleology, Darwinism does not include purposes and objectives among empirical properties of the real world: to explain why things happen, its key words are 'because of', and not 'in order to'.

To be sure, the behaviour of many organizations – ourselves included – may best be *described* by referring to objectives which they *appear* to pursue (possibly expressed as objective functions which they appear to maximize). In the Darwinian perspective, however, such a description is only a linguistic convenience, which is in no contradiction with the fact that the organization described is a causally working (possibly in a probabilistic sense) device. An elementary example is a thermostat: although clearly nothing more than a simple causally working mechanism, we often ascribe to it the objective of keeping a stable temperature; this is certainly a more condensed description of its behaviour than reporting the causal operations of its switching circuits and heating (or cooling) elements.[10]

This means that in the Darwinian perspective no organization really *has* objectives, but many may be *ascribed* objectives as a way of condensing the description of their behaviour.[11] To allow such a description, an organization only needs to contain some self-regulatory feedback circuits, which is indeed the case of virtually all biological and economic organizations (with the exception of erroneous variants which, without such circuits, cannot stay around for long). But we need not always take advantage of this possibility: we may very well – as many social scientists do – ascribe objectives only to human individuals, and not to their cells, or to their societies. We must only be aware that this is a subjectively chosen anthropocentric view, which cannot be substantiated in any empirical sense.

At first sight, Darwinism may thus seem to clash with both methodological and normative individualism. Upon a closer view, however, the clash turns out to be limited: methodological individualism is only qualified, while normative individualism is fully accommodated. The qualification is to see methodological individualism as only a special, anthropocentric case of reductionism which, however, makes it in no way illegitimate. And while ascribing objectives to organizations of different kinds and levels, and not only to ourselves, we may accommodate normative individualism by simply not valuing all these objectives equally, or necessarily giving higher-level objectives higher values. We may thus find it expedient, as we shall also do here, to speak of objectives of different levels in theoretical reasoning, and yet resolutely defend our own in practical actions – for instance, against both those of our cells, if they turn cancerous, and those of our society, if it turns totalitarian.[12]

INFORMATION

The term 'information' will be used here in a meaning close to its quantitative definition by Shannon and Weaver (1949), of which one of the first applications in biology is due to Ashby (1956), and in economics, to Theil (1967). For the present purposes, however, the intellectual costs of precise quantification would far exceed its explanatory benefits. The following rough definition appears to suffice: information is expressed by choices in a set of two or more possible messages (signals, symbols) and is used for guiding choices (decisions) in a set of two or more feasible alternatives (actions, states, beliefs).

Assuming that the alternative chosen is to have a certain desired property, for example to be best, or satisfactory, in terms of some success indicators, the quantity of the information required depends on the proportion of the alternatives that have this property. Roughly speaking (and, as noted, more precision will not be needed here), given the property desired, the smaller the proportion of the alternatives that have it, the more information the choice requires.[13]

This provides the basis for rough information accounting, following the elementary principle that information required also needs to be supplied. In general, the supply may come from several sources. What counts, however, is not all the information that a source makes available, but only the one *relevant* to the given choice: in other words, the one that helps to identify the alternative(s) with the desired property. For the present explanatory purposes, it will suffice to consider only the formally simplest form of this help, which is to eliminate a more or less large number of other alternatives, thus narrowing the initial choice set into a smaller one. In such cases, it is easy to see how pieces of relevant information can add up, and thus complement each other: they can be seen to successively narrow the initial choice set, with each additional piece further narrowing the choice set narrowed by the previous pieces.[14]

As it is not always obvious how to extract relevant information from the available one, the result may depend on the sophistication of the information processing used. For the information balance, however, only the relevant information actually extracted counts as supplied. If less information is supplied than required, whether owing to insufficiency of the information available or to its insufficient processing, an information deficit results. The only means to cover information deficits are sources of random messages – random in the sense that they are uncorrelated with the desired properties of the choice alternatives – sometimes called 'Monte Carlo devices', such as dice, lotteries or irrelevant fantasies and beliefs. The problem is that such sources are inseparably tied to risks of errors. But in choices which in one way or another must be made, and where therefore no information deficit can be left uncovered, there is no other way to proceed.[15]

To be sure, not all choices need be so decisive. For instance, when choosing among alternative beliefs or forecasts, we may retain several of them as plausible, and perhaps ascribe to them some probability distribution. But choices among alternative courses of actions, including alternative ways of forming organizations, must often boil down to one specific alternative, to the exclusion of all the others. All information deficits must then be fully covered, and risks of errors therefore cannot be avoided. The logic of the Darwinian answer thus starts to appear: organizing without an omniscient Creator – which is indeed nothing other than organizing with information deficits – must involve some random trial-and-error search.

ORGANIZING INFORMATION

With reference to the link between choices and information, o-information can be defined as the one relevant to choices among alternative ways of forming organizations from a given set of agents. O-information may be contrasted with current information, defined as the one used in choices within, and possibly also exchanged between, already formed organizations.

Brains and computers offer instructive examples. In brains, o-information or, more precisely, its initial part, is in the genes which guide their formation and growth, and current information in the nervous impulses that flow within them. In computers, o-information is in the design of their hardware, and current information in the data with which they operate (the classification of software raises a problem considered below).

O-information is more fundamental than current information in the sense that, without it, no information-using organizations could form, and there would therefore be no users of, and thus no use for, current information. As it often passes unnoticed (computer users typically ignore the o-information in the computer hardware, and social scientists typically ignore the genetic information for the forming of human brains) this point deserves emphasis.

What complicates the distinction between o-information and current information is that it may not be absolute, or exclusive. Definitions of organizations depend not only upon empirical properties of the real world, but also upon our perspective, which makes the distinction relative to the choice of the perspective. Thus, in the computer example, we may choose to limit the definition to an unprogrammed computer, or to extend it to a computer programmed by a certain software (for example, DOS or Windows). In the former case, only the information in the hardware is organizing, while all software information is current; in the latter case, the software included changes sides and its information is added to the organizing one.

The brain example illustrates why the classification may not be exclusive. As is well known, the forming of a brain depends not only on its genes, but also on the inputs actually received and processed. This means that the current information in nervous impulses must be recognized also as containing some o-information which can help the brain to form. In general, the two types of information may overlap in two cases: (a) in organizing which is observed, where a more or less large part of the o-information becomes current information for the observer, and (b) in organizing guided by an organizer, where a more or less large part of the o-information is first current information for the organizer. The brain example is a special case of (b), in which the organization itself contains (some of) its organizer(s). (This can also be seen as a special case of self-organizing, on which more will be said below.)

Here, however, none of these complications really matters. What we need is to identify the information that at least in some circumstances is organizing; we need not worry whether or not in other circumstances a more or less large part of it may also be current. For the identification, all we need is a clear picture of the choices in which o-information is used. It is in this picture that the notions of a-set, the possible o-set, and the successful o-subset, introduced earlier, are central. To recapitulate, a given a-set implies a possible o-set, which contains a successful o-subset. The o-information required for the forming of a successful organization is the one that can guide agents from the a-set to organize into a member of the successful o-subset. As follows from the rough definition of information, the smaller the part of the successful o-subset in the possible o-set, and thus the more unlikely it is that a successful organization might form by chance, the more o-information is required.

While the forming of an organization may consist of a long series of choices, each among few alternatives, or of a short series of choices, each among many alternatives, the o-information required remains the same, much as the size of a number remains the same, whether expressed as a long series of binary digits or as a shorter series of decimal digits. This independence of o-information accounting from the path that organizing may take in time makes it possible to reach interesting results – in particular about binding constraints and ranges of feasible outcomes – without any complex dynamic analysis.

INFORMATION, ENERGY, AND SCARCE RESOURCES

A brief reminder of the importance of energy in biology and scarce resources in economics is in order. Clearly, organizing needs not only information to be guided in a specific direction, but also some impetus to be driven in any direction at all. In the forming of living organisms, the impetus is the energy that activates the chemical agents involved: they must be made active enough to be ready to form a sufficient variety of complex compounds, including all those of which the organisms can be built. A simple illustration is a hen sitting on an egg: to form a chicken, the egg requires both the o-information in its DNA and the warmth of the hen.

In economic organizing, however, we cannot simply borrow the term 'energy' in its narrow physical meaning. To be activated, economic agents typically need a large variety of scarce resources: both as working capital and as promised rewards (incentives). We must also be careful about the use of the term 'information': in modern economics, some scarce resources, such as technologies and human capital, can also be said to be information, and this must not be confused with the organizing one. Organizing is only the information that guides economic agents to use available scarce resources, *including technologies and human capital*, to form certain economic organizations of certain performance, and not others. Although also this information is eventually internalized in human minds, and might thus be counted as a kind of human capital, this is a very special kind which standard theories of this capital do not include.[16]

In general, economists hardly need to be reminded of the importance of scarce resources; it is rather the role of o-information that they may underestimate. Indeed, while no modern biologist ignores the crucial role of genetic information in the forming of living organisms, most economists still appear to see economic development only in terms of quantities of resources. In particular, most theories of economic growth, from Solow (1956) through Grossman and Helpman (1991) to Romer (1994) and Barro (1997), pay little or no attention to the differences in o-information that can cause similar resources to be used in widely different ways and thus make different economies develop into very differently rich or poor creatures.[17] This is as if biology saw standard nutrients and the warmth of a hen to be the only factors that make an egg develop into a chicken, and then could not explain why basically the same nutrients and warmth may at other times produce a mouse or an elephant. The only growth theories in which o-information can be seen taken into account (be it only implicitly) are those about the growth effects of alternative institutions, with North and Thomas (1973) and North (1990) among the best-known examples.[18]

Here, however, as o-information is in the centre, this reminder of the role of energy/resources is useful as a protection against the opposite narrow-mindedness, which would make us see nothing but the information. To understand how the production, storage and use of o-information depend upon the supply of energy/resources, and how this in turn depends upon qualities of the o-information produced, is the key to the understanding of both biological and economic organizing.

SELF-ORGANIZING

Processes during which disorderly sets of agents spontaneously form orderly organizations have been described many times, but to my knowledge (and taste) not yet fully explained in clear operational terms. The perspective on o-organization is an effective remedy to this lack of clarity. Its contribution begins with a simple clear definition: *self-organizing is organizing for which some or all of the o-information required is supplied by the constituent agents themselves.*

To see what this definition implies, recall that all supply of o-information reduces the possible o-set. The property which allows agents to take part in this supply can be referred to as 'organizational selectivity' ('o-selectivity'), meaning their intrinsic abilities and/or willingness to establish only certain channels with only certain of their fellow agents, and refuse all the other channels and all the other agents. The more o-selective an agent is – in other words, the smaller the fraction of all the conceivable channels with other agents that the agent is actually able and willing to establish – the more o-information the agent supplies and the more the possible o-set is thus reduced. Moreover, as will be considered in more detail below, the larger this supply, the smaller the need, and the room(!), for o-information from Darwinian trial-and-error search.

At the lowest biochemical level of biological organizing, o-selectivity is implied by familiar properties of chemical agents: the chemical affinities (valences) which constrain the set of alternative compounds that a given set of atoms and molecules might possibly form. In economics, the characteristics of agents that imply o-selectivity are less familiar: as most economic analysis has been about the way given economic organizations function, and not how they form and reform, these characteristics have remained largely unnoticed. They may be thought of as *associative* rules and preferences, and defined as those characteristics that constrain and guide economic agents in their choices among different ways of joining, or avoiding, other agents in creating, enlarging or dissolving economic organizations. Their origins can be divided into the genetically determined human nature, cultural conditioning and personal idiosyncrasies (which in turn may be of genetic or cultural origins).

What causes difficulties in identifying and understanding self-organizing is that it may exist in many variants. A useful overview can be gained by classifying them along three dimensions: partial–complete, dispersed–concentrated and rigid–flexible.

In the *partial–complete* dimension, each variant can be described by a number between zero and one, showing, for a given organization, what share of its o-information is supplied by its agents themselves. 'Zero' means that the a-set resembles a universal construction set whose parts can be interconnected arbitrarily: all o-information must be supplied exogenously and thus no self-organizing takes place. 'One' means that the a-set resembles a self-assembling puzzle whose parts can form only one specific organization: no exogenous o-information need, nor can, be supplied; the self-organizing is complete.

Particularly clear examples of both these extremes can be found in biological organizing. The 20 amino acids exemplify a universal construction set: they can form any protein that any known living organism may ever need, while all the o-information required must be supplied from outside, by genetic messages. In contrast, the proteins formed are so specifically tailored that they often provide for several successive levels of self-assembling, from parts of cells to multicellular organisms and entire societies of organisms,[19] with the notable exception, on which more will be said in the last section, of societies of humans.

In the *dispersed–concentrated* dimension, each variant of self-organizing is described by the distribution of the supply of o-information over the a-set. At the dispersed extreme, all agents are equally o-selective, and thus contribute the same amount of o-information; this extreme might thus also be called 'associatively egalitarian'. In concentrated self-organizing, the a-set contains a more or less large subset of agents which are much more o-selective, and thus supply substantially more o-information, than the others. Such highly o-selective agents, which can be referred to as leading organizers, are exemplified by catalysts in chemistry, enzymes in biology and entrepreneurs in economics. To increase their supply of o-information, they may repetitively help less o-selective agents to interconnect by specific channels, without remaining part of such channels themselves.

An interesting parameter of concentrated self-organizing is the number of leading organizers. They may be several, or just one: the corresponding cases of self-organizing may be denoted as 'decentralized' and 'centralized'.[20] But the centralization of self-organizing must not be confused with the more familiar centralization of control of functioning. There is a fundamental difference between the two, which may perhaps best be seen by considering that centralized control may be formed by decentralized self-organizing, as in organisms with central nervous systems, and, vice versa, decentralized control may be centrally organized, as in multidivisional firms.

The rigid–flexible dimension requires much longer explanation than the first two. It grades variants of self-organizing according to the abilities of the agents involved to modify their o-selectivity, and thus the o-information they supply.

As pointed out, agents can supply o-information only thanks to some intrinsic abilities of theirs: in one way or another, they must be internally programmed for this supply. But these abilities may be differently rigid or flexible, depending on the sophistication of the programming. In the simplest cases, the programming rigidly prescribes the o-information supplied: examples include chemical agents, rigidly programmed by their internal atomic structures, and social insects, nearly as rigidly programmed by their genes. More sophisticated programming, however, may enable agents to modify their supply in response to current information, or even the ways of this response; in other words, such agents may learn, or even learn to learn, to self-organize. Examples include neurons, which respond to a certain series of impulses by a certain modification of their connections to other neurons, and thus allow current information (such as education) to contribute to the forming of brains. Similarly, human individuals respond to a certain cultural conditioning by forming a specific social behaviour, including specific preferences over joining or creating different organizations.

An important, although not always properly realized, point is that, however flexible an agent's o-selectivity might be, the form and the extent of this flexibility belong to the agent's intrinsic properties, which at a certain basic level cannot but be rigid. As anyone who tried to endow a computer with learning abilities knows, more flexibility requires more of basic rigid programming. Perhaps the most striking example is a human brain, which owes all of its enormous flexibility to the strict rigidity of the highly complex genetic information for its forming, part of the rigid genetic specification of each *Homo sapiens*. The rigidity is essential indeed: the entire difference between human brains and the much less flexible brains of apes is due to the rigid preservation of small differences in a few genes.[21]

This point is essential for a good understanding of the way flexible self-organizing arises and unfolds from intrinsic properties of individual agents. If the fundamental dependence of all self-organizing upon intrinsic properties of agents is overlooked, as has often been the case, even rigid self-organizing may appear as an unintelligible paradox or a holistic mystery. In flexible self-organizing, in which the relevant properties of agents are no longer o-selectivities themselves, but much more hidden selectivity-modifying abilities, this dependence is even more difficult to see: sophisticated agents which can modify their o-selectivity may seem to have fewer intrinsic properties than more primitive agents with rigid o-selectivity. A superficial observer may then get wrong the causal arrows of self-organizing and mistakenly conclude that such sophisticated agents do not form organizations but are, on the contrary, formed by them. This mistake has been quite widespread in the social sciences, where many authors used to claim, and some still do, that it is society which forms human individuals, and not vice versa.

The true problem with flexible self-organizing is that it can generate intricate organizing feedbacks: (a) agents start forming an organization using their initial given o-selectivities, (b) the organization leads to the production of certain current information, (c) the agents use their learning abilities to respond to this information by modifying their o-selectivities, (d) these in turn modify the organization; and so on. Much like feedbacks in automatic control, organizing feedbacks also may generate complex adjustment processes, during which both the organizations formed and their agents may undergo a long series of mutually caused modifications, possibly involving path dependency, or cycles which may or may not converge to stable states (attractors, equilibria).

What may confuse a superficial observer is that the feedback effects of an organization upon its agents are often more conspicuous than the forward effects of individual agents upon their organization. These effects may often be only infinitesimal, and thus easy to overlook, but without them the organization could not have been formed and maintained in the first place. To avoid such confusion, we need to keep in mind that the basic prerequisite, without which no flexible self-organizing can start, is the presence of a sufficient number of sufficiently sophisticated agents, endowed with certain o-selectivity-modifying (learning) abilities. In addition to such abilities, the agents must be endowed with certain initial o-selectivities that provide for the very first steps. For example, to form a developed brain, neurons must be able not only to modify their connections in response to impulses received, but also to grow by themselves certain primitive connections through which the first impulses could pass. Similarly, to arrive at forming developed societies, humans must be genetically endowed not only for adjusting their social behaviour in response to the education received, but also for building by themselves some primitive societies where their first social and cultural education could start.

As agents of the required abilities cannot be found free in nature, but must themselves be specifically organized, it follows that flexible self-organizing cannot be primary, but must be preceded by a lower-level organizing of another type, needed to form such agents. Hence no organization can be formed by flexible self-organizing alone. Although in some complex organizations, including both brains and human societies, flexible self-organizing may eventually contribute so much that it overshadows all the other sources, it can never supply all the o-information by itself. In particular, it cannot supply the initial part of this information, the one needed for the forming of suitable agents. Thus, however overshadowed this part might eventually become, it remains crucial in two respects: without it, no flexible self-organizing could start, and, moreover, depending on the sophistication of the agents formed, it sets limits to what flexible self-organizing can ever achieve.

As noted, flexible self-organizing is what in the context of both brains and economic organizations is often called ‘learning’. The finding that it essentially depends upon intrinsic properties of the constituent agents involved – neurons in brains and individuals in economic organizations – therefore has interesting implications for two current debates. One, relatively recent, is about organizational learning, often meaning the abilities of firms to adapt to new technologies and new market conditions. The implication is that such learning cannot be properly understood without carefully considering the roles and the learning abilities of the individuals involved. Perhaps the most striking example is the inability of theories which do not consider individuals to explain the well-known fact that similarly organized firms in similar conditions often show large differences in their adaptation abilities. Such theories simply miss what has been a commonplace in industrial practice, namely, that the learning abilities of each firm crucially depend upon the competence and learning abilities of a few key individuals. And although the competence and learning abilities of other individuals usually also matter, the key individuals strongly influence how the others are selected and what incentives and opportunities to contribute to the firm's performance they are given.

The second debate, of a much older date, concerns the learning of human brains, and in particular the issue of which part of their forming (self-organizing) is due to genetically given talents ('the nature') and which part is due to inputs from experience and education ('the nurture'). The main implication is that both are necessary in the following sense. Without the inputs any brain would remain seriously underdeveloped. Moreover, their contributions may be cumulative in the sense that the use of earlier inputs may increase a brain's abilities to use later inputs; or, in other words, a brain can also learn to learn. But, as a result, these contributions may become so overwhelming that they may give the impression of being the only ones, and thus mislead superficial observers into believing that the human brain is a *tabula rasa*, on which anything could be written by education. The main point here is, that however cumulative and overwhelming such contributions might be, they cannot but ultimately repose upon some genetically given o-information (inborn talents), without which no neurons able to self-organize into a brain could form, and which determines how such contributions can start to be used and sets limits to what they can possibly achieve.

Elementary empirical evidence is provided by the large differences between learning abilities of different species: there are now no doubts that it is differences in genetic endowments that allow monkeys to learn much more than dogs, and humans much more than monkeys.[22] But doubts still appear to persist about the responsibility of genes for the significant differences that can be observed between learning abilities of different humans. Although it is now generally agreed that both genes and education matter, how exactly they complement each other is still a matter of dispute. As opposed to the popular answer that they form a sum, the present implication is that they rather form a product, where the genetic endowment determines the maximum learning potential, of which education determines the actually exploited fraction. Thus, while it is true that lack of educational inputs can prevent even the genetically best-endowed brain from developing, it is also true that even the best education cannot teach more than what the genetic endowment allows to be learnt.[23]

ENERGY AND RESOURCES IN SELF-ORGANIZING

The issue of self-organizing has sometimes been confused by excessive if not exclusive attention to inputs of energy, for instance expressed in terms of distance from a thermodynamic equilibrium. A likely reason appears to be that such inputs are often so much more conspicuous than inputs of o-information that it is easy to mistake them for the only ones. This mistake engendered many spectacular but false 'order-out-of-disorder' paradoxes; for example, intricately organized patterns appeared to emerge in response to mere temperature changes, to the surprise of even some reputed authors.[24] More fundamentally, it also obscured the crucial difference between thermodynamic and organizational equilibria.

Concerning the paradoxes, the present perspective makes it easy to guess that 'the rabbit in the hat' is hidden in the inputs of o-information that the agents involved, thanks to their intrinsic properties, supply, but which, in the paradoxes, are ignored. Concerning the difference between thermodynamic and organizational equilibria, however, a more detailed clarification is in order. In general, as noted in the section 'Information, Energy and Scarce Resources', the importance of energy/resources for the forming of organizations is great, but nevertheless limited. In self-organizing, this importance can be described as follows. Without inputs of energy/resources, the o-selectivities of agents would not be activated, and the o-information of these selectivities would thus remain latent. Such inputs can thus be used as highly effective means by which self-organizing can be started or stopped. But they contribute little, if anything, to determining *which* organizations will form. Roughly, they can be compared to the developer which reveals the latent picture on an exposed film.

To be more precise, inputs of energy/resources may carry a limited amount of o-information in flexible self-organizing, if agents can modify their o-selectivities also in function of them. In biology, for example, it depends upon the supply of food whether a bee larva will use its genetic information to grow into a worker or a queen; in economics, it depends upon the supply of resources, both actual and conditionally expected (incentives), which of their intrinsic organizing abilities economic agents will actually use, and thus which types of economic organizations they will actually form. But even in such cases, most of the o-information clearly has origins other than inputs of energy/resources.

An instructive example is the role of temperature in biological organizing, which can be described as follows. At a low temperature, the chemical agents of biological organizing remain too little active to reveal their selective affinities by effectively searching for, and establishing bonds with, compatible neighbours. When the temperature rises, such bonds begin to be found and established, while it is clearly the agents' intrinsic o-selectivities, and not the rise in temperature, that determine the form of these bonds. But there is also an upper limit: if the temperature keeps increasing, the agents become overactive and start breaking the bonds they previously established at a lower temperature. It is indeed only within a rather narrow temperature range that the chemical agents of biological organizing can effectively make use of all their o-selectivities on which this organizing is based.[25]

The difference between thermodynamic and organizational equilibria can now be clarified as follows. It is perfectly true that the forming and maintaining of both biological and economic organizations require a continuing supply of energy/resources, and that such organizations can thus exist only in a thermodynamic disequilibrium. Yet if their agents, thanks to this supply *and to their own intrinsic o-selectivities*, can find and keep relatively stable positions within them, it is also perfectly sensible to recognize such states as another type of equilibrium, suitably called 'organizational'. Thus, if the two types of equilibria are properly distinguished, the existence of organizational equilibria may very well be admitted, in no conflict with the fact that, to be obtained and maintained, they need a thermodynamic disequilibrium.

DARWINIAN TRIAL-AND-ERROR SEARCH

Clarifying self-organizing first, before addressing Darwinian trial-and-error search, has the advantage of setting this search into a well-defined context, where its task and limits can in advance be clearly identified. The task is to contribute to the forming, from a certain a-set, of organizations that meet certain performance criteria (successful organizations) by producing that part of the o-information required which the self-organizing of the a-set does not supply. The limits can be expressed by three necessary conditions.

First, the forming of a successful organization must require more o-information than that supplied by self-organizing of the a-set. In other words, the a-set must not constitute a self-assembling puzzle but, to make room for some Darwinian search, the remaining possible o-set must have at least two members.

Second, the remaining possible o-set must contain non-empty subsets of both successful and unsuccessful organizations: if all of its members were unsuccessful, no search could help; if all of them were successful, no error could be committed and thus no trial-and-error search would be needed. Provided that the successful o-subset is non-empty, the smaller it is in relation to the remaining possible o-set, the more o-information Darwinian search is demanded and allowed to supply. However, to correctly estimate the size of these sets may not be easy: this requires, among other things, correctly estimating the o-information supplied by self-organizing. If this information is underestimated, the remaining possible o-set, and thus also the task of Darwinian search are overestimated.[26]

Third, the performance criteria must concern the supply of energy/resources on which organizations depend for their further existence (preservation, survival), and this supply must in turn depend upon the organizations' performance. The crucial test is whether or not the organizations formed are endowed with necessary behavioural (functional) competence to keep this supply sufficient, in spite of all the obstacles and disturbances which they may meet in their environments. These may, but need not, include competing organizations; whereas competition typically increases the difficulty of the test, even without it, the task of forming a coherent organization which holds together and keeps providing enough energy/resources for its further existence in a neutral environment is rarely trivial.

The supply of energy/resources is thus the main feedback of Darwinian search: it is this supply that ultimately decides which tentative o-information will be preserved and which one will be deleted. But it remains secondary in the sense that only little o-information can be added through it. Informationally rich tentative alternatives must first be produced by other means (more precisely, by combinations of self-organizing and lotteries) to which the energy/resources feedback can only answer 'yes' or 'no' (and thus add a single bit of o-information).

In the perspective on o-information, as noted, Darwinian search can be described in terms that are more general, and thus more suitable for economic applications, than the biology-specific 'genetic variety', 'replication' and 'natural selection'. Among several possible synonyms, perhaps the simplest and clearest ones are 'lotteries', 'memories' and 'tests'. General Darwinian search can thus be said to involve (a) some sources of random messages comparable to lotteries, needed to produce tentative variants of o-information, (b) some memory, or memories, needed to store the variants produced, at least while they are being tried, and longer if they prove successful, and (c) some tests, needed to determine which of the variants are successful and which are not. To distinguish the memories storing the tentative o-information produced by Darwinian search from other memories, let me denote them 'Darwinian'.

The biological interpretation is obvious. Darwinian memories consist of genetic messages (coded in DNA or RNA), maintained by means of heredity and replication; the lotteries produce genetic variety and mutations; and the tests correspond to natural selection. The genetic messages stored (genes, genotypes) guide the forming of, and thus become expressed in, organisms (phenotypes), which are tested for their abilities to function, survive and multiply; only if the organisms formed pass all of the tests are the messages which guided their forming preserved.

The economic interpretation, somewhat less obvious, will be considered in the section 'Particularities of Human Economic Organizing'. In a preliminary way, it may be useful to note that the main Darwinian memories will be found in the institutions ('rules of the game') that shape the forming and the working of economic organizations, are internalized in human minds, and repose on written and/or unwritten supports (for example, books of laws, oral traditions). The lotteries will be seen driven by imagination and fantasies of human minds, to the degree (until now quite high) to which they can generate ideas for institutional changes uncorrelated to the true consequences of these changes. The tests will be found close to natural selection for entire economies, but not for firms; rather than natural, the tests for them will be found more or less extensively organized by the economy's institutions in ways for which these institutions are themselves, sooner or later, tested.

The distinction between the Darwinian memories of o-information and the organizations that this information helps to form is essential, but not always easy to make. What may obscure it is that the memories typically belong to the organizations – for example, genetic memories belong to organisms, and institutions to economic organizations – and can often be preserved only if the organizations are preserved. This dependence of memories upon the organizations around them is indeed the keystone of the entire Darwinian feedback. This means that the memories must be distinguished *within*, rather than *outside*, the organizations.

It may be instructive to view the organizations formed as means by which the information stored in their Darwinian memories tries to protect itself. This generalizes the view suggested by Dawkins (1976, 1982) and Hull (1980), in which organisms are seen as means of protection and perpetuation of their genes. To express this view, Dawkins refers to genes as 'replicators' and to organisms as 'vehicles', whereas Hull speaks of 'evolvors' and 'interactors'. In present terms, replicators and evolvors are special cases of memories, and vehicles and interactors, of organizations.[27]

The distinction between Darwinian memories and organizations can also enlighten the long-standing issue of the units of selection: without this distinction, units of selection can be confused with units of *testing*. This confusion appears to be the main source of the disagreement about what the units of selection are. When the two are properly distinguished, it becomes clear that the units of selection can be nothing else than pieces of o-information stored in Darwinian memories: only such pieces can be produced by Darwinian lotteries and subsequently become subjects of selection for continuing storage.[28] The organizations that they help to form, sometimes mistakenly claimed to be also units of selection, can only be units of testing: it is the results of their performance tests that determine whether the o-information that formed them will be selected or rejected.

MULTI-LEVEL ORGANIZING

Multi-level organizations, in which organizations of one level are agents of organizations of a higher level ('organizations of organizations'), are common in both biology and economics. Proteins, parts of cells, cells, organs, multicellular organisms and societies of organisms exemplify ascending organizational levels in biology, and workshops, plants, firms, national economies and economic unions exemplify them in economics. Moreover, multi-level organizations in which economic organizations are seen to build additional organizational levels upon the particular biological organizations that are human individuals appear to be the only framework in which biology and economics can be interconnected in a well-defined sense.

A difficulty with multi-level organizations is that they complicate analysis, which makes most economists prefer to work with organizations of a single level. In standard analysis of resource allocation within a given firm or a given economy, many valuable results may be obtained in spite of, and often even thanks to, such a simplication. In the study of organizing processes, however, multi-level organizations cannot be avoided, for some of the most important ways in which self-organizing and Darwinian search can cooperate are precisely those that lead from one organizational level to another.

To comprehend such ways, the basic fact to be taken into account is that *the levels of organizations may not coincide with the levels of Darwinian memories*. For instance, if organizations of a certain level are formed by complete self-organizing, this level does not have Darwinian memories of its own. Nevertheless, much of the o-information for the forming of such organizations may be a result of Darwinian search, stored in Darwinian memories. But these can only be memories of a lower organizational level: the o-information they store determines the abilities of the agents to self-organize into the higher-level organization. In other words, such self-organizing agents act as relays which allow o-information from the lower level to guide the forming of the organizations at the higher level.

More generally, the o-information found by Darwinian search at lower level(s) may be transformed into o-information supplied by self-organizing at one or several higher levels. Or, to see it also from the other side, much of the o-information supplied by self-organizing at a higher level may be of Darwinian origins at a lower level. The important point is that the o-information from Darwinian memories of one level which helps to form organizations of several higher levels is submitted to tests at all these levels: to be preserved, all these organizations must be successful.

Biological organizing offers a particularly clear and relatively simple example: for all the levels of biological organizations, from proteins, through cells, to organisms and their societies, there is a single level of Darwinian memories: the level of genetic messages. For instance, the genes of ants store all of the o-information for forming the cells of ants, ants and entire anthills. This can be visualized, as noted in the section 'Self-organizing', by seeing genetic messages to guide the universal construction set of amino acids to forming so specifically tailored proteins that all the higher levels of biological organizing can subsequently unfold as a hierarchy of self-assembling puzzles.[29]

In this respect, however, economic organizing is more complicated. As the next section will consider in more detail, Darwinian search and self-organizing are combined there in more general ways. Darwinian search is conducted there at several levels, and possibly combined with self-organizing of the same levels. Economic self-organizing of any level is typically incomplete, and thus demands additional o-information from Darwinian search of the same level. As each level of Darwinian search needs its own Darwinian memories, the relationships with the organizations formed are complicated: not only may one level of such memories supply o-information for the forming of organizations of several higher levels – as in biological organizing – but also the forming of one level of organizations may be supplied with o-information from Darwinian memories of several lower (deeper) levels.

A further complication is that a higher-level organization, once it is formed, may encapsulate some or all of the lower levels within itself and submit them to its influence. The Darwinian lotteries and/or the criteria of selection at the lower levels may thus be modified: instead of remaining random, the lotteries may become filtered and some of their trials may even be entirely blocked; and, instead of remaining natural, the selection may become more or less organized, possibly protecting some agents which natural selection would eliminate, and/or eliminating some of those which natural selection would let stay. But such modifications are not free of charge. The organization bears responsibility for them during its own tests: for instance, if it blocked too many favourable trials and/or overprotected too many useless or harmful agents, it would cause its own downfall, and hence also rejection of the o-information which formed it in such a faulty way.[30]

The o-information found by a lower-level Darwinian search thus continues to be tested through the higher-level organizations which it helps to form, but these tests are less direct. As it now shares the responsibility for these organizations with the o-information found by a higher-level Darwinian search, it is tested less for the actual performance of these organizations than for the conditions it creates for this search. The organizations–agents which it helps to form at the lower level must be able to conduct the higher-level Darwinian search fast and fruitfully enough to find in time sufficiently successful higher-level organizations, needed to preserve it in its lower-level memories.

All this helps to clarify two often discussed issues. One is whether the evolution of human economic organizations is not Lamarckian rather than Darwinian. In present terms, the main difference between the two kinds of evolutions can be localized in the lotteries generating trials ('variety'): in Darwinian evolutions, the lotteries keep being random ('blind'), whereas in Lamarckian evolutions they contain a feedback which allows them to learn from past results, and thus keep increasing the probability of future successes and decreasing that of future errors. In the evolution of species, where it has not been possible to observe such feedback, Lamarckism is now considered definitely dead. But in the evolution of human economic organizations, where humans can definitely learn from their past mistakes (even if not as fast and as reliably as one might wish), Lamarckism may appear resuscitated.[31] In the present perspective, however, no such resuscitation is needed. Any evolution with learning can be explained in a clearer and simpler way as a combination of Darwinian search with increasing inputs of flexible self-organizing. In other words, an evolution may appear Lamarckian only if the agents involved are sufficiently sophisticated to be able to self-organize flexibly, and thus increase their own supply of relevant o-information and decrease the room left for Darwinian search. While all this search remains, by definition, random (blind), what may give the impression of Lamarckism is that its scope is being reduced.

The second issue is the one of group selection. To clarify it, the first step is to distinguish between societies ('groups') of non-human organisms for which all o-information is supplied by genetically prescribed instincts, and those of humans, where much of this information must be provided by conventional institutions: the two imply different answers. The former involves only one level of Darwinian memories: the genetic ones. Groups of such non-human organisms can thus only be units of higher-level testing of genetic messages in these memories, which remain the only units of selection. For instance, the genetic o-information of ants, to be preserved, must lead to the forming not only of successful cells and successful individual ants, but also of successful anthills. The only units of selection thus remain pieces of the genetic o-information, whereas anthills are just units of their higher-level testing.

It is mostly, if not only, in human societies that more than one level of Darwinian memories, and thus more than one type of units of selection, are significantly involved. Much like ants, humans need to live in societies, but as opposed to ants, not all of the o-information for the forming of their societies is in their genes. They may seem free to choose their societies themselves, but much of this freedom is only apparent. Nature keeps submitting their societies to severe tests – both for the efficiency of the means used and for the wisdom of the ends pursued – but without telling them in advance which of their societies may eventually succeed. It thus forces them to guess, and punishes them with social crises and individual suffering if they guess wrong. They must therefore provide themselves with higher-level Darwinian memories of o-information for their societies, and conduct a higher-level Darwinian search for such o-information that would lead them to make their societies successful.

These tests appear indeed more severe than those of anthills: in addition to coping with its external environments, such as natural laws, available natural resources and prevailing terms of trade on the world markets, a human society must also be able to cope with its own members. This is because humans, as opposed to ants, can change or destroy the institutions of their society if a sufficient number of them sufficiently dislike its performance. To be successful, a human society must therefore be able to reach and maintain a certain equilibrium between the outcomes it obtains – or, more precisely, allows its members to obtain – and the outcomes that its members demand. In principle, there are two complementary ways in which a society can reach such an equilibrium: by adapting, through economic efficiency, its performance to its members' demands and/or, through cultural conditioning, their demands to its performance.[32] But each way has its constraints. The adaptation of demands is constrained by the basic requirements of physical and psychical health of human beings (for example, no cultural conditioning can make humans stop demanding food, and perhaps also a minimum of personal freedom). And the adaptation of performance is hampered by resource constraints and production frontiers. Human societies are thus threatened by an additional risk of failure, unknown to anthills: the only societies which can cope successfully with their external environments might be rejected by their members.[33] The only hope is that people can learn in time to adapt their demands on their society to the constraints upon what the society can possibly deliver.

It is thus only in the case of human societies that the term 'group selection' can be given a meaning which reasonably reflects the idea of 'group'. Although such societies, including the economic organizations they contain, remain units of testing, the units of selection also include pieces of the society-specific higher-level o-information, stored, as noted, possibly in several levels of formal and informal institutions. The societies which pieces of such information help to organize are thus units of direct testing of these pieces.

Nevertheless, and this is an important example of the above-mentioned complications, human societies also remain units of indirect testing of the genetic o-information of *Homo sapiens*: success of human societies is obviously part of the necessary conditions for preserving this information. In contrast with the genes of ants, however, the genes of humans are tested less for the performance of actual societies than for the ability to conduct the search for successful societies safely and fast enough towards a happy end.

The central issue of this paper can now be seen as part of the problem of this search: a necessary condition for the success of human societies is the success of their economic organizations.

PARTICULARITIES OF HUMAN ECONOMIC ORGANIZING

Differences between economic and biological organizing start with differences in properties of the most elementary agents, especially in their information-processing abilities: obviously, human individuals are much more sophisticated and more heterogeneous than molecules of amino acids.

The high sophistication, which includes abilities to learn and to self-organize flexibly, implies that economic organizing contains a large component of flexible self-organizing already at its lowest level. In contrast, as noted, amino acids appear not to have any significant self-organizing abilities at all, which means that all o-information for their organizing must be supplied by Darwinian search.

The high heterogeneity makes the problem of economic organizing more complex, and thus in need of more o-information, than would be the problem of organizing the same number of similarly sophisticated but homogeneous agents. With homogeneous agents, as noted in the section 'Organizations', the task of organizing is limited to forming a network of channels, and thus implying the roles for individual agents, but without having to assign specific agents to specific roles. With heterogeneous agents, organizing must additionally provide for, and make use of, internal selection, with the task of assigning each role to a suitable agent and protecting it from all the unsuitable ones. Also some feedback must then be established to constrain the forming of channels and roles, in order to make this forming take into account how effective the selection can be made: it is important to prevent the forming of roles for which, given this effectiveness, suitable agents are unlikely to be selected and/or from which unsuitable agents cannot reliably be kept away.

Such internal selection connects self-organizing to two types of Darwinian trial-and-error search. To see these connections, consider that much of economic self-organizing, in addition to being flexible, is also highly concentrated: much more o-information must be supplied from a relatively few key roles, usually referred to as entrepreneurs or organizers, than from others. It is to these roles that the two types of Darwinian search are connected: (a) one for suitable pieces of this information, led by the agents assuming these roles, and (b) one for suitable agents for these roles. The reason for search (s) is that even the most suitable (relevantly competent, talented) human agents available are initially far from having all the necessary o-information for the forming of successful economic organizations in given specific conditions; even they must search for much of it in a Darwinian trial-and-error way. The reason for search (b) is the high heterogeneity of human agents, implying that some of them may generate much better trials in search (a), and learn much faster from their errors, than others.

To be precise, there may also be other key roles, such as investors, consultants or public policy makers, which may potentially contribute helpful information, and thus reduce the room for both these types of Darwinian search. But reduced in one place, the same two types of Darwinian search reappear in another: (a) for suitable pieces of actually helping information as part of these roles, and (b) for suitable agents for these roles.

For a given population of agents (a-set) and given key roles, the smaller the subset of suitable (sufficiently competent, talented) agents – and thus the larger the subset of the unsuitable ones, who would, in these roles, do more harm then good – the more effective the internal selection must be; or, in other words, the more o-information must be supplied by Darwinian search of type (b). Too difficult roles, for which this search cannot be made sufficiently effective, such as those of national planners or selective industrial policy makers, must thus be prevented from farming.

A difficult question is raised by Darwinian search of type (a). As this is conducted in the minds of selected agents, the question is how to distinguish there the already learnt relevant knowledge, the agents' contribution to self-organizing, from tentative conjectures (imaginations, beliefs) which constitute their Darwinian trials. What makes this question difficult is that the two are often intertwined – for example, knowledge usually influences, by various mental associations, even the probabilities of only weakly related conjectures – and that people often confuse the two even in their own minds. In particular, people often appear to mistake tentative conjectures, which will later prove to be gross errors for true relevant knowledge.[34]

Note that the use of learning is no criterion of distinction. Although learning is usually understood to mean acquiring knowledge, it may also mean acquiring possibly false conjectures of other agents. But note also that even such learning plays an important role in the Darwinian search for successful economic organizations: namely, it is needed whenever this search requires collective (for example, politically decided) Darwinian trials. While such trials, just as any other Darwinian trials, may, and often do, prove to be errors, if the relevant conjectures were not at least temporarily learnt and adopted by a critical majority of the agents – who must usually be fooled into believing that this is true knowledge – the trials could not be made and the search could not proceed.

Examples of such conjectures are those parts of ideologies and religions which imply precepts for economic organizing. They must thus be recognized as of high social value as bases for collective organizing trials in the absence of sufficient relevant knowledge, but with the warning that this value may rapidly drop and become negative if they are stubbornly maintained after the trials have proved them, empirically or theoretically, to be errors. Ideally, economic research might increasingly replace such conjectures with pieces of relevant knowledge, and thus reduce the room for, and the losses from, Darwinian search and its inevitable errors. But complete replacement cannot be expected, as relevant knowledge can hardly ever become complete. Although it appears possible, as discussed in more detail below, that a combination of suitably oriented theoretical research, and by it enlightened policies, can achieve progress, this progress is constrained by the very nature of the evolution of human economies, of which both such research and policies are endogenous parts.

In economic organizing, the o-information produced by Darwinian search and stored in Darwinian memories is perhaps best seen, as already noted, in the form of what modern institutional economics defines as 'institutions': legal and/or customary constraints upon agents' choice sets, or 'the rules of the game'. If we recall that reducing initial choice sets into smaller ones requires information, the information contents of institutions can easily be identified. Institutions thus appear to be the closest analogue to genes, which store the o-information produced by Darwinian search in biological organizing.

However, it is important to keep in mind the difference noted in the previous section: in contrast to biological organizing, all of which builds upon Darwinian memories of a single level, there may be several levels of them in economic organizing. In principle, each economic organization has institutions, and a corresponding Darwinian search, of its own. Perhaps the most instructive illustration, which also indicates connections to more familiar literature, can be obtained by considering two levels: (a) the overall institutions of a national economy, and (b) the internal institutions of its production organizations, in particular firms and government agencies. Level (a) can be seen addressed in the literature on the origins and evolution of institutions, pioneered in two somewhat different directions by F.A. Hayek and D.C. North, and level (b) in the evolutionary economics based on ideas of J.A. Schumpeter and A.A. Alchian.

Unless the different levels of Darwinian memories are carefully distinguished, confusion in economic applications of Darwinism can hardly be avoided. A minor complication is that human minds are again the places (with possible help of written supports) where all the different levels of Darwinian memories meet, and where the distinction must be made. But the complication is only minor because, compared to distinguishing relevant knowledge from imagination, distinguishing organizational levels from each other (for example, the institutions of a national economy from the internal institutions of a firm) appears much easier.

Evolutionary economics, to avoid confusion, must thus distinguish at least two types of evolutions: the Hayekian–Northian (H–N) one of the overall institutions of national and supranational economies, and the Schumpeterian–Alchianian (S–A) one of the internal institutions of firms and agencies within each such economy. While each of these evolutions has its own specific ways of generating trials and correcting errors, they are also interestingly interrelated. The overall institutions that are being tried in the H–N evolution significantly influence the prevailing conditions, for example by defining property rights, corporate and antitrust laws, and bankruptcy procedures – under which trials can be made and errors corrected in the S–A evolution. In turn, the firms and agencies formed by this evolution may influence, for example by inventing or imitating new habits, or by lobbying legislators, institutional changes in the H–N evolution.

So far, these evolutions have mostly been studied each for itself, with little contact between their respective students. Thus, for instance, Hayek and his followers rarely refer to Schumpeter's views of the creative and destructive aspects of market competition, and appear little interested in the role of industrial entrepreneurs and the evolution of industrial organizations in general. On the other hand, the students of this evolution usually assume standard capitalism, and thus pay little attention to the H–N evolution of national institutions.[35]

To study the two evolutions in relation to each other thus appears to be the only way to gain precise knowledge on the way economic organizations form and evolve. But attempts to actually follow this way must be left to other occasions.

ACKNOWLEDGMENTS

I am grateful for helpful comments to M. Lehmann-Waffenschmidt, J.S. Metcalfe, Anne Plunket, Gerhard Wegner and Ulrich Witt. The usual disclaimer applies.

NOTES

1. The usual reasons why evolutionary economists find it useful to learn from biology are enriched here by the fact that biology is the science in which the understanding of organizing processes has most advanced.
2. A puzzle, then, is why such an interesting question has remained so little studied. A possible reason may be that our brains are better equipped to deal with the functioning of already formed systems than with their forming. At least this is what appears to follow from the fact that, for so many centuries, humans could keep advancing their understanding of how complex systems, including living organisms, function, and yet until Darwin no one could clearly see how any such system might be formed otherwise than by an external, human or divine, hand (and many still cannot see it even today).
3. To introduce a corresponding perspective into the study of biological organizing, Ashby (1956) considered an ovum of a rabbit and noted that we might either (a) assume it to know how to grow into a rabbit and study from where it gets the energy to do so, or (b) assume it to be supplied with enough energy and study why it grows into a rabbit, and not a dog, a fish, or a teratoma. The section, 'Information, Energy and Scarce Resources' will note in more detail that most economic analysis, and in particular most theories of economic growth, can be seen to correspond to (a), and the present perspective to (b).
4. The possibilities of, and obstacles to, the application of Darwinism in economics have been the subject of a long-standing debate. For a recent round of this debate, with numerous references to earlier rounds, see Bowler (1997), Metcalfe (1997) and Witt (1999). It should be noted that, in most of the modern contributions (including this paper), where genes are recognized to play a key role in biological evolution, the names 'Darwinian' and 'Darwinism' are used to refer to what should more precisely be called 'neo-Darwinian' and 'neo-Darwinism'. The function of genes was unknown to Darwin and was initially believed incompatible with his idea of evolution. It was more than a half-century after him that the two were shown to be complementary, in what is called the Modern Synthesis, or neo-Darwinism.
5. The well-known suggestion by Nelson and Winter (1982) to characterize firms by behavioural routines, and to consider such routines as corresponding to the genes of living organisms, thus appears to require an important qualification. The information stored in genes directly guides the forming of organisms, and not their behaviour. While the behaviour does ultimately depend on the form, it is only in primitive organisms that this dependence is direct. In general, as discussed in more detail in the section 'Organizing Information', the dependence may be very indirect, mediated by more or less complex learning processes: the genes then only determine learning abilities, while the routines actually learned significantly depend upon information inputs from the environment (experience, conditioning, education).
6. That Darwinism cannot explain all the complexity of living organisms has been argued many times. While many of these arguments use naive sophisms in order to discredit Darwinism for religious reasons, some – of which an early example is Gould and Lewontin (1979) – deserve serious consideration. Although, in biology, insufficiency of Darwinism is still an open question, no evolutionary economist seems to doubt that all significant features of economic organizations cannot be explained by Darwinism alone.
7. I prefer to use the '-ing' form, as it more clearly indicates that the term refers to a *process*.
8. Much of the literature on self-organizing indeed lacks a clear definition of what self-organizing is and how it operates, and is more interested in criticizing than in complementing Darwinism. Attempts to synthesize the two are relatively recent; perhaps the most advanced attempt is in Kauffman (1993).
9. So far, however, the heterogeneity of human agents has failed to be fully recognized both in the 'orthodox' economic theories, which assume all humans to be perfectly rational optimizers, and in the 'heterodox' ones, which assume everyone to be of about the same bounded rationality. As considered in more detail later, important differences between successful and unsuccessful economic organizations cannot be understood

without recognizing that the rationality of human agents may be bounded in widely unequal ways.

10. In biology, the difference between the teleological claim that living organisms *have* some initially given objectives, and the view in which they are *ascribed* objectives as a way of condensing the description of their behaviour, is interestingly discussed by Monod (1972), who refers to this view as '*teleonomical*'. An economist may find in this discussion a diplomatic answer to the long-standing issue of whether economic agents optimize objective functions or just follow routines. The answer, which may remind of Friedman's (1953) 'as if' argument, is that they certainly do follow step-by-step routines, for in the last analysis also their brains must be recognized to be causally working devices, but the behaviour materialized by such routines can sometimes be conveniently described as optimizing under constraints.
11. A strict application of the Darwinian perspective thus erases Hayek's (1973) distinction between *cosmos* and *taxis*: in this perspective, all humans, including what they may see to be '*taxis*', are part of *cosmos*.
12. As reductionism and methodological individualism have often been claimed unable to explain either social or biological organizing, and this claim has been used to advocate some more or less mysterious holistic views, it should be noted that the present perspective on o-information will refute this claim and explain both forms of organizing in a clear, reductionistic way.
13. To indicate how this information might be quantified, let me mention its possible measuring in bits for a choice among N alternatives, of which only one has the property desired: $I = \log_2 N$. Roughly, I can be understood as the minimum number of binary digits, or yes-or-no questions, needed to identify that alternative (this is true exactly for N which are entire powers of 2: for example, for 64 alternatives, $I = 6$, and it is indeed six binary digits, or six yes-or-no questions, that are needed to identify one of them). To be more precise, this measuring is correct only if all the alternatives have the same a priori probability to be the right one. If some of them are initially known to be more likely to be right than others, the information that the choice requires is smaller than I. But such knowledge can be counted as a priori information on how promising the alternatives are. When this information is added to the one required, I reappears as their sum.
14. In its more general form, which is difficult to consider without mathematics, the help consists in modifying the probabilities with which different alternatives can be expected to be right: the probabilities for at least some of the right ones are increased, and those for at least some of the wrong ones are thus decreased – but not necessarily all the way down to zero, as in the currently considered simplest form.
15. To be precise, even without any information deficit, random messages may still be necessary, if two or more alternatives are known to have the desired property, but only one can be chosen. In agreement with the above definition, however, such messages contain no relevant information, for all the alternatives in such a narrowed choice are right. Our present attention is limited to random messages with relevant information, which thus do cover information deficits, although possibly (or even most likely) in the wrong way.
16. Some of this information may be seen contained in what sociologists call 'social capital'.
17. To include investment in education and research among the scarce resources considered, as modern growth theories started to do, can hardly help. As the now defunct socialist economies of central and eastern Europe strikingly illustrated (and Cuba still does), if the economy is wrongly organized, even high investments in education and research may contribute little to useful economic growth.
18. The term 'institutions' is understood here in the modern sense of 'constraints upon decision spaces', or 'rules of the game' – such as law and custom – common in neo-institutional economics (see, for example, North, 1990, p. 3).
19. An early noted example of self-assembling is ribosome, explained in Monod (1972).
20. Alternatively, borrowing terms from theory of market structures, the two cases might be called 'oligopolist self-organizing' and 'monopolist self-organizing'.
21. For an enlightening discussion of the relationship between flexibility and rigidity, see Hofstadter (1979).

22. More advanced evidence is now provided by modern neurophysiology, which shows with increasing clarity how such initial organizing information is provided by genetic instructions: they are shown to guide production of specifically tailored proteins which cause specific neurons to form and to grow the first specific interconnections. Although it is not yet entirely clear when exactly inputs from environment can begin to contribute, there is no doubt that a rather advanced neuronal structure must first be put in place under the sole guidance of genetic instructions, and that this structure sets limits to how large the contributions of environmental inputs can ever become.
23. However, it is also true that the learning potential of different individuals is difficult to estimate *ex ante*. For many practical purposes, in particular education policy, overestimating it appears to cause lower social and individual losses than underestimating it. In other words, wasting some resources on excessive learning offered to insufficient talents is likely to cause lower social losses than wasting talents by not providing them with sufficient learning opportunities.
24. Well-known examples of such paradoxes are in Prigogine and Stengers (1984). The source of the confusion is the use of thermodynamics well beyond the limits of its initial assumptions. Recall that thermodynamics is built upon the assumption of a perfect gas, made of particles which, much like billiard balls, bounce from each other in perfectly elastic and symmetric ways. If, instead of such particles, we observe ones that, thanks to their internal structures, exert asymmetric mutual attractions or even selectively cluster into specific larger particles – as is the case of most real atoms and molecules within suitable energy ranges – we should not be surprised that within these ranges the results of thermodynamics do not apply. For such cases, roughly speaking, we would need a thermodynamics that admits billiard balls with specifically patterned patches of glue on their surface.
25. This seems to indicate a certain asymmetry between biological and economic organizing. The upper limit of the supply of energy for the former does not seem to have a counterpart in the latter: there the generally accepted view is that the higher the supply of resources, the better. But it might be worth examining whether the asymmetry is real, or whether also this supply might eventually become excessive and have similarly destructive effects upon economic organizing: for instance, whether some excessively growing incentives to managers might make these overactive in their search for the best paid jobs and thus damage the stability of even good firms.
26. Such an overestimation is the basis of all the calculations meant to refute Darwinism by claiming that living organisms are too unlikely to be formed by a blind trial-and-error search.
27. Hull's terms appear better suited to economic applications than Dawkins': in general, economic o-information evolves, but, as noted, can rarely be said to replicate; and economic organizations as active entities appear better characterized as interactors than mere vehicles.
28. This brings qualified support to Dawkins' (1976) argument that the units of selection are genes, and not organisms. The qualification is that the units of selection are here only roughly identified as pieces of genetic information, without specifying whether or not their actual size is that of genes.
29. To be precise, it should be noted that some of these levels may involve flexible self-organizing, during which, as discussed in the section 'self-organizing', additional o-information may be produced from inputs of current information, such as in self-organizing of neurons into a brain. But, to recapitulate, the initial o-information remains basic: the ways of producing the additional o-information depend upon, and are limited by, the available self-organizing abilities, determined by the initial genetic o-information.
30. For economists, as discussed in more detail below, the most important examples are the ways in which national and supranational economies organize internal Darwinian search in the forming and reforming of their firms, and in the forming and reforming of their own institutions. But it may be instructive to note that analogous examples can also be found in biology. It appears that organisms may also act as filters which protect their genetic o-information from mutations in selective ways. The actual mutations are thus less random

than the outputs of Darwinian lotteries, which means that such filters must also be recognized as sources of some o-information. The important point is that, whatever selective capacities such filters may have, they must themselves be genetically prescribed in ways previously discovered by a Darwinian search. Beardsley's (1997) note on 'Evolution evolving' makes this point clear on the example of e.coli bacteria, found to be genetically programmed to cope with scarcity of sugars by increasing the rate of mutations of its enzymes-prescribing genes, and thus increasing the probability of discovering in time how to produce enzymes able to exploit alternative nutrients. (At first, before their genetic conditioning became clear, these mutations gave the impression of being directed in a Lamarckian sense and thus constituting a refutation of Darwinism.)

31. For instance, Nelson and Winter (1982) explicitly claim the evolution of firms by market selection to be Lamarckian.
32. The second way may appear to contradict individualistic liberalism, in which consumers' sovereignty is the highest norm and society has no other purpose than to provide favourable conditions in which each individual could best pursue her own objectives. But, in fact, it is precisely this way that individualistic liberals themselves try to use when they argue against egalitarian policies of wealth and income redistribution. Although they are most likely right that only a competitive market economy can be efficient enough to cope lastingly with adverse external environments (and in this respect, the present argument will give them full support) the problem is that such an economy cannot be lastingly accepted by the members of the society, unless these limit their demands for economic equality. To convince them to do so may indeed be seen as one of the main objectives of the liberal arguments.
33. This risk clearly appears if we recall Schumpter's (1942) old prediction that capitalism will fall because people will dislike it, and the more recent evidence which suggests that capitalism is the only type of society which can be economically successful.
34. Kenneth Boulding once remarked that the problem is not with what people do not know, but with what they know, and is not so.
35. Attempts to interrelate the two evolutions are relatively recent; perhaps the best known one is in North (1990). I tried my luck in Pelikan (1987, 1992, 1995).

REFERENCES

Alchian, A.A. (1950), 'Uncertainty, evolution and economic theory', *Journal of Political Economy*, **58,** 211–22.

Ashby, W.R. (1956), *Introduction to Cybernetics*, New York: John Wiley & Sons.

Barro, R.J. (1997), *Determinants of Economic Growth*, Cambridge, MA: MIT Press.

Beardsley, T. (1997), 'Evolution evolving', *Scientific American*, September, 9–12.

Bowler, P.J. (1997), 'The transfer of metaphors between evolutionary biology and economics', presentation at 'Symposium on Evolutionary Economics as a Research Program', Stockholm School of Economics, Stockholm.

Dawkins, R. (1976), *The Selfish Gene*, London: Paladin.

Dawkins, R. (1982), *The Extended Phenotype*, Oxford and San Francisco: W.H. Freeman.

Gould, S.J. and R.C. Lewontin (1979), 'The spandrels of San Marco and the Panglossian paradigm: a critique of the adaptional program', *Proceedings of the Royal Society of London*, **B 205**, 581–98.

Grossman, G.M. and E. Helpman (1991), *Innovation and Growth in the Global Economy*, Cambridge, MA: MIT Press.

Hayek, F.A. (1973), *Law, Legislation and Liberty*, London: Routledge & Kegan Paul, and Chicago: University of Chicago Press.

Hofstadter, D.R. (1979), *Gödel, Escher, Bach: An Eternal Golden Braid*, New York: Basic Books.
Hull, D.L. (1980), 'The units of evolution: a metaphysical essay', in U.J. Jensen and R. Harré (eds), *Studies in the Concept of Evolution*, Brighton: Harvester Press.
Kauffman, S.A. (1993), *The Origins of Order: Self-Organization and Selection in Evolution*, Oxford and New York: Oxford University Press.
Metcalfe, J.S. (1997), 'The strengths and weaknesses of modern evolutionary economics', presentation at 'Symposium on Evolutionary Economics as a Research Program', Stockholm School of Economics, Stockholm.
Monod, J. (1972), *Chance and Necessity*, London: Fontana.
Nelson, R.R. and S.G. Winter (1982), *An Evolutionary Theory of Economic Change*, Cambridge, MA: Harvard University Press.
North, D.C. (1990), *Institutions, Institutional Change and Economic Performance*, Cambridge: Cambridge University Press.
North D.C. and R.P. Thomas (1973), *The Rise of the Western World: A New Economic History*, Cambridge: Cambridge University Press.
Pelikan, P. (1987), 'The formation of incentive mechanisms in different economic systems', in S. Hedlund (ed.), *Incentives and Economic Systems*, London and Sydney: Croom Helm.
Pelikan, P. (1992), 'The dynamics of economic systems, or how to transform a failed socialist economy', *Journal of Evolutionary Economics*, **2**, 39–63; reprinted in H.J. Wagener (ed.) (1993), *On the Theory and Policy of Systemic Change*, Heidelberg: Physica-Verlag and New York: Springer-Verlag.
Pelikan, P. (1995), 'Competitions of socio-economic institutions: in search of the winners', in L. Gerken (ed.), *Competition Among Institutions*, London: Macmillan and New York: St Martin's Press.
Prigogine, I. and I. Stengers (1984), *Order out of Chaos*, New York: Bantam Books.
Romer, P.M. (1994), 'The origins of endogenous growth', *The Journal of Economic Perspectives*, **8** (winter), 3–22.
Schumpeter, J.A. (1942), *Capitalism, Socialism and Democracy*, New York, Harper & Row.
Shannon, C.E. and W. Weaver (1949), *The Mathematical Theory of Communication*, Urbana: University of Illinois Press.
Solow, R.M. (1956), 'A contribution to the theory of economic growth', *Quarterly Journal of Economics*, **70,** 65–94.
Theil, H. (1967), *Economics and Information Theory*, New York: American Elsevier and Amsterdam: North-Holland.
Witt, U. (1999), 'Bioeconomics as economics from a Darwinian perspective', *Journal of Bioeconomics*, **1**, 19–34.

Commentary: the origins of successful economic organizations – a Darwinian explanation with room for self-organizing

Bryan Morgan

INTRODUCTION

Processes involving innovations and selection lie at the heart of both biological and socioeconomic systems. The question we are confronted with in Professor Pelikan's chapter is whether a Darwinian explanation of such processes is appropriate to economic theories. I found the chapter to be very stimulating and, while there is much I agree with, in this response I will focus on the Darwinian mode of explanation and argue that it places unnecessary constraints on the development of economic theory.

Pelikan's chapter inquires into the origin of successful economic organizations, which are defined very broadly. Central to the Darwinian perspective developed in the chapter is the notion of organizing information or 'o-information'. O-information guides economic agents towards certain organizations rather than others and understanding the origins of o-information helps us understand the origins of successful economic organizations. Pelikan posits that o-information is stored in institutions, defined as 'rules of the game'. O-information has two sources, Darwinian trial-and-error search, and self-organizing which occurs when agents supply some of the required o-information themselves. The policy objective of this line of research is to develop theoretical knowledge that reduces the requirement for Darwinian search in acquiring o-information, thus reducing the losses from Darwinian errors in economic evolution. Pelikan describes this approach as 'enlightened constructivism', a middle path between the 'naive constructivism' of socialist planners and the 'pure spontaneism' associated with F.A. Hayek. Two types of evolution are identified. Hayekian–Northian (H–N) evolution involves the evolution of the institutions of national and supranational economies. Schumpeterian–Alchian (S–A) evolution pertains to the evolution of internal institutions of firms and agencies within each economy.

My response will consider some of the ways in which a 'Darwinian' mode of explanation limits our understanding of the two types of evolution identified in Pelikan's chapter. In the following section, I will look at the relationships between human intentionality and different forms of organization. The third section looks at how the general Darwinian search limits our understanding of socio-economic innovations and selection processes. In the final section I will outline some ideas for a non-Darwinian explanation.

DARWINIAN EXPLANATIONS, INTENTIONALITY AND ORGANIZATIONS

The central core of a Darwinian approach is the expulsion of the notion of deliberate action on the part of the unit of selection (Khalil, 1996). The units of selection in Professor Pelikan's chapter are pieces of o-information stored in Darwinian memories. However the expulsion of deliberative action extends beyond the units of selection. Professor Pelikan notes that, while the behaviour of many organizations including humans can be described as pursuing objectives, in the Darwinian perspective this is only a linguistic convenience.[1] The descriptive use of objectives only requires the presence of some self-regulatory feedback mechanism and applies equally well to individuals or organizations.

The problem with a position that puts the mechanistic, goal-oriented workings of a thermostat on a similar footing to purposeful human behaviour is that it ignores human self-reflexivity and consciousness of the goal itself (Hodgson, 1999). Ludwig Lachmann (1986, p. 49) notes:

> Phenomena of human action, unlike phenomena of nature, are manifestations of the human mind. Action has meaning to the agent. We are unable to understand phenomena of human action otherwise than as outward manifestations of human plans which exist before action is taken and which subsequently guide all action.

An important implication of the rejection of the notion of purposeful action is that Hayek's (1973) distinction between two forms of organization or order, *taxis* (made order) and *cosmos* (spontaneous order), is also rejected. The significance of the distinction between the two types of organization is reflected in the two types of evolution distinguished by Pelikan, H–N evolution and S–A evolution. Pelikan's starting point for distinguishing these two types of evolution is to consider two different levels of the socioeconomic system, but clearly the two types of evolution belong to two forms of organization, closely corresponding to *cosmos* and *taxis*. Intentionality is one of the things that differentiates spontaneous orders from made orders (Hayek, 1973).

Khalil (1996) points out some shortcomings in Hayek's (1973) dichotomy of orders which are pertinent to one of the questions addressed in this chapter: are humans able to produce and use knowledge relevant to forming successful organizations? Khalil (1996) proposes a trichotomy of orders by distinguishing two dimensions: intentionality and design. The acts that give rise to a form of social order may be intentional or non-intentional and the outcome itself, the social order, may be a design outcome or a non-design outcome. The three forms of organization or order identified by Khalil are *artificial order*, in which design outcomes match intentions; *structure order*, characterized by non-design outcomes and non-intention, and where there is no planner; and *organizational order*, characterized by non-design outcomes arising from intention. It is organizational order that is missing from Hayek's schema.

Khalil (1996) identifies artefacts such as watches with artificial order, firms and society with organizational order and markets with structure order. 'The trichotomy leads one to avoid lumping firms with artefacts, on one hand, and to escape confusing liberal polity with unhindered market forces, on the other' (ibid., p. 191). However, we should also recognize that the dimension of design is a continuum rather than two discrete categories. Some forms of organization arising from intention, for example army units, have a very high order of design outcome, while other forms, for example, as Khalil suggests, the liberal polity, have non-design outcomes.

Applying Khalil's (1996) trichotomy, H–N evolution incorporates two forms of order: organizational order (liberal polity) and structure order (market systems). In other words, some forms of H–N evolution are the result of intentional acts, others are not. Firms and agencies associated with S–A evolution lie on the continuum between organizational order and artificial order. Understanding the limits of 'enlightened constructivism' must entail, at least in part, understanding the nature of different forms of organization and the relationships between intentionality and design outcomes in those different forms.

Khalil's critique of Hayek's treatment of deliberative groups in spontaneous order provides an insight into the way theoretical research can contribute to relevant knowledge about H–N evolution. The type of knowledge that can be useful in policy formulation relates to organizational order, that is forms of organization that are *ex post* non-designed but none the less *ex ante* intended (Khalil, 1996). An important task of research in this area is to distinguish those forms of H–N evolution which belong to organizational order from those which belong to structure order.

One of the problems of adopting a Darwinian explanation such as that proposed by Pelikan is that it has no place for intentional behaviour. But human intentionality is central to understanding the differences between H–N evolution and S–A evolution and the associated forms of organization.

DARWINIAN SEARCHES, KNOWLEDGE AND SELECTION PROCESSES

'Darwinian searches' play a central role in the Darwinian explanation proposed by Pelikan. A 'general Darwinian search' involves the following:

- some source of random messages comparable to lotteries, needed to produce tentative variants in o-information;
- some memory or memories needed to store the variants;
- some tests needed to determine which of the variants are successful.

The three elements are generalizations of the biological Darwinian search which involves genetic variety, replication and natural selection. O-information can either be found through general Darwinian searches or it is supplied by the constituent agents themselves. The notion I will question here is the 'general Darwinian search'.

Socioeconomic evolution involves processes of innovation and processes of competitive selection, but are these processes a priori analogous to biological evolution where innovations are randomly generated and the selection processes are non-teleological? The frequent characterisation of socioeconomic evolution as Lamarckian rather than Darwinian suggests that it is not the case.

As outlined in the previous section, when human intentions are considered, there are several ways in which innovations give rise to new forms of economic organizations and, as Pelikan discusses, competitive selection takes place at a number of different levels in socioeconomic systems. A problem with applying the concept of a general Darwinian search to socioeconomic analysis is that it amalgamates the processes of innovation and competitive selection and treats innovation as the generation of random signals rather than the creation of knowledge. A better understanding of the system can be gained by considering innovation processes and competitive selection processes separately.

Innovation processes involve the creation of information and knowledge. However, the formulation of the Darwinian search as random trial-and-error search leads to information being defined in terms of Shannon and Weaver's (1949) information theory and variants in o-information being treated as random messages analogous to random genetic mutation. The role of knowledge in the Darwinian explanation and how it is defined are left unstated, although knowledge is central to both developing the explanation and subsequently realizing the policy objectives.[2]

The central role of knowledge in socioeconomic evolution is something identified by Thorstein Veblen a century ago:

> For the purpose of economic science the process of cumulative change that is to be accounted for is the sequence of change in the methods of doing things, – the methods of dealing with the material means of life. ... The physical properties of the materials accessible to man are constants: it is the human agent that changes, – his insights and his appreciation of what these things can be used for is what develops. (Veblen, 1898, pp. 70-71)

H–N evolution and S–A evolution involve the evolution of forms of knowledge, namely the 'rules of the game'. As Pelikan notes, an understanding of the nature of the two types of evolution and consequently the types of institutions is a prerequisite for understanding the origins of successful economic organizations. This is where Hayek (1973) provides some very useful insights, if it is accepted that there is a similarity between institutions, defined here as rules of the game, and Hayek's behavioural rules. Although the dichotomy of *cosmos* and *taxis* has its problems, Hayek's discussion of the differences between the types of rules that give rise to *cosmos* and the types of rules that give rise to *taxis* is very useful for understanding the relationships between H–N institutions, S–A institutions and the forms of organization with which each is associated. Unfortunately, space does not allow a more detailed discussion of this issue.

The emphasis on o-information as random messages rather than as knowledge creation leads to the conclusion that it is more difficult to produce relevant theoretical knowledge about S–A evolution than about H–N evolution. We may conclude that the relevant knowledge is of different kind rather than harder to produce if we consider the five forms of innovation identified by Schumpeter (1934): new consumer goods, new methods of production and of transportation, new markets and new forms of industrial organization. A successful firm, that is one which is long lived and grows in size, must be adept at most if not all of these forms of innovation. The production of relevant theoretical knowledge involves disciplines such as marketing, management and organizational psychology. The growth of these disciplines in recent decades suggests that the production of relevant knowledge, and the bureaucratization of entrepreneurial functions as suggested by Schumpeter, are taking place.

Pelikan discusses the multiple levels of testing in socioeconomic systems. We can see that the competitive selection of innovations identified by Schumpeter (1934) takes place at different levels and in different ways. For example, the final testing of products and firms themselves takes place in the arena of H–N institutions. Other purposeful selection processes are carried out within firms.

The outcomes of competitive selection processes are not known in advance. This is a point emphasized by Hayek (1978, p. 180); competition is a discovery procedure which 'is valuable *only* because, and so far as, its results are unpredictable and on the whole different from those which anyone has, or could have, deliberately aimed for'. However, it does not necessarily follow that competitive selection is a random trial-and-error search or that nothing useful can be said about the outcomes of selection processes. For example, Metcalfe's (1998) insightful analysis of competition at the level of the firm using replicator dynamics goes a long way to explaining why only a small number of firms are considered very successful.

CONCLUDING COMMENTS

Charles Darwin's big idea was natural selection. The modern neo-Darwinian synthesis developed from Darwin's theory incorporates two propositions that are almost universally accepted: genetic variations are randomly generated and natural selection is a non-teleological process. Can we build a useful socioeconomic theory on these foundations? This is where Pelikan and I have different views.

However, a proposition on which I do agree with him is that we can gain a better understanding of economic organizations by bringing together insights from Hayek and Schumpeter. I also wholeheartedly agree that we can do this by examining different forms of organization and the behavioural rules that give rise to them (institutions), innovation processes and processes of competitive selection.

An alternative interpretation of self-organization, one that does not rely on a biological analogy, may supply a way of linking the insights provided by Schumpeter, Hayek and others and so assist in the development of a theory of *socioeconomic* evolution. This interpretation of self-organization comes from complexity theory, and I think is related to the idea of organizational equilibrium discussed by Pelikan in the section 'Darwinian Trial-and-error Search' of his chapter.

According to complexity theorists such as Holland (1995) and Kauffman (1995), biological evolution is a particular example of the general principle of self-organization. Complexity theorists seek to uncover general principles of evolution rather than to generalize biological, that is Darwinian, theories of evolution. Holland (1995) considers socioeconomic systems to belong to a class of system he calls 'complex adaptive systems'. Complex adaptive systems, like other self-organizing systems, arise when rule-based interactions by agents at a microscopic level result in emergent features at a macroscopic level. What distinguishes complex adaptive systems from other forms of self-organization is that the rules governing interaction between microscopic agents can change over time and thus the system can evolve.

A feature that complex adaptive systems have in common with both Hayek's spontaneous order and Pelikan's explanation is rule-based interactions leading to higher-level organization. What is missing from both spontaneous order and the general Darwinian search is an explicit and prominent place for human intentionality. While the self-organization literature is, as Pelikan notes, not as developed as neo-Darwinian theories in biology, it is a framework that does not exclude intentionality. What is required is to develop theories of innovation and competitive selection that have explicitly socio-economic characteristics within such a general framework.

NOTES

1. Hodgson (1999) examines Darwinism and causality in economics. He distinguishes between reductive causal monism and emergent causal monism. Proponents of the former hold that the distinction between intentional and unintentional behaviour is an illusion or, alternatively, that intention can be readily explained in terms of unintended materialistic causes. Proponents of emergent causal monism regard intentions as emergent properties of the complex workings of materialist causes within the human nervous system. Intentions involve conscious prefiguration and self-reflexive reasoning with regard to future events or outcomes. Hodgson lists Charles Darwin as a prominent proponent of emergent causal monism.
2. Lachmann (1986, p. 49) provides useful definitions of information and knowledge. Information is the tradeable material embodiment of a flow of messages, while knowledge is a compound of thoughts an individual is able to call upon in preparing and planning action at any given time.

REFERENCES

Hayek, F.A. (1973), *Law, Legislation and Liberty: Volume 1, Rules and Order*, London: Routledge & Kegan Paul.

Hayek, F.A. (1978), *New Studies in Philosophy, Politics, Economics and the History of Ideas*, London and Henley: Routledge & Kegan Paul.

Hodgson, G.M. (1999), '*Darwin, Veblen and the Problem of Causality in Economics*', symposium on 'Darwinian Evolution Across the Disciplines', Dartmouth College, New Hampshire, USA.

Holland, J.H. (1995), *Hidden Order: How Adaption Builds Complexity*, Reading, MA: Helix Books.

Kauffman, S. (1995), *At Home in the Universe: The Search for Laws of Self-Organization and Complexity*, New York: Oxford University Press.

Khalil, E.L. (1996), 'Friedrich Hayek's Darwinian Theory of Evolution of Institutions: Two Problems', *Australian Economic Papers*, **35**, June, 183–201.

Lachmann, L.W. (1986), *The Market as an Economic Process*, London and New York: Basil Blackwell.

Metcalfe, J.S. (1998), *Evolutionary Economics and Creative Destruction*, London and New York: Routledge.

Schumpeter, J.A. (1934), *The Theory of Economic Development*, Cambridge, MA: Harvard University Press.
Shannon, C.E. and W. Weaver (1949), *The Mathematical Theory of Communications*, Urbana: University of Illinois Press.
Veblen, T. (1898), 'Why Is Economics Not An Evolutionary Science?', reprinted (1969) in *Veblen on Marx, Race, Science and Economics*, New York: Capricorn Books.

6. History-friendly theories in economics: reconciling universality and context in evolutionary analysis

Kurt Dopfer

PRELIMINARIES

The objective of this chapter is to explore the analytical possibilities of an evolutionary interpretation of long-run economic change. The analysis starts from the recognition that longitudinal economic change is, by its very nature, historical and that this basic characteristic must be allowed for in the process of theory making. *In nuce*, we need universal principles that explain the historical nature of economic processes. This perspective is rare, but not new. In a similar effort, Malerba *et al.* (1997) explore the historical nature of technological development with 'history-friendly modelling'. In sympathy with their approach, I have used their term 'history-friendly' in the title of this chapter too. However, though we are travelling in the same boat there are some differences, the major one being that my approach is not restricted to a single evolutionary trajectory (such as that of the computer industry) but deals instead with developmental sequences of which the trajectories are 'local' elements.

The longer time span brings the historical character of economic processes, and the problems of making a theory about it, into sharp focus. An economic short-run phenomenon, such as the formation of market prices under given institutional or technological conditions, can be analysed without bothering much about historical change; the conditions are kept constant. It has been considered to be a major achievement of neoclassical theorizing that its propositions, for instance optimization or constrained maximization, are universal. We contend that evolutionary theorizing can claim an analogous universality. Specifically, we will distinguish between three universal analytical categories: process regime, regime transition and developmental sequence of process regimes. The critical issue is how these universal categories relate to the historical nature of economic phenomena: does a developmental process repeat itself at a later date or in another space? To address this problem, we must define the concept of historical context analytically, and show how it relates to the notion of universal explanatory categories that address the issue of economic change.

It would be difficult to win the argument that the research pursued in this paper belongs to the mainstream of evolutionary economics. It certainly does not. On the one hand, emphasis in the current debate is on short- and medium-run issues that have, in a developmental perspective, a local character. For instance, there is a growing body of literature about the diffusion of technologies, selection processes, path dependence, critical masses and so forth – research areas that can be accommodated under the local umbrella of a process regime. An analysis that goes beyond the local 'time slices' is bound to make statements about the developmental succession of local events. The preoccupation with local issues falls short of bringing the 'whole' history into economic analysis.

We suggest that evolutionary analysis is not 'history friendly' if it employs evolutionary principles without referring to context. One way of supporting an ahistoric approach is to argue that only local issues are amenable to theoretical analysis. Evolutionary economists of this brand join the neoclassical chorus arguing that 'in the long run we are all historians'. The tenet of this chapter is that we can, and should, make theoretical statements about the historical nature of long-run economic change, without turning to historical laws or to the history department.

Another strand in evolutionary economics deals with historical features of economic processes in a formal–analytic way. A prominent candidate is chaos theory and analogous approaches that feature non-linearity. We do not object to the universality of the analytical categories applied: this is evident from our premises. However, it makes a difference whether or not universal principles are embedded in an analysis that allows for historical context. I would object to the notion of universality without context.

As many readers may be aware, there is a language deficiency in the current debate in evolutionary economics. Various 'dominant themes' have made their appearance in the theoretical discourse. They employ their language, follow particular research intentions and accept early closures within evolutionary subparadigms. It has therefore from time to time been suggested that the various approaches should be better integrated. However, researchers specializing in their fields usually shy away if an 'integrated' approach is suggested. If they accept it at all, 'specialists' are often prone to making it clear that some crucial detail is ill conceived or missing, and that, therefore, the entire approach is flawed. The *pars pro toto* fallacy is a powerful research device for demonstrating the significance of the narrow confines of a research field. The theoretical discourse produces a chorus with many distinct voices of soloists who show little willingness to orient their performance towards an orchestrated theme. There is, generally, a communication problem between researchers who specialize and those who take up the issue of integrating the disciplinary parts.

THEORIZING ABOUT THE HISTORICAL NATURE OF ECONOMIC PHENOMENA: THE HISTONOMIC APPROACH

The term 'historical' in theoretical analysis does not refer to the particular, the space–time unique event that is explored in its totality; it refers instead to historicity in a sense that recognizes the fundamental historical character inherent in economic phenomena. The distinction is thus not one between history and theory, but rather one between ahistorical theory and historical theory.

Changes of real phenomena over time can be analysed on the basis of the concept of a trajectory. It distinguishes between (a) initial and boundary conditions and (b) a theoretical assertion about the behaviour of a composite of real phenomena for which (a) is relevant. If we have information about (a) and (b), singular phenomena or events can be explained or predicted. The validity of (b) relates to (c) a temporal and (d) a spatial dimension. Depending on the assumptions made with regard to (c) and (d), we get various types of theories. Generally, we get the distinction between a theory type that assumes that theoretical statements are universally valid, and one that rejects the universality assumption and suggests that theoretical statements are confined in their validity to a specific space–time dimension.

The former is well known from methodology discussions as the nomological or nomothetic approach, and is used in classical mechanics as well as in mainstream economics. Its dominance may be demonstrated by referring to the fact that we lack even a term for the second approach to theory making. It is, however, the second methodological route to theory formation that is relevant for evolutionary economics (Herrmann-Pillath, 2001; Potts, 2000; Louçã, 1997). If we accept the idea that the issue is essentially one of making theoretical (nomic) statements about the historicity of economic phenomena, we can call that approach 'histonomic' (Dopfer, 1986; Foster, 1994). This terminology helps us to avoid misinterpretations when using the term 'historical', as in 'historical economics' or its econometric neologism 'cliometry'. The research programme of a histonomic approach is inspired by the idea that it is essential for us to state the necessary and the sufficient conditions of the irreversibility and non-repeatability of economic processes in an explicit manner.

The nomologic and histonomic approaches differ in the assumptions they make about the initial and boundary conditions and about the variancy or invariancy defined by (c) and (d). The nomological approach treats the antecedent conditions exogenously, and their application in the context of a theoretical argument is arbitrary. By contrast, a histonomic approach combines the conceptual elements of the initial and boundary conditions with the theoretical propositions about the events, and highlights their theoretical unity. The analysis rests methodologically on a fundamental circularity: economic events are dependent on initial and boundary conditions, that are, in turn, themselves influenced and shaped by those events. The contingency is not arbitrary but has a dynamic that must be recognized as endogenous to its historical nature. The process of theory formation cannot rely on a priori concepts of space and time, but instead must introduce a conceptual notion of historical time and historical space.

CONTEXT

The notions of historical time and historical space can be dealt with coherently by introducing the concept of context. The conceptual notion represents a composite of discrete space–time units, not a space–time continuum, as, for instance, in classical physics. Hence economic processes are viewed as occurring in many discrete space and discrete time contexts; they do not occur in homogeneous space or homogeneous time. (On this difference, see Potts, 2000.) Furthermore, we depart from the premise that discrete space–time contexts can, and often will, differ with respect to the values of essential variables. This, in fact, is an implication of making the analytical distinction in the first place.

It seems to be self-evident that in economics we accept the notion of context, but it is not. In neoclassical economics an event qualifies as being 'economic' because agents exhibit economic behaviours; for instance, they maximise their expected utility under constraints. Phenomena are hence not 'economic' because they belong to a context defined as economic, for instance, production or consumption. On the contrary, the rationality assumption and instrumental behaviour derived from it can be applied in all contexts, and it is this indiscriminate nature in relation to context that makes neoclassical theory universal. Its universality claim allows neoclassical theory to build bridges to other disciplines, such as sociology, and to produce hypotheses about marriage or suicide. More recently, the contextual scope has been extended to the animal kingdom, detecting economic behaviour in the behaviour of primates and bees. This research may result in surprises, but it provides little guidance when looking for theoretical propositions about cultural evolution or developmental sequences.

Once we take up the quest for a historical theory, we must accept the notion of context. Following Alice's advice to begin with the beginning, we refer to the spatial dimension of context. Generally, space is where people live. Climate, topography, distance and ecological conditions can be introduced as criteria to give the notion of context economic meaning. Arable land, drinking water, minerals and fossil energy supply represent some of the strategic economic variables. The classicals, particularly David Ricardo, employed a long-run production function with the marginal productivity of arable land as the limiting factor. From a present-day perspective, spatial context embraces the broader notions of a 'limiting production function' and a 'limiting consumption function'. Though the limiting entropic aspect of space critically determines the speed of, and differences in, global economic development, our enquiry will not proceed along this line, but will take up the second major variable that is considered to generate and sustain economic development – information and knowledge.

In this perspective, the concept of spatial context changes its clothes and takes on the appearance of cultural space. Contextual boundaries and distinctions therefore refer to cultural characteristics rather than topographic, climatic and ecological. The broad delineation of the concept invites various specifications. We suggest two criteria for determining the boundaries and differences of the spatial contexts conceived in this way.

A first criterion covers factors that refer to politicoeconomic governance and authority (Matzner and Bhaduri, 1998). Spatial context refers to nation states, state confederations or geopolitical regions. A systemic view can be employed which defines cultural context in terms of a societal or a politicoeconomic system. The systemic view emphasizes the boundaries and systemic interdependencies of a context. The concept of context is, in itself, context bound, and it has been shown that the cultural advances in its interpretation have coevolved with the scientific advances in political economy (Tribe; 1999, Ötsch, 1998). As an immediate consequence of this, we recognize that our concept of spatial context may be quite different from the one used a hundred years from now.

A second perspective brings developmental characteristics into the picture. The developmental view complements the systemic view. Systems can accordingly be seen as 'carriers' of development and, depending on the system referred to, we will speak of, for instance, economic, political or technological development. Boundaries and distinctions in the spatial context can be stated in terms of developmental variables and can be specified empirically on the basis of socioeconomic indicators, such as GNP, net national product or welfare index (NNP), or the Human Development Index of the United Nations Development Programme (UNDP). The division into contexts with different developmental characteristics will be of primary relevance for the present study. We shall propose that the developmental differences in contexts justify distinguishing between different genealogies of economic development.

There is a growing body of literature devoted to the analysis of national innovation systems (Nelson, 1993; Lundvall, 1998; Freeman, 1997; Andersen and Lundvall, 1988), national business systems (Whitley, 1996), national technological systems (Dosi *et al.*, 1988; Dosi and Cimoli, 1996), national systems of demand articulation (Gerybadze, 1999) or industrial districts (Becattini, 1990; Colli, 1999; Calafati, 1999; Mistri and Solari, 1999). The bimodal criteria suggested – allowing for both systemic and developmental distinctions when defining context – may provide a conceptual anchor and an elementary taxonomy for this work.

UNIVERSALITY IN EVOLUTIONARY ECONOMICS

The twin of space category is time. We relate time to the concept of process. We understand as process any physical actualization of generic information. A process refers to the inner nature of the mode of 'becoming' in time. We can distinguish between various time horizons, such as short-run, medium-run and long-run views. The essential point is that the differences in the duration of time result from differences in the nature of actual processes, such as economic, technological and institutional processes. The upshot is that an evolutionary approach does not accept the idea of an 'objective' external time but, on the contrary, it develops a notion of internal time from considering actual processes.

We distinguish between three analytical categories defined in terms of process, and thus in terms of internal time. The first type of process is captured by the analytical notion of process regime, R_j. It represents the smallest analytical process unit, the elementary 'time slice' of the evolutionary process. The Darwinian proposition of random mutation and selective retention is an example of a process regime. The Darwinian view employed in economics would analogously suggest thinking of a process regime in terms of the creation of novel generic information, its propagation in a selective environment and its retention in operational use. In economics, a process regime also has some Lamarckian features, whose recognition will prove significant later when dealing with intra- and intercontextual learning. Specifically, the Lamarckian notions of adaptation and intercontextual learning will provide analytical pillars for defining different development genealogies.

LOCAL UNIVERSALITY: EVOLUTIONARY REGIME

What gives an evolutionary regime its unity? First of all, its discrete nature suggests recognizing that the process has a beginning and an end. The process dynamics of a regime can therefore be described on the basis of three phases: origination, unfolding and termination of process. The process dynamics of a regime *R* can be stated as $r_1 \rightarrow r_2 \rightarrow r_3$, where *r* stands for a process phase of *R*. The arrows denote the temporal order of a regime process, the irreversibility of a process in real life. Organisms are born, live and die, and there is no way back. The ontogenetic metaphor has been used when dealing with the history of the growth of firms and businesses (Chandler, 1990; Foss, 2001; Mokyr, 1991).

In the following, however, the category of evolutionary regime has phylogenetics as its premise. The process dynamics of a regime applies to a species, and thus to a population, not to a single individual. This brings a whole range of macroscopic concepts, such as diffusion, selection and path dependence into the domain of enquiry. Approaches that deal with the phylogenetic characteristics of regime processes have been dealt with under the rubric of life cycle models. A life cycle applies in these models (perhaps somewhat misleadingly) not to the life of an individual but to that of a species. Dynamic regularities in macroscopic life cyles have been detected in the development of technologies, consumer products, and market shares of firms (Klepper, 1992; De Jong and Shepherd, 1986, *et al.*). What unifies ontogenetic approaches with phylogenetic approaches is a universal pattern that can be captured in the shape of a logistic curve.

A major research field in evolutionary economics deals with the issue of regularities in the process dynamics of a regime. The logistic curve represents a quantitative account of the observable 'surface structure' and invites further explorations into the nature of the 'deep structure' that makes for the regularities. An explanatory account (supplementing the descriptive one) may be provided by introducing various causal models. There is growing awareness in the current debate that breakthroughs in the discipline would require further enquiry into the specific causes of, say innovations, differential diffusion or circular reinforcing retention processes. The various partial causal models will provide an important element in the causal–explanatory account of the overall dynamics of an evolutionary regime.

At this juncture, we look for an approach that highlights the unity and leads in the direction of a coherent overall scheme that can serve as an umbrella for the various partial models. When they dig as deeply as that, in their abstractions evolutionary economists can rely on the process ontology developed by Pierce and Whitehead (Whitehead, 1978). We shall not attempt to offer here a representative picture of that approach, but a few essentials may be singled out and put coherently into perspective with a view to helping us develop the essential arguments on long-run issues of economic change. In this view, the world is composed of the constituencies of idea and matter–energy. The world being in a continual flux, ideas represent potentials that are actualized with matter and energy in time and space. The process phases previously introduced can be restated in ontological terms as a process of physical actualization of a regime potential, that is as $P(a_1) \rightarrow P(a_2) \rightarrow P(a_3)$, where P denotes a regime potential, for instance generic information about a technology, and a the actualization process, with 1, 2, 3 designating the phases. Ontological reasoning seems to be remote from a down-to-earth evolutionary enquiry, but it allows us to address in a reliable manner the aspect of unity characteristic of the analytical categories employed in such enquiries. An approach that allows ontological concepts to be linked with practical or instrumental concepts has been provided by Giovanni Dosi who distinguishes between a 'technological paradigm' and a 'technological trajectory' (Dosi, 1984). In an analogous vein, Nelson and Winter have introduced the concept of 'natural trajectory' which relates to the dominant general mode of solving a technological problem (Nelson and Winter, 1982). In an ontological sense, a paradigm represents a potential that is physically actualized as a trajectory in time and space. The conceptual notions can be extended to include other variables such as institutions, organizations or strategies. An institutional regime can thus be understood, for instance, as an institutional paradigm which unfolds as a trajectory that actualizes collective behaviours. The ontological and instrumental terminologies can be used interchangeably, depending on the demands of language and research communication.

A brief analytical exposition of the ontological abstractions is given in Figure 6.1. The horizontal line denotes the historical time in which a poten-

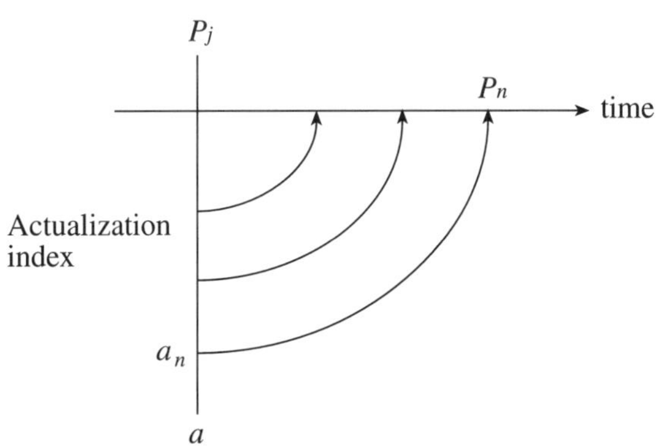

a = index of actualization $a_0, \ldots, a_n$
P = potential in historical time

Figure 6.1 Evolutionary regime: actualization of potential

tial P_j occurs. The vertical line, in turn, refers to an index of actualization of P_j in time. The index runs from zero, representing an unused potential, to a maximum where the adoption of a potential in a population is exhausted. Hence the historical nature of a potential is allowed for with respect to two time dimensions. A global dimension refers to the place of a potential in the history of the sequence of potentials (horizontal axis). The local dimension refers to the actualization process indicated by the curved arrows from the actualization index to the line of potential actualization.

The value of maximum actualization, represented by the index value a_n, is particularly interesting theoretically as it relates to values below the maximum, $a_k < a_n$. The classical economists provided an early explanation of regime process shown in this way by proposing that a technological innovation or analogous change leads to a temporary disequilibrium in the form of a surplus that is eroded under competitive conditions leading to a new equilibrium. The 'market price' converges to the technology governed 'natural price' that prevails in equilibrium. The classical economists did not specify the process but thought of it as a tendency for any process to gravitate eventually to the natural price. The introduction of an actualization index can be taken to mean that the rate of adoption of a novel variant correlates with competitive and other market behaviours. The quantitative index can serve as a common methodological denominator for diffusion, propagation or path dependence models. It is highly significant that the actualization index relates to a continuing process and not to a static configuration of the system. The vertical line in Figure 6.1 indicates that the actualization process stops at a_n, yet, as the horizontal line indicates, the potential P is still employed in the regime even though the adoption rate is zero. We have a 'recurrent equilibrium' which spreads out over time, and which may have a short or long duration. The process equilibrium can be given various theoretical interpretations. Schumpeter's concept of 'circular flow' and Veblen's 'circular causation' are theoretic applications of continuing adoption processes at an equilibrium $P_n\,(a_n)$.

ECONOMIC TRANSITIONS: NON-LINEAR AND GENERIC MODELS

A second universal analytical category used in a histonomic approach is regime transition, $R_{j-1} \rightarrow R_j$. The arrow denotes the transition process, and the question is how to give it a theoretical meaning. The significance of this category is intuitively clear and one may take it to be the *primus inter pares* of the fundamental analytical categories making up an evolutionary approach (Witt, 1997).

A simple approach is to see transition as a mechanical trajectory that is disturbed by some external force. If undisturbed, the trajectory takes course *A*, if disturbed it takes *B*. The 'transition' can be described on the basis of a nomological law which assumes that information about an external influence is given. Evolutionary economists are unlikely to accept the idea of transition as an exogenously disturbed mechanistic trajectory, and they may wish to take this model as a counter-heuristic to demonstrate what transition does not mean.

Another approach attempts to endogenize the mechanics that makes the path discontinuous. The bifurcation between *A* and *B* in this class of models is not generated by an external force but results from a specific mode of operation of the system itself. Although the non-linear models employed in this approach are still mechanistic–nomological, they differ from the linear ones in that they feature uncertainty and/or unpredictability. Non-linear dynamics has been employed to model transition phenomena in synergetics which introduce the ideas of potential function, phase transition and order parameter (Haken, 1978; on the relationship between feedback and 'feed forward' in economics, see Foster and Wild, 1994). Non-linear models with recursive equations using values in a specific range of discrete parameters have been used to depict chaos in time-series of economic magnitudes (Chen, 1993; Brunner, 1994). Another strand of non-linear modelling has dealt with transition probabilities that apply to changes in the behaviour of a population; non-linear master equations have been devised to determine the transition path (Weidlich, 1993). In physics, the concept of dissipative structure has revolutionized the entire ontological outlook since thermodynamics was linked to the generation of order – an anathema in classical mechanics (Prigogine, 1978). Recent developments in biophysics have been a source of paradigmatic inspiration, dividing the proponents into a group that claims that the concept of dissipative structures is universal (Prigogine, forthcoming) and one that recognizes its inherent limitations when dealing with complex biocultural phenomena (Brooks and Wiley, 1986). Joining the illuminating discourse, John Foster has interpreted the issue with regard to transition phenomena in economics (Foster, 1987 and forthcoming).

There is an alternative type of transition model that differs from the previous one in terms of ontological and methodological emphasis. In this view, transition goes from P_a to P_b, where *P* stands for generic information, specifically, *a*, *b*. Here, transition has a qualitative–generic nature. In the case of non-linear models, transition is conceived as a trajectory change that usually goes with a change in macroscopic structure. The models of non-linear dynamics share the feature that they relate to matter–energy, and not to ideas. From an epistemological viewpoint, a physical structure represents a 'constructed' idea (Glasersfeld, 1995), but the crucial point is that in these models ideas are not part of the theoretic story and thus cannot influence economic processes in a 'real' manner (Lawson, 1997).

We can contrast the quantitative–physical type of non-linear dynamics with the qualitative–generic type of evolutionary modelling. The approaches are, in my view, complementary rather than substitutionary, since the former brings the quantitative aspects of economic change into the picture and the latter the qualitative. The same rationale of complementarity applies when the relationship is considered in methodological terms. Methodologically, the quantitative–physical models feature a formal–descriptive analysis, while the qualitative–generic models rely more on a causal–explanatory approach. Recent studies of the non-linear dynamics of 'structural-breaks' have employed an 'integrated' approach which blends the formal–descriptive approach with the causal–explanatory approach (Lehmann-Waffenschmidt, 1997; Wagner, 1998).

What gives transition phenomena their qualitative–generic nature? The ontology introduced suggests investigating the causal nature of the constituencies of potential and actualization. A simple, but elementary, causal scheme results from doing this. First, transition can be seen as a process that is propelled by an 'autonomous' self-generation of potentials. Creativity, intentionality and epistemology are the stuff of which variables that relate to that process are made. Second, the process of actualization in time and space may itself have causal power with regard to the generation of potentials. The transition dynamics in this case is fuelled by the energy of an 'induced' self-generation. It follows from the ontological model that all existences are actualizations of potentials and that any monistic interpretation which deals with only one of the two constituencies would misstate the fundamental nature of economic phenomena. However, the ontological constituencies are causal powers in their own right. In the literature, both autonomous self-generation and induced self-generation have been taken up as theoretical concepts. The former has developed into research areas such as creativity analysis, cognitive science, and research and development, while the latter has taken up issues that deal with the impact that degenerating potentials, such as falling profit rates, exhaustion of the learning curve and growing selective pressures (Figure 6.1, actualization index *a*), have on the generation of innovation activities or on the renewed dynamics in general (Witt, 1993; Nelson, 1993).

HISTORY DEPENDENCE: FORWARD AND BACKWARD

It is conceivable that further theoretical progress will offer other interpretations, and this alone would suggest spelling out explicitly what makes the transition phenomena universal. We have argued that historicity is the all-pervasive feature of economic processes; thus the universal nature of transition will have to refer to its inherent historicity. The general proposition is that transition processes are history dependent. We are familiar with the notion of history dependence from path dependence models (David, 1985; Arthur *et al.*, 1994; Witt, forthcoming). However, path dependence models can be considered as a special case of a more general concept of history dependence. We distinguish between historical forward dependence and historical backward dependence.

In the Darwinian regime of mutation and selection mentioned earlier, mutation can, for instance, be viewed as a forward dependence in the system. At time t_0, the present, of the evolving process, there will be many generic variants resulting from mutation. The occurrence of mutation can be seen as the beginning of a new regime phase. However, the generic process itself, and hence its product, novel generic information, does not make the initial phase of the process universal since generic information may also be imported into the system from other contexts. Environmental contexts are, as Darwin had already recognized, rarely isolated and information can be transferred from one context to another. The initial phase takes on a Lamarckian flavour in that novel information is learned, not generated. The universality of forward dependence thus does not result from Darwinian mutation or Lamarckian learning, it results from the general availability of alternative variants at the initial time t_0 of the process. The specific provisioning that is instrumental for the first phase includes (a) self or auto-generic variants and (b) external or allo-generic variants. The universal concept of forward dependence accommodates both Darwinian and Lamarckian types of developmental genealogies.

Figure 6.2 may help to explain some of the features of the concept of historical forward dependence. The vertical axis shows the number of evolutionary bifurcations; more complex presentations would include a cascade of variants for each transition. The horizontal line represents the historical time axis, where t_0 stands for the present 'reality', t_{-1} for the past and t_1 for the future in which the transition process is historically embedded. The time asymmetry provides the domains in which backward and forward dependence become effective. Forward dependence means that at time t_0 we have the set of options P_1^1 and P_1^2; specifically, (a) system $P(t_0)$ has a range of future options open, and (b) a course of actual events is not arbitrary. This brings us back to the issue of how to model bifurcations or transition processes. Nonlinear models employ potential functions, master equations or phase transitions of synergetic and dissipative structures which fully (though unpredictably) determine a system at t_0. The pattern of bifurcations or transition thus does not relate to a historical context. Historical specificity does not explain a transition or developmental process 'causally'. The notions of forward and

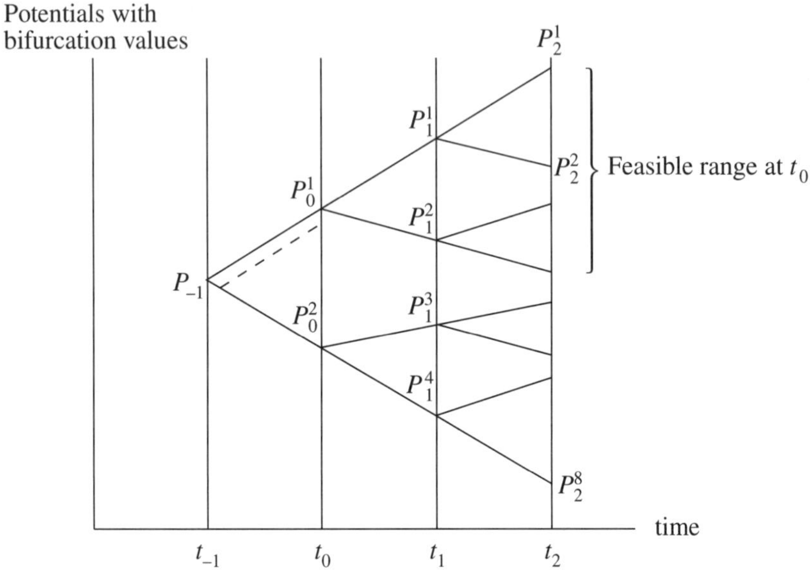

Figure 6.2 Transitions and the passage of time: historical dependence

backward dependence relate only to a formal–analytic pattern, not to a specific locus (other than *ad hoc*) of historical context.

A causal–generic approach leads to a different understanding of the historicity of the process. The production of novel generic information, such as Darwinian mutation, represents a break in time that clearly separates the past from the future. The present represents a state of the system in which novel generic information is revealed and henceforth available. A process regime has a distinct historical beginning. The range of bifurcations or cascade of variants define in the causal–generic approach informational potentials that offer historical opportunities at time t_0. The forward dependence is not given by the deterministic result of an equation whose time subscripts are labelled with positive natural numbers (indicating the future) but by a set of generic opportunities that are evolutionary open in terms of human intentions and boundedly rational choice of the agents facing the opportunity set. An evolutionary regime starts with a transition that is accomplished on the basis of self-generated or adopted generic information. It is a hallmark of a transition process thus interpreted that it operates with discontinuities which apply not only to critical mass phenomena or to changes from chaotic fluctuations, but also to the initial phase of the provisioning of generic variants.

There is, analogously, a backward dependence of transition processes. Since the system moves in time, decisions taken, and actions pursued, today are weaving the past of tomorrow. The argument can again be explained by referring to Figure 6.2. The figure shows an actual path that has occurred in the period t_{-1} to t_0, indicated by a dashed line going from P_{-1} to P_0^1. The actualized potential $P_0{}^1$ represents a lock-in of the system by historical backward dependence. At historical time t_{-1} a bifurcation was available which offered a set of historical opportunities, but this historical option was used up in the course of its historical actualization. Similarly, the opportunity set P_0^2, which would also allow the historical options P_1^3 and P_1^4, is now ruled out by way of backward dependence. The historical dependence on past events is independent of whether they have characteristics that derive from what is traditionally called path dependence. These models give an explicit account of processes in which individual adoptions are dependent on the frequency of previous decisions taken by other agents about some variant, and where the past thus feeds back in the form of an altered opportunity set for the remaining potential adopters. The backward dependence of conventional path dependence models is independent of the overall historical sequence of (possibly) antecedent path-dependent regimes.

BASIC DIACHRONICS: DEVELOPMENT SEQUENCE

The third analytical category refers to global evolution stated in terms of a sequence of evolutionary regimes R_j, or regime transitions, $\rightarrow R_{j-1} \rightarrow R_j \rightarrow R_{j+1} \rightarrow$, where the arrows again denote transition processes. It is likely that not all economists would agree that modelling transition processes is a worthwhile venture. They prefer to be silent about novelty generation, radical uncertainty, complexity or cross-contextual Lamarckian learning. Even fewer economists may be prepared to risk taking a step outside the confines of the second analytical category and embark on the exploration of the theoretical characteristics of the historical dynamics of a development sequence. However, the essential question once again is: is there any general sequential pattern that can be detected in long-run development, and what specifically accounts for the universality of such a pattern in time and space? Are we indeed all historians in the long run? The following discussion will suggest that we should object to the idea that economists who tackle long-run issues belong basically in the history department.

The proposition that the development sequence category is universal can be supported by referring again to the historical dependence of the process. The sequence can be viewed as a succession of regimes defined as transitions in which a historically specific backward and forward dependence is effective. The histonomic rationale that has been applied when analysing transition phenomena also applies to the global scope of a sequence of transitions. We propose that the duration of the path of discontinuous punctuations, or number of transitions, will be closely related to the historical lock-in associated with an actual developmental sequence. Figure 6.2 again allows us to clarify the issue. We have discussed the first transition previously, and now introduce the second transition shown by the line from P_1^1 to P_2^1 and P_2^2. The cumulated backward dependence of the forward historical actualization has led to a range of historical opportunities that exclude other ranges of historical options. The distance which encompasses the entire feasible and non-feasible ranges for P_0^1 is shown at t_2 with the boundary values P_2^1 and P_2^8. The domain of non-feasible development paths is a source of inspiration for models that feature counterfactual history and analogous conjectures.

We consider that the three analytical terms – process regime, regime transitions and regime sequence – represent universal categories of evolutionary economics. We contend, as mentioned, that they are comparable in terms of their universal status with analogous categories of neoclassical economics, such as constrained maximization. Our further contention is that universal evolutionary categories are essentially context bound. The contextual 'boundedness' of the analytical categories is, we recall, essential for it being possible to arrive at meaningful theoretical propositions about intrinsically historical phenomena. Before turning to these aspects, we shall look briefly at what determines the synchronic properties of universal context bound processes.

THE EVOLUTIONARY SYSTEM

A process regime is part of a whole. Adding the interconnected regimes gives them their unity as a system (Allen, 1994). Keeping the slowly changing variables of a system constant, the 'frozen' time allows us to look into the structure of the system. In an evolutionary perspective, synchronicity does not mean timelessness as, for instance, in static equilibrium theory; it refers to the recurrence of processes within a given historical regime. The systemic interconnectivity of process regimes thus represents a state of an economic system specified in terms of a composite of local evolutionary trajectories. Although the connectivities are governed by a systemic organization, they also represent interconnected processes which are actualized in time and space. The routines of a firm, for instance, represent a 'gene-pool' that is actualized as a structured composite of behavioural trajectories (Nelson and Winter, 1982), path-dependent interconnected 'technological systems' (Carlsson, 1997). In a similar vein, the dynamics of technology diffusion processes may be interlinked with network structures, Markov random fields or channel schemes (David and Foray, 1994; Antonelli, 1997).

The following analysis does not attempt to go more deeply into the synchronic issue. A main observation must suffice. Any theoretical account of economic evolution over time is linked to the notion of complexity defined by the connectivities of the entire economic system. The analyses conducted in terms of technological systems, industrial sectors, and so on are partial by assumption, and require further integration using an overall economic systems analysis.

We proceed to the diachronic areas of investigation 'as if' we understood the synchronic operation of the system and explore the dimensions of evolution 'as if' they were systemic wholes. The provisio, 'as if', is not a *ceteris paribus* clause designed to restrict further enquiry into the issue. On the contrary, it makes it explicit that the systemic analysis belongs to the core domain of the research agenda awaiting further exploration.

HAMLET AS A METHODOLOGIST: TO REPEAT OR NOT TO REPEAT

The ahistorical character of nomological theories is not described just by saying that the antecedents of the proposed 'laws' are valid. It is also related to the 'internal' nature of the phenomenon under investigation. Given the premise that the law holds universally, the implication that the 'representative' nature of the real phenomena does not change is also accepted. Methodologically, a set of single phenomena is seen as representing a class whose members are invariant entities. By contrast, the histonomic approach turns the ontological premises upside down by accepting that we live in a world of continual change. The notion of typology is thus alien to the evolutionary mode of thinking. Instead, the conceptual ideas of taxonomy, for instance evolutionary family trees or genealogies, in which the classes themselves are the very product of the historical process, are featured. A century ago, Thorstein Veblen proposed that economics should be a taxonomic science that defines the complex set of individual events within the conceptual confines of a descendence analysis using a genetic causality approach (Veblen, 1898). The suggested term 'histonomic' in its prefix 'histo' refers to the 'inner' nature of real phenomena, while the term 'nomic' addresses the theoretical (not historical) status of the statements about their change and their continuity.

The notion of time brings into focus the fundamental difference between a historical and a histonomic analysis. In a nutshell, the former refers to the past only, while the latter deals with the entirety of historical time comprising both time past and time future. A histonomic analysis centres on the issue whether or not the past and the future are symmetric. Historical analysis does not recognize the 'history of the future', and the issue of (a)symmetry is an anathema.

The differences among historical and ahistorical theories come into focus if we review some of the major strands of doctrinal history. The *Methodenstreit* of the German Historical School was not primarily fought against the Austrian neoclassicals of their time (as may appear retrospectively in orthodox thinking) but rather against the early classical economists of Anglo-Saxon origin. The historicals attempted to replace the 'empty' classical theories with ones that were based firmly on empirical or historical grounds (Ebner, 2000). Their basic tenet was that human history allows us to detect a universally valid law that depicts the development process as a unique sequence of successive stages. In our time, Walt W. Rostow has revived the 'historical spirit' and suggested that all societies pass through five stages which he called traditional society, preconditions for take-off into self-sustaining growth, take-off, drive to maturity and age of high mass consumption. 'These stages have an inner logic and continuity … they constitute, in the end, both a theory of economic growth and a more general, if still highly partial, theory about modern history as a whole' (Rostow, 1960).

The hypothetico-deductive approaches of modern growth theory share with (what may be called) the empirico-deductive approaches of historical stages the idea that development is basically a deterministic process. A process 'law', which resembles a trajectory in classical physics, allows us to predict the terminal state of a system once information about the initial conditions is known. A development strategy based on this model is effective if the political authorities succeed in meeting the necessary 'preconditions' for the sequence. The developmental sequence postulated is (under the assumed conditions) repeatable – expounding a law that holds over the whole of historical time and space. The model does not provide any systematic information about the possibility and probability of meeting the conditions, nor does it provide a theoretical rationale for conceivable changes in the developmental sequence (other than the reference to disturbances). The deterministic trajectory models – growth theory and stages theory – do not see development as a historically open evolving process.

An evolutionary alternative to the received theories of economic development and growth can be discussed on the basis of the analytic categories introduced. Rejecting *a priori* repeatability, an evolutionary approach has to take at face value the question of whether a development sequence describes a universal order that is repeated in all space–time contexts. We propose that a complete and coherent theoretical statement about the repeatability, or non-repeatability, of development sequences is possible if a few necessary and, as a whole sufficient, conditions are met:

- capacity to store generic information in a multi-systems context; public 'gene-pool', available as potential for development;
- capability of systems or populations to learn from one another; Lamarckian intersystemic and intergenerational knowledge transfer,
- available knowledge has impact on actual economic behaviour and actual development processes in general.

Accepting these quite 'mild' – necessary and, as a whole sufficient, – conditions, various types of developmental or growth genealogies can be distinguished.

GENEALOGY OF SUCCESSIVE SEQUENCE

A first genealogical approach views development as a sequence in which new regimes emerge gradually from old ones, and the genealogy of development can thus be described as a successive sequence (Ayres, 1997; Dopfer, 1979; coincidentally, both authors introduce the term). A necessary condition for a successive sequence to occur obeys a simple logic and argues that, for instance, the fire comes before the steam engine, the wheel before the mail coach, and that again before the railway; or, referring to our own times, post-Newtonian physics necessarily had to precede nuclear power, or Joe Shockley's invention of the transistor had to precede the PC. (On the technophysio evolution of the last three centuries, see Fogel, 1999.) The logic of historical succession can also be observed in single industries or technological sectors. Malerba *et al.* describe the pattern of technological change in the computer industry, suggesting that the introduction of technical innovations marks various distinct punctuations in the history of the industry. Specifically, the sequence of technological punctuations runs through four phases, from early experimentation and mainframe computers (phase 1), to integrated circuits and minicomputers (phase 2), to the PC made possible by the invention of the microprocessor (phase 3) and finally to the networked PCs and the use of the Internet (phase 4) (Malerba, *et al.*, 1997). The methodological significance of the technological history told by the authors makes it a clear example of 'appreciative theorizing' (Nelson and Winter, 1982; Nelson and Ostry, 1995). In an analogous vein, Paolo Saviotti has documented, referring to the technology of telegraphy, the evolutionary dynamics of increased differentiation and complexity in a single regime of a successive sequence (Saviotti, 1995).

What is the historical logic that is linked to this developmental dynamics? A generalization of the stories can be suggested as follows: there is a genealogy of development that typically follows a succession of events, where *A* necessarily occurs before *B*, *B* necessarily before *C*, and so on. Specifically, if, say, A_j comes before B_k we can say, *ex post*, that A_j was necessary for the actual emergence of an evolutionary regime B_k. However, we cannot say at time present that A will be necessary for B or that B is bound to follow necessarily from A. A prediction of a successive sequence is impossible since we do not know at time $A(t)$ *ex ante* (a) whether there will be inventions or novel ideas or what they will be like, (b) whether, and in what forms, innovations will appear, for instance, as B_l or B_k, and (c) whether innovations will survive selection and make it through the process of adaptation, and which of them will do so, and thus shape the subsequent phase in the development process.

General statements about the historicity of long-run economic change are possible in a definite way. A development regime A can be said to be necessary for a subsequent regime B to occur. The determination, however, cannot be stated *ex ante*; it is unpredictable owing to radical uncertainty in the face of novelty. In a nomological model, necessity and prediction are intrinsically linked. A law claims typically universal validity, and the analysis can reach at any time into both time past and time future, producing equally deterministic results. At time $B(t)$ the past sequence $A \rightarrow B$ can be derived uniquely from retrodiction, and analogously a future course $B \rightarrow C$ from prediction. In a histonomic view, the time of observation has a direct bearing on the statement about what makes the future and the past of a successive sequence. Time present (the 'real' time that refers to actual events) divides time into a historical past and a historical future. The time asymmetry derives from causal forces that can be given a rationale on the basis of evolutionary principles.

Methodologically, a theoretical statement about the past can rest on solid empirico-inductive foundations – only historians can change facts. A theoretical statement about the future deals with novelty and radical uncertainty, and it is not a factual–inductive account that guides the rationale of a forward-looking theory but, rather, imagination and creative anticipation. Retrodiction and prediction are in evolutionary economics horses of quite different colours. Novelty constitutes for a participant observer – the actual agent and the scientist – a surprise. The neo-Austrian subjectivists have long stressed this point and, coincidentally, modern information theory values information content more highly the more improbable an actual event is.

GENEALOGY OF SIMULTANEOUS SEQUENCE

Finally, the litmus test: does the successive sequence-type development repeat? Are we dealing here with a universal genealogy of development that applies in all contexts? We started from the premise that there are contextual differences, and we have proposed that these have a causal significance for the actual development paths. We propose that the genealogical pattern of a successive sequence does not repeat – naturally not in its own context, *X*, where it unfolds, but also not in another context, *Y*, which is a candidate for its repetition. The causal rationale in a nutshell: just because a successive sequence occurred in *X* it will not necessarily be followed in *Y*.

The non-repeatability proposition follows directly from the premises of contextual differences, knowledge transfer and historically late knowledge use. Figure 6.3 provides a bird's eye view of what happens in a *simultaneous sequence* type of development. The horizontal axis depicts the time of actual development. The present is denoted by t_0 and divides the past from the future. The past development course of the successive sequence is shown by the letters *R*, where the subscripts again represent various regimes. The development process is backward-dependent, in that it cannot be reversed in a sense that, at present time t_0, all options that were available at an earlier time could still be chosen. The successive sequence is locked in by the historical opportunities used up. The forward dependence of the development process is linked to the forerunner's capacity to generate and proliferate novel variants. The successive sequence cannot rely on informational spill-overs available from the overall context of which it is part. A forerunner country, or context, *X* is a public goods exporter, not an importer.

The situation appears to be quite different if we look at how the historical dependence operates in a latecomer country, or context, *Y*. The successive sequence becomes a compounded historical experience for context *Y*. In Fig-

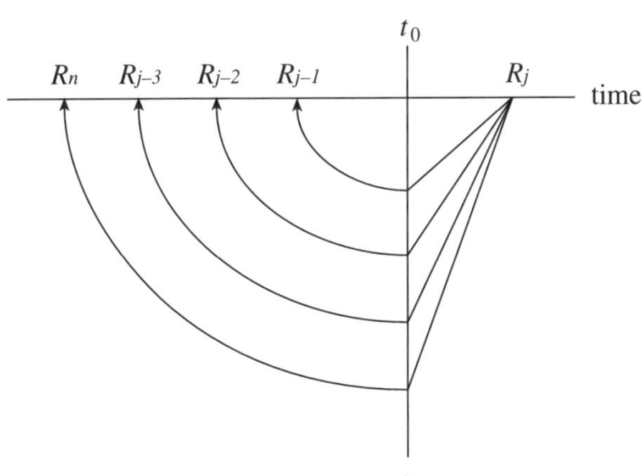

Figure 6.3 Simultaneous sequence: Lamarckian genealogy of economic development

ure 6.3, the vertical line represents the set of historical opportunities made available simultaneously at t_0 by the previous development process of the successive sequence. The various letters R represent pieces of historical experience that reveals itself in two dimensions. First, it relates to knowledge about potentials that enable, say, novel technologies, organizational routines, institutional arrangements or decision-making algorithms to be actualized. Second, the experience relates to the actual occurrence of a development process or the practice of actualizing generic information. The latecomer learns from what the forerunner has learned. Locally, a learning process is still a cognitive effort in terms of adapting to a new idea or generic information, but the latecomer can also enjoy a 'learning advantage' in terms of knowledge available from previous trial-and-error processes that were uncertain, risky and costly at the time.

An important aspect of generic learning thus conceived relates to the exhaustion of the actualization process as indicated in Figure 6.1. There is no inherent tendency for a given potential to go through the complete course of actualization up to the index value a_n. Particularly in a dynamic growing economy, novel variants will have an 'early entry' into the continuing process and will carry the system towards a new initial phase, possibly keeping it in a state of dynamic disequilibrium in the long run. A latecomer country has knowledge about this historical experience and thus benefits not only from the information about the generic potential itself, but also from its specific 'ontogenesis'.

At time t_0 the successive sequence type of development also has the entire stock of historical knowledge available, but it has had to build up its vintages over time. This process is well captured in recent contributions of endogenous growth theory and specifications made in the analysis of embodied technology (Silverberg and Verspagen, 1996; Romer, 1986, 1993; for a critique, see Philip, 1997). What makes the simultaneous type of development distinct is the simultaneous availability of historically accumulated knowledge at time t_0. In a successive sequence, simultaneity exists *ex post*, and the set of historical options has been consumed at t_0. In a context Y, the compound historical experience represents a set of unused historical opportunities. We have argued that the proliferation of historical opportunities as such, and not the mechanism that brings them into being, is what makes the origins of a development sequence universal. The conclusion corroborates our earlier conjecture that differences in contexts to which explanatory principles apply lead to different genealogies of development.

Nomological models, such as the stages theories mentioned, operate with the notion of preconditions. Once necessary initial conditions are met, the development trajectory is put into motion. The histonomic perspective emphasizes the self-generated dynamics stated in terms of the principle of historical dependence. The historical time when a latecomer enters a simultaneous sequence type of development makes a decisive difference. A country may be isolated, and this will yield a development sequence that differs essentially from one that opened up earlier when introducing the then simultaneously available set of historical opportunities. The dynamics of the historical opportunities can be visualized with a rightward shift of the (vertical) t_0 curve in Figure 6.3. The preconditions in the form of social and technological capacities are themselves generated in the emerging process and it is not a classification of preconditions that leads to an understanding of what is considered as the initial boundary conditions of economic development; it is an understanding of the implications of backward dependence.

CONCLUSIONS

The genealogies of the successive and simultaneous sequences start from specific premises with regard to differences in development contexts. Another group of models has been proposed that operate on the assumption of a single global context and focus on differences between forerunners and latecomers along the evolutionary trajectory of a single technology or single industry. Various studies have concentrated on the interactions of international technology gaps with international trade, particularly North–South trade (Cheng, 1984; Helpman, 1999). The dynamic interactions between technology gaps and international trade have been modelled along evolutionary lines by referring to factors of non-price competition and of firm routines, where they determine global investments and production decisions (Maggi, 1993). It is possible, and is by now a popular belief, that the whole world will become a single context with big firms as its global players, but we may ask whether this is necessarily so. The profoundest triviality of evolutionary economics is: we do not know what our future will be. From a 'northern' viewpoint, the notion of single technological or institutional trajectories that diffuse in a homogeneous global context seems reasonable. Irrespective of its positive theoretic validity, this serves the interests of large companies which belong by and large to the cultural context in which most of us, as scientists, live. The present proposal to distinguish between two major types of development genealogies should be seen as an additional research strand which should not be a substitute for, but rather be a complement of, the continuing efforts in the related research of evolutionary economics. Global technological trajectories may go through various countries with very different development levels and economic structures, but we would suggest that the overall historical dynamics of these cannot be grasped theoretically on the basis of those tendencies alone. Further advances in the presentation of development genealogies may provide not only a classificatory scheme, but also a causal framework that connects the single trajectory studies through their dynamic interactions, for instance, between international trade and differential technical progress.

As a minimum of analytical clarity, in the analysis of the differences that exist for the entry into development processes we can distinguish between whether it relates to a successive sequence or to a simultaneous sequence. We can think of the agents participating in a successive sequence either as first adopters or as second adopters, and accordingly, we can discuss first- and second-mover advantages and further extensions of this dynamic relationship. If we turn to the issue of entry into a development process in the context of a simultaneous sequence, we can talk instead of early adopters and late adopters. An early adopter may be able to participate in the race between first and second adopters (the rankings may change during the race). A late adopter, who will be confronted by possibly insurmountable development differences, is likely to be out of the race from the very beginning. The 'homogeneous model' of global technological and related trajectories therefore cannot cover the entire development dynamics – the 'heterogeneous model' can.

REFERENCES

Allen, P.M. (1994), 'Evolutionary Complex Systems: Models of Technology Change', in L. Leydesdorff and P. Van den Besselaar (eds), *Evolutionary Economics and Chaos Theory: New Directions in Technology Studies*, London: Pinter.

Andersen, E.S. and B.A. Lundvall (1988), 'Small National Systems of Innovation Facing Technological Revolutions: An Analytical Framework', in C. Freeman and B.A. Lundvall (eds), *Small Countries Facing the Technological Revolution*, London: Pinter.

Antonelli, C. (1997), 'The economics of path-dependence in industrial organization', *International Journal of Industrial Organization*, **15**, 643–75.

Arthur, W.B., J.M. Ermoliev and J.M. Kaniovski (1994), 'Path Dependent Processes and the Emergence of Macro-Structure', in W.B. Arthur (ed.), *Increasing Returns and Path Dependence in the Economy*, Ann Arbor: University of Michigan Press.

Ayres, R.U. (1997), 'The Kuznets curve and the life cycle analogy', *Structural Change and Economic Dynamics*, **8**, 413–26.

Becattini, G. (1990), 'The Marshallian Industrial District as a Socio-economic Notion', in F. Pyke, G. Becattini and W. Sengenberger (eds), *Industrial districts and inter-firm co-operation in Italy*, Geneva: International Institute for Labour Studies.

Brooks, D.R. and E.O. Wiley (1986), *Evolution and Entropy: Toward a Unified Theory of Biology*, Chicago: University of Chicago Press.

Brunner, H.P. (1994), 'Technological Diversity, Random Selection in a Population of Firms, and Technological Institutions of Government', in L. Leydesdorff and P.

Van den Besselaar (eds), *Evolutionary Economics and Chaos Theory: New Directions in Technology Studies*, London: Pinter.
Calafati, A. (1999), 'On Industrial Districts', discussion paper for workshop on 'The Evolution of Industrial Districts', September, Jena: Max-Planck-Institute.
Cantner, U. and H. Hanusch (1991), 'New Developments in the Economics of Technology and Innovation', Volkswirtschaftliche Diskussionsreihe, No. 64, Institut für Volkswirtschaftslehre der Universität Augsburg.
Carlsson, B. (1997), 'On and Off the Beaten Path: The Evolution of Four Technological Systems in Sweden', *International Journal of Industrial Organization*, **15**, 775–99.
Carlsson, B. and S. Jacobsson (1996), 'Technological Systems and Industrial Dynamics: Implications for Firms and Governments', in E. Helmstädter and M. Perlman (eds), *Behavioral Norms, Technological Progress and Economic Dynamics*, Ann Arbor: University of Michigan Press.
Chandler, A. (1990), *Scale and Scope*, Cambridge, MA: Harvard University Press.
Chen, P. (1993), 'Searching for Economic Chaos: A Challenge to Econometric Practice and Nonlinear Tests', in R. Day and P. Chen (eds), *Nonlinear Dynamics and Evolutionary Economics*, Oxford: Oxford University Press.
Cheng, L.K. (1984), 'International Competition in R & D and Technological Leadership: An Examination of the Posner–Hufbauer Hypothesis', *Journal of International Economics*, **17**, 17–40.
Coats, A.W. (1988), 'What Can We Accomplish with Historical Approaches in an Advanced Discipline such as Economics?', mimeo, London.
Coats, A.W. (1992), 'On the History of Economic Thought: British and American Economic Essays', **1**, London: Routledge.
Colli, A. (1999), 'Lessons from the History of Italian Industrial Districts', discussion paper at the Economic History Institute, Bocconi University, Milan.
Cunningham, W. (1892a), 'The relativity of economic doctrines', *Economic Journal*, **2**, 1–16.
Cunningham, W. (1892b), 'The Perversion of Economic History', *Economic Journal*, **2**, 491–506.
Dannreuther, C. and R. Lekhi (1999), 'Globalisation and the Political Economy of Risk', ISA Annual Conference.
David, P.A. (1985), 'Clio and the Economics of QWERTY', *American Economic Review*, **75**, 332–7.
David, P.A. and J.A. Bunn (1988), 'Gateway technologies and the evolutionary dynamics of network industries: lessons from electricity supply history', *Information Economics and Policy*, **3**, 165–202.
David, P.A. and D. Foray (1994), 'Percolation Structures, Markov Random Fields and the Economics of EDI Standard Diffusion', in G. Pogorel (ed.), *Global Telecommunications Strategies and Technological Changes*, Amsterdam: North-Holland.
Day, R.H. (1996), 'Macroeconomic Evolution: Long Run Development and Short Run Policy', *Papers on Economics and Evolution*, No. 9606, Max-Planck-Institut zur Erforschung von Wirtschaftssystemen, Jena.
De Jong, H.W. and W.G. Shepherd (eds) (1986), *Mainstreams in Industrial Organisation*, Dordrecht and Boston: Kluwer.
Delorme, R. and K. Dopfer (eds) (1994), *The Political Economy of Diversity: Evolutionary Perspectives on Economic Order and Disorder*, Aldershot, UK and Brookfield, US: Edward Elgar.

Dopfer, K. (1979), *The New Political Economy of Development: Integrated Theory and Asian Experience*, London and Basingstoke: Macmillan.
Dopfer, K. (1986), 'The histonomic approach to economics: beyond pure theory and pure experience', *Journal of Economic Issues*, **20**(4), 989–1010.
Dosi, G. (1984), *Technological Change and Industrial Transformation: The Theory and an Application to the Semi-Conductor Industry*, London: Macmillan.
Dosi, G. and M. Cimoli (1996), 'Technological Paradigms, Patterns of Learning and Development: An Introductory Roadmap', in K. Dopfer (ed.), *The Global Dimension of Economic Evolution: Knowledge Variety and Diffusion in Economic Growth and Development*, Heidelberg: Physica-Verlag.
Dosi, G., C. Freeman, R.R. Nelson, G. Silverberg and L. Soete (eds) (1988), *Technology and Economic Theory*, London: Pinter.
Ebner, A. (2000), 'Schumpeter and the "Schmoller program": Integrating Theory and History in the Analysis of Economic Development', *Journal of Evolutionary Economics*, **10**, 355–72.
Fogel, R.W. (1999), 'Catching Up with the Economy', Presidential Address delivered at the One-Hundred Eleventh Meeting of the American Economic Association, 4 January, New York.
Foss, N.J. (2001), 'Evolutionary Theories of the Firm: Reconstruction and Relations to Contractual Theories', in K. Dopfer (ed.), *Evolutionary Economics: Program and Scope*, Dordrecht: Kluwer.
Foster, J. (1987), *Evolutionary Macroeconomics*, London: Allen.
Foster, J. (1994), 'The Self-Organisation Approach in Economics', in P. Burley and J. Foster (eds), *Economics and Thermodynamics: New Perspectives on Economic Analysis, Recent Economic Thought Series*, Dordrecht and Boston: Kluwer.
Foster, J. (1997), 'The Analytical Foundations of Evolutionary Economics: From Biological Analogy to Economic Self-Organization', *Structural Change and Economic Dynamics*, **8**, 427–51.
Foster, J. (forthcoming), 'The Self-Organisational Perspective on Economic Processes: A Unifying Paradigm', in K. Dopfer (ed.), *The Evolutionary Foundations of Economics*, Cambridge: Cambridge University Press.
Foster, J. and P.H. Wild (1994), 'Self-organization and Synergetics in Economics – The Revitalization of Economic Science?', *Papers on Economics and Evolution*, 9402, ed. European Study Group for Evolutionary Economics.
Freeman, C. (1997), 'Innovation Systems: City-state, National, Continental and Subnational', mimeo, paper presented at the Montevideo conference, University of Sussex, SPRU.
Gerybadze, A. (1999), 'Nationale Innovationssysteme und nationale Systeme der Bedarsartikulierung', discussion paper, Universität Stuttgart Hohenheim.
Glasersfeld, E.V. (1995), *Radical Constructivism: A Way of Knowing and Learning*, London: Falmer Press.
Gordon, R.J. (1999), 'U.S. Economic Growth Since 1870: One Big Wave?', *American Economic Review*, **89**, 123–8.
Gowdy, J.M. (1992), 'Higher Selection Processes in Evolutionary Economic Change', *Journal of Evolutionary Economics*, **2**, 1–16.
Haken, H. (1978), *Synergetics: An Introduction*, Berlin: Springer.
Hanusch, H. (1988), *Evolutionary Economics: Applications of Schumpeter's Ideas*, Cambridge: Cambridge University Press.
Helmstädter, E. and M. Perlman (eds) (1996), *Behavioral Norms, Technological Progress and Economic Dynamics*, Ann Arbor: University of Michigan Press.

Helpman, E. (1999), 'The structure of foreign trade', *Journal of Economic Perspectives*, **13**(2), 121–44.
Herrmann-Pillath, C. (2001), 'On the Ontological Foundations of Evolutionary Economics', in K. Dopfer (ed.), *Evolutionary Economics: Program and Scope*, Dordrecht: Kluwer.
Hodgson, G.M. (1993), *Economics and Evolution: Bringing Life Back Into Economics*, Cambridge: Polity Press, Ann Arbor: Polity Press and University of Michigan Press.
Hodgson, G.M. (2000), 'Economics, History and General Thorey: Specificity in Social Science', draft.
Klepper, S. (1992), 'Entry, Exit, Growth, and Innovation over the Product Life Cycle: The Dynamics of First Mover Advantages, Declining Product Innovation and Market Failure', discussion paper, Carnegie Mellon University.
Lawson, T. (1997), *Economics and Reality*, London: Routledge.
Lehmann-Waffenschmidt, M. (1997), 'Strukturähnlichkeiten ökonomischer Prozesse im Zeitablauf', paper presented at the Jahrestagung des Ausschusses für Evolutorische Ökonomik im Verein für Socialpolitik, 3–5 July, Osnabrück.
Louçã, F. (1997), *Turbulence in Economics – An Evolutionary Appraisal of Cycles and Complexity in Historical Series*, Cheltenham, UK and Lyme, US: Edward Elgar.
Lundvall, B.A. (1998), 'Why study national systems and national styles of innovation?', *Technology Analysis and Strategic Management*, **10**(4), 407–21.
Maggi, G. (1993), 'Technology gap and international trade: an evolutionary model', *Journal of Evolutionary Economics*, **3**, 109–26.
Malerba, F., R. Nelson, L. Orsenigo, S. Winter and L. Giorcelli (1997), '"History Friendly" Models of Industry Evolution: The Case of the Computer Industry', *Industrial and Corporate Change*, **1**.
Matzner, E. and A. Bhaduri (1998), 'The socioeconomic context: an alternative approach to Popper's situtational analysis', *Philosophy of Social Sciences*, **28**(4).
Metcalfe, J.S. (1997), *Evolutionary Economics and Creative Destruction*, London: Routledge.
Mistri, M. and S. Solari (1999), 'Local Self-Organising Economic Processes: Industrial Districts and Liquidity Preference', discussion paper, University of Padua.
Mokyr, J. (1991), 'Evolutionary Biology, Technical Change and Economic History', *Bulletin of Economic Research*, **43**, 127–49.
Nelson, R.R. (ed.) (1993), *National Innovation Systems: A Comparative Analysis*, Oxford: Oxford University Press.
Nelson, R.R. and S. Ostry (1995), *Techno-Nationalism and Techno-Globalism: Conflict and Cooperation*, Washington, DC: Brookings Institution.
Nelson, R.R. and S.G. Winter (1982), *An Evolutionary Theory of Economic Change*, Cambridge, MA: Harvard University Press.
Nightingale, J. (1998), 'Jack Downie's Competitive Process: The First Articulated Population Ecological Model in Economics', *History of Political Economy*, **30**, 369–412.
Ötsch, W. (1998), 'Zur Geschichte und Zukunft von Grundkategorien des ökonomischen Denkens: Raum, Zeit, Objekt und Ich', *Arbeitspapier Nr. 9826*, Johannes Kepler Universität Linz.
Philip, V.P. (1997), 'Economic Growth: Evolutionary and Self-Organisation Perspectives on the Micro-Foundations of Knowledge and the Process of Technological Change', PhD thesis, University of Queensland.

Potts, J. (2000), *The New Evolutionary Microeconomics, Complexity, Competence and Adoptive Behaviour,* Cheltenham, UK and Northampton, MA, USA: Edward Elgar.
Prigogine, I. (1978), *From Being to Becoming*, New York: Freeman.
Prigogine, I. (forthcoming), 'The Rediscovery of Value and the Opening of Economics', in K. Dopfer (ed.), *The Evolutionary Foundations of Economics*, Cambridge: Cambridge University Press.
Romer, P.M. (1986), 'Increasing Returns and Long Run Growth', *Journal of Political Economy*, **94**, 1002–37.
Romer, P.M. (1993), 'Two Strategies for Economic Development: Using Ideas and Producing Ideas', *Proceedings of the World Bank Annual Conference of Development Economics, Supplement to the World Bank Economic Review*, March.
Rosenberg, N. (1976), *Perspectives on Technology*, Cambridge: Cambridge University Press.
Rostow, W.W. (1960), *The Stages of Economic Growth: A non-Communist Manifesto*, London: Cambridge University Press.
Saviotti, P. (1995), *Technological Evolution, Variety and the Economy*, Aldershot, UK and Brookfield, US: Edward Elgar.
Saviotti, P. (1997), 'Innovation Systems and Evolutionary Theory', in C. Edquist (ed.), *Systems of Innovation: Technologies, Institutions and Organizations*, London: Pinter.
Silverberg, G. and B. Verspagen (1996), 'An Evolutionary Model of Long Term Cyclical Variations of Catching Up and Falling Behind', in K. Dopfer (ed.), *The Global Dimension of Economic Evolution: Knowledge Variety and Diffusion in Economic Growth and Development*, Heidelberg: Physica-Verlag.
Stahl, S. (1999), 'Kulturelle Beschränkungen im Transformationsprozess: Eine sozialpsychologisch-kognitive Theorie institutionellen Wandels', dissertation: Universität Jena.
Tribe, K. (1999), 'Adam Smith: critical theorist?', *Journal of Economic Literature*, **37**, 609–32.
Veblen, T.B. (1898), 'Why is Economics not an Evolutionary Science?', *The Quarterly Journal of Economics*, **12**, 373–97; reprinted in T. Veblen (1990), *The Place of Science in Modern Civilisation and Other Essays*, New Brunswick: Transaction.
Wagner, A., (1998), 'Zur Transformation von Wirtschaftssystemen', RWI-Mitteilungen, **48**(1 & 2), 47–60.
Weidlich, W. (1993), 'The Master Equation Approach to Non-linear Economics', in U. Witt (ed.), *Evolution in Markets and Institutions*, Physica: Würzburg.
Whitehead, A.N. (1978), *Process and Reality: An Essay in Cosmology*, London: Macmillan.
Whitley, R. (1996), 'The Social Construction of Economic Actors: Institutions and Types of Firm in Europe and other Market Economies', in R. Whitley (ed.), *The Changing European Firm*, London: Routledge.
Witt, U. (1992), 'Evolutionary Concepts in Economics', *Eastern Economic Journal*, **18**, 405–19.
Witt, U. (1993), 'Emergence and Dissemination of Innovations', in R.H. Day and P. Chen (eds), *Nonlinear Dynamics and Evolutionary Economics*, Oxford: Oxford University Press.
Witt, U. (1997), 'Lock-in vs. "Critical Masses" – Industrial Change under Network Externalities', *International Journal of Industrial Organization*, **15**, 753–73.

Witt, U. (forthcoming), 'Path-dependence in Institutional Change', in K. Dopfer (ed.), *Evolutionary Foundations of Economics*, Cambridge: Cambridge University Press.

Commentary: history-friendly theories in economics – reconciling universality and context in evolutionary analysis

Jason Potts

INTRODUCTION

Professor Dopfer addresses the fundamentally important question of the proper relation between history and theory in economics. In the conventional view of things, history is the construction of 'localized stories' that depend upon some specific context, and theory is the construction of 'universal stories' that have no specific contextual reference. The type of storytelling engaged in, and the language used (for example, mathematical closure or prose narrative) are determined by the extent, scope and prevalence of event regularities; where these are identifiable, and suggestive of universality, the mode of storytelling is called theory. Historians, on the other hand, mostly reject the notion that there are 'laws of history' in the developmental (for example, Marxian) sense and sagely counsel initiates against the folly of ascribing such universality to their particulars. Neophyte economists, whose primary art will be model making, receive the opposite counsel: on the folly of being seduced by wanton particulars that do not conform to the sacred universalities. History and theory represent extrema of storytelling and are plainly dialectical constructs. It follows, then, that there must be a state of storytelling that is both history and theory at once. This, it seems to me, is what Dopfer means by the *histonomic* approach (see also Dopfer, 1986).

Heterodox economists seem mostly to accept, or at least claim to accept in principle, the Marshallian methodological dictum that a proper description of economic phenomena involves a melding of both history and theory that is irreducible to one or the other.[1] The difficulty of this task notwithstanding, Dopfer cautions that many of the self-styled evolutionary economists have nevertheless tended to neglect the primacy of historical context. Indeed, there seems to be much confusion about the meaning of an historic(al) approach, and the extent of its methodological demands. The histonomic approach requires a conceptual translation of 'history' towards a more abstract notion of 'context' in which dimensionality is permitted but continuity is not. In this way, context becomes an identification of *state*, and a changed context is due to a state transition. History is then read as a sequence of state transitions.

Dopfer defines the concept of a trajectory as the analytical object representing changes in real phenomena over time. He then distinguishes the nomological and histonomic approaches in terms of whether the antecedent conditions are, respectively, exogenous or endogenous. In doing so, Dopfer expressly abandons the 'analytical context' of the Newtonian space–time continuum and instates 'discrete space and discrete time contexts'. Still, it remains unclear what the essential nature of the new 'analytical context' actually is, for it seems to me that what the histonomic approach involves, manifest as emphasis on the specific spatial and temporal conditions/context, is more fundamentally an enquiry into the (temporal and spatial) *geometry* of an economic system. And if this is the correct interpretation, then the notion of context can be usefully interpreted as referring to a specific *geometry of economic space*. In turn, 'universality without context' is then an extreme state of the potential form of the geometry of economic space. The comments I wish to make relate to the implications of this geometric interpretation of the histonomic approach. As such, reconciling universality and context involves recognition of the existence of a complex and variable geometry of economic space. This centres the notion of a system (defining a state) and from that the notion of an adjacent state, which is the basic analytical unit of (histonomic) dynamics. Dopfer illustrates this with the notion of an evolutionary regime, but this concept of context has more general application.[2]

ON THE MEANING OF CONTEXT: HISTORY, ENVIRONMENT, FIELD

The notion of 'context' is pivotal to a histonomic approach, so let us first distinguish between several abstract notions of context, namely, *history*, *environment* and *field*.

History as context generally refers to a known set of chronologically ordered antecedent events (a sequence) leading to a singular event. The act of writing history is subjective in the sense not of the ascription of truth or otherwise to various events, but in the attribution of specific events as elements within a sequence, without which the final events would have been otherwise. The subjective element in the construction of context is the specification of causal connections (see Lawson, 1997, chs 9, 10; also Burke, 1998). Note that history, in this constructed sense, also entails the recognition of potentia as the possibility that events *could have been* otherwise. If one is attempting to find universals in historical sequence, then these relate not to the actualized events *per se*, but rather to the extent and definition of the potentia surrounding them. History implies temporal connectedness and ordering as sequence.

Environment as context refers to the contemporaneous value of other variables that affect an element, and implies a sense in which an element is connected to a set of other elements and as such embedded within a larger process.[3] Concepts of local boundedness, such as niche or industry for example, are derivatives of the notion of environment, recognizing that an environment can be partially decomposed into local systems.[4] Environment implies spatial connectedness and ordering as structure.

The concept of a regime or a trajectory is a synthesis of the concept of history and the concept of environment to create a spatiotemporal connectedness as an ordered structure. Dopfer argues that regimes or trajectories, as emergent systems, can themselves manifest dynamics that are amenable to theoretical capture.[5] I have elsewhere termed the ontological aspect of this theoretical property, in which a complex set of interactions effects a closure such that the system emerges as an element in a higher-level system, 'system–element duality' (Potts, 2000). A trajectory or regime is an institutional/technological/paradigmatic context that can be thought of as an 'element' in a broader histonomic theory of long-run economic growth.

It is important, I think, to be clear about why this approach is different from the (neoclassical) orthodoxy. In formal orthodox economic theory, context is defined with the meta-mathematical construct of a field (Mirowski 1989; Potts, 2000), which is a way of representing generalized interactions between each and every element within a system and thus defines the space as the field R^n. The field construct, which underpins all equilibrium analysis, entirely eliminates concern with individual interactions (Kirman, 1997) and, with that, all concern with specific event sequence, region of effect, locality and other such historical/environmental details. A field is an analytical context that effectively eliminates ontological context. The histonomic approach, as I interpret it, is diametrically opposed to the mathematical and conceptual use of the field construct as analytical context.

THE GEOMETRY OF ECONOMIC SPACE, ADJACENCY AND THE CONSTRUCTION OF POTENTIAL

Suppose there exists a geometry of states, such that each state is represented by a set of elements and a set of connections between them. Each state (graph) will have identifiable antecedents (a sequence of connections that were required to be made to reach the present state) and from this state a finite set of neighbouring (or adjacent) states, each of which also has a neighbourhood and so on as a combinatorial expansion (see Kauffman, 1993). The forward set of neighbourhood states represents the potential of the system. The history of the system is an actualization of potential states, with each transition closing off a set of potentials (irreversibility) and opening up a further set of potentials (imagination, entrepreneurship, expectations). A system is then a *path* (cf. a *trajectory* in continuous dynamics) through state-space, but the crucial aspect is that each time step represents not a dynamic *in* space but rather a dynamic *of* space: a change in the connections in a system constitutes an historical event (endogenous time) and changes the geometry of economic space. The geometry of these transformations is the object of study.

An evolutionary regime (a technological trajectory) is a sequence of actualization that moves through a self-generating front of potentiality. From my perspective, what is of interest here is the nature (that is, the geometry) of the potentiality that defines the regime. We must recognize that 'regime potential' does not have a priori existence, at least not in the way that physicists and the like think about the concept, but is something that is actually constructed by agents. Agents actively construct potential. When we look more closely at this, it is apparent that this is not something done by the representative agent, but is a key service of the entrepreneurial agent, who forms potential as possibility, which is then refined into expectations (Kirzner, 1973; Shackle, 1972). Actualization is then the movement through a set of adjacent states within the set of potential states (the regime). The microeconomic question, which we are yet to answer, is – how are potentials constructed?

In a field-based framework, this question does not even make sense, because the potentials do have a priori existence. This is illustrated by the concept of a production function, in which all possible input combinations are predefined. However, it is apparent, I think, that the sort of potentials of interest to the institutional and evolutionary analysis are not field concepts but rather are combinatorial concepts. For this reason, models of search that employ a specifically combinatorial operator, such as a genetic algorithm, are more likely to capture the dynamic nature of the underlying process of potential construction.

However, I do not think that the notion of regime potential is yet suitably formulated. Specifically, there seems to be missing a concept that refers to the basic process of change (which Dopfer associates with a process regime). I suggest that the graph theoretic notion of adjacency is such a concept. Adjacency refers to the set of neighbouring states that are one 'move' away from a present state. A 'move' occurs when a connection in the system is changed. Any given state (a system of elements and specific connections) will have a number of adjacent states. This number will be the key variable in addressing process dynamics. For instance, the inflection points in the logistic curve can be interpreted as a system initially having a low number of adjacent states, and thus only a few pathways for development, but with exploration many more become apparent (are constructed). This is associated with the rapid growth of the system. Eventually, as the pathways are exhausted, the number of adjacent states begins to decline, as associated with the terminal phase of the logistic curve (see Kauffman, 1993).

Furthermore, potential defines the boundaries of an evolutionary regime, and when potential changes (an imaginative, creative act) this becomes the necessary precondition (an endogenous precondition) for regime transition. Whereas the above process regime can be conceptualized as the exploration of the dynamics of connections, a regime transition would perhaps correspond to the introduction of a new element into the primary set, which thus changes the basic geometry (number of adjacent states, and so on) of the system. The other way that this can occur is when the system itself affects a kind of closure so that it becomes an element in a higher-level system. This sort of emergence can be analytically represented with the notion of *hyperstructure* (Baas, 1997; Potts, 2000), which is a way of representing power sets (sets of sets of…).[6] I would argue that Dopfer's notion of a developmental sequence of regimes is, if understood in terms of the geometry of economic space, a hyperstructure. A hyperstructure describes the process by which a new technology, say, does not replace the old technology (for example, Schumpeter's mail-coaches and railways) but rather embeds it within itself (the system becomes an element in a new system). For example, programmes are elements that, when combined with appropriate hardware elements, lead to the emergence of the system 'computer'. A computer then becomes an element in systems such as a manufacturing process or a network, a network then becomes an element in a higher-level system such as the Internet, and so on. Some systems have much more potential to become elements in higher-level systems than others. Arguably, when this happens, we have a 'revolution' (such as the steam engine, the internal combustion engine, the transistor, the PC and so on). The total evolutionary dynamic is the process of elements combining to form systems and these systems then having the potential to become elements in higher-level systems.

FINAL COMMENT

In sum, Dopfer's notion of context underpinning notions of local universality, evolutionary regimes and regime transitions, and indeed history dependence in general, can, I think, be formally interpreted as arguing that the correct basis for the development of a synthetic evolutionary economics is to proceed within the analytical context of a hyperstructured non-integral (partially connected) geometry of economic space. The core aspect of this is to recognize that the fundamental elements of investigation are complex systems, and that these can be universally represented with graph theoretic structure (Green, 1996). Systems are sets of elements and sets of connections between them. It is the specificity of the connections that defines a discrete geometry of states, and, *in toto*, an historical and environmental context. Context refers to the notion of systems embedded within systems, and this can be given analytical closure with the construct of a hyperstructure. The histonomic approach, therefore, is perhaps best defined not by methodological criterion, but rather with respect to an ontological criterion of context that involves beginning with analysis and definition of the geometry of economic space.

NOTES

1. Cf. the Bourbaki school of microeconomic orthodoxy (see Weintraub and Mirowski, 1994).
2. Examples I suggest are Tony Lawson's social ontology (Lawson, 1997), artificial life modelling (see Tesfatsion, 1998) and game theory with endogenous rules.
3. An element can have both an historical and an environmental context, and these are not necessarily related (for example, an immigrant is an agent whose historical and environmental context are different). Concepts such as coevolution are special cases of the above, wherein the environment is defined in terms of some specific other element.
4. It is perhaps also worth pointing out that the entire notion of selection, in the Darwinian sense (for example, Alchian, 1950), is a statement about context. The concept of fitness as the qualitative measure of selection is at heart the concept of appropriateness of something *in the context of a situation*.
5. It is perhaps worth noting that systems biologists and ecologists theorize in such terms as well.
6. A hyperstructure is a plausible geometric and algebraic formulation of Herbert Simon's notion of emergent hierarchy.

REFERENCES

Alchian, A.A. (1950), 'Uncertainty, evolution and economic theory', *Journal of Political Economy*, **58,** 211–22.

Baas, N. (1997), 'Self-Organization and Higher Order Structures', in F. Schweiter (ed.), *Self-Organization of Complex Structures: From Individual to Collective Dynamics*, Amsterdam: Gordon and Breach.

Burke, E. (1998), *The Pin-Ball Effect*, New York: Addison-Wesley

Dopfer, K. (1986), 'The histonomic approach to economics: beyond pure theory and pure experience', *Journal of Economic Issues*, **20**, 989–1010.

Green, D. (1996), 'Towards a Mathematics of Complexity', *http:/www.csu.edu.au/ci/vol3/meas.meas.html*

Kauffman, S. (1993), *The Origins of Order: Self-Organization and Selection in Evolution*, Oxford: Oxford University Press.

Kirman, A. (1997), 'The Economy as an Evolving Network, *Journal of Evolutionary Economics*,**7**, 339–53.

Kirzner, I. (1973), *Competition and Entrepreneurship*, Chicago: Chicago University Press.

Mirowski, P. (1989), *More Heat than Light: Economics as Social Physics*, New York: Cambridge University Press.
Potts, J. (2000), *The New Evolutionary Microeconomics: Complexity, Competence, and AdaptiveBehaviour*, Cheltenham: Edward Elgar.
Shackle, G. (1972), *Epistemics and Economics: A Critique of Economic Doctrines*, Cambridge: Cambridge University Press.
Tesfatsion, L. (1998), *http://www.econ.iastate.edu/tesfatsi/getalife.htm*
Weintraub, E. and P. Mirowski (1994), 'The pure and the applied: Bourbakism comes to mathematical economics', *Science in Context*, **7**, 245–72.

PART II

Empirical Perspectives

7. Considerations about a production system with qualitative change

Paolo Saviotti

INTRODUCTION

The central problem underlying this and other texts by the same author is the emergence of qualitative change and its implications for economic development. Qualitative change is defined here as the emergence of new entities, qualitatively different and distinguishable from pre-existing ones, and the disappearance of some pre-existing ones. New entities can be defined as new types of activities (for example, production processes), of actors (for example, firms, organizations, enterprises) and objects (goods and services). Qualitative change leads to changes in the composition of the economic system and to structural change.

Qualitative change is not taken into account explicitly by most economic models of production and growth. Such neglect would be without consequences for economic theory if the composition of the economic system were only an effect of previous economic development. However, there are good reasons to believe that the composition of the economic system at a given time is also a determinant of future economic development. To the extent that this is true, it becomes important to be able to define variables that can allow us to treat analytically the composition of the economic system and to create models of production and growth that include such variables. The study of qualitative change can be considered one of the most important challenges for economic theory and for evolutionary theory in particular.

Previously, Saviotti (1996, 1998a, 1998b) has used the variable called either variety or diversity to describe analytically the changing composition of the economic system. Variety was there defined as 'the number of actors, activities and objects necessary to characterize the economic system'. The role of variety in economic development was discussed in terms of two hypotheses: (a) the growth in variety is a necessary requirement for long-term economic development; (b) variety growth, leading to new sectors, and productivity growth in pre-existing sectors, are complementary and not independent aspects of economic development.

The justification and the implications of these hypotheses are given in previous papers (for example, Saviotti, 1996). Here we concentrate on the problem of constructing a production/growth model that can take into account qualitative change. We start by pointing out that it cannot be taken into account explicitly by macroeconomic models, in the sense in which the term 'macroeconomic' is normally used in these models. Such models are constructed largely independently of the structure of the economic system. It is not the intention of this paper to dispute the usefulness of a macroeconomic approach to growth. The use of models that establish relationships between aggregate variables is an important simplificative device used successfully in several disciplines. The considerations in this chapter are rather intended to bridge the gap between a microeconomic and a macroeconomic approach. Such a gap can be overcome if we reconstruct the macroeconomic level by aggregating micro units (firms, industrial sectors and so on). Here a replicator dynamics approach developed in previous papers will be adapted to the objective of aggregating different sectors in order to reconstruct the output of a whole economic system. The nature of equilibrium in a multi-sector system undergoing qualitative change will be discussed. It will be argued that the state of the economic system will be defined by the balance between inter-population dynamics, that is, the rate at which new sectors emerge and old ones become extinct, and intra-population dynamics, that is, the rate at which the firm population of each sector adjusts to the perturbation of equilibrium determined by inter-population dynamics. Finally, it will be argued that the near-equilibrium solutions of replicator dynamics and the input–output approach both correspond to a subset of the dynamic system undergoing qualitative change. They can only represent changes of the economic system taking place near equilibrium and thus they are essentially approaches at constant composition.

POPULATION APPROACH

In this chapter a population approach is used. This approach, often used in biology but not in economics, has been advocated by several evolutionary economists (see, for example, Metcalfe and Gibbons, 1989; Saviotti and Metcalfe, 1991). In order to represent a population we can concentrate on several of its properties. In the typological approach which is very often used in economics, we concentrate on the representative individual and on the average properties of the population. On the contrary, in a population approach we take into account that the members of a population are not identical and that, in order to characterize the population, we must consider both its average properties and their distribution within it.

In what follows in this section we will try to establish some general features of an approach applicable to economic agents (firms, consumers and so on) with the purpose of understanding and representing qualitative change in economic development. A very important property of all populations is the number of their members. Here we can realize immediately that a population approach is intrinsically dynamic. Even when the number of members of a population is constant in the course of time this apparent invariance is the result of a dynamic equilibrium, in which the entry of new members exactly compensates for the exit of old members. The terms 'entry' and 'exit' correspond to those of birth and death respectively in the biological applications of replicated dynamics (RD). The dynamics of entry and exit is not the only type of change that can take place in a population in the course of time. Especially where populations of economic agents are concerned, other changes can take place. For example, if we consider a population of firms producing a comparable output, such an output can undergo very considerable changes in the course of time. In the meantime the size, organization and strategy of the firms can undergo very substantial changes. In general, we can say that both the number and the nature of the members of a population can change in the course of time. If we are interested in the study of qualitative change the analysis of the evolving nature of population members must be an additional concern. In what follows we will refer to the study of the dynamics of entry and exit of members into and out of a population as a simple RD approach and to the analysis of other types of change as an augmented RD approach. Let us now observe that this adaptation of an RD approach, while taking inspiration from biological models, is essentially driven by the nature of the economic problem to be analysed.

The changing nature of the members of existing populations already represents an example of qualitative change. A Boeing 747, a latest model car or personal computer are very different from their analogues at the beginning of the life cycles of the respective technologies. However, the most significant dimension of qualitative change is represented by the emergence of completely new populations and by the extinction of pre-existing ones. In this sense an economic system can be equated to a population of populations, with a macrodynamics represented by the entry and exit of populations, and with a microdynamics represented by the entry and exit of members into and out of each population. Let us also observe that, in this framework, a population of firms producing a differentiated output corresponds to an industrial sector. It must be observed that in this approach each firm produces a differentiated product, but that the extent of differentiation does not necessarily correspond to that of a multi-product firm.

Summarizing, then, the representation of a production system by means of RD requires three levels of analysis. First is *the change in the number of members of existing populations*. This is a form of intra-population dynamics that corresponds to quantitative change only. This level of analysis is called a simple RD approach.Second is *the change in the nature of the members of existing populations*. This is a form of intra-population dynamics that introduces qualitative change. Third is *the change in the number of distinguishable populations*. This is a form of inter-population dynamics that makes the greatest contribution to qualitative change. The combination of these three constitutes an augmented RD approach.

In order to proceed further, we need to give some more information about the nature of the populations that will be referred to in the rest of the chapter. The starting point of the approach is the twin characteristics representation of product technology (Saviotti and Metcalfe, 1984). Each product technology is thus represented by two sets of characteristics, one describing the internal structure of the technology (technical characteristics) and the other describing the services performed for the users (service characteristics). Any product (good or service) is thus considered the output of a product technology. In this sense we can call the population either technological or product population. It is to be remarked here that, while this twin characteristics representation has been developed for material products, it can be adapted to services (Gallouj and Weinstein, 1997). Each product model is then represented by a point in characteristics space, and a product population is given by the distribution of product models in the relevant dimensions of characteristics space. Such a distribution takes the shape of a 'cloud' which, in the course of time, changes its position, size and density. Such populations will show a dynamics as the nature of the products changes, as they become more differentiated and as new populations emerge.

A product population is, so to speak, underlying other types of population. Thus, as a new product population is created, firms can start producing it and consumers purchasing it, creating a firm population and a consumer population, respectively. The dynamics of the firm population and of the consumer population interact with that of the underlying product population. As the new product becomes cheaper and acquires greater performance, more consumers can purchase it. Firms increase their production and adapt it to consumers' tastes.

Let us here start dealing more explicitly with qualitative change. The distinction between radical and incremental innovation corresponds to that between qualitative and quantitative change. In extreme cases such a difference is quite clearly established. For example, the first emergence of aeroplanes or of computers was obviously a radical innovation because no analogue of these products or technologies existed previously. On the other hand, the *n*th vintage of an already existing product (toothpaste, washing machine and so on) represents only quantitative change. However, if we compare some existing vintages of products to their analogues in the early phases of their life cycles it is quite doubtful whether only incremental innovations have led these products to be what they are now. For example, the emergence of jet aircraft can be considered a change of paradigm in aircraft technology (Constant, 1980; Frenken *et al.*, 1999). Thus we need a more analytical approach to the problem of qualitative change. The characteristics representation referred to above can be very useful for this purpose. A completely new technology differs from any previous ones, at least in its technical characteristics, and possibly also in its service characteristics. Thus a jet engine needs to be represented by variables/characteristics different from those required to represent a piston engine. In other words, a radical innovation leading to qualitative change needs to be represented in new dimensions of technical characteristics space. It is also possible for the new technology to create completely new services, but that is not a necessary condition for the innovation to be radical and for the change to be qualitative. On the other hand, an incremental innovation will only lead to changes in the values of the existing characteristics. Thus the time evolution of a product population will be given by the displacement of its centre of gravity and by a change in the distribution of models in the *same dimensions of characteristics space*. Yet both radical innovations and the accumulation of incremental innovations within existing populations can give rise to the emergence of new, *distinguishable* populations and thus lead to changes in variety. As regards radical innovations, the fact that their output needs to be represented in new dimensions of characteristics space makes them separate and distinguishable from any pre-existing population. However, an existing population in the course of its evolution can fragment into several populations, which remain in the same dimensions of characteristics space (Figures 7.1 and 7.2). The new populations are distinguishable to the extent that they occupy separate and non-overlapping regions of characteristics space. Thus new distinguishable populations can be created both by radical innovations and by the accumulation of incremental innovations. Thus it seems that qualitative change can be driven by both incremental and radical innovations.

We need to distinguish several types of different but interrelated populations. In the model that follows a population of products is underlying any population of firms. Each time a new and distinguishable product is created the corresponding population comes into being. Then the population of firms producing the new product can be created. It could be argued that products can only be produced by firms and that a firm population should precede a product population. Yet a new product could be created by a lone inventor. Even if it were created in the R&D laboratories of a firm, its existence as a prototype would create the new product population. Any other firm, either existing or new, could start producing the new product. Furthermore, once the

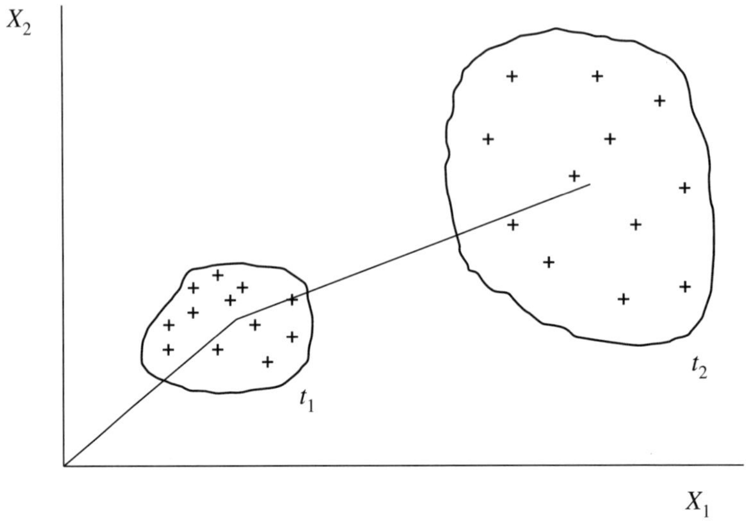

Figure 7.1 *Change of the position and density of a technological population between t_1 and t_2*

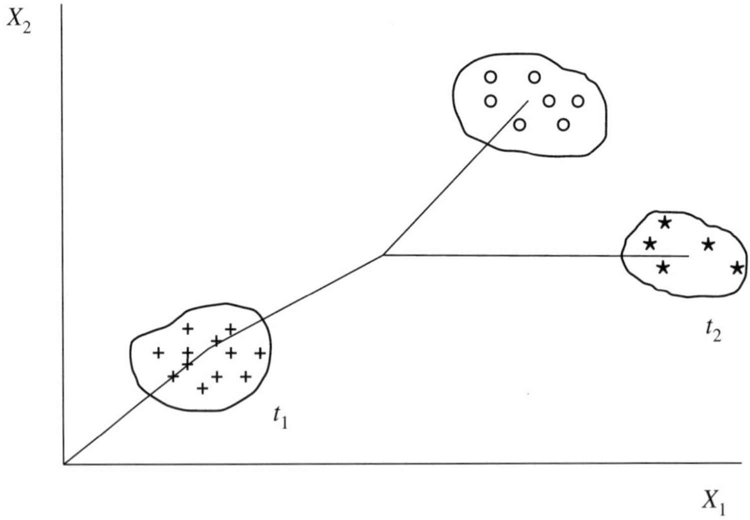

Figure 7.2 *Specialization/segmentation of a technological population between t_1 and t_2*

new product population exists, consumers can start purchasing it, thus creating a new consumer population. However, what is more important is that a population of products and a population of firms are interacting. The product can diffuse, be modified and evolve if firms produce it. Being produced the product will undergo incremental innovations, thus going through its life cycle. Were the firms that produce it not successful, the evolution of the product would be stunted and truncated. On the other hand, the success of the firms producing it will lead to imitation and, by the accumulation of incremental innovations, to a rich and highly differentiated evolution.

Any qualitative change leads to a change in the composition of the economic system. The composition can be established by means of a list of sectors that constitute the system itself. In this sense qualitative change would be equivalent to structural change and both our previous and subsequent analysis amount to saying that economic development by necessity involves structural change. However, the qualitative change taking place within the system exists at a deeper level than what is commonly referred to as structural change. Once a new sector is created its internal composition does not remain constant in the course of time. As we have seen before, once a new population has been created it can fragment or differentiate into two or more populations. While in principle these populations can be considered two or more sectors, industrial classifications do not necessarily take into account the emergence of these populations. Furthermore, even when a given population remains undifferentiated in the course of economic evolution, the product models of which it is constituted do not remain unchanged. The aircraft, cars and microcomputer models now constituting the respective populations are very different from the corresponding models at earlier stages of their product life cycle. From this reasoning we can now draw two conclusions.

First, the composition of the economic system can be established at three levels: (a) the number and type of populations constituting the system, (b) the internal composition of each population, and (c) the internal composition of the product models constituting the population. Second, existing industrial classifications do not reflect adequately changes in the composition of the economic system. An appropriate type of industrial classification would be based on a taxonomy of the economic system matching the number and type of distinguishable populations constituting the system.

Going back to the introduction of this paper we can now see that any change in the composition of the system at the three levels defined earlier leads to a change in variety. Variety is thus an appropriate variable to measure the composition of an economic system and its changes in the course of time.

Having defined the composition of the economic system in terms of the populations constituting it, we can now proceed to analyse the factors most likely to be responsible for the dynamics of emergence of new populations and for the extinction of old ones. The creation of new product populations can be influenced by two types of factors. First, the dynamics of growth and of development of existing populations can create inducements for incumbent firms present in these populations to exit and to establish themselves in new niches where they would have a temporary monopoly. Second, the negative inducements to exit existing populations need to be accompanied by positive inducements to the creation of new niches. The negative inducements are essentially related to some form of crowding or saturation. Examples of these inducements are as follows.

1. An increasing intensity of competition creates inducements for incumbent producers to exit a population and negative inducements for potential entrants to enter. Producers will then, in a Schumpeterian fashion, leave the overcrowded population (Andersen, 1999) and create a niche where they will have a temporary monopoly. We expect that the profit rate will decline as the intensity of competition is raised by the entry of imitators, which erodes the temporary monopoly enjoyed by the early innovators.
2. The saturation of demand will create positive inducements for incumbent firms to exit and negative inducements for potential entrants to enter. Again, these inducements will lead to the creation of new niches, where an adjustment gap will be present in the form of a largely unsatisfied demand.
3. The two previous factors constitute inducements to exit or not to enter an existing population. These must be accompanied by positive inducements to the creation of new niches. These can be of two types: first, the results of search activities both within the differentiated product technology involved and in other technologies create opportunities for the establishment of new niches; second, the number of niches that can be created varies according to the scope of the product technology considered. Such scope is partly determined by the technological opportunity of the product technology considered. In what follows the scope of a technology will be represented by the volume of a product population in service characteristics space. This is based on niche theory, which tells us that, the wider the range of services performed, the greater the number of niches that can be created within it (Saviotti, 1996; Frenken *et al.*, 1999).

These general considerations will be given a more analytical form in the next section.

A REPLICATOR DYNAMICS MODEL OF FIRM BEHAVIOUR WITHIN A SECTOR

As pointed out at the beginning, the model presented in this chapter is an example of replicator dynamics, a technique of biological origin. Here a replicator means anything that can reproduce. The model developed here can describe the evolution of interacting populations. The model can describe both quantitative change in the number of members of the population, and qualitative change, as regards both the nature of the existing populations and the emergence of completely new populations. Quantitative change is represented by the combination of the basic processes of birth and death, where any phenomenon that contributes to raising the number of members of the population is a component of birth and any phenomenon that contributes to lowering the number of members of the population is a component of death. As already pointed out, birth is equivalent to entry and death to exit. Qualitative change in the members of existing populations can take place in a number of ways. For example, in a previously developed model of technological evolution (Saviotti and Mani,1995) incremental innovation gave rise to changes in the characteristics of population members. On the other hand, qualitative change can be created by the emergence of completely new populations. Of course, the structure of the equations that represent the evolution of a particular system is specific to the system itself. For example, the phenomena contributing to birth and death are specific to the system. On the other hand, the model is capable of considerable generality, in the sense that we can represent the evolution of very large classes of populations in terms of birth, death, changes in the nature of the members of existing populations and emergence of completely new populations.

The particular version of replicator dynamics (RD) that constitutes the starting point for the analysis in this paper has been developed in previous chapters and applied to different types of populations (Saviotti and Mani, 1995; Saviotti, 1998a, 1998b). It contains three types of equations, corresponding to the three levels of analysis: type 1, representing the net number of members of the population; type 2, representing the change in the nature of the population members; and type 3, representing the change in the net number of distinguishable technological/product populations. A product population is the set of all product models that the given product technology can create in characteristics space. Such a population is always preceding the development of populations of firms or of consumers. Once the new product population has been created, firms can start producing it and consumers purchasing it. A type 1 equation represents quantitative change, while type 2 and 3 equations represent qualitative change. A type 2 equation represents the most incremental type of change, such as the gradual increase in performance of existing product models, the changing size of the firms producing a given type of differentiated output, or the changing income share allocated by a population of consumers to a given product class. A type 3 equation represents the emergence of completely new types of populations or the extinction of pre-existing ones. Examples of new types of populations are a completely new product, the population of firms producing a completely new product, or the population of consumers purchasing a completely new product. The population of a new product anticipates, then, the emergence of the corresponding populations of firms and of consumers. Once the new product exists, firms can start producing it and consumers purchasing it, thus creating the two corresponding populations. Here it must be observed that a completely new product can be the result of a radical innovation, creating completely new dimensions in characteristics space, or of the specialization of a pre-existing population, creating a new and distinguishable population in the same dimensions of characteristics space previously occupied.

A type 3 equation is, then, the representation of a Schumpeterian process of creative destruction, and it is the most important contributor to the change in composition and in variety of the economic system. It must also be observed that, while type 1 and 2 equations are specific to each population, a type 3 equation is unique for the whole economic system, since it represents the change in the net number of technological/product populations within the system.

Finally, before getting into the details of the model, we have to point out that its level of aggregation is that of product technology, defined as a distinguishable population in characteristics space. That is, all firms in a population produce some variant of the product. It is a micro model because it contains the composition of the system. However, the same technology can be produced all over the world. As a consequence, the population of firms can be distributed over the world economic system. Furthermore, the model can describe the evolution of several interacting populations. Therefore its level of aggregation can be greater than that of a national economy. In principle we can use it to reconstruct aggregated features starting from the lowest possible level of aggregation, that of the firm.

BIRTH AND DEATH PROCESSES

The inducement for new firms to enter, leading to birth, can be split into two principal components: (a) the inducement for firms to exit from pre-existing populations; (b) the inducement to create a niche that will subsequently become a population. In turn, part (b) can be separated into the knowledge base and competencies that firms must possess in order to create the niche, financial availability and expected growth potential of the sector. Furthermore, even when firms have the right knowledge base and competencies, their decision to enter is always subject to uncertainty. The example of existing firms can be expected to reduce uncertainty about the prospects of a new technology, to create routines which can be followed by imitating firms and to establish legitimation (Hannan and Freeman, 1989), in terms both of market acceptance and of institutions that can support the market.

$$\frac{dN_i}{dt} = k_1 N_i^{\beta} FA_i (F_i - \overline{F}) V(Y_i) \sum_{j \neq i=1}^{n_1} \frac{N_j \rho_j m_j(t)}{D_y(i,j) M_j} \tag{7.1}$$

where N_i is the number of members of the *i*th population, FA_i is a measure of financial availability, F_i is the fitness of the technology, F is the average fitness of all technologies, $V(Y_i)$ is the expected volume of the *i*th technological population in service characteristics space, and ρ_j is the density of another, pre-existing population. Being an expected volume $V(Y_i)$ corresponds to a time subsequent to the one at which the behaviour of the agents is considered. $V(Y_i)$ represents, then, the growth potential of the system. F_i is related to the knowledge base of firms (Saviotti, 1998b). FA_i is financial availability, which does not mean only money, but money coupled to the knowledge required to assess the probability that the investment can be successful. The presence of this type of knowledge is particularly important for firms creating or using radical innovations at the beginning of their life cycles. We can expect FA_i to depend on the number and size of financial institutions and on the degree of confidence they have in the new technology *i*. Thus FA_i is likely to depend on the number of firms already present in the new technology (N_i), on $V(Y_i)$ and on $(F_i - F)$.

F_i is the fitness of firms entering population *i* and F is the average fitness of firms in the other, pre-existing populations. Fitness is generally defined as the capacity of a firm, a technology or a species to adapt to the external environment in which it lives or operates. This is a very general definition, useful in principle but difficult to apply to specific situations. An approximate but more easily applicable definition of fitness, similar to the one previously proposed by Saviotti and Mani (1995) and by Kwasnicki (1996) is the following:

$$F_i = \frac{\overline{Y}_i}{P_i^{\xi}} \tag{7.2}$$

where Y_i is an aggregator of the services performed by product *i*, p_i is the product price and ξ is the price elasticity of demand. In this definition fitness is an indicator of the value for money provided by the product. With this definition the fitness of a firm depends uniquely on the quality and price of its products. It is possible to use different definitions of fitness. For example, Silverberg *et al.* (1988) also include delivery times amongst the variables determining fitness. However, the analysis of the effect of different forms of fitness is outside the scope of this paper.

It must be observed that the fitness of a given product is not fixed, but changes during its life cycle as both Y_i and p_i change. Furthermore, F_i is also relative to a population of users or a subset of it. In other words, F_i changes in different regions of characteristics space. Typically, when a new technology i is created, F_i has a very high value in the niche, but not necessarily everywhere else. Thus a new product technology may be very expensive and therefore be adapted only to the requirements of a small subset of a population of potential users. However, in later phases of the product cycle, as Y_i grows and p_i falls, the new technology may have become adapted to a much larger population of potential users. This implies that there is likely to be a very strong interaction between fitness and expected market size.

The first term on the right of the equals sign, $k_1 N_i^{\beta}$ in the equation (7.1) represents the effect of imitation. The presence of firms already in place reduces uncertainty, creates routines and helps to establish institutions and organizations for the new technology. Since $\beta < 0$, the imitation effect falls with the number of firms already in place. The second term represents the capacity of a firm to enter the new technology i. It is the product of FA_i, financial availability, and of $(F_i - F)$, the differential fitness of the new technology with respect to the average fitness of all other technologies in niche i.

The term $\Sigma N_j\ \rho_j\ /D_Y(i,j) * [m_j(t)/M_j]$ altogether represents the inducement to exit from pre-existing technological populations (j). Following the previous considerations on competition, the term $N_j\rho_j$, the product of the number of competitors and of the density of the technological population, represents the intensity of competition of a technological population that pre-existed the ith one. $N_j\rho_j$ represents the extent of overcrowding of an existing product population and thus the inducement to exit from such a population in order to establish a niche, where there will be temporary monopoly. Alternatively, $N_j\rho_j$ is a measure of the intensity of intra-product competition; $m_j(t)/M_j$ represents the fraction of the population of households that has already adopted a good. On the other hand, $FA_i(F_i{-}F) * V(Y_i)$ represents the combination of the inducements and the capabilities required to enter population i. $V(Y_i)$, the expected volume of the ith technological population in service characteristics space, measures the scope or potential of the ith technology and thus the growth potential of the ith product technology. The greater $V(Y_i)$, the greater the number of niches (Saviotti and Mani, 1995) that can be established within the technological population, and the greater the expected development potential of the technology.

The inducement of firms to exit from the ith technological population, leading to death, depends on both intra- and inter-technology competition and on demand saturation. Intra-technology competition is measured by the term $N_i\rho_i$, the intensity of competition within the ith technological population, while inter-technology competition depends on the distance, or on the degree of similarity, between technology i and other potentially competing technologies in service characteristics space. As already pointed out, the closer two technological models are in characteristics space, and thus the smaller their distances the more similar they are. Thus distances are inversely proportional to degrees of similarity. Demand saturation is, as before, represented by $m_i(t)/M_i$, the fraction of the population of households that can adopt the good/service i. Moreover, it has been observed that death rates vary considerably with firm size, large firms having substantially lower mortality rates than smaller ones (Carroll and Hannan, 1990). Consequently death rates are given by the expression:

$$\frac{dN_i}{dt} = k_3 \sum_{i \neq j = n_1}^{n_2} \frac{N_i \rho_i m_i(t)}{D_y(i,j) M_i} + \alpha t_i^{\alpha-1} S_{i,t}^{-\gamma} \tag{7.3}$$

where N_i is the number of competitors in technology i, ρ_i is the density of the ith technological population, $D_y(i,j)$ is the average distance between technologies i and j in service characteristics space, $S_{i,t}$ is the average size of firms in technology i at time t, $0 < \alpha < 1$, $0 < \gamma < 1$. Therefore size decreases mortality at a decreasing rate.

Carroll and Hannan (1990) suggest that death rates depend also on the age of firms. While we do not want to dispute this suggestion, for the time being we leave this factor out of consideration.

The net rate of birth, that is the balance of birth and death rates, is given by:

$$\begin{aligned} \frac{dN_i}{dt} = {} & k_1 N_i^{\beta} FA(F_i - \overline{F}) V(Y_i) \sum_{j \neq i = 1}^{n_1} \frac{N_j \rho_j m_j(t)}{D_y(i,j) M_j} \\ & - k_3 \sum_{i \neq j = n_1}^{n_2} \frac{N_i \rho_i m_i(t)}{D_y(i,j) M_i} - \alpha t_i^{\alpha-1} S_{i,t}^{-\gamma} \end{aligned} \tag{7.4}$$

In order to simplify the model, we will consider that population i interacts only with two other populations i– and i+, created before and after i, respectively. As the intensity of competition and the saturation of demand in i– increase there are growing inducements to exit from i– and to create i. In due course, after the temporary monopoly enjoyed by the entrepreneurs that created i is gradually eroded, there are decreasing inducements to enter i and increasing inducements to exit from it; *i*+ will thus be created. Equation (7.4) can then be rewritten as:

$$\frac{dN_i}{dt} = k_1 N_i^{\beta} FA(F_i - \overline{F})V(Y_i)\frac{N_i - \rho_i - m_i - (t)}{D_Y(i-,i)M_{i-}} - k_3 \frac{N_i \rho_i m_i(t)}{D_Y(i,i+)} - \alpha t_i^{\alpha-1} S_{i,t}^{-\gamma} \tag{7.5}$$

An even simpler form of (7.5) is the following:

$$\frac{dN_i}{dt} = k_1 N_i^{\beta} FA_i(F_i - \overline{F})V(Y_i)IC_{i-}DS_{i-} - k_3 IC_i DS_i - \alpha t_i^{\alpha-1} S_{i,t}^{-\gamma} \tag{7.6}$$

where:

$$IC_i = \frac{N_i \rho_i}{D_Y(i,i+)} \qquad DS_i = \frac{m_i(t)}{M_i} \tag{7.7}$$

IC_i and DS_i represent the intensity of competition and the degree of demand saturation, respectively.

Firm Size

The size of a firm can vary either through internal growth or through mergers and acquisitions. Internal growth will be influenced by the rate of growth of demand and by the differential fitness of firms in the technology.

$$\frac{dL_{i,l}}{dt} = k_4(1 - \frac{m_i(t)}{M_i})VA(F_{i,l})L_{t-1}\exp(-\delta L_{t-1}{}^2) + (V_a - V_f) \tag{7.8}$$

where $L_{i,l}$ is the size of a firm (*l*) in the *i*th technological population measured by its total employment, $(1-m_i(t)/M_i)$ is the rate of growth of demand for the output of the technology at time *t*, here considered exogenously determined; $VA(F_{i,1})$ is the variance in the fitness of the firms within the *i*th technological population, L_{t-1} is the average size or firms within the *i*th technological population at time $t-1$, V_a and V_f are the assets and financial values of the firms in the *i*th technological population.

We can expect that the opportunities for the growth of the best firms will be greater the larger the variance in the firms' fitness. Conversely, we can expect that, when this variance falls as the less efficient firms go out of business, the rate of size growth is going to fall. This situation is similar to that described by Fisher's fundamental theorem in biology (Nelson and Winter, 1982), which says that the rate of growth of a population is proportional to the variance in the fitness of the population. Also we can expect that, beyond a minimum size level, larger firms will have advantages in a number of situations, for example in obtaining loans from banks and in setting up alliances with other firms. Such positive influence of size on growth is represented by the term $L_{i,t-1}$, the average firm size at time t–1. The disadvantages of large size are represented by the term $\exp(-\delta L_{i,t-1}{}^2)$. The term $(V_a - V_f)$, the difference between the average assets and financial values of firms, represents the contribution of mergers and acquisitions.

Here it must be pointed out that the rate of size growth can also be written in terms of firm output $Q_{i,l}$. This equation can be derived from equation (7.8) in the following way:

$$\frac{dQ_{i,l}}{dt} = \frac{dQ_{i,l}}{dL_{i,l}} \frac{dL_{i,l}}{dt} \tag{7.9}$$

where:

$$Q_{i,l} = q_{i,l} L_{i,l} \tag{7.10}$$

$q_{i,l}$ being the labour productivity in the production of good/service i by firm l.

We can expect to derive $dQ_{i,l}/dL_{i,l}$ from the following:

$$q_{i,l} = f(HC_{i,l}, K_{i,l}) \tag{7.11}$$

where $HC_{i,l}$ is the human capital and $K_{i,l}$ is the physical capital in firm l.

Firm Structure

Firm structure is represented in this model by the number of divisions or departments $n_{D,i,j}$:

$$n_{D,i,l} = k_5 L_{t,i,l} V(Y_i) V(X_i) N_x \tag{7.12}$$

where $L_{t,i,l}$ is the size of firm l in the ith technological population at time t, and $V(Y_i)$ is the volume of the ith technological population in service characteristics space, $V(X_i)$ is the volume of the ith technological population in technical characteristics space, and N_x is the number of dimensions in technical characteristics space. Equation (7.10) tells us that the expected number of divisions or departments in a firm is likely to increase with firm size, with the degree of product differentiation in the technology and with the differentiation of the competences required, here represented by $V(X_i)N_x$. The effect of firm size can be considered to lead to a multifunctional, or U, structure, and that of product and of competences differentiation to a multidivisional, or M, structure.

The Number of Distinguishable Technological Populations

New product technologies lead to new product populations, whose firms can be distinguished from those of previous populations both by the competences and knowledge bases they use and by the nature of their output. The net number of technological populations is one of the most important components of the qualitative change, and therefore of the variety or diversity of the system.

$$\frac{dn}{dt} = k_6 \sum_{j \neq i=1}^{n_1} \frac{N_j \rho_j m_j(t)}{D_Y(i,j) M_j} V(Y_i) \left[SE_i + \frac{k_7 \sum_{j=1}^{n} SE_j}{D_X(i,j)} \right] - \sum_{j=N_1}^{n_2} \frac{N_i \rho_i m_j(t)}{D_Y(i,j) M} \left[\sum_{j=n_1}^{n_2} \frac{V(Y_j) SE_j}{D_X(i,j)} \right] \tag{7.13}$$

where n is the net number of distinguishable technological populations at time t; SE_i represents the search efforts in technology i, SE_j the search efforts in technology j; $D_x(i,j)$ is the distance between technologies i and j in technical characteristics space, $D_Y(i,j)$ is the distance between technologies i and j in service characteristics space; $N_i\rho_i$ and $N_j\rho_j$ represent the intensities of competition in technologies i and j, respectively, $m_i(t)/M_i$ and $m_j(t)/M_j$ the extent of demand saturation for good i and j.

Equation (7.13) tells us that the rate of creation of new populations (i) increases with the saturation of pre-existing populations (j=1,n_1), both linked to increasing intensity of competition and to the saturation of demand, and with the scope of the new product technology, determined by its expected volume in service characteristics space and by the accumulated search activities. Search activities carried out in technologies j can be used by technology i to the extent that the absorption capacity of technology i allows it. Equation (7.13) also tells us that the absorption capacity of technology i for the results of the search activities carried out in technologies j varies inversely with the distance between i and j in technical characteristics space. In other words, the greater the difference between technology i and another technology j in knowledge space, the lower the capacity of i to absorb knowledge created in j. Once the new technology i has been created, it can be expected to follow the same life cycle as any of the pre-existing product technologies. That is, we can expect increasing intensity of competition and saturation of demand to reduce the incentives to stay in population *i*. This, coupled with the opportunities created by search activities in newer product technologies, induces the creation of further niches, that in turn follow the same life cycle. Thus those that begin their life as niches subsequently become growing markets and then saturated markets.

Equation (7.13) can be rewritten in a simpler way by assuming, as was done previously, that a product technology (*i*–) pre-existed *i*, and another product technology (*i*+) is created after *i*:

$$\frac{dN}{dt} = k_6 IC_{i-} SD_{i-} V(Y_i)\overline{SE_{T,i}} - k_8 IC_i SD_i V(Y_{i+})\overline{SE_{T,i+}} \tag{7.14}$$

where:

$$IC_{i-} = \frac{N_{i-}\rho_{i-}}{D_y(i-,i)} \tag{7.15}$$

$$SD_{i-} = \frac{m_{i-}(t)}{M_{i-}} \tag{7.16}$$

$$SE_{T,i-} = \int SE_i dt + \int \frac{SE_j}{D_X(j,i)} dt \tag{7.17}$$

The meaning of these terms is as follows. IC_{i-} tells us that the intensity of competition in population *i*– increases with the number of firms N_{i-}, with the density of the corresponding product population in characteristics space ρ_{i-}, and with the presence of technologies providing inter-technology competition.

SDi– tells us the extent of demand saturation. The combination of IC_{i-} and of SD_i– gives the inducement to exit from population *i*–.

The meaning of $SE_{T,i}$ is the same as in equation (7.13).

A PRODUCTION SYSTEM

In the previous sections it was established that the firms constituting the *i*th population produce a differentiated product, represented by a distribution of product models in characteristics space. Thus each population *i* corresponds to an industrial sector. We can then imagine representing a whole production system containing *n* sectors, where in each sector a differentiable product is produced, by means of a system of n equations of type 1, plus one equation of type 3. At any time type 1 equations would give us the rates of entry and of exit into each sector/population. Type 2 equation would tell us how the nature of the members of each population would change, and a type 3 equation would tell us whether new populations need to be added to the system or old ones eliminated. In what follows, for simplicity of exposition, we will limit our considerations to types 1 and 3.

In order to develop our considerations more analytically, we now proceed to outline a strategy for the transformation of the previous sectoral production model, called EVTEFI, into a multi-sector model. We start from the assumption that a model like EVTEFI, which has been developed in a partly inductive way to be a realistic model, is unlikely to have analytical solutions. Leaving aside for the moment the possibility of a numerical solution, we try to simplify the EVTEFI equations by transforming them into Lotka-Volterra-type equations. Furthermore, for the time being, we use only type 1 equations. In general, a Lotka-Volterra equation can be written (Roughgarden, 1996, p. 505) as:

$$\mathrm{N}\frac{dN_i}{dt} = r_i N_i \frac{(K_i - \sum_j \alpha_{ij} N_j)}{K_i} \tag{7.18}$$

where r_i is the rate constant of population growth, N_i is the number of members of population i at time t, α_{ij} is the competition coefficient between populations i and j, and K_i is the carrying capacity of population i.

In our case we can expect these terms to have the following form:

$$r_i = k_1 V(Y_i) * \dot{F}_i * FA_i * \overline{IC_{j \prec i}} * \overline{DS_{j \prec i}} \tag{7.19}$$

$$K_i = k_2 \frac{V(Y_i) * IC_{i,\max} * KC_i}{p_i * E_i * RA_i} \tag{7.20}$$

$$\alpha_{ij} = \frac{\overline{F_j} / \overline{F_i}}{D_X D_Y} \tag{7.21}$$

Equation (7.18) tells us that the rate constant of population growth r_i is determined by the scope of the technology, here represented by the volume ($V(Y_i)$) of the population in service characteristics space, by the rate of performance growth and price fall, here represented by the rate of change of fitness, by the financial availability FA_i, by the average intensity of competition in all populations that preceded i, and by the average demand saturation in technologies j that pre-existed i. The carrying capacity of technology i increases with the expected market size of technology i, here represented by $V(Y_i)$, with the maximum intensity of competition that can be tolerated in i ($IC_{i,\max}$), with the level of infrastructures and complementary technologies (KC_i), and decreases with the price of i, with the environmental impact of the technology (E_i) and with the returns to adoption RA_i. As regards the last variable, it must be remembered that we are dealing with a population of firms and that the carrying capacity refers to the maximum number of firms that the product technology can support. If RA_i becomes greater than 1 (increasing returns to adoption) the number of firms supported falls. The coefficient of interaction between technologies i and j should be determined by the relative average fitness of the product technologies that preceded i ($j<i$), by the distances in technical and service characteristics space, D_X and D_Y, where for simplicity the indices of populations i and j have been omitted. The form of α_{ij} indicates that a greater fitness in populations j relative to i would reduce the equilibrium level of population i, but that this effect is limited by the distances in technical and service characteristics space. The distance in service characteristics space is a measure of the degree of non-substitutability of product technologies i and j. If this distance is zero, that is if product technologies i and j are perfect substitutes, an infinitesimal superiority of j with respect to i would lead to the extinction of population i. This situation corresponds to perfect competition. When two products have the same position in service characteristics space ($D_Y(i,j) = 0$) and thus have the same quality, even a minimum price difference, leading to a corresponding difference in fitness, will lead all consumers to adopt the lower-priced product. On the other hand, the greater the distance in service characteristics space, the less substitutable products i and j are, and the more monopolistic the competition becomes. The effect of α_{ij} will then vary in different regions of service characteristics space, corresponding to the fact that even a high-priced product can have a very high fitness in a niche where its services are highly valuable. Thus as $D_Y(i,j)$ grows, competition passes from perfect like to monopolistic. $D_X(i,j)$, the distance in technical characteristics space, represents the knowledge barrier that users of product technologies j have to face when they start using product i. When such a barrier is very high, even a superior product i ($F_i>F_j$) might not displace j and thus not have an effect on the equilibrium level of population i.

It must be observed that the term F appearing in the rate constant r_i, is the rate of change of fitness in the course of time. We can expect that:

$$\dot{F} = k\left(SE_i + \sum_j \frac{SE_j}{D_X(i,j)}\right); \qquad (7.22)$$

that is, fitness is likely to grow with increasing search activities in technology i and in other technologies j, from which spin-offs or externalities can flow to i. The possibility that search activities performed in technology j can be used in technology i depends inversely on their distance in technical characteristics space. This is an expression of the local character of knowledge (Nelson and Winter, 1982; Saviotti, 1996, 1998b): a firm is more likely to be able to internalize an external technology similar to the one it was using before than a very different one. Alternatively, the inverse dependence on the distance between the two technologies in technical characteristics space can be considered a measure of the absorptive capacity (Cohen and Levinthal, 1989, 1990) of technology i.

We can then rewrite equation 7.18 in a Lotka-Voltera form as follows:

$$\frac{dN_i}{dt} = k_1 V(Y_i) * \dot{F}_i * FA_i * \overline{DS_{j \prec i}} \qquad (7.23)$$

$$\frac{\dfrac{k_2 V(Y_i) * IC_{i,\max} * KC_i}{p_i * E_i * RA_i} - \sum_j \dfrac{F_j / F_i}{D_X(i,j) D_Y(i,j)} N_j}{\dfrac{k_2 V(Y_i) * IC_{i,\max} * KC_i}{p_i * E_i * RA_i}}$$

Our production system is then represented by a system of equations of type (7.17) or (7.21). In principle, such equations may have solutions, although to find them is not necessarily easy. An alternative to solving systems (7.17) or (7.22) is to linearize the system near an equilibrium. The concept of equilibrium is for the moment used without any attempt to define it. We will later reflect on the possible nature of equilibrium in the systems investigated in this chapter.

Let us consider that our system of equations is constituted by a series of equations which are in principle non-linear, that can be written in the following way:

$$\frac{dN_i}{dt} = G_i(N_1, N_2, \ldots\ldots, N_m) \qquad (7.24)$$

where N_i is the number of members of population i, and G_i is a function of N_1, N_2, ...N_m, m being the maximum value of i in the system. We can first of all find an equilibrium position for the system as the situation in which all $dN_i/dt = 0$, and Taylor expand the functions G_i around the equilibrium point. Expanding around the equilibrium for each population, we find (May, 1973, pp. 21–3):

$$N_i(t) = N_i^* + x_i(t) \tag{7.25}$$

where N_i^* is the number of members of the ith population at equilibrium, and $x_i(t)$ is a (small) perturbation term. By Taylor expanding each of the equations (7.24) above, we find:

$$\frac{dx_i(t)}{dt} = \sum_{j=1}^{m} \alpha_{ij} x_j(t) \tag{7.26}$$

This set of m equations describes the population dynamics in the neighbourhood of the equilibrium point. In matrix notation we have:

$$\frac{d\overline{x(t)}}{dt} = A\overline{x(t)}, \tag{7.27}$$

where $\overline{x(t)}$ is a column matrix ($m \times 1$) and A is the $m \times m$ community matrix whose elements a_{ij} describe the effects of species j on species i near equilibrium.

At this point we have available two routes to solve the type 1 equations of our system: we can transform our equations into a Lotka-Volterra form and use the solutions that are available for them, or we can linearize the system near equilibrium. In the former case, we can find the competition matrix α and in the latter case the community matrix A. These matrices are different because they describe different types of interactions of the populations constituting our system.

REFLECTIONS ON THE NATURE OF EQUILIBRIUM IN POPULATION DYNAMICS

We can now try to summarize the features of population dynamics as previously discussed. A population of firms can have an *intra-population* dynamics, constituted by the birth/entry of new firms and by the death/exit of old ones. The whole production system has an *inter-population* dynamics, constituted by the emergence of new populations and by the extinction of pre-existing ones. The replicator dynamics system considered here is constituted by an equation of type 1, describing the change in the net number of members of the population, by one or more equations of type 2, describing the change in the nature of the population members, and by an equation of type 3, describing the change in the net number of distinguishable technological/product populations. As we have done so far in this paper, we concentrate on type 1 and type 3 equations. In other words, we assume that each population will have its own intra-population dynamics with births/entry and death/exits. Such dynamics will not change the composition of the system in a qualitative way. On the other hand, a type 3 equation tells us under what conditions new populations are going to be created and old ones become extinct. Thus we can consider a type 3 equation as a transformation operator that by adding and subtracting sectors changes the composition of the system. Each time a new population emerges a new equation of type 1 needs to be added and correspondingly a type 1 equation will have to be deleted when a population becomes extinct. Alternatively, a type 3 equation can be said to represent the population of populations constituting the production system.

We can in general assume that a state of equilibrium will involve an invariance of the state variables of the system. Such invariance may be dynamic, in the sense that fluctuations at the micro level can cancel one another out, thus leaving the macro variables of the system unchanged. An example of this situation can be found in a type 1 equation, where the net number of firms N_i in population i can remain constant in the presence of entry and exit. If we were to observe that N_i reaches a given value and subsequently remains constant, we could say that the system has achieved an equilibrium. In ecology the community of a given species that has achieved a constant number of members is considered to be in equilibrium with its habitat. Once the system had achieved an equilibrium of this type the marginal displacements from it would lead the system back to equilibrium. Only a perturbation of large size could move the system away from equilibrium irreversibly.

Let us now move to a type 3 equation, describing the number of distinguishable populations n constituting the production system. By following the same reasoning as before, if we were to observe that, beginning at a given time, the number of populations n remains constant, we could say that the production system has achieved an equilibrium and that this equilibrium is stable to the extent that any perturbation is not enough to change the net number of populations in the system. Again this equilibrium could be dynamic, since the entry of new populations and the exit of old populations could compensate each other.

The situation becomes more complicated if we take into account that the (intra-population) equilibria of a type 1 equation and the (inter-population) equilibria of a type 3 equation are interdependent. When a new firm population i is created, the number of its members can be expected to change until it reaches an equilibrium. If at this point one (or more) new populations are created and one (or more) old populations become extinct, the equilibrium of population i becomes unstable. Some of the new populations may represent opportunities previously unavailable and induce incumbent firms to switch from population i to one of the newly created populations. This process will continue until a new equilibrium both for population i and for the newly created one has been achieved. In other words, the entry of new populations or the exit of old ones represents a strong perturbation of the equilibria of individual populations within the system, to which the system reacts by means of a series of adaptation processes eventually leading to a new set of equilibria. These adaptation processes can only occur at a finite rate. Thus, if the entry of new populations were to make the equilibrium number of firms in population i, N_i^* unstable, the new equilibrium number of firms in population i, $N_i'^*$, would be achieved only a finite period of time after the new population(s) had been created. The long-term evolution of the system could thus be represented by entry of new product populations followed by the adjustment processes taking place within each of the firm populations producing the differentiated products.

We have thus taken into account two types of equilibrium: the equilibrium in the number of firms constituting each population and the equilibrium in the number of distinguishable populations constituting the production system. The dynamics of displacement and of adjustment of the two types of equilibrium are unlikely to be the same. To begin with, we can expect the dynamics of entry and exit of firms into and out of a firm population to be faster than the dynamics of creation and extinction of populations. In our case we could consider that new populations of firms are added rather infrequently to the economic system by means of radical innovations. The adjustments constituted by the change in the equilibrium value of the number of firms in the interacting populations should take place long before a new population can be created. If this were the case, the processes represented by a type 1 equation and by a type 3 equation would be examples of the fast and slow dynamics identified by Lordon (1997) in the development of modern capitalism. However, if we take into account that new populations can also be created by the accumulation of incremental innovations in the same dimensions of characteristics space, we realize that this process can be almost continuous and thus represent a permanent perturbation applied to the various intra-population equilibria. Even when two populations, i and $i+$, have not yet become completely separate, their changing features during the process of separation will lead to a change in the interactions with the remaining populations of the system. To the extent that the processes of creation of new populations, including the effect both of radical and of incremental innovations, can be accelerated by a growing intensity of search activities, the rates of intra-population adjustment and of the creation of new populations could become comparable. In this case the system might never be able to achieve the equilibrium number of firms in each population constituting it. Before such an equilibrium number of firms is achieved, the emergence of one or more new populations will establish new target values for intra-population equilibria. Furthermore, if we consider that changes in the nature of the members of the interacting populations (a type 2 equation) can also influence the interactions of different populations, we realize that the system may be in a state of continuous adjustment towards equilibria that are never reached. These considerations are not incompatible with the achievement of a steady state characterized by constant or quasi-constant rates of change of the state variables of the system.

Finally, we can notice that the emergence of new populations is endogenously generated by the inducements created by the saturation of old populations and by the focusing devices represented by the expected size of the new markets and by the technological opportunities afforded by the results of search activities. In other words, and although exogenous shocks cannot be excluded, an economic system constituted by a set of interacting populations of products, of firms and of consumers, such as the one described earlier, will never achieve a static equilibrium, but it will constantly be undergoing processes of transformation, including transformation of its composition.

ON THE RELATIONSHIP BETWEEN REPLICATOR DYNAMICS AND INPUT–OUTPUT ANALYSIS

The main objective of this chapter is to start constructing a model of a production system compatible with qualitative change. As was previously pointed out, macroeconomic growth models cannot take into account changes in the composition of the economic system other than in very indirect ways. Input–output-based models take into account explicitly the composition of the economic system, but they do it in a static way. Having previously discussed the nature of a dynamic model of production in which qualitative change takes place, we are now in a position to discuss the limitations of both an input–output-based approach and of a simple RD approach. It must be pointed out that in both cases the representation of the economic system is based on the interactions occurring between different sectors. However, the interactions considered are not the same in the two cases. In an input-output system the interactions represented are flows of inputs and outputs between different sectors, while in a simple RD approach they are competitive interactions between the same sectors. The coefficients of interactions derived by means of a simple RD approach tell us how strongly sectors i and j are competing for the resources required to perform their basic functions. Thus the comparison does not involve the types of interactions, but the ability of each type of representation to take into account the emergence of new sectors and the disappearance of old ones.

Let us begin with an input–output (IO) approach. Here the number of sectors constituting the system is given. Within an IO approach we can only observe *ex post* the emergence of new sectors and add them to the IO matrix. Admittedly, even though in an input–output approach the composition of the system is fixed, we have an idea of the possible bottlenecks that can hinder the development of the system. Thus in Pasinetti's approach (1981, 1993) the imbalance between the rates of productivity and of demand growth leads to a bottleneck in the development of the system. Such bottlenecks can be eliminated by the emergence of new sectors. However, we do not have any indication of what the new sectors are likely to be or of the circumstances under which they are likely to emerge. A proper long-run analysis of the development of an economic system needs to include a transformation operator, such as a type 3 equation, that tells us what new sectors are going to be added, what old sectors are likely to disappear and under what conditions this is likely to happen. Of course, to predict accurately the composition of an economic system at some future time is impossible. Even though we can predict the inducements to the creation of a new population or some likely features of a future innovation, its exact nature is impossible to predict, at least for sufficiently radical innovations. It is not only the uncertainty surrounding the introduction of a radical innovation that makes it impossible for us to predict its exact nature, but also the possibility that such innovation may not be unique. At least some innovations are subject to increasing returns to adoption, thus leading to path dependence, to multiple equilibria and to possible inefficiency (see Arthur, 1988, 1989, 1994; David, 1985). Thus we will have to be content with an analysis that gives us the inducements to and the possible trends in the creation of innovations.

The solutions of a simple RD approach, obtained either by solving the Lotka-Volterra equation or by linearizing the system near equilibrium, correspond to a system at constant composition. Especially if we linearize the system near equilibrium the approach is applicable only for very small displacements around the equilibrium position. Thus, although an IO and a simple RD approach represent very different types of interactions occurring within the economic system, they have in common the limitation that they can represent such interactions in a very narrow range around the chosen equilibrium position.

Following the reasoning of the previous section, if all sectors were always at or near equilibrium, long-range economic development would not take place. Thus both an IO approach and a simple RD approach, while being adequate modes of analysis for short-range interactions within the economic system, are not suitable for the analysis of long-range economic development. In order to transform them into models of long-range economic development they need to be complemented by a mechanism that creates new sectors and eliminates some pre-existing ones. Such a mechanism is provided in an augmented RD approach by a type 3 equation, that tells us how many sectors exist in the economic system at each time as a result of the creation of new sectors and of the extinction of old ones. A type 3 equation can then be considered a transformation operator, that changes the composition of the economic system while the rest of the model (either an IO approach or a simple RD approach) analyses the interactions that take place at constant composition. Thus both an IO approach and a simple RD approach can be considered representations of quasi-static subsets of the more complex object of study of an augmented RD approach.

We can now go back to consider the equilibria for a simple RD approach and for an IO system, as described before. In an RD approach the equilibrium position for each population corresponds to a constant number of firms (members in each population). The solutions that can be found for a system of type 1 equations either by transforming them into a Lotka-Volterra form or by linearizing them near an equilibrium point describe the interactions of the different populations near such an equilibrium. On the other hand, the equilibrium in an IO system is characterized by an equality of flows within the system, that is by the condition that supply equals demand in the relevant markets.

Following the previous considerations, such equilibria could only be stable if no new populations emerged or old populations became extinct. Analytically, in an RD approach this would happen if:

$$\frac{dN_i}{dt} = 0 \tag{7.28}$$

$$\frac{dn}{dt} = 0, \tag{7.29}$$

where N_i is the net number of members of population i and n is the net number of distinguishable product/technological populations. However, given that an IO approach represents a system at constant composition, equation (7.28) is a component of the overall equilibrium definition even in this case. In the presence of equilibria defined in this way, no economic development would take place. The economic development represented by the emergence of new populations would destroy the equilibrium as defined in a simple RD approach or in an IO approach.

We can conclude this section by saying that the equilibria that are normally defined for either a simple RD approach or for an IO approach are static equilibria, incompatible with economic development. Such static equilibria could only be achieved by performing the (impossible) experiment of 'freezing' economic development and of observing the effects of marginal displacements on the equilibrium thus obtained. Of course, although the experiment of freezing economic development is in principle impossible, it can lead to a suitable approximation to economic behaviour in the short run, to the extent that the rate of change in the composition of the system can be considered slow or very slow with respect to the adjustment processes within each population. However, such an approximation becomes inadequate the longer the time horizon in which one is interested. If economic development involves in a fundamental way changes in the composition of the system, equilibrium as previously defined is incompatible with it and only useful for the analysis of short run behaviour.

SUMMARY AND CONCLUSIONS

The main objective of this paper is to define the nature of a production model that can take into account explicitly qualitative change. The paper starts with a type of replicator dynamics (RD) approach previously applied to populations of product models, of firms and of consumers. This type of RD approach represents two separate but interacting types of dynamics. The first is an intra-population dynamics, corresponding to all the changes (entry and exit of firms, changing competitive conditions and so on) taking place within each population of firms producing a differentiated output and thus representing a sector. The second is an inter-population dynamics, representing the entry of new populations, corresponding to new types of products, and the exit of some pre-existing ones. It is the latter dynamics that represents the Schumpeterian process of creative destruction. The two dynamics are interacting because, for example, the saturation of pre-existing populations, due to the increasing intensity of competition and to the saturation of demand, increases the pool of potential entrants into new sectors, and because any particular sector can use the results of search activities created in other sectors.

A production system will then be represented by a system of equations (of type 1 in this chapter), each of which describes the dynamics of entry and of exit into and from an existing technological/product population, plus the transformation operator, a type 3 equation, that from time to time adds or subtracts technological/product populations.

Type 1 equations, constituting the simple RD approach, are usually difficult to solve. In order to try and solve them it is possible to transform them into a Lotka-Volterra (LV) form. This can in principle enable us to take advantage of the knowledge existing about the solutions of this type of equation. Furthermore, whatever the form of the equations, it is possible to linearize the system of equations of type 1 near equilibrium. In this way we can calculate the interactions of the different populations constituting the system. All the solutions of the LV equations or of the linearized system near equilibrium are solutions of a system at constant composition.

This augmented RD model provides us with the opportunity to reflect on the meaning of equilibrium in economic systems undergoing qualitative change and on its relationship to economic development. Equilibria can be conceived for each population within the system as a constant number of firms. On the other hand, for the economic system as a whole an equilibrium would correspondingly be constituted by a constant number of populations. If we imagine starting from a state of the system where each population is in equilibrium, either the emergence of a new population or the extinction of a pre-existing one will displace the equilibrium of each of the individual populations. We can then expect a process of adaptation to take place, whereby all populations start moving to their new equilibrium position. The evolution of the system as a whole then depends on the relative rates of intra- and inter-population dynamics. If the rate of creation of new populations and of extinction of old ones were much slower than the rates of inter-population dynamics, economic development would be constituted by long periods of equilibrium separated by shorter disequilibrium shocks. If, on the other hand, the process leading to the creation of new populations were to happen at a rate comparable to that of adjustment of each population to its new equilibrium, individual population equilibria might never be reached, but the system might continuously be in a state of adjustment towards a new equilibrium position. All this does not prevent the system from showing some stability: in its adjustment process the system might show a constant rate of change of many or most of its state variables for very long periods of time. However, this steady state corresponding to an adjustment process ought to be clearly distinguished from an equilibrium. The equilibria of each individual population might very well be virtual states, that are never reached but that represent a moving target that the system is continuously attempting to approach. In fact, it is the processes that continuously redefine and displace the various equilibria described that constitute economic development.

Amongst the existing production/growth models, macroeconomic models, while very useful for other purposes, are not well suited for the analysis of qualitative change. Input–output models, on the other hand, take into account explicitly the composition of the economic system, but represent a system at constant composition. In a sense they correspond to a simple RD approach, although the interactions that they describe, flows of inputs and of outputs between sectors, are very different from the competitive interactions of a system of LV equations. An IO approach and a simple RD approach can then be considered complementary representations of a production system at constant composition. Both for a simple RD approach and for an IO approach qualitative change is only introduced by adding a transformation operator (a type 3 equation) that adds new populations and eliminates some old ones.

Given that the approaches compared in this paper come from different research traditions, it is important to reflect on the meaning of equilibrium used. In a simple RD approach the equilibrium within each population (intra-population) can be defined as the achievement of a constant number of firms as a result of the balance of the processes of entry and of exit. If all populations of firms were independent each one would eventually reach its own equilibrium. However, the populations of firms are interdependent. Thus the introduction of a completely new population, or even changes in the nature of existing ones, influences the equilibria of all the other populations within the system. The evolution of the system can then be represented as the combination of two types of processes: first, the emergence of completely new populations or the changing properties of the existing ones, and, second, the adjustment of the equilibrium position of each of the populations. If the emergence of completely new populations were much slower than the adjustment of the intra-population equilibria, the system would be most of the time at equilibrium. However, if we take into account also that changes in the nature of the existing populations can influence intra-population equilibria and that such changes occur almost continuously, we realize that the processes leading to the displacement of intra-population equilibria and the consequent processes of adjustment could be of the same order of magnitude, especially in a knowledge-based society. Thus it is quite conceivable that a steady state of the whole economic system would not necessarily correspond to a set of equilibria. If the rates of displacement of intra-population equilibria and the processes of adjustment were of the same order of magnitude, the system might always be moving towards equilibrium without ever reaching it.

Summarizing, the RD approach considered here, including a simple RD approach and a transformation operator, is a more general representation of production than an IO approach, or conversely, an IO approach is a subset of the type of RD approach used here. To both a simple RD approach and to an IO approach a transformation operator must be added in order to introduce qualitative change.

REFERENCES

Andersen, E.S. (1999), 'Railroadization as Schumpeter's standard example of capitalist evolution: an evolutionary–ecological interpretation', paper presented at the workshop on the History of Evolutionary Thought in Economics, Max-Planck-

Institute for Economic Research, Evolutionary Economics Unit, 26–8 August, Jena.

Arthur, B. (1988), 'Competing technologies: an overview', in G. Dosi, C. Freeman, R. Nelson, G. Silverberg and L. Soete, *Technical Change and Economic Theory*, London: Pinter.

Arthur, B. (1989), 'Competing technologies, increasing returns and lock-in by historically small events', *Economic Journal*, **99**, 116–33.

Arthur B.W. (1994), *Increasing Returns and Path Dependence in the Economy*, Ann Arbor: University of Michigan Press.

Carroll, G.R. and M.T. Hannan (1990), 'Density delay in the evolution of organizational populations: a model and five empirical tests', in J.V. Singh (ed.), *Organizational Evoluton: New Directions*, London: Sage.

Cohen, M. and D. Levinthal (1989), 'Innovating and learning: the two faces of R&D', *Economic Journal*, **99**, 569–96.

Cohen, M. and D. Levinthal (1990), 'Absorptive capacity: a new perspective on learning and innovation', *Administrative Science Quarterly*, **35**, 128–52.

Constant, E.W. (1980), *The Origins of the Turbojet Revolution*, Baltimore and London: Johns Hopkins University Press.

David P. (1985), 'Clio and the economics of QWERTY', *American Economic Review Proceedings*, **75**, 332–7.

Frenken, K., P.P. Saviotti and M. Trommetter (1999), 'Variety and niche creation in aircraft, helicopters, motorcycles and microcomputers', *Research Policy*, **28**, 469–88.

Gallouj, F. and O. Weinstein (1997), 'Innovation in services', *Research Policy*, **26**, 537–56.

Hannan, M.T. and J. Freeman (1989), *Organizational Ecology*, Cambridge, MA: Harvard University Press.

Kwasnicki, W. (1996), 'Innovation regimes, entry and market structure', *Journal of Evolutionary Economics*, **6**, 375–409.

Lordon, F.F. (1997), 'Endogenous structural change and crisis in a multiple time-scales growth model', *Journal of Evolutionary Economics*, **7**, 1–21.

May, R.M. (1973), *Stability and Complexity in Model Ecosystems*, Princeton: Princeton University Press.

Metcalfe, J.S. and M. Gibbons (1989), 'Technology, variety and organisation: a systematic perspective on the competitive process', *Research on Technological Innovation, Management and Policy*, **4**, 153–93.

Nelson, R. and S. Winter (1982), *An Evolutionary Theory of Economic Change*, Cambridge, MA: Harvard University Press.

Pasinetti, L.L. (1981), *Structural Change and Economic Growth*, Cambridge: Cambridge University Press.

Pasinetti, L.L. (1993), *Structural Economic Dynamics*, Cambridge: Cambridge University Press.

Roughgarden, J. (1996), *Theory of Population Genetics and Evolutionary Ecology: An Introduction*, Upper Saddle River: Prentice-Hall.

Saviotti, P.P. (1996), *Technological Evolution, Variety and the Economy*, Cheltenham, UK and Brookfield, US: Aldershot: Edward Elgar.

Saviotti, P.P. (1998a), 'Variety, growth and demand', paper presented at the Conference of the International Schumpeter Society, 12–14 June, Vienna.

Saviotti, P.P. (1998b), 'Technological evolution firm behaviour', in Lesbourne, J. and

A. Orléan (eds), *Advances in Self-Organizaion and Evolutionary Economics*, Paris: *Economica.*

Saviotti, P.P. and G.S. Mani (1995), 'Competition, variety and technological evolution: a replicator dynamics model', *Journal of Evolutionary Economics*, **5**, 369–92.

Saviotti, P.P. and J.S. Metcalfe (1984), 'A theoretical approach to the construction of technological output indicators', *Research Policy*, **13**, 141–51.

Saviotti, P.P. and J.S. Metcalfe (eds) (1991), *Evolutionary Theories of Economic and Technological Change: Present State and Future Prospects*, Reading: Harwood Publishers.

Silverberg, J., G. Dosi and L. Orsenigo (1988), 'Innovation, diversity and diffusion: a self-organisation model', *Economic Journal*, **98**, 1032–54.

8. Heterogeneity and evolutionary change: empirical conception, findings and unresolved issues

Uwe Cantner and Horst Hanusch

INTRODUCTION

This chapter summarizes part of the research performed during the 1990's at the University of Augsburg. This research has been concerned with the issue of heterogeneity of actors at various levels of aggregation, its sources and its consequences in the context of innovation and technological change. In this respect we have taken up the issue from a theoretical and an empirical side. The theoretical work has dealt mainly with the question of how knowledge spill-overs arising out of technologically different actors influence the direction and intensity of technological change,[1] the structural development in sectors,[2] the cross-fertilization effects between sectors,[3] and the comparative development of countries.[4]

This chapter, however, will report on the empirically oriented research, where we have been concerned with the issue of measuring the heterogeneity within a population of actors and tracking its development over time. This again has been performed on several levels of analysis, the intrasectoral,[5] the sectoral,[6] the regional[7] and the international level.[8] Although quite different levels of aggregation have been approached, the respective research has in common a certain conception about heterogeneity with respect to the productive structure of the sample under consideration, that is, the firms, the sectors or the countries. These structures are built up (a) by differences in *total factor productivity* and (b) by differences in *input intensities*, *output intensities* and/or *output coefficients*.

In order to identify such heterogeneous structures and to track their development and their change over time, we suggest a specific empirical approach. For this purpose we introduce a two-step analysis consisting of the *non-parametric procedure* to construct production or efficiency frontiers and the *Malmquist productivity* index to track the change of this structure over time.

The plan of the presentation is as follows. In the next section we will briefly refer to some theoretical issues: first, we describe the role heterogeneity plays in the evolutionary framework; second, we ask for the criteria to be applied in order to determine the analytically relevant heterogeneity in empirical data and put forward four requirements for the empirical approach to be employed. In the third section we refer to the measure of total factor productivity, distinguish our procedure from the traditional way of computing this measure and briefly introduce the main methodological approach we have chosen in order to detect heterogeneity and to track its development over time. The fourth section presents a selected number of results pertaining to different levels of aggregation. The conclusion summarizes our approach and discusses some as yet unresolved issues and problems.

THE CONCEPT OF HETEROGENEITY

In this section, what we attempt to discuss briefly is the concept of heterogeneity both in a more general way and more specifically with respect to the economic theory of technological change and innovation. For the further discussion this initial step allows us to propose a rather well-defined analytical frame constructed on the basis of a conception of heterogeneity which aims at differences in the technological performance of agents. This, of course, is an extraction from all possible sources and instances of heterogeneity, but it enables us to focus on that kind of heterogeneity we consider analytically relevant in the economic theory of technical change.

Theoretical Issues

In economics, there are a number of distinguishing elements of the neoclassical and the evolutionary approach. Probably one of the most important ones, however, is the *heterogeneity* of behaviour, attitudes, characteristics and so on of agents.[9] Thus what heterogeneity is all about is *asymmetry* among the agents in a set. However, it is not at all obvious whether this asymmetry matters for the description of the state of this set or for its development over time. In neoclassical approaches one would deny this in general, with the consequence that the theoretical models suggested are characterized by symmetry of agents or even by a representative agent.[10] All the approaches designed in this way are justified by the attitude that for the final outcome of a certain process, the differences in agents' behaviour during this process do not matter – it is just average behaviour which is determining the result and which analytically is relevant and interesting. Hence heterogeneity is only of an temporary nature and consequently it is a phenomenon only showing up during transitory dynamics.

Evolutionary approaches

Contrariwise, heterogeneity or asymmetry is a fundamental principle in the theories of economic evolution. Selectionist approaches, synergetic approaches and developmental approaches rely on it and discuss how the system's nature or structure, on the one hand, and, on the other hand, based on this, how its (structural) dynamics are affected or driven by it. However, in each approach the way heterogeneity affects evolutionary development is quite specific. In the selectionist approach it is heterogeneity which is reduced by competition and generated by innovation. In the synergetic approach it is heterogeneity which brings about specific structural, self-organizing features with respect to learning, co-operation and so on. In the developmental approach, finally, heterogeneity is a matter of stages of development (to be) passed.

Heterogeneity as asymmetry and variety

Heterogeneity is a concept which refers to the degree of difference within a population of observations, whether that be households, firms, sectors or even regions or countries which differ with respect to their efforts, behaviours and/or success due to (among other things) the artefacts they consume or produce, the modes of production they employ, the direction and intensity of innovative activities they pursue, or the organizational setting they choose. This heterogeneity of agents is, on the one hand, considered the result of technological change, that is, of different innovative/imitative/adaptive activities and differential innovative/imitative/adaptive success; on the other hand, it also serves as a source for further progress in the sense that this heterogeneity puts pressure on technologically backward actors to improve performance when the gaps become too large and on leaders when the gaps become too close; and in the sense that it provides for different kinds of learning processes (imitative and adaptive learning, cross-fertilization and so on).

In order to account for the heterogeneity of agents driven by and driving technological change, one draws on the close relationship between the characteristics and the behaviour of agents, on the one hand, and the kind of inputs which, on the other hand, they transform into outputs. In fact, in the theory of technological change the actors are characterized by the nature, level and degree of their innovative activities, either on the input or on the output side.

In this respect, heterogeneity can be accounted for by the conception of *variety* (Saviotti, 1996). This concept is based on the number of distinguishable elements of a set of artefacts.[11] In this sense Saviotti (p. 94) distinguishes output and input variety, the former being the number of distinguishable outputs and the latter taking account of the number of distinguishable types of processes.

However, heterogeneity in general and within the context of innovativeness in particular is not only a matter of simply counting distinguishable elements.

Any innovator attempts to perform better than his competitors, and this 'better' may show up in providing goods and services with superior price–quality ratios, compared to those of the competitors. Thus very often one would like to have a conception which allows for a quantification of the differences on which heterogeneity rests. Hence, with respect to output variety, one would be interested in whether the variety observed is also built upon measurable quality differences ('higher' and 'lower' quality) or whether this variety is found within a more narrow or more broad range of the specific characteristic under consideration ('more' or 'less' built-in features). Equivalently, with respect to input or production variety, we should have an account of whether the several techniques in use are rather similar or very different with respect to their efficiency ('more' or 'less' efficient) or their relative input requirements ('more' or 'less' capital-intensive).

An appropriate conception in this respect is found in Dosi (1988, pp. 1155–7), who is concerned with the asymmetry of activities and distinguishes *variety* as a special case of asymmetry. Both are to be seen in a context where firms engaged in innovative activities are affected differently by technological change in terms of their process technologies and quality (or kind) of output. Whenever firms can be ranked as 'better' or 'worse' according to their distance from some technological frontier he refers to this as *asymmetry*. The degree of asymmetry of an industry is then its dispersion of input efficiencies for a given (homogeneous) output and price-weighted performance characteristics of firms' (differentiated) products. For all differences or asymmetries among firms which cannot be ranked as unequivocally better or worse, he refers to *variety*. This may be the case when (a) firms producing the same good with identical costs employ different production techniques or (b) when firms search for their product innovations in different product spaces, embodying different product characteristics, and aim at different corners of the markets.

The concept of heterogeneity

Based on this discussion, the following will be concerned with heterogeneity which is as closely as possible related to technological performances and their differences; thus heterogeneity is meant to be technological heterogeneity and it is based on the local application of certain technologies. This includes, first, performances which can be compared directly to each other and by this means be ranked: that is, producing a certain product with a higher or lower quality or running a specific production process more or less efficiently. Second, this conception also comprises technological performances which cannot be compared to each other directly: producing different products in the sense of old and new or running quite different production techniques. These latter performances cannot be compared directly (in terms of some physical measures) and one has to rely on some other measures such as the comparative economic success of those performances (as measured in terms of profitability, market share, growth rates and so on).

Technological heterogeneity at higher aggregation levels

Moreover, the technological heterogeneity we are concerned with is not only confined to the technological performance of individual actors. It is also applicable to higher levels of aggregation such as the sectoral, the regional or the national level. By way of aggregation, of course, any sublevel heterogeneity gets covered and only some – here no matter how defined – *average* characterizes the higher-level unit. Despite the inevitable loss of information involved here, we nevertheless expect considerable and relevant heterogeneity in technological performance of sectors, regions or economies with respect to the product and quality range produced (for example, agricultural products, Germany compared to India) and/or the kind and degree of certain production techniques employed (for example, cotton production, United States compared to Pakistan). Accordingly, what we mean by locally applied technologies does – with a loss of specific description – also apply in a more aggregate sense to sectors, regions and countries.

Heterogeneity and dynamics

Heterogeneity as just introduced can be considered as a snapshot description of a sample of observations. Especially in the context of technological progress, it is quite obvious and has to be expected that heterogeneity is subject to change. One could easily think of exogenous forces which affect all agents in the same way. However, for endogenous changes which are provoked by individual action, it is just as obvious that the respective changes are to a considerable degree specific to a certain agent or group of agents; that is, the change we are concerned with is *local technological change*.[12] And even if we considered a number of agents to behave rather similarly, for example in catching up with the technology leaders, such progress as well is local in the sense that only a subgroup of the agents under consideration achieved it.

Equivalently to our discussion of heterogeneity the concept of local technological change is applicable to several levels of aggregation. In this respect, technological change is specific to a certain country (for example, the United States compared to Togo), to a certain region (for example, East Asian Tigers compared to Western Europe), or to a certain sector (for example, in machinery, Germany compared to Japan). Of course, and again equivalent to the above, local change at higher levels of aggregation hides local changes at lower aggregation levels, so that only an 'average' change shows up.

Empirical Issues

Heterogeneity everywhere

To state the importance of heterogeneity is one side of the coin; the other is to specify clearly in which unit we should measure or observe heterogeneity, and this in such a way that it is also analytically relevant.

To clarify this, it is obvious that we are not all the same. But is this extreme degree of heterogeneity of analytical relevance to explaining, for example, any difference in language among us? Probably we have to be more crude or even more abstract. We thus could suggest that it is only nationality that matters – and for analysing the differences in structure and content of the comments we could give here, each one of in his native language, this might be a helpful distinction.

Consequently, to identify heterogeneity in empirical work is not an easy and straightforward task at all. In principle, one is facing a problem similar to the one the typological approach is confronted with: what is essential for analysing the issue under consideration? Whereas the typological approach searches for some reliable average characteristic, the population perspective is confronted with the task of finding characteristics which are diverse, that is heterogeneous, and which are essential for the performance and progress of the population under consideration. Looking for variables which can render this, one very often has to be engaged in rather detailed analyses almost of a case-study type. Although the results are often very illuminating and interesting, it is often not possible to transfer the methodology and the results of one study to another; the aggregation of several results is often not possible, because the relevant variables are not of the same type.

Heterogeneity and innovation

Let us now look more carefully at the theory of technological change and innovation. How can we measure technological performance? To give an answer we start with another question: what does technological progress lead to, how do we distinguish an innovation from a well-known old artefact?

Here it is quite obvious that innovations provide for heterogeneity because something new – a 'new combination' in Schumpeter's (1912) words – is introduced into the market. This may be a better technique of production, a better organizational structure, a better product quality or an entirely new product. Hence the innovator introducing this new combination can be distinguished from competitors just by his or her innovation.

Thus, more generally, technological heterogeneity is just the consequence of differential innovative success cumulated up to the present. In a dynamic context, with respect to several features of the process of technological change, such as path dependency, cumulativeness and so on, this heterogeneity can also serve as an indicator for the direction and success probability of further innovative activities, such as innovation, imitation and adoption.

The central question arising out of this is concerned with the measure we should apply in order to account for this innovation and technology-related or determined heterogeneity.

Specific versus general measures

Of course, we could have a long list of possible characteristics or features which perform the task of detecting the effects of technological change and innovations. All of the characteristics used in *technometrics* are based on rather technical issues. Look, for example, at the technological development of helicopters, so well studied by Saviotti: technological progress here is represented by the development in technical characteristics such as engine power, rotor diameter or number of engines. Or look at computer chips, where technological progress is indicated by steadily increasing storage capacities. Finally, look at car production, where technological progress or organizational progress shows up in the increased number of cars assembled in an hour (Fordism) or in the decreased number of bad-quality cars assembled (Toyotism).

However, for all its merits, this quite specific and quite exact technical measurement also has its drawbacks:

- Despite the respective specific characteristics of a technology and despite the fact that its development can be represented relatively exactly, it also means that the more exactly one measures specific features the less a comparison between different observations will be possible and meaningful.
- Whenever different technologies and their respective progress are analysed, a comparison of the results is less likely to be possible.
- Any aggregation from the business unit to the firm, to the sector and industry, to the regional or even to the macroeconomic level is no longer possible. The reason for this is quite obvious: it is impossible to aggregate the products of different firms in a sector, the products of different sectors in an economy when they are measured differently by technical attributes such as pieces, kilos or megabytes.

On the basis of the following four central requirements we suggest and introduce a measure and empirical procedure which attempts to circumvent the problematic issues just raised and which makes it possible to analyse empirical observations within a theoretical framework aiming at locally applied technologies and local technological change. For each requirement we give a brief suggestion here. A full discussion is found in the next section.

Requirement 1 The task therefore is to find a measure which may help to overcome these problems. Thus what one has to look for in this context is a measure which, on the one hand, is exact enough and, on the other hand, is not too specific, so that the above-mentioned deficit will not show up. Hence, what we are looking for is a measure which serves this purpose and is applicable to a broad range of innovative phenomena at different levels of aggregation.[13]

Suggestion 1 In order to show the way to set up a broadly applicable taxonomy we suggest the measure of total factor productivity (TFP) and its change over time to play a major or even pivotal role in this endeavour. This suggestion, at first glance, might look somewhat old-fashioned as the concept of total factor productivity has been much criticized in the past, mainly in the context of growth accounting exercises where its construction is based on equilibrium assumption and conditions of traditional production theory combined with the notion of the same production to be applied to all observations. This leads us to a second requirement.

Requirement 2 The way TFP is measured should differ considerably from standard procedures. By this, in a first step, it should make it possible to distinguish innovators from imitators and account for better and for worse technological performance. Moreover, it should deliver a quantitative account of these differences.

Suggestion 2 With respect to requirement 2, we suggest applying a frontier analysis where the frontier function or technology frontier is set up by the best-performing observations. All worse-performing observations are at some distance from this technology frontier where this distance can be used as a measure for differences in technological performance.

Requirement 3 Related to the need to distinguish better from worse performance is the requirement that, following the evolutionary approach, the empirical analyses should not be restrictive in the sense that functional relationships, such as a specific production function, are a priori assumed to hold for all observations. One rather should allow for an open number of these relationships and also take into account *variety* in productions functions or output mixes.

Suggestion 3 For satisfying requirement 3, we suggest the computation of TFP measures by a non-parametric procedure to determine technology frontiers which – at least when compared to the traditional approaches of TFP index numbers, parametric production functions and parametric production frontiers[14] – are rather unrestrictive in the functional form employed for the aggregation of inputs and outputs, respectively. In principle, there are as many functional forms allowed for as a sample contains observations.

Requirement 4 The measure applied should be tracked over time. The respective measure of the change in TFP should be able to take account of local technological change.

Suggestion 4 In this respect we suggest employing the procedure to compute the Malmquist productivity index which just measures the change in TFP. The important feature of this measure is that it allows us to identify local technological change at the technology frontier as well as for the below best-practice observations.

TFP, TECHNOLOGICAL PROCESS AND EVOLUTIONARY THEORY

TFP as a Measure of Technological Performance

Referring to requirement and suggestion 1, we consider total factor productivity and its change over time as an appropriate measure for technological performance and technological change. This, of course, requires some qualifications.

Generality

As already claimed, we are interested in a generally applicable measure which allows us to track technological change on several levels of aggregation and in several fields of application. Thus what we have to accept is a loss of specificity, especially found if one applies the analysis on lower levels of aggregation often coming close to pure case studies. The loss of specificity, however, is counterbalanced (and in our view even overcompensated) by the opportunity to detect more general insights into structure and change whose driving elements are found on the individual level of actors and firms, whose collective outcome then shows up in a characteristic manner on the next level of aggregation, and so forth. In this respect the measure of total factor productivity is applicable to all levels and areas of aggregation whenever we have at hand appropriate data on outputs and inputs.

Construction

Index numbers for total factor productivity (TFP) have found a prominent application in growth accounting exercises. There it is aggregate output Y, prominently GDP, set into relation to an aggregate I of various input factors, prominently labour and capital:

$$TFP = \frac{Y}{I}.$$

One can easily apply this measure to lower levels of aggregation, such as the sectoral level,[15] and to the firm level. Any change in total factor productivity, in the sense that this indicator rises, is considered the effect of technological progress: that is, change in output which cannot be accounted for with a change in aggregate inputs:

$$\Delta TFP = \Delta Y - \Delta I.$$

It is this so-called 'residual' which attracted so much research especially in the analysis of economic growth. And it is also this residual that Abramovitz called 'our measure of ignorance'.

A first question arising in this context refers to whether TFP can be taken as a measure of technological performance and whether a change in total factor productivity can adequately account for technological change. Let us take up this issue accordingly.

TFP as performance indicator

In order to account for the performance of an observation the indicator applied is to be interpreted always as a relative measure, either with respect to some known optimal performance or with respect to the best performance observed. In empirical work it is always the latter relativization which is employed. For this comparison to work, however, one has to provide for that the categories used for measuring inputs and outputs, and the respective way of aggregating inputs and outputs in order to compute the TFP, are identical among the observations. Otherwise the comparison is inadequate.

To cope with the first problem, one has to look for measures which allow for homogeneous input and output categories. By some degree of abstraction or cleverly chosen units of measurement – in the sense of real units (hours worked, kilos and so on) – one might be able to cope with this problem, at least partly.

As to the aggregation functions for inputs and outputs, with respect to inputs it is just the production function that is searched for and which has a number of specific problems. We do not want to go into detail here but only to recall that, on the theoretically founded perceptions of techniques applied locally and local technological change, an aggregation or production function identical for all observations cannot be expected *a priori*: to the contrary, heterogeneity is to be expected.

With respect to outputs, the problem is similar whenever we are not in the lucky situation of having to consider only one homogeneous output. Again this is not the normal case and among the observations we normally have to expect both differences in the quality of the output and differences with respect to the number of outputs produced. A common way to deal with this is to accept *product prices* as weights which account for quality differences as well as differences in kind.[16] This leads to output measures such as GDP, sectoral sales or firm sales. Besides this, however, one might also be interested in dealing with output variety in an disaggregated way, such as splitting up GDP into the output of various sectors or of firms' sales into the sales of different products. A possible way of performing this is presented below.

Change of TFP as measure of technological change

Interpreting the change of TFP as a measure for technological progress faces the same problems as just stated. Whenever we consider process innovations allowing the given resources to produce more of a homogeneous output, the change in TFP appropriately takes account of this. However, dealing with quality improvements or new products, whenever quantity and price changes account for this in a proper way we can use the aggregate output. But if we were interested in the development beneath the level of aggregation it would be helpful to have the respective TFP change determined on the basis of a disaggregated TFP index.

Other influences on TFP

A final remark here refers to differences in the TFP which are not due to the respective technological performance of the observation. Proper candidates are vintage structures as well as economies of scale.[17] For the change in TFP we should additionally be aware of substitution effects at work. With respect to substitution effects, according to Rosenberg (1976), substitution along a traditional isoquant is to be considered as applying a technique not applied before and this could also be considered as technical change.

Having given some justification and qualifications on the TFP measure as a response to requirement 1, we now want to go one step further and introduce a method taking care of requirements 2 and 3.

Structure: a Non-parametric Frontier Function Approach

Requirements 2 and 3 ask for a method which allows us to determine TFP in such a way that technological heterogeneity in the sense of asymmetry and variety shows up. For this purpose we suggest a non-parametric frontier function approach.

Unrestricted performance measure

The non-parametric frontier function approach, Data Envelopment Analysis (DEA), basically relies on index numbers to measure total factor productivity in a fashion similar to the one used in more standard productivity analysis. In a sample of n observations for each observation j (j=1,…,n) a productivity index h_j is given by:

$$h_j = \frac{u^T Y_j}{v^T X_j}. \tag{8.1}$$

Here Y_j is an s vector of outputs (r=1,…,s) and X_j an m vector of inputs (i=1,…,m) of observation j. The s vector u and the m vector v contain the aggregation weights u_r and v_i, respectively.

The h_j in (8.1) is nothing other than an index of TFP. The respective aggregation functions (for inputs and outputs respectively) are of a linear arithmetic type, as also employed in the well-known Kendrick–Ott productivity index.[18] There, however, by special assumptions the aggregation weights, u_r and v_i, are given exogenously. The non-parametric approach does not rely on such assumptions; in particular, it is not assumed that all observations of the sample have a common identical production function. With this (at least to a certain degree) unconstrained way of aggregating both inputs and outputs, we are able to account for requirement 3 above. The parameterization of the aggregation functions and thus the aggregation weights which may be specific to a certain observation are determined endogenously. They are the solution to a specific optimization problem (as discussed below), and therefore they are dependent on the empirical data of the sample. Critics often argue that a linear arithmetic aggregation nevertheless presupposes at least a special type of production function,[19] such as the Leontief-type production function.[20] Since the aggregation weights are determined endogenously and can be different between observations, there ultimately exist a number of parametrically different possible aggregation functions, although they are all of the same type.[21] For the input side, moreover, the fact that the Leontief production function fits well into this framework suits well the widely held assumption of short-run limited substitutability of production factors whenever techniques employed are of a local character.

This unrestricted form of the total factor productivity measure is central to an application of this method to evolutionary analysis and to detecting heterogeneity in particular. For computing this index we can include all kinds of inputs and different types of outputs. This implies also that new products and, equivalently, new production factors, can be taken care of. Since the non-parametric approach does not require all inputs to be employed or outputs to be produced by each observation, we are readily able to take into account both product innovations and new techniques of production.

Having found a rather unrestricted means of measuring the performance of an observation, we would also like to provide a comparison of this performance with those of the other observations, in the sense that we find statements about 'unequivocally better' or 'unequivocally worse', or even 'not comparable'.

Comparison of performance

In making this comparison, the basic principle of the non-parametric approach is just to determine the indices h_j in such a way that they can be interpreted as efficiency ratings, which implies a comparison of each observation with the best observation(s). The (relatively) most efficient observations of a sample are evaluated by $h = 1$, less efficient observations by $h<1$. Hence, by comparing all observations with each other, we achieve an account of different technological performance where the differences are quantified in the measure h; this is just what requirement 2 asked for.

The following constrained maximization problem is used to determine such an h value for a particular observation l, $l \in \{1,\ldots n\}$:

$$\max h_l = \frac{u^T Y_l}{v^T X_l}$$

$$s.t.: \frac{u^T Y_j}{v^T X_j} \leq 1; j = 1,\ldots,n; \tag{8.2}$$

$$u, v > 0.$$

Problem (8.2) determines h_l of observation l subject to the constraint that the h_j of all observations (including l itself) of the sample are equal to or less than 1. The constraints provide that h is indexed on (0,1). Moreover, the elements of u and v have to be positive. This requirement is to be interpreted so that for all inputs used and outputs obtained there must exist at least a positive efficiency value.[22]

Best practice or frontier functions

Since we employ linear arithmetic aggregation functions for inputs and outputs, (8.2) is a problem of linear fractional programming.[23] To solve such optimization problems, there exist a number of methods, the best known of which is from Charnes and Cooper (1962), who suggest transforming (8.2) into a standard linear programme which can then be solved with the well-known simplex algorithm. Performing this step and transforming the resulting primal to its corresponding dual problem, one arrives at the well-known Charnes/Cooper/Rhodes[24] envelopment form of the non-parametric approach:

$$\begin{aligned} &\min \theta_l \\ &s.t.: \\ &Y\lambda_l \geq Y_l \\ &\theta_l X_l - X\lambda_l \geq 0 \\ &\lambda_l \geq 0. \end{aligned} \tag{8.3}$$

y_l and X_l are the r and s vectors of outputs and inputs, respectively, of observation l; Y and X are the $s{\times}n$ matrix of outputs and $m{\times}n$ matrix of inputs of all observations of the sample. The parameter θ_l to be minimized expresses the percentage level to which all inputs of observation l have to be reduced proportionally in order to have this observation producing on the production frontier representing the best practice technologies; it is identical to h_l and is a relative measure of technological performance. With $\theta_l = 1$, the respective observation belongs to the efficient observations on the frontier. Proceeding in this way and solving (8.3) for all observations in the sample, the non-parametric approach determines an *efficiency frontier* or *technology frontier* constructed by the best-practice observations. The efficiency rating of each observation is measured relative to this frontier.

Figure 8.1 shows this result for a sample of observations which produce, with two inputs, x_1 and x_2, one unit of output. The technology frontier determined is *DAB*. The technological performance is the relative distance of an observation from the technology frontier. In the case of observation *C*, the measure θ_C is given by the ratio OC' to OC.

The n vector λ_l states the weights of all (efficient) observations which serve as reference for observation l. For the efficient observation l (with θ_l = 1), we obtain 1 for the lth element of λ_l and 0 for all other elements. Grouping all observations according to their respective reference observations allows us to detect fields of similarity. These fields are distinguished by different input intensities, output intensities or input coefficients. In terms of Figure 8.1, for observation *C* the reference observations are *A* and *B*. Consequently, only λ_A and λ_B are different from 0. The respective values state the degree to which *A* and *B* are used, respectively, to construct C'.

A first characterization of the structure of a sample

So far the discussion has delivered an account of a sample which makes it possible to detect and quantify heterogeneity in productive performance.

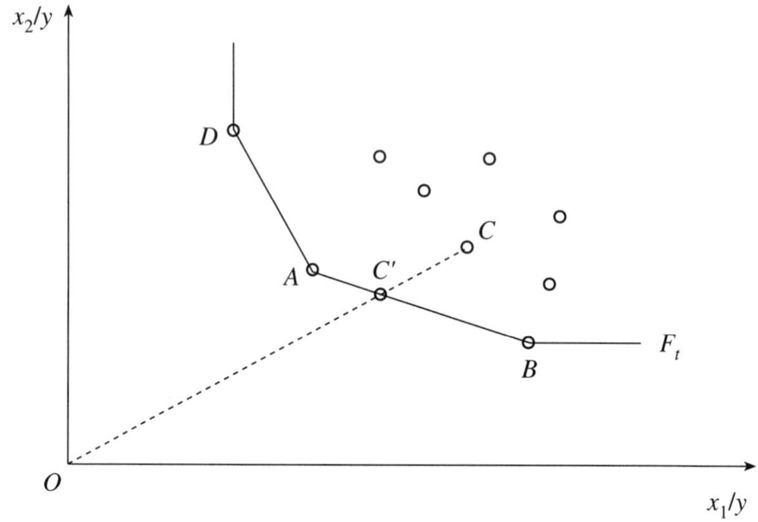

Figure 8.1 *Technology frontier and the measure*

With programme (8.3) we are now readily able to characterize the structure of a sample of observations:

- θ as a measure of performance indicating and quantifying whether an observation is best practice or below best practice;
- λ as a measure of structural (dis)similarity (Cantner, 1996).

However, modifying programme (8.3), some measures can be computed which shed additional light on the structure of a sample.

Comparison of best practice

Since the frontier function quite regularly is constructed by several best-practice observations which cannot be ranked as better or worse, one might additionally be interested in a comparison between them. The following modification of programme (8.3) allows for this where now the observation under consideration l is not a member of the reference set:

$$\begin{gathered} \min \theta_l^* \\ s.t.: \\ Y_{-1}\lambda_l \geq Y_l \\ \theta_l^* X_l - X_{-1}\lambda_l \geq 0 \\ \lambda_l \geq 0. \end{gathered} \tag{8.4}$$

The matrices Y_{-l} and X_{-l} contain the outputs and inputs of all n observations except observation l. The modified efficiency measure is θ_l^*. For all below best-practice observations it is identical to θ_l determined by programme (8.3). However, for all best-practice observations θ_l^* is different. For them it holds $\theta_l^* \geq 1$ and the difference $\theta_l^* - 1$ can be interpreted as the buffer or lead observation l holds compared to certain other observations. This θ_l^* is a measure to distinguish observations which with programme (8.3) are determined as not comparable (Cantner and Westermann, 1998).

Figure 8.2 shows the result of programme (8.4) for observation A. The respective frontier for A in this case is DB and θ_A^* is equal to the ratio OA' to OA, which is larger than 1.

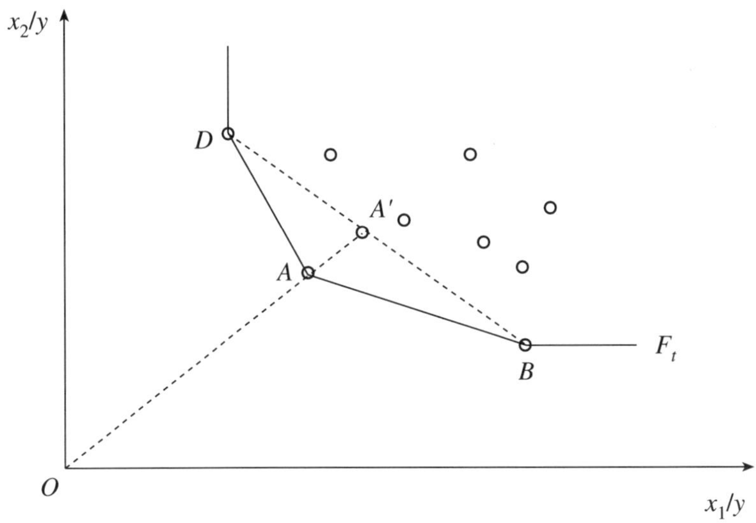

Figure 8.2 Comparison of best-practice observations

Besides this mode of comparing best-practice observations, an alternative or additional way is to look at the dynamic performance, that is, their comparative ability to shift the frontier function (by technological progress). This issue will be taken up below.

Accounting for scale effects

Finally, since the programmes used so far have been discussed under the assumption of constant returns to scale technologies, one might be interested in taking into account size effects. This is done by first setting up a programme allowing for non-constant returns to scale. This leads to a formulation where the elements of the λ_l vector have to sum to 1 (e^T is a vector containing only elements 1):

$$\begin{gathered} \min \theta_l^v \\ s.t.: \\ Y\lambda_l \geq Y_l \\ \theta_l^v X_l - X\lambda_l \geq 0 \\ e^T\lambda_l = 1. \end{gathered} \tag{8.5}$$

For the efficiency measure determined by programme (8.5) we get $\theta_l^v \geq \theta_l$. Taking the ratio of these two measures, $\sigma_l = \theta_l/\theta_l^v$, states the level of efficiency which is due to scale with $1 - \sigma_l$ accounting for that degree of below best practice which is caused by a size different from the minimum efficient scale size.

Besides these measures, the non-parametric frontier approach does deliver a number of other measures allowing us to deal with allocative efficiency, non-radial inefficiencies, specific forms of returns-to-scale and so on. These are of minor importance in the context of this paper. More interesting, however, is the dynamic extension of the analysis.

Structural Dynamics: Local Technological Change, Catching up and Falling behind

The following discussion refers to requirement 4, asking for an appropriate way of dealing with localized technological change and thus the structural dynamics induced.

Dynamic analysis

In order to track the structure, determined by the measures introduced above, it is by no means sufficient to compare the structural results of consecutive periods. Because for each period these measures are of an only relative type, such a comparison makes no sense. Consequently, consecutive periods have to be compared with each other, that is we have to compute relative measures which compare period t with $t + 1$ and vice versa. Doing this pairwise for all consecutive periods allows us to track structural change over time. The procedure chosen for this purpose is based on the *Malmquist index*, which states a specific observation's change in productivity between two periods. A quite interesting feature of this index is that it can be decomposed into a measure for technological change and one for catch-up – or, of course, technological regress and falling behind.

Malmquist index

The theoretical basis of the Malmquist productivity index is found in the work of Malmquist (1953), Solow (1957) and Moorsteen (1961). For productivity measurement, this index has been applied by Caves *et al.* (1982a, 1982b). Färe, Grosskopf, Lindgren and Roos (1994) have shown how the efficiency measure θ above can be used to compute the Malmquist index. We will follow this line of reasoning.

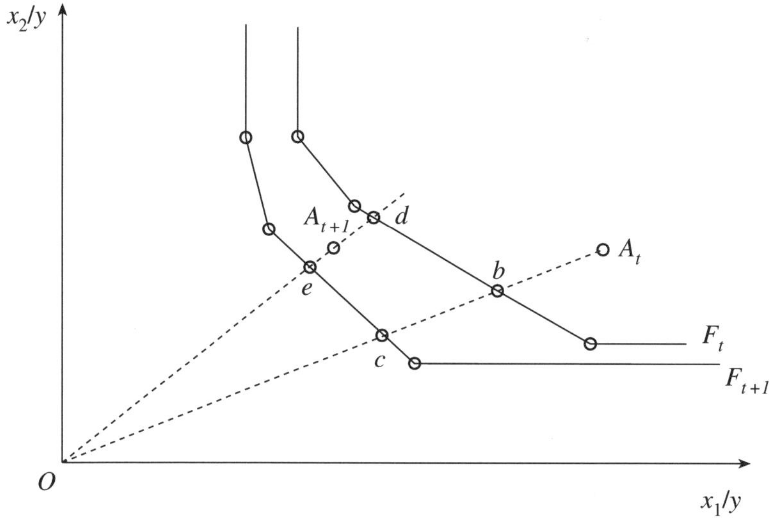

Figure 8.3 Malmquist productivity index

In order to explain what the Malmquist productivity index measures we refer to Figure 8.3, which contains a simple example of two non-parametric production frontiers F_t and F_{t+1} pertaining to period t and $t + 1$. For measuring the productivity change of observation A from A_t to A_{t+1}, consider the following. First, evaluate A_t and A_{t+1} towards the frontier F_t and compute the ratio of the two results. For this we get Ob/OA_t divided by Od/OA_{t+1}; if this ratio is less than 1 the productivity of A was increased. Second, and in addition to that we could also evaluate A_t and A_{t+1} towards the shifted frontier F_{t+1}; again we determine the ratio, here Oc/OA_t divided by Oe/OA_{t+1}; this ratio, less than 1, implies a productivity improvement. In a final step the geometric mean of these two computations is taken.

The resulting index,

$$M_A^{t+1} = \left(\frac{Ob / OA_t}{Od / OA_{t+1}} \frac{Oc / OA_t}{Oe / OA_{t+1}} \right)^{0,5},$$

the Malmquist productivity index, states the productivity change of A between t and $t + 1$. In a general way, the Malmquist productivity index M_l^{t+1} measuring the productivity change of observation l from t to $t + 1$ is defined as follows:

$$M_l^{t+1} = \left(\frac{\theta_l^{t,t}}{\theta_l^{t+1,t}} \frac{\theta_l^{t+1}}{\theta_l^{t+1,t+1}} \right)^{0.5}. \tag{8.6}$$

$\theta^{t,s}$, $t, s \in T$, is the efficiency of observation l in period t whenever the frontier function of period s serves as a reference measure.[25]

Decomposition of the Malmquist index

With some manipulation we can develop (8.6) to the following expression for the Malmquist index:

$$\begin{aligned} M_A^{t+1} &= \left(\frac{\theta_l^{t,t}}{\theta_l^{t+1,t}} \frac{\theta_l^{t,t+1}}{\theta_l^{t+1,t+1}} \right)^{0.5} \\ &= \frac{\theta_l^{t,t}}{\theta_l^{t+1,t+1}} \left(\frac{\theta_l^{t,t+1,t+1}}{\theta_l^{t+1,t}} \frac{\theta_l^{t,t+1}}{\theta_l^{t,t}} \right)^{0.5} \\ &= \mathrm{MC} \cdot \mathrm{MT}. \end{aligned} \tag{8.7}$$

The second line in (8.7) states the decomposition of the productivity change in technological progress (MT) and change in the technology gap (MC).

Whenever MC < 1 (MC > 1) we find catch-up (falling behind). The second term, MT, indicates the movement of the frontier. This is measured twice: first with the factor intensities of l in t, and a second time with those of l in t + 1. With MT < 1 (MT > 1) we have technological progress (technological regress) at the frontier. Looking at our example in Figure 8.3, this decomposition is given by the following ratio of distances:

$$\begin{aligned} M_A^{t+1} &= \frac{Ob/OA_t}{Oe/OA_{t+1}} \left(\frac{Oe/OA_{t+1}}{Od/OA_{t+1}} \frac{Oc/OA_t}{Ob/OA_t} \right)^{0.5} \\ &= \mathrm{MC} \cdot \mathrm{MT}. \end{aligned}$$

By this, we can state that the first bracket term measures the change in the distance of A towards the frontiers F_t and F_{t+1}. The second term in brackets takes account of the (geometric) mean change of the frontier part pertaining to A. In this example both terms will be smaller than 1, indicating that observation A performed technological progress and was able to catch up to the frontier.

Local change

As is readily apparent from Figure 8.3, the productivity change in (8.6) is local, in the sense that it is specific to the observation under consideration. In this respect the degree of this local change depends (a) on the observation's ability to shift in direction to the origin and (b) on the behaviour of the frontier. As to (b), the respective change is also local in the sense that, for observation l, it is only relevant how the respective part of the frontier assigned to l (by the way of the elements of the λ vector) shifts. The decomposition of the index allows us to distinguish these two movements.

Moreover, the decomposition also allows us to evaluate best-practice observations in a dynamic context by comparing them by way of the MT index and thus by the ability to shift the frontier function locally. An application of this is found in the macro-meso application below.

Summary of the Issue

In face of the theoretical and empirical requirements stated in the second section we have suggested measuring total factor productivity by a procedure which is as unconstrained as possible but nevertheless allows us (a) to systematize heterogeneity and (b) to track its change accomplished by technological progress in general and local technological progress in particular. For this purpose we apply a non-parametric procedure to determine frontier functions. These consist of the best-practice observations in a sample and do not rely on any common a priori parametrically given production function. We thus dispense with any notion of the neoclassical production function and rely entirely on production techniques which, in the short run, show no substitutability among production factors; that is, which could be described by a Leontief-type relationship between output and input.

For the dynamics we apply the Malmquist index measuring productivity change by comparing the non-parametric production frontiers and observations of consecutive periods. By this we dispense with the notion that technological progress shifts the entire production frontier and instead we allow for (a) parts of the frontier shifting and (b) this shift not being proportional.

With respect to heterogeneity and its change, this two-step procedure performs or detects the following. The first step of this two-step procedure allows us to detect heterogeneity – here technological heterogeneity – and classify the observations into the following categories: (a) heterogeneity in the performance of running a specific technique, class or range of techniques, and (b) heterogeneity in applying a specific technique out of a larger range of possible techniques.

The second step then tracks this heterogeneity over time and allows for (a) measuring local technological change, and (b) distinguishing between progress of the best-practice techniques or forging ahead and dynamics of catching up or falling behind.

Taken literally, the procedure suggested does classify the observations in a specific way in both a static and a dynamic context. By this we do not a priori have to rely on restrictive assumptions or constraints which force the observations to behave in a certain way, for example to obey the same parametrically given production function.

SELECTED EMPIRICAL RESULTS

In the following we will briefly present some empirical results found by using the methods introduced above. In this respect, our focus will be on heterogeneity and its development over time. Of course, this kind of exercise *does not prove* any of the evolutionary concepts or theories. In order to perform this task, the respective results have to be analysed in a further step by applying other statistical techniques such as regression analyses. Only then can one give answers on questions such as whether heterogeneity is the result of different innovative success, of different abilities to imitate and so on; or whether there are spill-over effects arising out of heterogeneity which influence the structural development; or how macro growth is influenced by meso or micro dynamics. Whenever they are available for our empirical analyses we will also briefly report on the results of these required third steps.

Intrasectoral Analysis of Technological and Structural Change: Industrial Dynamics

The first of our selected empirical applications is concerned with the dynamics of productivity within industrial sectors (Cantner, 1996, 1998). This dynamics is characterized by a certain structural stability with respect to best-practice performance as well as some regularities as to which firms are more likely to catch up than others. We concentrate here on *heterogeneity*, 'defined' on the basis of the performance differences between best- and below best-practice firms.

For the purpose of presentation we refer to a number of investigations into the German manufacturing sector. Here we report on the plastics (22 firms), machinery (83 firms) and electronics (36 firms) sectors. The analysis is performed for the period 1981–93. We use three inputs: labour (labour hours), capital (machinery and equipment, capacity adjusted) and materials. Output is sales corrected by change in stocks. Hence the non-parametric frontier approach is run with three inputs and one output.

In Figure 8.4 we present results for the three sectors. Using the efficiency values determined by the non-parametric approach, we draw Salter curves of 1986 and 1993 for the three selected sectors. Here the order of firms (which are distinguished by an identification number, 'firm i.d.') on the abscissa is always in accordance with the efficiency ranking as found in 1986. Comparing the Salter curves for the two selected years we find:

- some degree of *persistency* because
  a number of best-practice firms in 1986 are still ahead in 1993;
  the efficiency ranking of firms is rather similar in 1993 to that of 1986, at least in plastics and machinery;
- tendencies of overall *convergence* or *divergence*,
  where in plastics the 1993 curve is almost everywhere above the 1986 curve, implying that the efficiency levels came closer together; the contrary applies to electronics; no clear answer is possible for machinery;
- characteristic *structural dynamics*,
  where the 'falling back' from 1986 to 1993 is more often the case in regions of higher efficiency in all three sectors;
  where 'catching up' from 1986 to 1993 is more likely in the lower regions of efficiency in plastics and machinery and only in regions of middle efficiency levels in electronics.

To explain these results, additional analyses have to be performed. For the structural dynamics of catching up and falling behind one could test for the hypothesis of 'advantage of backwardness' and the role of absorptive capacities for the followers in catching up.

The results of this analysis are stated in Tables 8.1a–c. We regress the catch-up variable MC_i (which measures the change in efficiency from 1986 to 1993) as the dependent variable on the technology gap in 1986, θ_i, and proxy variables for absorptive capacity, AC_i. SRDSL is the R&D capital stock per worker of firm *i* (determined by the capital inventory method) and SRDWORK is the number of R&D personnel in the total working force of firm *i*.

Moreover, we distinguish a linear relationship from a non-linear one; the latter presumes that, first, catching up is easier when the gap is larger because much more can be learned; this is the 'advantage of backwardness' hypothesis. Alternatively, and secondly, it is assumed that, although much more can be learned with a larger gap, it becomes more difficult to absorb the respective knowledge when the gap increases. Thus the ability to catch up is dependent on the firm's absorptive capacity. For this case a bell-shaped relationship between catching up and technology gap can be deduced stating that, up to some point, a larger gap allows for higher spill-overs, but with the

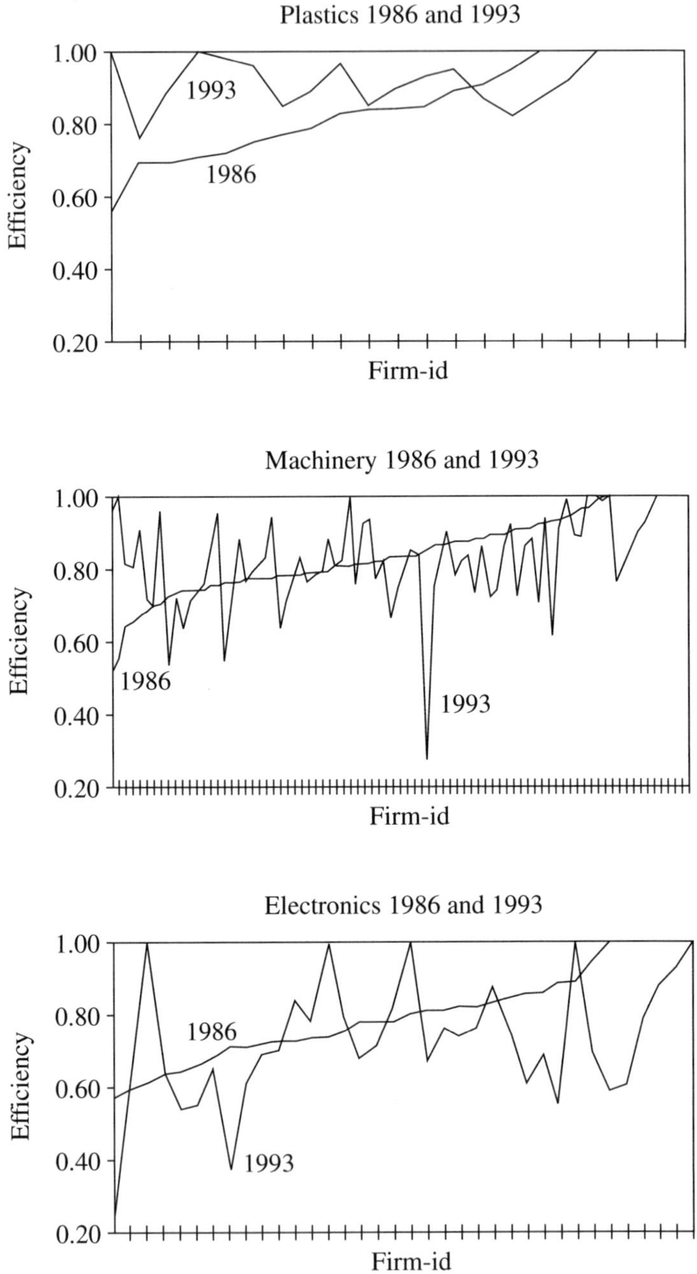

Figure 8.4 Salter curves, 1986 compared to 1993

Table 8.1a Regression results for plastics (t-*values in brackets)*

Dep. MC_i	Const.	Gap θ_i	Absorptive capacity AC_i SRDSL	SRDWORK	R^2 F-value
OLS	0.117	–0.244			0.37
	(4.390)	(–6.415)			(11.47)
OLS	0.02	–0.267	0.151		0.47
	(0.497)	(–6.422)	(3.211)		(7.987)
OLS	0.027	–0.332		0.110	0.45
	(0.231)	(–6.172)		(1.288)	(7.17)
NLS	0.280	–0.893	–0.587		0.51
	(5.719)	(–4.687)	(–5.392)		(9.73)
NLS	0.297	–0.806		–0.371	0.54
	(6.556)	(–5.908)		(–5.871)	(10.56)

Table 8.1b Regression results for machinery (t-*values in brackets)*

Dep. MC_i	Const.	Gap θ_i	Absorptive capacity AC_i SRDSL	SRDWORK	R^2 F-value
OLS	0.148	–0.345			0.34
	(14.16)	(–12.88)			(32.02)
OLS	0.149	–0.357	–0.005		0.35
	(14.85)	(–12.98)	(–1.494)		(16.68)
OLS	0.150	–0.359		–0.002	0.36
	(14.33)	(–13.04)		(–1.841)	(17.44)
NLS	0.125	–0.249	0.296		0.37
	(9.358)	(–5.574)	(2.472)		(18.02)
NLS	0.129	–0.268		0.239	0.36
	(9.543)	(–5.633)		(1.935)	(17.90)

gap further increasing the absorptive capacity puts a constraint on the level of spill-overs, which then are decreasing.

For both specifications the signs of the coefficients except the constant are all expected to be negative. The linear version is estimated by using ordinary least squares (OLS) whereas the bell-shaped relationship requires non-linear least squares (NLS).

Table 8.1c Regression results for electronics (t-values in brackets)

Dep. MC_i	Const.	Gap θ_i	Absorptive capacity AC_i SRDSL	SRDWORK	R^2 F-value
OLS	0.048	–0.107			0.08
	(0.491)	(–1.45)			(2.26)
OLS	0.050	–0.107	–0.0001		0.08
	(0.497)	(–1.42)	(–0.246)		(1.17)
OLS	0.050	–0.107		–0.0001	0.08
	(0.495)	(–1.42)		(–0.229)	(1.17)
NLS	0.135	–0.318	–0.570		0.23
	(1.463)	(–2.874)	(–2.332)		(3.73)
NLS	0.107	–0.262		–0.657	0.19
	(1.103)	(–2.553)		(–1.834)	(2.93)

The results show that the linear version of the catch-up hypothesis and thus the 'advantage of backwardness' hypothesis holds in all sectors, whereas the non-linear one shows up in the expected way only in plastics and in electronics. This result fits quite well with the Pavitt classification (1984) of sectors where machinery is considered a specialized supplier, implying that progress is mainly dependent on user–producer contacts rather than on knowledge flows among the machinery sector firms.

Similar results are found in other sectors of the German manufacturing industry (Cantner, 1996) and in the French manufacturing sector for machinery, electronics and chemical products (Bernard and Cantner, 1998).

Comparative Macroeconomic Growth

The second group of empirical results refer to a study concerned with comparative macroeconomic growth of economies, as analysed by Cantner, Hanusch and Krüger (1999, 2000) and Cantner and Krüger (1999a, 1999b). Similar to the intrasectoral analysis above, we are here interested in a heterogeneity based on the performance differences among countries. Additionally, we take into account the local character of progress and explicitly consider internationally different 'technological approaches', meaning that countries differ in the technology mix they employ, where the input intensity is used as a proxy for those differences.

The data we use for these investigations are taken from Penn World Table 5.6. As input we use the labour force L and the capital stock K (computed by the perpetual inventory approach). Output is gross domestic product Y in international prices. We thus run a non-parametric frontier model with two inputs and one output; we assume constant returns-to-scale in production so that the following analysis can rely on the input requirement per unit of output L/Y and K/Y.

Taking into account 87 countries, the frontier functions and their dynamics are computed for the period 1960–90. Figure 8.5 shows the world technology frontiers of the selected years, 1960, 1970, 1975 and 1990.

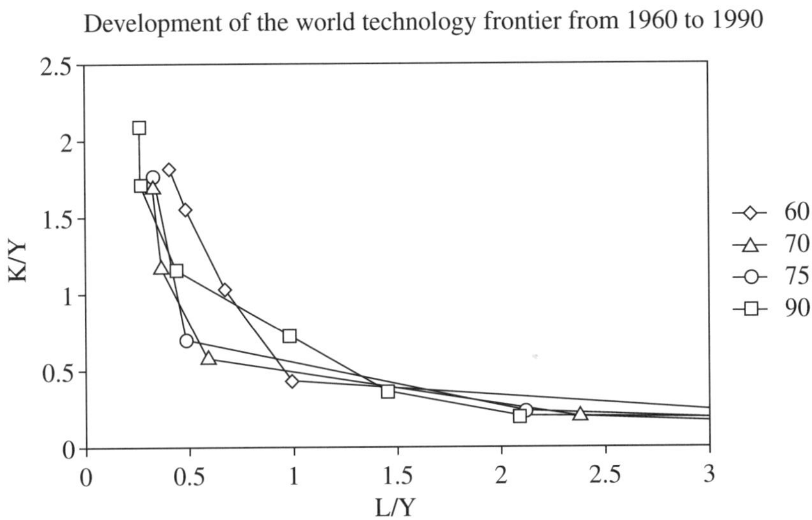

Figure 8.5 The world technology frontier for selected years

The local character of change clearly shows up as best-practice performance increases only in the range of relatively high capital intensities; this range of capital intensities is where the G7 countries are located, with the United States being continuously on the world technology frontier. In this range of capital intensity a continuous improvement of the respective frontier parts is observed. In the range of middle capital intensities the backward shift of the frontier in the late 1970s and the 1980s is considerable and quite obvious. Here we have mainly countries from Latin America, Northern Africa and the Middle East, with Venezuela and Iran often having the leading position. At the lowest range of capital intensities we have countries from Africa; here some improvement of the frontier is to be observed which is mainly due to the development of Egypt.

Figure 8.6 shows the development of several groups of countries. Most interesting is the development of the 'Tiger states' compared to the countries

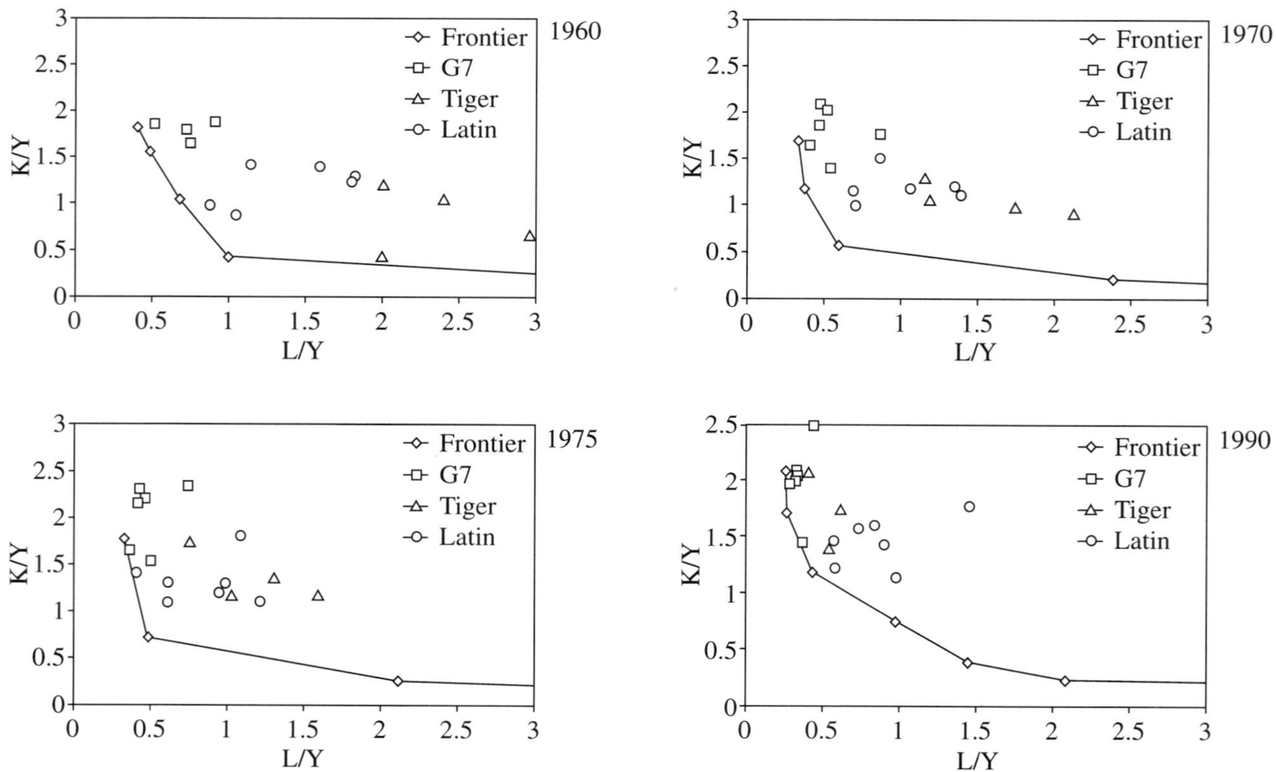

Figure 8.6 Tigers versus Latin American countries

from Latin America. During the whole period under consideration, the Tigers increase their capital intensity much more than Latin America. By this they first were not able to achieve high productivities as they were falling behind the frontier in the periods up to 1972. Later on, they were able to catch up to the frontier (for example, Japan in the range of the G7 capital intensities), overtake the Latin American countries, and even come to dominate part of the world technology frontier, as in the case of Hong Kong.

For this phase of catching up one can distinguish two sub-groups within the Tiger states. The first one, consisting of Japan (which now is in the G7 but in the 1960s and 1970s could be considered an early Tiger state), Singapore and possibly South Korea, managed to achieve capital intensities as high as in the G7 countries. Consequently, their productivity development is rather similar to the G7 development. For this group the assimilation hypothesis seems to hold at least for the second part of the period 1960–90. Productivity growth and growth rates were very high, although when compared to 1960–73 the intensity of investment had slowed down.

A second group of Tiger states did not manage to raise capital intensity to G7 values. These countries stick to technologies, much closer to those in Latin America. In doing so, they managed to catch up to the frontier and even to shift it. However the respective frontier parts do not show much technological progress and we even find considerable backward shifts. Thus these Tigers succeeded in improving the application of relatively labour-intensive technologies which did not show much technological improvement.

In order to explain these developments in a third step, an analysis is performed which attempts to explain the internationally different *technology levels* the countries achieved. These technology levels are computed by using the efficiency level in 1960 and then accumulating the productivity changes of each country from 1960 to 1990. Doing this we distinguish between the productivity level, the efficiency level and the technology level, each one related to the measures M, MC and MT, respectively.

As explanatory variables we used patents granted in the United States, human capital, share of years open, investment ratio and so on.[26] Some selected results are stated in Table 8.2.

Most interesting are differences in results between the efficiency and the technology levels. Patents granted are insignificant for the MC regression but significant at the 1 per cent level in the MT regression with a much higher coefficient estimate. This implies that patents represent the amount of research activities leading to technological progress. In catching up through efficiency improvements there seems to be no strong case for activities that lead to inventions which are valuable enough to become granted in the United States. For the years open to international trade we have exactly the reverse pattern. There is a substantially stronger relation

Table 8.2 Basic regressions on the technology levels

Dependent variable Regressors	Productivity level (M)	Efficiency level (MC)	Technology level (MT)
Constant	0.50913	0.67648	0.47422
	(9.595)	(11.374)	(7.640)
Patents granted in the USA	0.05478**	0.00898	0.08994
	(2.606)	(0.799)	(2.989)
Human capital	0.04098	0.03319	0.04781
	(4.434)	(3.340)	(4.310)
Share of years open	0.17552	0.20457	0.02574
	(3.126)	(3.517)	(0.465)
Investment ratio	–0.0082**	–0.0113	–0.0099**
	(–2.071)	(–2.818)	(–2.377)
Sample size	70	70	70
$\bar{R}^2$	0.558	0.346	0.492
RESET(3): F robust	0.1242	0.4335	0.2494
ANN test: F robust	1.3960	0.3631	2.1868*
White: F (no cross)	1.4584	4.1275	0.1933
White: F (cross terms)	1.0721	2.6202	0.2330
Jarque–Bera residuals	2.7820	0.5452	6.6695**

Note: *t*-statistics (in parentheses), the RESET and the ANN test are based on Jackknife corrected heteroscedasticity-consistent covariance matrix; significance is indicated by * on 10%, ** on 5% and on 1% level.

between openness and the efficiency levels than between openness and the technology levels.

Finally, and contrary to the other variables, public and private investment in physical capital is significantly negative correlated with all total factor productivity levels. Positive externalities from capital accumulation seem to arise here. However, this result has to be taken with caution because the investment ratio data are the same as the ones used in the construction of the capital stocks for the non-parametric analysis and rapid accumulation of capital naturally depresses the efficiency parameter θ and also the Malmquist index.

Productivity Growth: a Macro–Meso Approach

The following results refer to a paper by Cantner and Hanusch (1999) which deals with the analysis of productivity growth for the OECD countries for the years 1970–91. The analysis performed builds upon the advantage of the non-parametric frontier approach to allow the analyst to include output data in a disaggregated form. See equation (8.1), where we also have an aggregation function for outputs; the non-parametric frontier approach computes the respective aggregation weights (they are determined endogenously) and using them computes the productivity or efficiency index.

Referring to this feature of the non-parametric approach our analysis focuses on the difference between an analysis where the aggregated output is used and an analysis where output is included in a disaggregated way. In this respect we attempt to analyse whether and how 'heterogeneity below the aggregate' matters for the performance of the aggregate.

The data for the analysis are taken from the ISDB database of the OECD. For 13 countries,[27] we run the following two computations:

1. a so-called 'macro' analysis with one output and two inputs. Output is the economy's real value added in international prices of 1990. Labour is the number of employed persons; capital is gross capital formation in prices of 1990;
2 a so-called 'macro–meso' analysis where the inputs are just the same as in the previous design. Output, however, is now disaggregated into six subsectors: natural resources, services, consumer goods, wood and paper, chemicals, remaining manufacturing.

These six subsectors have been selected in a first step in order to include all 13 countries in the analysis – which otherwise would not work. Obviously, some more disaggregation as well as a focus on other subsectors would be preferable. This is work for the future.

For both analyses the efficiency indexes are computed for each year from 1970 to 1991. Then the Malmquist productivity index and its decomposition were computed for 21 years from 1971 to 1991. Here we have discussed mainly the results we obtain for the Malmquist computation.

Best-practice performance

Comparing the results of the two-yearly efficiency analyses reveals that in the 'macro–meso' case many more countries are on the technology frontier (Table 8.3) than in the 'macro' case. This, of course, is as expected for the non-parametric frontier analysis where the number of efficient observations (those with $\theta = 1$) increases with the number of outputs and inputs included. In the 'macro' we have for each year three to four best-practice observations, whereas for the 'macro–meso' this number increases to between five and nine.

For the purpose of interpretation we read this as follows: disaggregating the output real value added into subsectoral output implies looking at the

Table 8.3 Best-practice observations for the 'macro' and 'macro–meso' analyses

	BEL	CAN	DEU	DNK	FIN	FRA	
Macro	89–91	70–91					
Macro–meso	75–91	70–91	70–91		80–91		
	GBR	**ITA**	**JPN**	**NDL**	**NOR**	**SWE**	**USA**
Macro			70–77				70–91
Macro–meso		73–91	70–91	80–91	70–91		70–91

specific importance each subsector has in a country's 'portfolio', which could also be its international specialization. Take an example where several countries are compared to each other on an aggregate basis. As to Figure 8.7 the ranking is *B*, *C*, *A*, …, *D*,… .

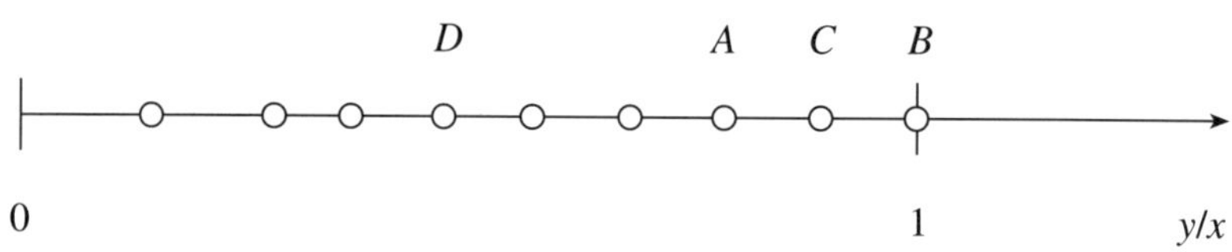

Figure 8. 7 Ranking at the macro level

On a disaggregated basis we would get the frontier function shown in Figure 8.8, which in this case is a transformation function.

Obviously, there are more best-practice observations, because they differ in their output mix. Observations with an extreme output mix, such as *D*, become best practice and even overtake an observation which in the 'macro' performed better, such as *C* compared to *D*.

Thus, if a country compared to the other countries specializes to the extreme in natural resources (as is the case for Norway) then it may well happen that it becomes efficient in the 'macro–meso' although it is not in the 'macro'. Consequently, the performance in the 'macro' can be further analysed in the 'macro–meso', where the following results may occur (Table 8.3):

1. The result in the 'macro–meso' still states only below best practice, indicating that some other country or a combination of countries have a

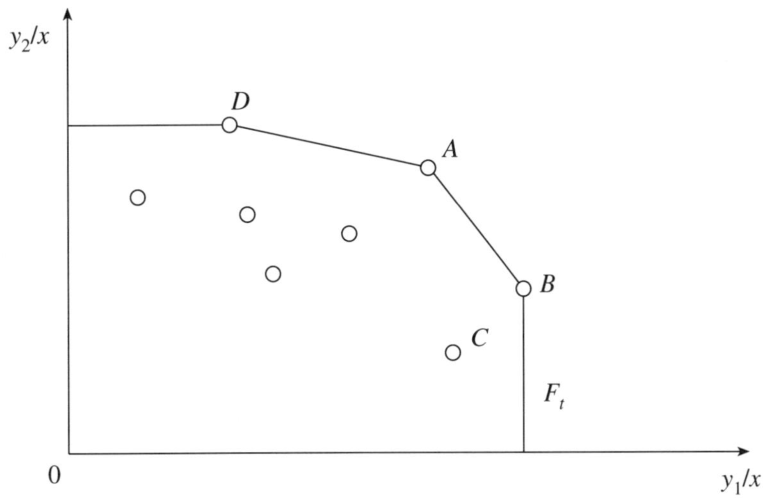

Figure 8.8 Performance at the disaggregated level

better performance in producing the same output mix of the country under consideration. This applies to DNK, FRA, GBR and SWE.

2. The result shows that in the 'macro–meso' the country under consideration is now being evaluated as performing best practice. Consequently, its output mix shows some specificity, to be considered further. This applies to DEU and JPN which specialize in manufacturing, with DEU relatively capital intensive and JPN relatively labour intensive. Equivalently, NOR and FIN specialize in mining, with FIN more labour intensive and NOR more capital intensive.

Performance dynamics

For both the 'macro' and the 'macro–meso' the Malmquist computations and the decomposition allow us to look at the performance dynamics of the countries. Most interesting is to compare the results of the two settings. Take, for example, the average productivity changes, as stated in Table 8.4a. For countries where productivity change in 'macro' is less than in 'macro–meso', we conclude that the progress due to the specificity in the country's output mix is larger than the overall rate of progress. Thus the 'specialization' of the country is in sectors with relatively higher progress. This obviously holds for DNK, FIN, ITA and NDL. The contrary case, where progress in 'macro–meso' is less than in 'macro', is to be interpreted as a 'specialization' of a country in less progressive sectors. This holds for BEL, DEU, GBR and JPN. For GBR, with a positive macro progress, the 'macro–meso' is even negative,

Table 8.4a Average productivity change

	BEL	CAN	DEU	DNK	FIN	FRA	
71–91							
Macro	1.81	–0.26	0.86	0.85	1.05	0.97	
Macro–meso	0.78	–1.10	0.13	1.38	1.79	0.97	
71–80							
Macro	2.91	0.31	0.90	0.59	1.10	1.39	
Macro–meso	0.91	–0.54	0.04	1.88	2.81	1.27	
81–91							
Macro	0.82	–0.77	0.82	1.09	1.01	0.59	
Macro–meso	0.67	–1.60	0.22	0.92	0.87	0.69	
	GBR	ITA	JPN	NDL	NOR	SWE	USA
71–91							
Macro	0.55	0.76	–1.91	1.00	2.47	0.38	0.43
Macro–meso	–1.34	1.28	–2.51	2.35	2.92	0.55	0.41
71–80							
Macro	0.38	1.39	–3.32	1.26	2.81	0.37	0.15
Macro–meso	–1.49	2.72	–4.82	3.71	0.62	0.32	–0.15
81–91							
Macro	0.71	0.18	–0.62	0.76	2.17	0.38	0.68
Macro–meso	–1.21	0.00	–0.37	1.12	5.05	0.77	0.92

indicating that the 'specialization' contributes even negatively to overall progress. An equivalent argument holds for JPN.

The decomposition of the productivity change into technological progress and catching up sustains these findings. Tables 8.4b and 8.4c contain the respective changes. In Table 8.4b, the shaded cells indicate that the country under consideration is best practice and is therefore responsible for the shift of the frontier.

For the subperiod 1981–91, the results show that there are countries which are able to manage a higher rate of technological progress in their 'specialization' than at the macro level, such as BEL, FIN, NDL, NOR and USA. The contrary holds for CAN (regress), DEU and ITA.

With respect to catching up, a comparison for the not best-practice countries shows again that in some cases, such as DNK and NDL, the performance

Table 8.4b Average technological progress

	BEL	CAN	DEU	DNK	FIN	FRA	
71–91							
Macro	0.49	–0.26	0.37	0.28	0.37	0.30	
Macro–meso	0.33	–1.18	–0.04	0.53	0.52	0.67	
71–80							
Macro	0.48	0.31	0.27	0.02	0.22	0.20	
Macro–meso	0.09	–0.72	0.04	0.42	0.14	0.55	
81–91							
Macro	0.48	–0.77	0.46	0.52	0.51	0.39	
Macro–meso	0.58	–1.60	–0.13	0.63	0.87	0.77	
	GBR	**ITA**	**JPN**	**NDL**	**NOR**	**SWE**	**USA**
71–91							
Macro	0.24	0.36	–1.83	0.30	0.68	0.42	0.43
Macro–meso	–1.14	0.90	–2.49	1.55	2.92	0.74	0.37
71–80							
Macro	0.50	0.6	–3.22	0.13	0.39	0.29	0.16
Macro–meso	–0.91	1.8	–4.82	1.00	0.62	–0.04	–0.15
81–91							
Macro	0.02	0.46	–0.54	0.47	0.95	0.53	0.68
Macro–meso	–0.36	–0.09	–0.32	1.10	5.05	1.30	0.89

in the 'macro–meso' is better than in the 'macro'; the contrary holds for FRA, GBR and SWE. However, here one has to be careful with the interpretation because catching up is indicated also for a backward shift of the frontier.

CONCLUSION

This chapter deals with empirical analysis in evolutionary economics in general and innovation economics as a prominent application of evolutionary ideas in particular. Within the latter, heterogeneity, in the sense of different innovative activities, different production processes employed, different qualities or goods produced, is a major analytical element – all the greater because innovative actors aim at creating heterogeneity and imitators attempt to re-

Table 8.4c Average catching up

	BEL	CAN	DEU	DNK	FIN	FRA
71–91						
Macro	1.32	0	0.49	0.57	0.68	0.67
Macro–meso	0.39	0	0	0.84	1.27	0.30
71–80						
Macro	2.41	0	0.63	0.57	0.88	1.19
Macro–meso	0.82	0	0	1.45	2.69	0.71
81–91						
Macro	0.33	0	0.36	0.58	0.50	0.20
Macro–meso	0	0	0	0.29	0	–0.08

	GBR	ITA	JPN	NDL	NOR	SWE	USA
71–91							
Macro	0.31	0.39	–0.09	0.69	1.78	–0.04	0
Macro–meso	–0.20	0.40	0	0.79	0	–0.22	0
71–80							
Macro	–0.11	1.13	–0.10	1.13	2.41	0.07	0
Macro–meso	–0.59	0.85	0.00	1.67		0.12	0
81–91							
Macro	0.69	–0.27	–0.08	0.29	1.21	–0.15	0
Macro–meso	0.15	0	0	0	0	–0.52	0

duce it again. This heterogeneity has an additional feature to be accounted for: the performance of the different techniques, activities, goods and so on under consideration. Thus there is not only a counting of different elements in a set but also the evaluation of these elements due to static or dynamic performance.

The task to be performed by empirical analyses contains three steps or problems: (1) defining the heterogeneity which is analytically relevant, (2) evaluating the performance of the heterogeneous entities, and (3) testing whether the structural development of the entities can be explained by evolutionary conceptions.

In this chapter we focus mainly on the two first steps. The third one requires much more space and cannot be presented in an appropriate way here. With respect to steps (1) and (2) we suggest a measure and procedure which are applicable to all levels of aggregation (micro, meso and macro) and which rest on a comparison of total factor productivities of the entities under consideration. The procedure we suggest is as unrestricted as possible: in the static analysis of the non-parametric frontier function approach aiming at the identification of structures there is no restriction on the production technique employed or the output mix produced. In the dynamic analysis performed by the computation of Malmquist productivity indexes the local character of technological change is allowed to work and to be identified. By this 'twin procedure' the heterogeneity and the differences in performance, so central to innovation, can be accounted for.

With the help of three empirical analyses we show how the method suggested works and what results can de deduced. In an intrasectoral study we focus on the stability and instability of certain technological structures. The study on macroeconomic growth throws some light on the dispute between accumulation and assimilation hypotheses concerning the East Asian Tigers. The macro–meso study finally shows how (meso) heterogeneity below a (macro) aggregate of countries may help to explain the differences in the macro performance.

These examples already show what the future research agenda could look like. On all three levels much more work has to be done, especially referring to the step (3) analysis aiming at testing for evolutionary mechanisms. There the main problem is to find appropriate hypotheses to be tested. Some hypotheses are readily available, such as the relationship between market share dynamics and local technological progress, or spill-over relationships in the international context.

The third empirical example, however, shows an additional line of further research. Here we focus on the dependence of macro performance on the behaviour or heterogeneity below the aggregate. In an evolutionary context, where the innovative activities of individuals or groups of individuals are the main driving force for progress on several levels of aggregation, this focus seems to us of great importance. The following questions arise in this respect. What structures provide for which characteristic development? How does this development translate to the next level of aggregation? What performance is to be expected there? Which characteristic development will then be observed? How does this translate to the next level of aggregation?

Of course, the twin procedure presented provides opportunities for further development. For example, stochastic elements could be included or the frontier conception chosen could be switched. An example of the latter is found in Cantner and Hanusch (1996) where we investigate a frontier function in the sense of best practice up to period t.

A major problem is also the rather unrestricted form of the procedure which by definition allows as many production functions or output mixes as observations. Does this imply that a representative sample cannot be used to explain the behaviour of the whole population?

Obviously, all the results presented and the future research agenda are dependent on the quality and the number of the data available. The coverage of the data with respect to the time period under consideration is one point. Another is the degree to which the respective variables are an appropriate measure for the technology under consideration.

Finally, the research we attempt to follow aims at shedding some light on the phenomenon of total factor productivity and its development. In many applications this still is a black box or residual. To achieve a better understanding for this residual, the procedure we have suggested may be a promising way to go.

NOTES

1. See, for example, Cantner, Hanusch and Pyka (1998).
2. See, for example, Cantner and Pyka (1998a, 1998b), Cantner (2001).
3. See, for example, Cantner (1996).
4. Pyka *et al.* (1999).
5. See, for example, Cantner (1996), Cantner, Hanusch and Westermann (1998), Cantner and Westermann (1998).
6. Cantner and Hanusch (1999).
7. Bernard and Cantner (1999).
8. Cantner, Hanusch and Krüger (1999, 2000).
9. Other distinguishing features include the different conception of uncertainty and of rationality.
10. Analyses dealing with asymmetric information are an exception to this.
11. An obvious candidate would be this number itself. According to Saviotti (1991, p. 177) in information theory the variety of a set is just the logarithm in base 2 of the number of distinguishable elements.
12. See Atkinson and Stiglitz (1969); a good overview is found in Antonelli (1994).
13. Saviotti (1996, p. 52) claims: 'a taxonomy at all levels of aggregation in such a way that the relationships of the various units of analysis within and between each level of aggregation can be analysed'.
14. For a discussion and comparison of the non-parametric approach with more traditional methods, see Cantner and Krüger (1999a).
15. See, for example, Wolff (1997).
16. This comes close to what Dosi (1988, pp. 1155–7) claims to be price-weighted performance characteristics of firms' (differentiated) products.
17. Differences might also be due to scale effects and/or vintage structures (Dosi, 1988, p. 1156).
18. See Ott (1959).
19. See also Chang and Guh (1991, p. 217).
20. Leontief (1947) has shown that a linear aggregation exists for a Leontief-type production function. Instead of a Leontief function, one could also use a linear production function.
21. Employing parametric methods, such as the COLS or the EM-algorithm, a specific production function is assumed. The coefficients of this function are estimated using the available data and the resulting production function is used to determine technical (in)efficiencies of all the firms in the sample. This procedure, however, suggests that there

is only one 'best-practice' technology. With the non-parametric approach, a number of 'best-practice' technologies can be determined.
22. This procedure is also known from activity analysis.
23. An overview of linear fractional programming is given in Böhm (1978).
24. There obviously exists a range of possible model specifications where the one chosen is known as CCR. Applying this, one has to keep in mind that possible scale inefficiencies are included in the technical inefficiency measure. For a more general formulation see Appendix I.
25. For the respective programmes required to compute the several θ measures, see Appendix II.
26. *Patents granted* are the sum of the per capita number of patent grants for inhabitants from the country under consideration in the United States over the period 1963–90 from the US Patent and Trademark Office; *human capital* is the average schooling years in the total population over age 25 averaged over all six five-year values from 1960 to 1985, as reported in Barro and Lee (1993); *openness to foreign trade* is the fraction of years open to international trade between 1960 and 1990 according to a classification of Sachs and Warner (1995); *investment ratio* is the average percentage share of public and private investment in real GDP during 1960 to 1990 obtained from the Penn World Table 5.6.
27. These countries are Belgium (BEL), Canada (CAN), Germany (DEU), Denmark (DNK), Finland (FIN), France (FRA), the UK (GBR), Italy (ITA), Japan (JPN), the Netherlands (NDL), Norway (NOR), Sweden (SWE) and the United States (USA).

REFERENCES

Antonelli, C. (1994), *The Economics of Localized Technological Change and Industrial Dynamics*, Dordrecht: Kluwer Academic Publishers.

Atkinson, A. and J.E. Stiglitz (1969), 'A New View of Technological Change', *Economic Journal*, **79**, 573–8.

Barro R.J. and J.W. Lee (1993), 'International comparisons of educational attainment', *Journal of Monetary Economics*, **32**, 363–94.

Bernard, J. and U. Cantner (1998), 'Retombées technologiques, effets de rattrapage et dynamique intra-sectorielle', in J. Bernard and M. Catin (eds), *Les Conditions Économiques du Changement Technologique*, Paris, Montreal: L'Harmattan.

Bernard J. and U. Cantner (1999), 'French Regional Performance and Variety – A Non-Parametric Frontier Approach', in P.Y. Badillo and J.C. Paradi (eds), *La méthode DEA – analyse des performances*, Paris: Hermes Science Publications, 255–73.

Böhm, K. (1978), *Lineare Quotientenprogrammierung – Rentabilitätsoptimierung*, Frankfurt a.M.: Haag+Herchen Verlag.

Cantner, U. (1996), 'Heterogenität und technologische Spillovers – Grundelemente einer ökonomischen Theorie des technologischen Fortschritts', *Habilitationsschrift*, Universität Augsburg.

Cantner, U. (1998), 'Industrial Dynamics and Structural Development: R&D, Spillovers and Absorptive Capacity', EARIE Conference, 27–30 August, Copenhagen.

Cantner, U. (2001), 'Heterogenität, Technologischer Fortschritt und Spillovers', in M. Lehmann-Waffenschmidt and H.W. Lorenz (eds).

Cantner, U. and H. Hanusch (1996), 'Intrasektorale technologische Dynamik', in E. Helmstädter, G. Poser and H.J. Ramser (eds), *Beiträge zur angewandten Wirtschaftsforschung*, Festschrift K.H. Oppenländer, Berlin: Duncker & Humblot.

Cantner, U. and H. Hanusch (1999), 'Productivity Development – A macro–meso approach', mimeo, University of Augsburg.

Cantner, U. and J. Krüger (1999a), 'An empirical account of technological progress on the macro-level – DEA versus growth accounting', mimeo, University of Augsburg.

Cantner, U. and Krüger, J. (1999b), 'Assessing the Robustness of Malmquist Index-based productivity changes and levels – an empirical investigation for 20 OECD countries', mimeo, University of Augsburg.

Cantner, U. and A. Pyka (1998a), 'Absorbing technological spillovers – simulations in an evolutionary framework', *Industrial and Corporate Change*, **7**(2), 369–97.

Cantner, U. and A. Pyka (1998b), 'Technological Evolution – An Analysis within the Knowledge-Based Approach', *Structural Change and Economic Dynamics*, **9**(1), 85–108.

Cantner, U. and G. Westermann (1998), 'Localized technological progress and industrial dynamics – an empirical approach', *Economics of Innovation and New Technology,* **6**, 121–45.

Cantner, U., H. Hanusch and J. Krüger (1999), 'Explaining International Productivity Differences', Congress of the International Joseph A. Schumpeter Society, 13–16 June.

Cantner, U., H. Hanusch and A. Pyka (1998), 'Pushing Technological Progress Forward: a Comparison of Firm Strategies', in J. Lesourne and A. Orlean (eds), *Advances in Self-organization and Evolutionary Economics*, London, Paris and Geneva: Economica.

Cantner, U., H. Hanusch and G. Westermann (1998), 'Technological Performance and Variety – The Case of the German Electronics Industry', in K. Nielsen and B. Johnson (eds), *Institutions and Economic Change – New Perspectives on Markets, Firms and Technology*, Cheltenham, UK and Lyme, US: Edward Elgar.

Caves, D.W., L.R. Christensen and W.E. Diewert (1982a), 'Multilateral comparisons of output, input and productivity using superlative index numbers', *Economic Journal*, **92**, 73–86.

Caves, D.W., L.R. Christensen and W.E. Diewert (1982b), 'The economic theory of index numbers of the measurement of input, output and productivity', *Econometrica*, **50**, 1393–414.

Chang, K.-P. and Y.Y. Guh (1991), 'Linear production functions and the data envelopment analysis', *European Journal of Operations Research*, **52**, 215–23.

Charnes, A. and W.W. Cooper (1962), 'Programming with linear fractional functionals', *Naval Research Logistics Quarterly*, **9**, 181–6.

Charnes, A., W. Cooper, A.Y. Lewin and L.M. Seiford (eds) (1994), 'Data Envelopment Analysis – Theory, Methodology and Applications', Dordrecht: Kluwer.

Dosi, G. (1988), 'Sources, procedures and microeconomic effects of innovation', *Journal of Economic Literature,* **XXVI**, 1120–71.

Färe, R., S. Grosskopf, B. Lindgren and P. Roos (1994), 'Productivity Development in Swedish Hospitals: A Malmquist Output Index Approach', in A. Charnes *et al.*

Krüger, J., U. Cantner and H. Hanusch (2000), 'Total factor productivity, the East Asian Miracle and the World Production Frontier', *Weltwirtschaftliches Archiv*, Jahrgang 136, 111–36.

Leontief, W.W. (1947), 'Introduction to a theory of the internal structure of functional relationships', *Econometrica*, **15**, 361–73.

Malmquist, S. (1953), 'Index numbers and indifference surfaces', *Trabajos de Estatistica*, **4**, 209–42.

Moorsteen, R.H. (1961), 'On measuring productive potential and relative efficiency', *Quarterly Journal of Economics*, **75**, 451–67.

Ott, A.E. (1959), 'Technischer Fortschritt', in: *Handwörterbuch der Sozialwissenschaften*, Volume 10, Stuttgart.

Pavitt, K. (1984), 'Sectoral patterns of technical change: towards a taxanomy and a theory', *Research Policy*, **13**(6), 343–73.

Pyka, A., J. Krüger and U. Cantner (1999), 'Twin-Peaks – What the knowledge-based approach can say about the dynamics of the world income distribution', paper prepared for the 'European Meeting on Applied Evolutionary Economics', 7–9 June, Grenoble.

Rosenberg, N. (1976), *Perspectives on Technology*, Cambridge: Cambridge University Press.

Sachs, J.D. and A. Warner (1995), 'Economic reform and the process of global integration', *Brookings Papers on Economic Activity*, **1**, 1–118.

Saviotti, P.P. (1991), 'The Role of Variety in Economic and Technological Development', in P.P. Saviotti and J.S. Metcalfe (eds), *Evolutionary Theories of Economic and Technological Change: Present State and Future Prospects*, Chur: Harwood Academic Publishers.

Saviotti, P.P. (1996), *Technological Evolution, Variety and the Economy*, Cheltenham, UK and Brookfield, US: Edward Elgar.

Schumpeter, J.A. (1912), *Theorie der Wirtschaftlichen Entwicklung*, Berlin: Duncker & Humblot; first published 1935.

Solow, R.M. (1957), 'Technical change and the aggregate production function', *Review of Economics and Statistics*, **39**, 312–20.

Wolff, E.N. (1997), 'Productivity Growth and Capital Intensity on the Sectoral and Industry Level: Specialization among OECD countries, 1970–1988', working paper, New York University.

APPENDIX I: THE ENHANCED LINEAR PROGRAMME OF NON-PARAMETRIC FRONTIER ANALYSIS

The version of the envelopment form including possible excess inputs and output slacks reads as

$$\begin{gathered}\min \theta_l - \varepsilon e^T s_l^+ - \varepsilon e^T s_l^- \\ s.t.: \\ Y\lambda_l - s_l^- = Y_l \\ \theta_l X_l - X\lambda_l - s_l^+ = 0 \\ \lambda_l, s_l^+, s_l^- \geq 0\end{gathered} \tag{8A.1}$$

A proportional reduction of inputs (as given by θ_l) does not necessarily lead to efficiency in the Pareto–Koopmanns sense. In order to correct for this the remaining excess inputs (s^+) and output slacks (s^-) are taken into account in the objective function. Vector e^T contains only elements 1. (Of course, one should here distinguish two vectors e^T, for inputs and output, respectively, which contain s and i elements, respectively. To simplify notation we do not take account of this. The further analysis is not affected.) ε is a positive non-Archimedean small number. Thus, additionally to the θ programme (8A.1) takes into account the remaining output slacks or excess inputs. Only then is a clear-cut selection of efficient and inefficient observations possible.

APPENDIX II: LINEAR PROGRAMMES REQUIRED FOR COMPUTING THE MALMQUIST INDEX

In computing the Malmquist productivity index, for each observation l and for each periodical change, four different linear programmes have to be solved. In the case of $\theta^{t,t}$ and $\theta^{t+1,t+1}$ the programmes are just the ones given by (8.3) and we will always get results obeying $\theta \leq 1$. In the case of $\theta^{t,t+1}$ the observation in period t will be compared to the frontier function of period $t+1$; and in the case of $\theta^{t+1,t}$ the observation in t+1 will be compared with the frontier in t. In both cases the efficiency values θ are not necessarily constrained to the interval (0,1) but they may be larger than 1. In this case technical progress would be detected.

For these four computations different linear programmes are required. They are given as follows, with t as the period under consideration and s as the period of the reference frontier:

$$\begin{gathered}\min \theta_l^{t,s}\\ s.t.:\\ Y^s\lambda_l \geq Y_l^t\\ \theta_l X_l^t - X^s\lambda_l \geq 0\\ \lambda_l \geq 0\end{gathered} \tag{8A.2}$$

With these programmes T–1 index number can be computed for all observations, with T being the length of the period under investigation.

Commentary: heterogeneity and evolutionary change – empirical conception, findings and unresolved issues

John Nightingale[1]

The chapter under discussion is both a defence of a method and a review of its use. Cantner and Hanusch have both published numerous articles using the method. What could be called 'the Augsburg Research Programme' involves, first, the collection of individual entity or agent data, then the fitting of data envelopment functions to estimate differences in total factor productivity (TFP) between members of the population in question. Finally, evolutionary theories are used to explain changes of population TFP and economic performance statistics over time.

The fact that the first part of their chapter is devoted to a defence of a method involving heterogeneity of economic agents, and the analysis of populations rather than the representative agent method of orthodox economics, is a comment on the state of economic science at the end of the twentieth century. Apologists for capitalism make much of the central importance of variety and innovation in distinguishing capitalism from centrally planned economies. However, the dominant strand of economic theory pretends variety is merely an inconvenient generator of noise in applied economics. How much longer will this remain a comfortable assumption rather than a scandal? Given this state of affairs, a full defence of population thinking would require a fuller analysis of the concepts underlying selectionist Darwinism and synergistic self-organization theory. This is not provided in this chapter. I would like to add a mere two sentences by way of defence. All that comes between representative agent theory and reality is the absence of mechanisms for agents to adapt seamlessly to optimality. Agents cannot know what is required for optimality and, even if they did know, they could not get to that position costlessly or immediately.

Given a population perspective, the complexities of reality set in. This is important for evolutionary theory, as it has been convincingly argued that such a research method as this belongs to the class of realism and naturalism. (Lawson, 1995; Jackson, 1995). Modelling becomes a matter of reducing complexity in ways which do not compromise scientific explanation beyond belief. The choices available to modellers are enormous, given that economic systems embody many different focal elements. Firms and technologies may be the unit of analysis in modelling an industry. Work groups, product lines, financial flows or functions may be the unit of analysis in modelling a firm. Attempting to model everything at once, even at a particular hierarchical aggregation with its own emergent properties, falls victim to excessive detail that can make even numerical models impossible to interpret. The simple verities of such a relation as that of Fisher's Principle quickly become vague once more than a couple of coevolutionary processes are operating. And, just in case it might be thought the biologists have it easy compared to us (as an excuse for our tardiness in developing adequate evolutionary models), a browse through Elliot Sober's *Philosophy of Biology* (1993) will disabuse you. Biologists have the same difficulties with defining the unit of analysis and the appropriate level of aggregation.

The Augsburg programme is an alternative to directly confronting coevolution. The solution its proponents implement is one long used for econometric analysis of the firm, and used by one of the pioneers of modern evolutionary theory, Jack Downie, in estimating the speed and strength of the competitive process. Downie calculated a measure of total factor productivity to estimate firm efficiency (1958). The Augsburg workers carry out a more sophisticated version of Downie's calculations. They use index number theory to boil down complex multivariate systems into a vector that has a scalar representation, a summary statistical variable, the distance function. Micro systems, such as households, firms or localities, can be further aggregated into markets, industries or countries. The population in question then has a single efficiency statistic on which each member is observed. It is this statistic which, Cantner and Hanusch say, presents 'performances which can be compared directly … and by this means be ranked'. Only those variables that can validly be embodied within an index can be potentially used in creating the distance function statistic. The distance function, a measure of relative performance, can then become the selection variable in testing evolutionary hypotheses.

The argument is rather stilted, as the authors present phenomena in an explicitly atheoretical context, then ask how theory might be used on these phenomena. Their exposition of the significance and nature of heterogeneity has to be carried without recourse to theoretical concepts that might resolve the problem before they have a chance to argue to it. But having argued to it, we can see its significance. The generation and reduction of variety is the core of an evolutionary system. Heterogeneity is the evidence of variety. Mapping heterogeneity in a population over time is the essence of empirical evolutionary economics. Their use of data envelopment analysis, which gives the distance function as the efficiency statistic, is a bold stroke of simplification. It just may work.

They distinguish between two types of variation. The first is between incomparable attributes, such as alternative products or input mixes, the second is between inferior and superior efficiencies in use of an input mix or in an index of quality of an output. Such distinctions are absent from orthodox theory because perfect information, and the efficacy of competition, eliminates inappropriate product and input mixes, and enforces maximum efficiency.

The four requirements, with their suggestions for resolution, take them, seemingly inevitably, to data envelopment analysis and the Malmquist index (Coelli *et al.* 1998). Comparability of different phenomena, a quantitative account of performance, generality of functional form, and the temporal dimension to allow identification of change, all are argued to be satisfied by the Malmquist index.

The conditions are lexicographical. Comparability must come first. Disparate phenomena have to be brought to a common measure. TFP boils down the many input/output metrics to the one scalar. Critique of TFP measures centres on how input dimensions are measured. It is not possible to avoid the difficulties of using such metrics as market prices or historical costs of machinery and buildings, rentals paid, interest charged, and so on, where markets are not regarded as perfect. Such is the ubiquity of the general equilibrium neoclassical model, and its CGE (computable general equilibrium) child in applied economics, that TFP measurement relies on the Walrasian outcome for comparability. Benchmarking exercises, in lively demand from business and government enterprise to validate their actions, depend on the benchmarked enterprises being in the same economic environment, of prices and acceptable rates of return on investment. Only at the most disaggregated level, where physical measures can be used, is it possible to benchmark accurately, and then the implications are not so easy to draw if differences in economic environment make different physical performance inevitable. The textile factory in Hamburg will rightly have different physical productivities from that in Calcutta.

The constant reference to 'local technological change' refers to marginal, or local, movement around a production frontier of whatever non-parametric kind, but it may also have to refer to comparability within a single economic environment in which relative prices and acceptable returns can be presumed roughly the same. But is this not strictly inconsistent with the boundedness of rationality and temporally limited speed of reaction that is required to observe an evolutionary process?

The authors also mention variables for which direct comparison is invalid, where inferences about these variables depend on the use of other measures, or proxies, to give them any sort of metric. Such variables, they suggest, can be proxied by the results of their action. But such procedure is the mark of a highly developed and well-accepted body of theory about the interrelationship between the variable thought to be significant and its proxy. Such a body of theory is not present in economic theory of whatever kind. The history of proxies in industrial economics, for example, is a history of misleading inference and mistaken policy conclusions (Scherer and Ross, 1990). The suggestion made by our authors, that one can rely on measures of outcomes to infer the causes, is a dangerous one. It can be mere *ex post* rationalization, a sin of which many economists have been guilty. New Institutional Economics is perhaps the best known location for this sin, with its rationalizations of alternative institutional structures by reference to vaguely measurable transactions and agency costs. In the present context, the temptation to explain superior performance by reference to vaguely measured selection advantages can be difficult to pass up. Evolutionary biology is similarly full of *ex post* rationalization of successful propagation by dubious adaptive features. This suggests that the composition of an index of inputs or causes must be independent of any performance characteristics to be explained. There is no place for output measures which are proxied by inputs (for example, output of financial institutions used to be proxied by number of employees of financial institutions).

The second requirement, a quantitative account, also includes a request for distinguishing between innovation and imitation. The suggestion is that a frontier analysis allows us to distinguish between an entity moving towards the frontier, moving along the frontier or moving beyond, creating a new frontier. But what does this mean in terms of the realities behind the Malmquist TFP index? The economics of technological change has had plenty of trouble with the idea that imitation can be distinguished from innovation. In a world of proprietary information and local knowledge, is a firm's attempt to match a rival an imitation of the rival if it does something new, but does not match the rival's performance? What if the new routine or method is patented; what if it leads to superior performance, but not for some time before development of the new thing matches the rival's performance? This is a normal part of innovation. On the Malmquist method, a firm which used slave labour intensively, from a large supply of slaves, and beat them mercilessly to produce faster and without fault, would be judged to have innovated if its TFP inputs were measured by number of workers rather than by hours or intensity of those hours. Some might argue that modern corporations work their staff in such a manner, following 'downsizing', and thus record higher TFP at least in the time period used for the measurement of TFP (partly by not recording unpaid overtime). One is reminded of the pastime of engineers in days when blast furnace records were being set, to run the furnace for the record, not caring that near-future downtime for relining had been brought forward by furnace abuse. Thus measurement of inputs becomes a very significant issue for TFP identification of innovation versus imitation. A definition of innovation which requires that innovation involve a new way of combining inputs, a leap into the unknown, is also problematical in that it is not comparable across activities, or generally quantifiable. But it should be recognized that the Malmquist method can lead to false identification of innovation, the more so the shorter the time period of observation. The two major reasons, above, are transitory reasons for superior performance and time lags in technological development of ultimately superior methods.

In light of these features of TFP, it is a surprise that there is no discussion of the distinction long made in consumption analysis, that between transitory and permanent aspects of observations. A feature of data sets on benchmarking (which is the usual origin of disaggregated data revealing heterogeneity) is the tendency for outliers to retreat towards the mean of the distribution, the original regression principle. The data sets used here are not exceptions. To what extent does this indicate that the data are, like household income data, measured with error in the variable? That is, the true variable is permanent TFP, the underlying efficiency measure. The measured variable includes factors that are transient, such as over- and under-runs of demand, very short-run pecuniary factors such as blips in factor prices, natural disasters and accidents, and so on. These transient factors would account for at least some of the regression toward the mean seen in these data sets, and for churning around the mean by observations closer to the mean.

It makes little sense to ask TFP analysis about the characteristics of technique which are of interest to the business historian or the historian of technology. Frontier analysis measures the dimensions of inputs and outputs quantitatively. Our authors refer to this in the third section of their chapter as the counterbalancing of loss of specificity by opportunity to detect more general insights. Here may be the place to mention some types of technological progress common in the literature of evolutionary economics, and their significance for TFP analysis. First, there is the Marshallian marginal adjustment to changing environments, an adaptationist view that is somewhat at odds with a hard-line selectionist position, given that the unit of analysis for Marshallian economics is the entrepreneur. This type of technological change may be commonly taken as the theory behind what is observed as learning by doing effects, and is the activity which the growth accountants imagined. Second, there are selection effects as represented by Downie's Transfer Mechanism, reallocation of resources from less to more efficient uses. There is no need for further comment on this as it is the nub of much evolutionary economics. Third, there is the explicit innovation of Schumpeter and his followers. Here we have the actions and reactions of the entrepreneurial market place. The problem for TFP measurement, even of the Malmquist kind, is how to go beyond improvements to real material welfare from price and cost falls due to improved processes and also deal with qualitatively uncertain effects on price and output indices of new products and new capabilities of products. Our authors attempt to justify a limited consideration of new products, but their answer rather depends on neoclassical assumptions about markets. This is the only way I can interpret their statement, 'whenever quantity and price changes account for this in a proper way we can use the aggregate output'. This again emphasizes the fundamental problem with TFP analysis: its reliance upon equilibrium assumptions about market observations. Not even a perfect market would give the right answers without there being a modification of the index regimen to deal with the new products or capabilities. The question remains not very tractable as far as TFP analysis is concerned.

In the same section the authors mention, in passing, the famous residual in the growth accounting literature. This deserves more detailed treatment as it is of significant interest to evolutionary economists. This residual is an artefact of a representative agent analysis. The assumption behind growth accounting is that all agents achieve efficient outcomes, therefore improvement is due to either more inputs or improved technique. Evolutionary economics suggests that this improvement comes from the reallocation of resources as selection pressures shift economic weight from the less efficient (in whatever sense) to the more efficient. The task of the Augsburg method is to measure and quantify that reallocation, thus explaining what we can of the residual by this means. Growth accountants measure average practice, rather than best practice. Over time, any shift of weight towards better practice means an improvement of average practice. The Malmquist scheme shows us a measure of best practice, in terms of either the Figure 8.1 isoquant frontier or the Figure 8.8 PPF (production possibility frontier). An economic system which allows or encourages selection or self-organization of resource use will be measured by Malmquist as the interior observations declining in weight. A system which encourages innovation will show the frontier expanding. Orthodox growth accounting imagines that only the latter process is occurring. Evolutionary theory makes its special contribution by focusing on the former, the selection process. Malmquist allows these distinctions to be made clear.

The empirical examples proffered suffer some rough edges, both in presentation and in analysis. The analysis suffers from econometrician's disease. This is the tendency to explain results in terms of data and overly simple economics. This is paradoxical in this case, as the point of the paper is to demonstrate the significance of evolutionary economic theory. The main problem for this example, of industrial structure in three industries, plastics, machinery and electronics, is that the elementary industrial organization of the industries is not sketched first. A few lines about industrial concentration, rate of technological change (the Salter curves are relative performance curves), diversification and profitability would set the scene for interpretation of the information presented. Given this, the hypotheses tested by the Salter curves and regression analysis would be more explicable. An evolutionary perspective, informed by the industrial organization of the case, would encourage conjecture and speculation on the basis of these results, and provide the motivation for the steps which should follow, the evolutionary hypotheses that remain to be tested.

The second, and perhaps more troubling, problem is the acceptance that the observations are reasonably accurate measures of the phenomena they purport to measure. I commented earlier that TFP is not merely measured with error (that is, an error term required) but that the variable itself is an inaccurate metric for actual TFP. Perhaps it is appropriate to see it as being an error in the variable problem. This would imply that econometric modelling requires an approach which recognizes this, such as the method of instrumental variables (though this may be very old fashioned now). It may be that much more data are needed to wash out the effects of transitory factors in observed TFP. Permanent TFP cannot, in principle, be directly observed, any more than permanent income for a household.

That being said, it is still true that the Malmquist index is a potent technique for evolutionary economists. Much remains to be done to deal with its problems, the neoclassical remnants within its assumptions, measurement problems and the restrictive nature of the technical changes it can deal with. But it is fundamentally consistent with the basic assumptions of evolutionary theories, of disequilibrium processes, structural change over time and limits on knowledge and information.

NOTE

1. The author would like to thank Tim Coelli for his guidance through the TFP literature. Remaining errors are due to my residual ignorance.

REFERENCES

Coelli, T., D.P. Rao and G. Battese (1998), *An Introduction to Efficiency and Productivity Analysis*, Boston: Kluwer Academic Publishers.

Downie, J. (1958), *The Competitive Process*, London: Duckworth.

Jackson, W.A. (1995), 'Naturalism in economics', *Journal of Economic Issues*, **XXIX**(3), 761–80.

Lawson, T.A. (1995), 'Realist perspective on contemporary "economic theory"', *Journal of Economic Issues*, **XXIX**(1), 1–32.

Scherer, F.M. and D. Ross (1990), *Industrial Market Structure and Economic Performance*, Boston, MA: Houghton Mifflin.
Sober, E. (1993), *Philosophy of Biology*, Oxford: Oxford University Press.

9. Measuring complexity: puzzles and tentative solutions

Francisco Louçã

INTRODUCTION

Formal reasoning in economics flowered in the wake of the development of the neoclassical theory of price formation, and was in consequence dominated by a strictly deterministic vision. In this framework, the dynamics of economic processes should be given by a simple linear function:

$$dx / dt = F[x(t)] \tag{9.1}$$

But a purely deterministic dynamics could not explain the irregularities in the observed trajectories, and as a consequence Frisch suggested that the evolution of economic variables should be analysed as the juxtaposition of deterministic processes and stochastic events. That approach became the standpoint of the Cowles Commission research programme and of the econometric modelling of macro variables during the 1940s, under the impulse of Marshack, Koopmans and Haavelmo. They posulated that

$$dx / dt = F[x(t)] + \omega(t), \tag{9.2}$$

where $\omega(t)$ is a random process. Yet recent investigations pointed to the fact that economic dynamics, both that represented by analytical models and that represented by the description of real-life economies, can generate a much more complicated outcome. That is the case when a large number of oscillators creates a phenomenon of resonance and therefore generates aperiodic orbits, or when, as a result of non-linear interactions, strange geometric forms attract the orbits of the system. We have

$$dx / dt = G[x(t), \omega(t)], \tag{9.3}$$

where G is a non-linear function. In that case, given the necessary conditions, the process generates both intrinsic and extrinsic randomness. A pragmatic view suggested accepting both the non-linear nature of our world and the inevitability of analysing it with the tools of traditional statistical inference. Any economy is in theory essentially non-linear in nature with complex interactions among many variables of economic significance. However, at the current state of the art there is no good way to capture the richness of these models in testable form. At the level of applied works the models are linearized and the corresponding error terms modelled as residuals. The question remains: do we live in an essentially linear economic world with unforecastable events exogenous to the model? Pragmatism dictates that we continue to develop better estimation methods for a world having both non-linear interactions and unforecastable shocks. We are led to the conclusion that probabilistic methods are for the time being the most appropriate technique for analysing economic time-series data (Liu and Granger, 1992, S38).

An alternative view, on the other hand, suggests that constitutive non-linearities are decisive in our world, and therefore that they must be part of the analysis. In this sense, the purpose of this paper is to reflect on the most widely used method in economics for studying this type of process, emphasizing its requirements, implications and shortcomings.

Non-linear dynamics has been assessed through two distinctive narratives in the economic literature, which in some way reproduce and amplify the traditional divide between deductive and inductive work. On one hand, there is a growing literature about abstract models leading to chaos and, on the other hand, there has been a sustained although inconclusive effort to measure and to identify chaos in historical macroeconomic and financial time-series. Although their relation has not been deeply explored, the argument of this paper is that it may provide important insights both about statistical method and about economic theory.

Indeed, the two trends in the study of non-linear dynamics in economics did not converge for quite a while. The first developed suggestions that chaos was relevant for economics emerged from empirical research leading to new theoretical intuitions: Benoit Mandelbrot, an IBM scientist, took the opportunity of a question by a colleague to study the distribution of the changes in prices of cotton and financial assets on the Chicago market and published in the 1960s a series of very polemic papers introducing the first sketch of the notion of the fractal (Mandelbrot, 1963, 1967). On the other hand, there was the previous and almost unknown incursion by Von Neumann in the dynamics of the tent map but, as with so much of what he wrote, the implications of the insight were not understood by his contemporaries. More recently, Robert May, a zoologist from Oxford University, suggested in 1975 an application of chaos to the study of cycles in economics (May and Beddington, 1975).[1] This paper was rejected for publication by a major econometrics journal, which is an indication of the strangeness of the subject for our discipline at the time;

nevertheless, a version was published in *Nature*, and it still is the most quoted paper on chaos.

It took a further ten (since May) to fifteen years (since Mandelbrot) for chaos to become a relevant topic in economics – and it was via the theoretical work and modelling. One of the papers which had a large impact, published in *Econometrica* by Grandmont, proved that, in the case of the traditional overlapping generations models and in cases of models of economies with a finite number of infinitely lived agents, under the assumptions of utility maximization and orthodox intertemporal choice, chaos could still emerge. The author concluded that this feature re-established in some way the Keynesian problem (the paradox of savings and investment, and the lack of effective demand generating unemployment) and that public intervention was necessary and possible under these circumstances, although long-term prediction is eventually useless in a chaotic framework. In the same vein, Kehoe (1988), proved that a Walrasian *tâtonnement* process could lead to chaos, under some simple assumptions. These and other examples confirmed the intuition that many textbook models, gives some minor adjustments not at odds with a realistic approach, would lead to instability and chaos. Furthermore, as the economies can be modelled as the non-linear interaction of distinctive agents and institutions, this outcome is more than a theoretical possibility and is becoming a research task.

In spite of this, the study of non-linear dynamics generated some curiosity but not a major impact in economic theory (Boldrin, 1988, p. 49). Linear specifications of simple models, and a pragmatic approach based on classic probability theory, dominated and dominate economic modelling.

There is of course at least one good reason for this. The implicit challenge of chaos to the postulate of rationality (and perfect information) and its implications for equilibrium, rejecting the restriction of the models to a specific class of very low-dimensional attractors – a rest point or a steady-state growth – made it a very unwelcome development in economics. The paradox was that, nevertheless economics has adopted the paradigm of maximizaion mimicking physics, but now the new science of chaos and complexity is developing in physics, which is still the epistemological reference for economics, and that made its importation compulsory as well. As a consequence, some economists accepted the challenge, crossed the bridge, installed their tents in the battlefield and bravely modelled chaotic systems – hopefully in order to generalize the traditional equilibrium postulates which have been (almost) unreservedly accepted for 120 years.

This endeavour is now reassessed from the point of view of one of the dominant methods of identifying the structure of a dynamical system, the BDS[2] statistics based on the Grassberger–Procaccia correlation dimension (Grassberger and Procaccia, 1982, 1983; Grassberger *et al.*, 1991). This method provides a new and telling example of the potentialities and implications of the incorporation of tools developed in physics and brought into economic theory and applied work.

DATA AND METHODS

The BDS statistics was introduced in the second half of the 1980s and will not be described here since they are quite well known (Brock, 1986; for recent surveys and extensions, see Brock *et al.*, 1991; Brock and Potter, 1993; Brock *et al.*, 1996). This section discusses some of the problems related to the treatment of data, which are at the root of part of the scepticism about the statistical tests based on this or on alternative approaches. The next sections deal with more general implications of the statistics.

The application of any method in order to identify the structure of a complex series is of course highly affected by the quality of the available data. In general, long-term statistical information in economics is rather poor, is based upon the use of distinct and even contradictory criteria, and spurious conclusions can be introduced by errors of measurement. Furthermore, the macroeconomic series are very short, may concern different institutional settings and are roughly rounded measurements of very complex evolutionary processes with undetected qualitative features. If no other difficulty were present, these ones would be large enough to require a careful treatment of the conclusions from the tests on macroeconomic data. In order to minimize this problem, the variable to be used must be an important one, and the quality, stability and comparability of criteria for measurement are essential. Of course, the amount of data required – but not their quality – depends on the test to be performed: if the theory postulates high dimensional chaos, the case is hopeless, since it is virtually impossible to distinguish it from a white noise process without an extravagant amount of data (Liu and Granger, 1992, S27). And even if the hypothesis of a low dimension is under discussion, a large number of data points is still needed, although these can be provided for some cases. Anyway, no complete solution to this problem of availability of a good quantity of good-quality data is ever possible for the real historical macroeconomic series.

The second difficulty was also noted by several researchers but, unlike the first one, its implications are highly disputed: it concerns the aggregation effect in the macroeconomic measurement, since most series are Laspeyres or Paasche indices combining a large mass of heterogeneous information, parts of it based upon pure guesswork. Some noted that the likelihood of finding chaos is superior for series of desegregated variables (Baumol and Benhabib, 1989, p. 101; Terasvirta, 1990, p. 112), that aggregation may introduce spurious evidence of a white noise process (Barnett and Chen, 1988, p. 280) and reduce the evidence of short-term non-linearity (Granger, 1991, pp. 272, 275). Therefore false evidence of linearity can be imposed by aggregation (Brock, 1986, p. 191; Brock *et al.*, 1991, pp. 187, 193; Westlund, 1991, p. 280), namely by averaging (Dechert and Gencay, 1992, S48). Granger also suggested that aggregation may be related to the evidence in favour of fractional differenced processes, or 1/f noise (Granger, 1991, p. 272).

But, in spite of these insights, not much time was spent on the effects of aggregation on the results of the tests, although that topic became a major point of concern in other disciplines. The importance of the aggregation bias was demonstrated, for instance, for some cases of empirical series in epidemiology: Sugihara *et al.* (1990), proved that the evolution of measles in British cities could be better explained by chaotic processes, but that no such evidence was present in the country as a whole. Louçã (1997) developed a similar experiment in economics using the BDS test which is here under scrutiny, and proving that linearity could not be rejected in the historical UK GDP series, whereas there is strong evidence of non-linear structure in some of its main components. This suggests the importance of studying desegregated series in order to check for non-linear structure and complexity.

EMPIRICAL RESULTS

A large number of historical series have beeninspected for chaos: for instance, macroeconomic series of GDP (Brock, 1986; Brock and Sayers, 1988; Frank and Stengos, 1988; Scheinkman and LeBaron, 1989a; Sayers, 1989; Potter, 1991), of unemployment (Sayers, 1988a, b, 1989; Lee *et al.*, 1989), of pig iron production (Sayers, 1989), of industrial production (Schmidt and Stahlecker, 1989), of exchange rates (Hsieh, 1989; Lee *et al.*, 1989; Papell and Sayers, 1990; Meese and Rose, 1991; Dechert and Gencay, 1992), of gold and silver returns (Frank and Stengos, 1989), of stock market returns (Eckmann *et al.*, 1988; Scheinkman and LeBaron, 1989b, 1992a, b), of monetary aggregates (Barnett and Chen, 1988; Barnett and Choi, 1989; Lee *et al.*, 1989; Ramsey *et al.*, 1990), of interest rates (Lee *et al.*, 1989), of the S&P 500 Index (Mantegna and Stanley, 1995). Many of these studies used the Grassberger–Procaccia algorithm and the BDS statistics in order to measure the dimension of the series and to test for non-linearity. Indeed, the diffusion of the BDS has been responsible for a major step in empirical research on chaos in economics.Table 9.1 summarizes some examples of the early findings.

These results are certainly surprising, since some of the obtained dimensions are very low, which is at odds with the theory (but not with common

Table 9.1 Correlation dimension in historical series

Author(s)	Time series	Correlation dimension
Brock (1986)	US GNP 1947–85	~3.0–4.0
Sayers (1988a, b)	US man-days lost due to work stoppages	~1.3–1.5
Frank, Stengos (1988)	Canada GNP	~2.4–4.0
Frank, Gencay, Stengos (1988)	Germany, Italy, UK, Japan GNP	~6.0–7.0
Scheinkman, LeBaron (1989b)	Exchange rates	~5.0–6.0
Barnett, Choi (1989)	Divisia monetary aggregates	~2.0
Frank, Stengos (1989)	Gold and silver returns, London market	~6.0–7.0
Brock (1990a)	Detrended real US GNP	
	Real US industrial production	~2.0–3.5
	Real US civilian employment	
	US unemployment rate	
	US pig-iron production	

practice in modelling). Brock addressed this problem as follows: 'I was initially intrigued with this finding because low dimension is consistent with the presence of low-dimensional deterministic chaos, yet no one in economics had expected low-dimensional deterministic chaos in economic data' (Brock, 1990a, p. 435). Common sense eventually postulates a larger dimension, whereas most of the current models fix very low dimensions and deal with the non-explicit variables as part of the (infinitely dimensional) vector of random shocks. This evidence of low-dimensional processes obviously suggested the hypothesis of a deterministic non-linear process, of chaos.

Another reason for caution is that several tests on non-linearity do not reach the same conclusions. Lee *et al.* (1989) proceeded to an experiment comparing the results of several tests for the same series, and concluded, as Table 9.2 indicates, that the BDS and other tests do not agree in a number of cases. This of course strengthens the scepticism previously pointed out.

Granger and his colleagues concluded that no test outperformed the others, although the author's own preference was for the neural network test (Granger, 1991, p. 272). Later on, they indicated that other tests could have more power than the BDS (Liu and Granger, 1992, S34).

Prudence in the interpretation of BDS results is also called for by the fact that the applicability of the Grassberger–Procaccia concept of correlation dimension is questionable in noisy and evolutionary series. Ruelle (1990, p. 244–5) and Sugihara and May (1990, p. 741) share a clear lack of confidence

Table 9.2 Comparison between results from a BDS test and other tests (bispectrum, neural network test, Tsay, McLeod-Li) by Lee, White and Granger (1989)

Series	Results of tests
US/Japan exchange rate (1973–87)	No proof of neglected non-linearity
Three months US Treasury Bill interest rate (1958–87)	Linearity rejected by all tests
US M2 money stock, monthly (1958–87)	Linearity rejected (neural network, BDS, bispectrum, McLeod-Li); accepted (Tsay, information matrix)
US personal income, monthly (1958–87)	Linearity rejected (bispectrum); accepted by the others
US unemployment rate, monthly (1958–87)	Linearity rejected (neural network, BDS, Tsay, McLeod-Li, bispectrum); accepted by the Tsay test

in a direct estimation of the Grassberger–Procaccia measure in so short series, if this low dimension is at odds with the theory.

The evolution of the writings of Ruelle, who voiced the most drastic opposition to the current trend in empirical investigation, is a very curious one. Ruelle was part of the inaugural 1987 Santa Fé Institute (SFI) meeting, which brought together ten natural scientists and ten economists, in which he presented a short paper with his collaborators Eckmann and Kamphurst and also with Scheinkman. It concerned the results of the computation of a recurrence plot and Lyapunov exponents for a financial series, and they found two slightly positive values (Eckmann *et al.* 1988, pp. 301–4). In the same conference, Ruelle considered the correlation dimension obtained by Scheinkman and LeBaron for other series as 'encouragingly low' (Ruelle, 1988, p. 200). But shortly afterwards he initiated a sharp critique of the use of the Grassberger–Procaccia algorithm in economic series. In his Claude Bernard Lecture, in 1989 (published as Ruelle, 1990), Ruelle presented some cases discussed both by Grassberger and by Procaccia for which the theory precludes the existence of a low-dimensional attractor, and for which the evidence obtained from the G–P dimension could not be believed (Ruelle, 1990, p. 247). Next year, Ruelle was even more conclusive: the G–P algorithm is 'without value' for short series[3] (Ruelle, 1991, p. 234 n.) and the efforts in that sense at the SFI meeting were 'vain' (ibid., p. 113). His argument is that one should not believe estimates of the correlation dimension measure which are not well below $2log_{10}N$, the formula for the upper bound of the dimension, or, in general, $2log_aN$, N being the number of data points in our series measured over the a period. But several authors argued that there is no a priori justification for the choice of a, and therefore that the formula has no practical use (Essex and Nerenberg, 1991, pp. 287f; Tsonis, 1992, p. 172). Ruelle (1988) suggested the alternative computation of the Lyapunov exponents:

> If there were an underlying deterministic dynamics, which changes slowly over time (drift), then the drift would affect dimension estimates more than it would affect the larger characteristic exponents. In fact, drift would essentially amount to introducing a new characteristic exponent close to zero. In view of this, the determination of characteristic exponents may be more useful than the determination of dimensions for the time series of economics. (Ruelle, 1988, p. 200; see also, in the same sense, 1990, p. 246)

Nevertheless, the Lyapunov exponent cannot be defined in the presence of noise. Thus the researcher must use several complementary statistical measures in order to identify the qualitative features of the series.

DATA PREPARATION

Although there are some scarcely discussed claims, such as presenting the test as a 'nonlinear Granger causality test' (Brock, 1990b, pp. 233, 239), this test has been widely used in economics as well as in other fields in order to test the null of IID (independant and identically distributed residuals). It proved to be a powerful diagnostics for model specification, and it is still the single most widely used non-parametric method in non-linear dynamics in economics.

In common use, the researcher must obtain a stationary representation of the series before testing the hypothesis, and that is typically obtained by detrending and linearly filtering it in order to avoid non-stationarity in mean and in variance.[4] This is possible, since it was proved by Brock that linear filtering preserves the same correlation dimension and the measure of the largest Lyapunov exponent, given the invariance of chaotic equations to linear transformations (for example, Brock, 1990a, p. 436; Lorenz, 1993, p. 223). This allows for the linear filtering used in pre-whitening, with some precaution, since the introduction of nuisance parameters from the filter apparently has no asymptotic effects on the result of the test; yet the implication of non-linear transformations such as that imposed by several detrending methods is not covered by this theorem. In spite of that, it is accepted that fitting a linear model to a time-series introduces dependence in the residuals, lags and estimation noise (Scheinkman and LeBaron, 1989b, p. 318; Brock,

1990a, p. 436), which is not considered to challenge the conclusion. In this case, the authors suggested the application of the test to the residuals, and then the use of a reshuffling diagnostics: in the case of the presence of chaos, the correlation dimension should be approximately the same for the series and for the residuals, but should increase dramatically if the residuals of the series were randomly resampled. In that case, the geometric ordered form would be destroyed and the computed dimension should approximate the infinite dimension of the white noise process.

Although the technical need to stationarize the data is a simple requirement for the application of the test, its theoretical justification is not trivial. A short survey of the procedures used by different researchers highlights this point. Lee *et al.* (1989) pre-whiten the series with an AR process fit to the first differences of data or of logs of data, which cleans most of the evidence of dependence and non-stationarity. But Brock *et al.* (1991, p. 95f) analyse the S&P 500 index from 1928 to 1962 but drop the years 1940–49 because of the irregularities attributable to the war period. Scheinkman and LeBaron (1989a) rejected linearity in per capita US GNP for 1872–1986 and then – hypothesizing that the rejection was due to heteroscedasticity – used GLS (considering 1872–1946 and 1946–86) and dummy variables for the periods of the Great Depression (1930–39) and for the Second World War (1940–45), so that the BDS test could no longer reject the null.

The authors interpret this procedure in the following way: 'The introduction of dummy variables destroys certain similarities of patterns across distinct periods, for example, making a period that includes years in 1940–45 that was previously similar to a period at the end of the eighteenth century now distinct' (Scheinkman and LeBaron, 1989a, p. 226). This is possible, but the reverse is also, if not more common: the smoothing out of the periods of abrupt change may hide evidence of non-linearities, and the weighted standardization assumes the necessity of destroying the structural difference between two periods, both choices eventually leading to a spurious similarity of distinct historical periods. The final results are thus theoretically indeterminate: even if the statistics and hypotheses testing on the transformed series are conclusive, what are they conclusive about?

Since it is common knowledge that macroeconomic time-series are often heteroscedastic and have infinite variance, the empirical and theoretical analysis cannot avoid the problem of interpretation of related historical change and growth. In fact the results previously obtained

> seem to suggest to the world of nonlinear researchers to proceed with caution. These tests have not been able to find uniform results between time periods. Also, much of the structure seems to be coming from changes in variance. This research indicates that the nature of the nonlinearities may not remain stationary long enough for researchers to reliably detect them. (Brock *et al.*, 1991, p. 107)

Both Brock (1988) and LeBaron (1988) proved that the NYSE weekly returns stock index registered a structural shift between 1962–74 and 1975–85, which is of course explainable by the major crises which occurred in 1974 and thereafter. And although Hsieh (1991) rejected the hypothesis of structural changes across subperiods, evidence from stock returns shows otherwise (Brock *et al.*, 1991, p. 28). In this sense, De Lima proved that the impact of the 1987 crash was responsible for the rejection of linearity (De Lima, 1994).

Another objection may be raised against the effects of the preparation of data for the computation of the correlation dimension and for testing for IID. The widespread use of the Frischian and Cowles paradigm for the treatment of time series – which amounted to considering the series to be generated by the addition of stochastic shocks to the well-behaved neoclassical equations leading to equilibrium – required a double decomposition in order to annihilate what Mandelbrot called the 'Joseph effect' and the 'Noah effect', long memory persistence and fat tails. That censorship of variance is obviously necessary in order to describe the universe of Brownian motions, which is so decisive for the paraphernalia of the efficient market hypothesis and similar theoretical settings. But this strategy is counter-intuitive in itself, since one is supposed to look for evidence of non-linearity after making a considerable effort to wash it out: 'It reverses the conventional methodology by imputing chaos to the residuals remaining after as much of the data's variability as possible has been explained by conventional stochastic processes' (Barnett and Hinich, 1993: 255). The procedure is an imposition of a prejudice against the chaotic hypothesis.

There is still a further reason for the reconsideration of these methods and eventual alternatives: the technical adequacy and even the technical necessity of a certain procedure is no sufficient theoretical motivation for its use. For instance, detrending by fitting an exponential function assumes the existence of two completely separate and separable economic processes, the cycles and the trend, the latter being accounted for by a constant rate of growth. There is no justification whatsoever for these assumptions.

In fact, which is the strictly separable social process represented by the 'trend'? Capital accumulation or technological progress do not qualify, since they are not separable from the remaining economic movements; the same applies to population growth – and none of them has a constant growth rate over long periods.[5] Indeed, detrending is a mathematically arbitrary procedure, implying the abandonment of any evolutionary perspective since the object of the research becomes the reversible fluctuation around a theoretical line, instead of the irreversible evolution of the actual historical process. This has been the outstanding price paid for the divorce between the growth domain and the cycle domain, which still dominates the theoretical and empirical work. Of course, the question is not specific to the techniques used in non-linear dynamics, but rather general, as it is related to the role of statistical inference in assessing historical data.

As a consequence, there is a dramatic trade-off between the necessary technical requirements for the test and the lack of their theoretical justification: the antinomy deterministic equilibrating system versus random shocks but scarce economic substance, and the pre-whitening procedure concentrates on the elimination of high-frequency signals ignoring long memory processes and taking for granted that they are independent. The dismissive treatment of these implications is a consequence of the acceptance of the epistemic primacy of simplistic versions of mechanics, for science in general and for economics in particular.

IMPORTATION FROM PHYSICS

The introduction of methods and techniques derived from physics is not new in economics, but it usually led to not enough reflection on the specificity of both subject-matters. Indeed, direct conversation between scientists from these two fields has been scarce, although the case under scrutiny provided one of the few exceptional examples of an exchange of views. One of the leading researchers in non-linear statistics in economics, José Scheinkman, clearly pointed out that the new methods applied in chaos theory in economics were derived from statistical developments in physics:

> The earlier efforts in applying the ideas of chaotic dynamics in order to uncover nonlinear dependence in economic data consisted simply of using certain tools developed in the mathematical and physics literature in a rather direct way. The most promising of these practices make use of the correlation dimension. (Scheinkman, 1990, pp. 39–40)

This inspiration was quite natural, since physics, receiving inputs from meteorology and mathematics, led the research on non-linear dynamical systems and on the detection of chaos – both in theory and in practical applications. But this is the beginning of the story and not the end of it, since the differences between the experimental framework of physics and the theoretical space of the social sciences are quite substantial and could not go undetected by both kinds of user of the metaphor.

In fact, some physicists raised doubts on the common assumptions of economic models (Palmer, 1988). This was quite obvious when economists and natural scientists met at the 1987 Santa Fé inaugural meeting. Brock, one of the participants at that meeting, recognized that open confrontation and its rationale: 'Many scientists from other fields are appalled at the economists' modelling of rationality. They are specially rankled by the hypothesis of rational expectations' (Brock, 1991, p. 127). The author recommended reading the volume of proceedings of that conference, with the argument that it is 'well worth reading, not only for the ideas it contains, but also for the reactions of natural scientists when confronting this self-referential aspect of economic modelling. The implications of this self-referentiality (...) are difficult for many natural scientists to grasp' (Brock, 1990b, p. 233).

Although the answer somewhat lessens the critical remarks made against the equilibrium postulate and the rational expectations hypothesis put forward by Palmer, Anderson and other participants at the meeting, Brock acknowledged that, for economists, the metaphor of chaos implied major difficulties as well. Chaotic economics tends to challenge the description of the economy as the juxtaposition of independent deterministic and dampening propagation systems plus exogenous, small and random impulses.[6] In other words, without the unexplainable shocks, the system inevitably converges to a steady state as time goes to infinity, whereas in a chaotic model such a distinction is irrelevant and the deterministic part creates by itself intrinsic randomness and therefore drives the system (Brock, 1990b, p. 258). As a consequence, this type of model seems more adequate to investigate phenomena such as the strong persistence detected in economic series, in spite of the fact that these 'ideas are not part of the mainstream economic literature'[7] (Brock, 1991, p. 140). Brock once even suggested that some version of Hicksian non-linear models could displace the Frischian paradigm for good (Brock, 1988, p. 9). Yet, in spite of this, Brock and his colleagues generally take the standpoint of orthodoxy:

> A rather large literature has emerged in economic theory on the possibility of chaos being consistent with rational expectations in intertemporal general equilibrium macroeconomic models. (...) The conclusion is: yes. Chaos is consistent with standard assumptions used in dynamic economics. This raised interest in testing for the presence of chaos in data. (Brock and Potter, 1993, p. 220)

There is certainly a paradox in this story: against the physicists challenging the adequacy of the equilibrium and rationality postulates, Brock evokes orthodoxy; but, when the time comes for empirical work, the shortcomings of these postulates are acknowledged and the analyst proceeds without them. Furthermore, accepting Mirowski's history of the neoclassical revolution as a word-for-word transcription of the concepts and equations of middle nineteenth-century energetics (Mirowski, 1989 or, for an example, see Louçã, 2000), Brock suggests that economics can only be emancipated from this type of 'physics envy' if more 'precise theoretical structures' and a list of 'stylized facts' to be explained are incorporated in the research programme (Brock, 1991, p. 120) – both requirements still being largely unmet.

The topic, as suggested in the last paragraph, is related to the very nature of historical data. David Ruelle argued that economic systems, by analogy with turbulence, are the product of the coupling of several modes of oscillation, namely through trade or technological development, and that their intense interaction is eventually responsible for chaos, defined as sensitivity to initial conditions (Ruelle, 1988, p. 199; 1991; pp. 108f.). But this concept is at odds with traditional economic theory, which emphasized starting with Adam Smith all the way to Walras that such an interaction should produce order and equilibrium. In a nutshell, this is the difference between physicists and economists: whereas the former group accepts the null of chaos or non-linear dynamics as the standard, the latter adopts the a priori concept of simple and linear systems leading to equilibrium.

This difference between the insights from physics and the economists' assumptions was noted not without some persiflage both by Ruelle (1988, 1991) and by Anderson (1988), two of the physicists who criticized the mainstream economist's concept of equilibrium at the 1987 Santa Fé meeting:

> In mechanics and physics one would often say that (a 'fixed point for time evolution'(*x* is an equilibrium (in fact, a stable equilibrium), but note that the economists use the world 'equilibrium' to denote a state which is not necessarily time independent. The issue (the coupling of sub-systems(is slightly confused by the fact that 'equilibrium' as understood by economists does allow for time dependence in the form of anticipation of the future. Here, however, we question some standard economic assumptions, and specifically the 'perfect foresight' of economic agents in the presence of sensitive dependence on the initial conditions. (Ruelle, 1988, pp. 198–9)

And thus Anderson, choosing a very polite formula:

> From William Brock's summary and José Scheinkman and Thomas Sargent's discussion of the concept of the Arrow–Debreu theory, we learned that even theories which appeal to the concept of 'equilibrium' do not necessarily avoid the apparently random fluctuations in the course of time which are characteristics of driven dynamical systems in physics. In physics these are called 'non-equilibrium' systems; a liberal education on the various meanings of the word 'equilibrium' was a bracing experience for all. (Anderson, 1988, p. 265)

The nature of the difficulty is obviously related to the difference between the controlled protocols in experimental physics, which were translated into economics with the application of classical probability theory with scarce adaptation, and the organic framework of evolving complex systems in real economies. The adherence to this metaphor of the economic process as a mechanical system allowed for conceptualization and estimation in the traditional positivist mood. But mechanics is not a fair representation of social evolution, as noted by Mandelbrot: 'The only reason for assuming continuity

[Gaussianity] is that many sciences tend, knowingly or not, to copy the procedures that prove successful in Newtonian physics (…). But prices are different: mechanics involves nothing comparable' (Mandelbrot, 1983, p. 335).

Nevertheless, this epistemic primacy of physics also implies the danger of contamination: indeed, that was the case with the study of non-linear self-organized dynamical systems, originating in meteorology, physics, chemistry and mathematics. In such a framework, the paradigmatic gravitation around equilibrium tragically loses its charm: rest points or limit cycles are not the relevant attractors for these systems that create both order and disorder. Alternatively, the adherence to the analysis of economies as non-linear processes imposes major difficulties on their analytical treatment, since their crucial property is the evolutionary character:

> The current chaos theory treats recurrent time series, that is, those in which the systems necessarily return to states near those already visited in the past. This 'eternal return' is not present except in moderately complex systems. The historical evolution of very complex systems, on the other hand, is typically in one sense: history never repeats itself. To the very complex and non-recurrent systems, we generally have sensitive dependence on initial conditions, but the problem arises of knowing whether it is limited by regulative mechanisms, or whether it provokes important effects in the long term. (Ruelle, 1991, p. 110, my translation),

Ruelle continues: 'We are in an irritating situation in which we observe time evolutions that are quite similar to those of the chaotic physical systems, but nevertheless different enough to prevent us from analysing them' (ibid., p. 114). In spite of this, Ruelle accepted the traditional formulation of economic models,[8] although suggesting that the specificity of economics implied a new interpretation of randomness. Historical evolution or coevolution is unidirectional;[9] the arrow of time has no reversion. In other words, economic series are highly complex, and chaos may be expected from active coupling of subsystems in the framework of an evolutionary process that makes it difficult to measure and to model. Furthermore, if a non-linear process is at work, intrinsic and extrinsic stochasticity may emerge, determining an irregular time path in which coordination of unstable trajectories is decisive and structural change is frequent but bounded. Thus, we may hypothesize that most of the technical and analytical difficulties of measuring chaos in economics are related to the inadequacy of the currently used methods, derived from different problems and unable to interpret evolutionary complexity.

Obviously, these difficulties are not exclusively imputable to the use of the Grassberger–Procaccia algorithm, since they are generally applicable to the available measures of complexity.

STRUCTURAL INSTABILITY AND ITS MEASURE

The limitations of the current methods are even more general, since they do not allow for the distinction between non-linear attractors in low-frequency processes, that is with long memory, and linear time-varying processes. Furthermore, the statistics based on the Grassberger–Procaccia correlation dimension are unable to interpret bifurcations, since it presumes that the data describe the evolution of a system under the heroic proviso that it did not go through a bifurcation:

> Since they [the BDS-related techniques] test for motion on a strange attractor, they necessarily cannot adjudicate whether or not the dynamic system has undergone a bifurcation during the time span covered by the data, thereby perhaps creating or destroying such a hypothetical attractor. Empirical methods presuming one qualitative type of motion cannot be used to identify transitions between qualitatively distinct phases. In particular, they presume that the data follow one trajectory along a given manifold generated by an unknown process whose parameters are fixed. Thus, the primary evidentiary devices economists use presuppose a constancy itself inconsistent with the fundamental insights achievable from the qualitative analysis of dynamics. (Bausor, 1994, p. 120)

As a consequence, this approach is unsuitable to directly identify fundamental change, the modification of the economic and social structure over historical time. Indeed, there is no statistical device to deal with it (ibid., p. 125n). The statistical test based on the Grassberger–Procaccia dimension cannot perform that task, and therefore it should be reassessed in its original framework: as an estimate of the self-similar characteristics of a certain object. In that sense, it should be used either to test the absence of structure in a stationary environment (Mirowski, 1995, p. 593) or to discriminate between linear and non-linear stochastic processes (Liu and Granger, 1992, S25). In any case, it rests on the traditional interpretation of randomness, which is precisely what is at stake in non-linear dynamics. These and other topics are today widely discussed (Anderson *et al.*, 1988; Arthur *et al.*, 1997; Day and Chen, 1993; Gabisch and Lorenz, 1989; Scheinkman and Woodford, 1994; Smith, 1992).

IS CHAOS OUT THERE?

The empirical work based on the BDS statistics presents does not deny the presence of non-linearity and, on the contrary, suggests the relevance of studying the eventual presence of chaos in some economic series. The computation of low dimensions, the general rejection of the null of IID and the detection either of positive Lyapunov exponents in some of the macroeconomic series (for example, Brock, 1986; Scheinkman and LeBaron, 1989b; Brock, 1990a; Dechert and Gencay, 1992) or of self-similar scaling properties (Mantegna and Stanley, 1995) provide a good case for studying chaos. Yet the general consensus is that the existence of chaos could not be proved: 'Hence the weight of the evidence appears to be against the hypothesis that there is chaos in economics and finance' (Brock, 1990a, p. 430), or 'The direct evidence for deterministic chaos in many economic series remains weak' (LeBaron, 1992b, p. 1).[10]

In fact, in spite of the indicative empirical results obtained so far and as a consequence of the difficulties of the proof, a large number of authors tend to present a dismissive conclusion about chaos: for example, Brock and Malliaris (1988), Baumol and Benhabib (1989). The only authors strongly claiming to have provided a conclusive demonstration of the existence of chaos are Barnett and Chen (1988), who used Divisia monetary aggregates, but their conclusion was challenged almost immediately by Ramsey *et al.* (1990), who transformed the data in order to obtain stationarity and then rejected the conclusion of chaos. DeCoster and Mitchell (1991) obtained similar conclusions to those of Barnett and Chen.

Inspecting a series of exchange rates and obtaining a fractal dimension and a positive largest Lyapunov exponent, Scheinkman and LeBaron (1989b) applied the reshuffling diagnostics, getting a larger dimension measure, and consequently did not reject the hypothesis of chaos. Likewise Frank and Stengos (1989) for the gold and silver returns in the London market. In other cases, Brock (1986) excluded the existence of chaos in spite of the positive Lyapunov value and the fractal dimension, since the computed values were not invariant to the magnitude of the radius ε, measuring the local distance. Frank *et al.* (1988), Sayers (1988a, b, 1989) and Granger (1991, p. 263) reached the same conclusion, accepting the non-linear hypothesis but rejecting chaos.

One of the interesting features of the debate between Barnett, Chen and Hinich and their critics, Ramsey, Sayers and Rothman, was the topic of the definition of non-linear dynamical systems as opposed to chaotic systems. In fact, the strict distinction between the two types of systems – in the sense of considering chaotic systems a very peculiar and well identified subset, clearly distinguishable from the other members of the general class of non-linear dynamics – seems to be a unique characteristic of economists involved in complexity theory. This is striking, since the available methods for identifying dynamics and discriminating between a general non-linear structure and a peculiar chaotic process are still so rough and underdeveloped.

In the study of moderately complicated dynamical processes in physics, the generally accepted attitude is to put the burden of proof on those denying chaos, and to accept chaos while no refutation is presented. Yet, in economics, the current attitude is the opposite one. The reason for the difference is obvious: physics is not constrained by the constitutive concept of equilibrium, and therefore can dispense with the notion of an intrinsic, well-defined and unique order.

The acceptance of the null in the test of hypotheses is therefore eased by this general option. It is true that current technical limitations impose that form for the BDS test, since the distribution under the alternative hypothesis is not known; but it is also remarkably adjusted to the questionable a priori view dominating mainstream economics. Therefore the BDS does not test for chaos and not even for non-linearity: a rejection of the null may arise from any sort of dependence in the process. The crux of the matter is that common practice, in the face of a situation in which both an autoregressive process of low order *n* and a non-linear alternative may explain the variability in data, is to accept the linear specification.

It is true that it is virtually impossible to progress in the detection of chaos in economic series while we have no definition of a statistical procedure or a test of chaos defined as the null, but it is also arguable that the current choice of the basic assumptions constrains the development of the theory, imposing a bias against chaos.

Furthermore, some general philosophical problems cannot be avoided in this context. A sophisticated inductive inference, such as the Popperian infirmationist strategy, is also incompatible with the use of the Neyman–Pearson framework, since there is no prediction derived from the alternative hypothesis under inspection, which is accepted simply if the null is rejected and is not by itself submitted to any sort of test; in other words, it is not the basis for any refutable prediction.

However, the crucial question about the use of probability theory in this framework concerns the role of randomness and determinism in models of the economy. The lack of controlled experimental protocols in economics imposes a clear limitation on the use of classical inductive inference and on the definition of the size and power of the tests. Yet it is unreasonable to accept that purely deterministic models can ever explain the working of an economy (Scheinkman, 1990, p. 35). The traditional trade-off between purely deterministic systems and purely exogenous small, random and unimportant shocks is a response to this difficulty, which has been traditionally solved by the postulate of the juxtaposition of both concepts of evolution.

But chaos theory introduced a major shift from this point of view, since it suggested and proved for a specific class of models that deterministic systems could account for time paths virtually indistinguishable from those of traditional systems driven by stochastic impulses: 'white chaos' is not statistically distinguishable from stochastic series (Liu and Granger, 1992, S27). However, one cannot conceive of a deterministic model accounting for all the possible social interactions, as Scheinkman noted, and some noise is always present. Therefore the problem can be redescribed as interpreting the complex generation of intrinsic and extrinsic noise. Moreover, the question arises whether they are separable, and whether their distinction can indeed be established in a non-linear system: 'There is indeed a deep philosophical question concerning the difference between determinism and stochasticity or "randomness"' (Brock and Sayers, 1988, p. 74). This difficulty was noticed in the early discussions about the detection of chaos in economics (Ruelle, 1994, p. 27). In the same sense, Barnett and Hinich argued that this 'deep philosophical question' is virtually unsolvable:

> It is well known that solution paths produced from chaotic systems look very much like stochastic processes. This produces a virtually unsolvable problem: should we view chaos as a potential explanation for stochastic appearing data (Barnett, Chen), or should we view stochastic processes as a potential explanation for chaotic appearing data (Ramsey, Sayers, Rothman). (Barnett and Hinich, 1993, p. 255)

Or, paraphrasing Boldrin (1988, p. 250), the question remains whether we should take Laplace or Poincaré's point of view. Granger suggests keeping to the tradition:

> As economic data include measurement error that is almost certainly stochastic, it seems unlikely that chaos can be observed with the length of series currently available. It seems that econometricians are well advised to continue using the techniques of classical probability theory. (...) The inherent shocks to the economy plus measurement errors will effectively mask any true chaotic signal. Thus, it follows that it will be a sound, pragmatic strategy to continue to use stochastic models and statistical inference as has been developed in the last two decades. (Granger, 1991, p. 268)

Poincaré's alternative points in another direction: randomness ceases to be considered either as a perturbation or as a meaningless encapsulation of all other factors, and is defined as the very substrate of the economic evolution, as a constitutive part of the evolutionary process itself. In that sense, the economies are defined as complex processes with sensitive dependence on initial conditions. Consequently, the distinctions between intrinsic and extrinsic randomness, as well as between deterministic and stochastic processes, are overruled. In economic series, the holistic framework that accounts for the creation of both order and disorder blurs these antinomies.

CONCLUSION

Tremendous work has been developed in recent years using the tools here described and it has contributed to important breakthroughs in statistical methods as well as new theoretical insights. These efforts challenge the old certainties, as the postulates of rationality and equilibrium, a peculiar characteristic of economics that distinguishes it from physics, where these techniques originated.

Although one should acknowledge the difficulty, for these and for other methods, of assessing structural change and specifically the bifurcation between attractors, this line of work provided valuable contributions and rigorous analyses. Their inadequacy for the detection of chaos or for the identification of the non-linear structure, which are presumably important features in the historical evolution of macro variables, is imposed by the assumption of a constant setting represented by a deterministic system, and by the impossibility of redefinition of the model once a bifurcation occurs. In spite of this, the statistics can be used for investigating the qualitative evidence of non-linearity, namely of heteroscedasticity as a representation of the structural breaks in the series.[11]

For chaotic or highly complex real systems, one cannot determine their precise trajectory, but instead can hypothesize the nature of the motion and the general structure of the flow. The BDS statistics, the Lyapunov exponents and other measures can therefore be used as tools for identification of critical points in the evolutionary process, in order to elaborate conjectures about the turbulent interaction of political, economic and technological factors in concrete historical time.

The simultaneous and combined enquiry into non-linearity and non-stationarity is still a task for the future. Once the relevance of the complexity approach has been accepted, the dogma of their epistemic distinction must be challenged: non-stationarity may be an effect or a cause of non-linearity, and vice-versa; the variation in variance may be evidence for changes either of the 'trend' or of the structure, in other words the form of a non-linear process. This suggests the analysis of changes in variance as symptoms of non-linear relations, and the use of several complementary statistical tests, eyeball evidence, topological, graphic and geometric inquiries, as part of the theoretical investigation.

In this sense, history is brought back into economics: it is thanks to history and not because of mechanical representations that we understand, describe with the help of macro variables, and may eventually explain, the turning points, the structure of the epochs in economic evolution, the social constraints, the main innovations, the rise and fall of institutions. And that is the subject of economics: back to real life; statistics and formal methods are challenged to interpret bifurcations, non-linearities and mutations. This is a task for the future.

ACKNOWLEDGMENTS

An earlier version of this paper was presented to the CEMAPRE Conference on Mathematical Applications to Economics and Management, Lisbon, May 1997. I must express my thanks for comments from C.W.J. Granger and other participants, as well as from William Brock, Blake LeBaron, David Lane and José Scheinkman on a previous version of this chapter. The usual disclaimer applies.

NOTES

1. This is indicated as the first reference to chaos in economics, ignoring the previous authors, by Baumol and Benhabib (1989, p. 80n.). It must be emphasized that the history of the incorporation of the notions of chaos and complexity into economics is still to be done. Some topics on the evolution of debates and concepts are discussed in the next sections.
2. The name BDS was taken from the authors: Brock, Dechert and Scheinkman.
3. The Grassberger–Procaccia dimension is downwards biased in small samples and the bias increases with the embedding dimension, as Ramsey, Granger, Barnett, Hinich and others have emphasized.
4. The authors here surveyed suggest that 'shifts in the unconditional variance could explain common findings of persistence in the conditional variance' (Brock and De Lima, 1995, p. 24). In the case of stock returns, which is a non-stationary process, one might ask if this is caused by discrete shifts in the unconditional variance, representing structural or institutional change, or by non-linear complex processes. The current methods are unable to discriminate between these two hypotheses.
5. Yet this is assumed without margin for doubt or a second thought by virtually all the authors surveyed (for example, Barnett and Chen, 1986, p. 22).
6. Frisch's 1933 paper and the large cohort of followers he ignited in economics defined 'the standard way economists view time series: there are impulses (club movements) and a propagation mechanism (rocking horse) which together produce the fluctuations or cycles of economic time series around their upward movements' (Brock and Potter, 1993, p. 195). This system is represented by linear difference equations or by mixed differential–difference equations driven by random shocks, and it established the primacy of linear methods in economics and econometrics. But there are at least two severe objections to it, and one is indeed formulated by Brock and Potter: it is unable to account for large structural changes: 'However, if we return to the physical analogy introduced by the rocking horse example it is not clear that the behaviour of the rocking horse is accurately described by a linear difference equation for movements far away from its resting position' (ibid.). The second objection concerns the cursory treatment of the concept of randomness and, although that ought to be a major contribution from chaos theory, no precise reference is made to that point: Brock just minimizes the role of random shocks (Brock, 1993, p. 7). On this topic, see Louçã (1997).
7. In the same text, Brock emphasizes another crucial difference of economic modelling in relation to physics: 'Unlike some of the physics and nonlinear science literature on cellular automata and interacting particle systems we shall stress global connectors as well as local connectors and non-symmetric interactions as well as symmetric interactions. Also the role of conservation principles and invariance principles under symmetries will be minimal in

economic applications many of which suggest no natural counterparts to these concepts of central importance in some natural science applications' (Brock, 1991, p. 120). This is an obvious although implicit denunciation of the neoclassical foundations of economics since, without a conservation principle, maximization becomes meaningless, and the abandonment of the principle of invariance over time challenges the procedure of inductive inference. Note that there is a contradiction between these well-taken points and the defence by the author of neoclassical standards against the physicists' critiques.

8. 'Finance, economics and social science phenomena yield time evolutions of great interest but perplexing difficulty. One has the impression that, while there is an element of deterministic low-dimensional dynamics, a useful model should also include noise (shocks) and perhaps drift of the deterministic dynamics (that is, some of the parameters of the deterministic part of the dynamics change with time). Here, basically, one has not been able to obtain quantitatively useful models. One tentative conclusion of studies in this domain is that many time evolutions in finance or economics are chaotic in the sense that a small change in the initial conditions would have important consequences for late-evolution' (Ruelle, 1994, p. 28).
9. The Nobel prizewinner Philip Anderson (physics) evokes this difficulty for economics, giving the examples of the 'changes of regime' introduced by the Napoleonic wars, the Great Depression and the period of the world wars, and the structural changes of the 1980s (Anderson, 1988, p. 271). In other words, history matters.
10. The arguments against chaos are powerful indeed, but paradigmatically bounded: they are based on predictive value either of the efficient markets hypothesis in financial processes or of the random walk hypothesis in foreign exchange analysis. Both assume the independence of events in relation to the past – but both were rejected in the concrete empirical work (Brock, 1990a, p. 430; Brock *et* al. 1991, p. 143). Yet these theoretical settings remain largely undisputed.
11. Granger made the well-taken point that heteroscedasticity may cause the test to reject the null (Granger, 1991, p. 265). Based on that, one may reverse the argument and defend the contentious claim that heteroscedasticity is evidence for the specific form of non-linearity that is relevant to the analysis of macroeconomic historical series.

REFERENCES

Anderson, P. (1988), 'A Physicist Look at Economics: An Overview of the Workshop', in Anderson *et al.* (eds).

Anderson, P., K. Arrow and D. Pines (eds) (1988), *The Economy as an Evolving Complex System*, Redwood City: Addison-Wesley.

Arthur, B., S. Durlauf and D. Lane (eds) (1997), *The Economy as an Evolving Complex System II*, Redwood City: Addison-Wesley.

Barnett, W. and P. Chen, (1986), 'The Aggregation-Theoretic Monetary Aggregates are Chaotic and Have Strange Attractors', in W. Barnett, E. Berndt and H. White (eds), *Dynamic Econometric Modelling: Proceedings of the Third Austin Symposium in Economics*, Cambridge: Cambridge University Press.

Barnett, W. and P. Chen, (1988), 'Deterministic chaos and fractal attractors as tools for nonparametric dynamical inferences', *Mathematical Computing and Modelling*, **10**, 275–96.

Barnett, W. and P. Choi (1989), 'A Comparison between the Conventional Econometric Approach to Structural Inference and the Nonparametric Chaotic Attractor Approach', in Barnett *et al.* (eds).

Barnett, W. and M. Hinich (1993), 'Has Chaos been Discovered with Economic Data?', in R. Day and P. Chen (eds).

Barnett, W., J. Geweke and K. Shell (eds) (1989), *Economic Complexity: Chaos, Sunspots, Bubbles and Nonlinearities*, Cambridge: Cambridge University Press.
Baumol, W. and J. Benhabib (1989), 'Chaos: significance, mechanism and economic applications', *Journal of Economic Perspectives*, **3**(1), 77–105.
Bausor, R. (1994), 'Qualitative Dynamics in Economics and Fluid Mechanics: A Comparison of Recent Applications', in P. Mirowski (ed.), *Natural Images in Economic Thought*, Cambridge: Cambridge University Press.
Boldrin, M. (1988), 'Persistent Oscillations and Chaos in Dynamic Economic Models: Notes for a Survey', in Anderson *et al.* (eds).
Brock, W. (1986), 'Distinguishing random and deterministic systems: abridged version', *Journal of Economic Theory*, **40**(1), 168–95.
Brock, W. (1988), 'Hicksian Nonlinearity', SSRI Working Paper 8815.
Brock, W. (1990a), 'Chaos and Complexity in Economic and Financial Series', in G. Furstenberg (ed.), *Acting Under Uncertainty: Multidisciplinary Conception*, Boston, MA: Kluwer.
Brock, W. (1990b), 'Causality, Chaos, Explanation and Prediction in Economics and Finance', in J. Casti and C. Kalquist (eds), *Beyond Belief: Randomness, Prediction and Explanation in Science*, Boca Raton: CRC Press.
Brock, W. (1991), 'Understanding macroeconomic time series using complex systems theory', *Structural Change and Dynamics*, **2**(1), 119–41.
Brock, W. (1993), 'Pathways to randomness in the economy: emergent nonlinearity and chaos in economics and finance', *Estudios Económicos*, **8**(1), 3–55.
Brock, W. and P. De Lima (1995), 'Nonlinear Time Series, Complexity Theory and Finance', SSRI Working Paper 9523.
Brock, W. and A. Malliaris (1988), *Differential Equations, Stability and Chaos in Dynamic Economics*, New York: North-Holland.
Brock, W. and S. Potter (1993), 'Nonlinear Time Series and Macroeconometrics', in G.S. Maddala *et al.* (eds), *Handbook of Statistics*, vol. 11, Elsevier.
Brock, W. and C. Sayers (1988), 'Is the business cycle characterized by deterministic chaos?', *Journal of Monetary Economics*, **22**, 71–90.
Brock, W., D. Hsieh and B. LeBaron (1991), *Nonlinear Dynamics, Chaos and Instability: Statistical Theory and Economic Evidence*, Cambridge: Cambridge University Press.
Brock, W., W. Dechert, B. LeBaron and J. Scheinkman (1996), 'A test for independence based on the correlation dimension', *Econometric Reviews*, **15**(3), 197–235.
Day, R. and P. Chen (eds) (1993), *Nonlinear Dynamics and Evolutionary Dynamics*, Oxford: Oxford University Press.
Dechert, W. and R. Gencay (1992), 'Lyapunov exponents as a nonparametric diagnostics for stability analysis', *Journal of Applied Econometrics*, **7**, S41–S60.
DeCoster, G. and D. Mitchell (1991), 'Nonlinear monetary dynamics', *Journal of Business and Economic Statistics*, **9**, 455–62.
De Lima, P. (1994), 'Nonlinearities and Nonstationarities in Stock Returns', mimeo, Department of Economics, John Hopkins University.
Eckmann, J.P., S. Kamphurst, D. Ruelle and J. Scheinkman (1988), 'Lyapunov Exponent for Stock Returns', in Anderson *et al.* (eds).
Essex, C. and M. Nerenberg (1991), 'Comments on deterministic chaos: the science and the fiction by D. Ruelle', *Proceedings of the Royal Society of London*, **A435**, 287–92.
Frank, M. and T. Stengos (1988), 'The stability of Canadian macroeconomic data as measured by the largest Lyapunov exponent', *Economic Letters*, **27**, 11–14.

Frank, M. and T. Stengos (1989), 'Measuring the strangeness of gold and silver rates of return', *Review of Economic Statistics*, **56**, 553–67.
Frank, M., R. Gencay and T. Stengos (1988), 'International chaos?', *European Economic Review*, **32**, 1569–84.
Gabisch, G. and H.W. Lorenz (1989), *Business Cycle Theory: A Survey of Methods and Concepts*, New York: Springer Verlag.
Grandmont, J. (1985), 'On endogenous competitive business cycles', *Econometrica*, **53**, 995–1046.
Granger, C.W.J. (1991), 'Developments in the nonlinear analysis of economic series', *Scandinavian Journal of Economics*, **93**(2), 263–76.
Grassberger, P. and I. Procaccia (1982), 'Characterization of strange attractors', *Physical Review Letters*, **50**, 346–9.
Grassberger, P. and I. Procaccia (1983), 'Measuring the strangeness of strange attractors', *Physica 9D*, 189–208.
Grassberger, P., T. Schreiber and C. Schaffrath (1991), 'Nonlinear time sequence analysis', *International Journal of Bifurcation and Chaos*, **1**, 521–47.
Hsieh, D. (1989), 'Testing for nonlinear dependence in foreign exchange rates', *Journal of Business*, **62**, 339–68.
Hsieh, D. (1991), 'Chaos and nonlinear dynamics: applications to financial markets', *Journal of Finance*, **46**, 1839–78.
Kehoe, T. (1988), 'Computing and Multiplicity of Economic Equilibria', in Anderson *et al.* (eds).
LeBaron, B. (1988), 'The Changing Structure of Stock Returns', working paper, Department of Economics, University of Chicago.
LeBaron, B. (1992a), 'Some relations between volatility and serial correlation in stock market returns', *Journal of Business*, **14**, 199–219.
LeBaron, B. (1992b), 'Chaos and Nonlinear Forecastability in Economics and Finance', SSRI Working Paper 9446.
Lee, T., H. White and C.W.J. Granger (1989), 'Testing for Neglected Nonlinearity in Time Series Models: A Comparison of Neural Network Methods and Alternative Tests', working paper, Department of Economics, University of California; reprinted (1993), *Journal of Econometrics*, **56**, 269–90.
Liu, T. and C.W.J. Granger (1992), 'Using the correlation exponent to decide whether an economic series is chaotic', *Journal of Applied Econometrics*, **7**, S25–S39.
Lorenz, H.W. (1993), *Nonlinear Dynamical Economics and Chaotic Motion*, Berlin: Springer-Verlag.
Louçã, F. (1997), *Turbulence in Economics – An Evolutionary Appraisal of Cycles and Complexity in Historical Series*, Cheltenham, UK and Lyme, US: Edward Elgar.
Louçã, F. (2000), 'Intriguing pendula', *Cambridge Journal of Economics.*
Mandelbrot, B. (1963), 'The variation of certain speculative prices', *Journal of Business*, **36**, 394–419.
Mandelbrot, B. (1967), *Fractal Manifesto*, reprinted in B. Mandelbrot (1981), 'Towards a second stage of Indeterminism in Science', *Interdisciplinary Science Review*, **12**, 117–27.
Mandelbrot, B. (1983), *The Fractal Geometry of Nature*, New York: Freeman.
Mantegna, R. and H. Stanley, (1995), 'Scaling behaviour in the dynamics of an economic index', *Nature*, **376**, 46–9.
May, R. and J. Beddington, (1975), 'Nonlinear Difference Equations: Stable Points, Stable Cycles, Chaos', unpublished Msc.

Meese, F. and A. Rose (1991), 'An empirical assessment of nonlinearities in models of exchange rate determination', *Review of Economic Studies*, **58**, 603–19.
Mirowski, P. (1989), *More Heat than Light – Economics as Social Physics, Physics as Nature's Economics*, Cambridge: Cambridge University Press.
Mirowski, P. (1995), 'Mandelbrot's economics after a quarter century', *Fractals*, **3**(3), 581–600.
Palmer, R. (1988), 'Final Plenary Session', in Anderson *et al.* (eds).
Papell, D. and C. Sayers (1990), 'Nonlinear Dynamics and Exchange Rate Frequency', working paper, Houston University.
Potter, S. (1991), 'A Nonlinear Approach to US GNP', working paper, UCLA.
Ramsey, J., C. Sayers and P. Rothman, (1990), 'The statistical properties of dimension calculations using small data sets: some economic applications', *International Economic Review*, **31**, 991–1020.
Ruelle, D. (1988), 'Can Nonlinear Dynamics Help Economists?', in Anderson *et al.* (eds).
Ruelle, D. (1990), 'Deterministic chaos: the science and the fiction', *Proceedings from the Royal Society of London*, **A427**, 241–8.
Ruelle, D. (1991), *Hasard et Chaos*, Paris: Odile Jacob.
Ruelle, D. (1994), 'Where can one hope to profitably apply the ideas of chaos?', *Physics Today*, July, 24–30.
Sayers, C. (1988a), 'Diagnostic Tests for Nonlinearities in Time Series Data: An Application to the Work Stoppage Series', working paper, University of North Carolina.
Sayers, C. (1988b), 'Work Stoppages, Exploring the Nonlinear Dynamics', working paper, University of Houston.
Sayers, C. (1989), 'Chaos and the Business Cycle', in S. Krasner (ed.), *The Ubiquity of Chaos*, Washington, DC: American Association for the Advancement of Science Publications.
Scheinkman, J. (1990), 'Nonlinearities in economic dynamics', *Economic Journal*, Supplement, **100**(400), 33–47.
Scheinkman, J. and B. LeBaron (1989a), 'Nonlinear Dynamics and GNP Data', in W. Barnett, J. Geweke and K. Shell (eds), *Economic Complexity: Chaos, Sunspots, Bubbles and Nonlinearities*, Cambridge: Cambridge University Press.
Scheinkman, J. and B. LeBaron (1989b), 'Nonlinear dynamics and stock returns', *Journal of Business*, **62**, 311–38.
Scheinkman, J. and M. Woodford (1994), 'Self-organized criticality and economic fluctuations', *American Economic Review*, **84**(2), 417–21.
Schmidt, K. and P. Stahlecker (1989), 'Gibt es Chaos im Industriellen Sektor der Bundesrepublik Deutschland?', *Jahrbuch Fur Sozialwissenschaft*, **40**, 332–41.
Smith, R. (1992), 'Estimating dimension in noisy chaotic time series', *Journal of the Royal Statistical Society*, **B54**, 329–51.
Sugihara, G. and R. May (1990), 'Nonlinear forecasting as a way of distinguishing chaos from measurement error in time series', *Nature*, **344**, 734–41.
Sugihara, G., B. Grenfell and R. May (1990), 'Distinguishing error from chaos in ecological time series', *Philosophical Transactions of the Royal Society of London*, **B330**, 225–35.
Terasvirta, T. (1990), 'Structural Change in Swedish and Finnish Monthly Industrial Output Series', in P. Hackl and A. Westlund (eds), *Economic Structural Change – Analysis and Forecasting*, Berlin: Springer Verlag.

Tsonis, Anastasios (1992), *Chaos – From Theory to Applications*, New York: Plenum Press.

Westlund, Anders (1991), 'Comment on C.W.J. Granger, developments in the nonlinear analysis of economic series', *Scandinavian Journal of Economics*, **93**(2), 277–81.

TECHNICAL ANNEX: THE BDS STATISTICS

Consider a model of the form

$$x_t = f(z_t, b, e_t) \quad (1)$$

where $\{\mathbf{x}_t\}$ is a strictly stationary vector of observable variables including lagged z_{t-n}, $\mathbf{b}$ is a vector of parameters that can be estimated $\sqrt{n}$-consistently, $\{e_t\}$ is an IID process with zero mean and finite variance.

In order to check the existence of a strange attractor in this process, one might measure the Hausdorff dimension of the series $\{\mathbf{x}_t\}$; obviously, if the series is chaotic, this measure will be non-zero and fractional. However, this is a very difficult computation, and Grassberger and Procaccia (1982, 1983) suggested a simpler algorithm in order to approximate the dimension of a series. The Grassberger–Procaccia correlation dimension has ever since been widely used in physics and was adapted to economics, as we shall see. It provides a measure of a lower bound to the state space dimension,[1] so that we have

G–P correlation dimension < information dimension < Hausdorff dimension

The *correlation dimension* measures the geometric correlation of nearby points and indicates for trajectories generated under different initial conditions how close two points on those trajectories came to be in the phase space. As some authors suggest, this measurement may be viewed as indicating the minimum dimension or number of degrees of freedom which could generate the time series under inspection (Gabisch and Lorenz, 1989, p. 189, Brock *et al.*, 1991, p. 2). The correlation dimension tends to a stationary and small value with increasing embedding dimension if a low-dimensional deterministic process generates the process, whereas it tends to infinitely if the process is purely stochastic.

Brock and Sayers (1988) intuitively perceive the notion of dimensions from the following illustration: a computer program generating random numbers, IID uniformly distributed in [0.1] is used to generate a series $\{x_t\}$. The distribution of the data in the interval is inspected in order to check whether they fill it or if they cluster around some points. If the first case happens, then it is supposed that the dimension is ≥ 1. If **m**-vectors (*m*-histories) generated by this program can also fill an *m*-cube, $[0.1]^m$, and do not cluster around some lower dimensional subset, then the dimension must be ≥ *m*. Of course, a truly random process should fill all the *m*-cubes for all *m*.

Brock, Dechert and Scheinkman have developed since 1986 a statistical procedure which is based on this notion of dimension, in order to discuss some of the qualitative features of the series whenever the precise function (1) is not known, and generally not knowable. An *m*-geometric object, an *m-history* – that is, a possible subset $\{x_s, \ldots, x_{s+m-1}\}$ from the original series – is created in an *m*-dimensional space: it was proved by Takens in 1981 that this reconstructed attractor is topologically equivalent to the object formed by the trajectory of the original dynamical system (Lorenz, 1993, p. 206). A *correlation integral* generated by the series $\{x_t, \mathrm{t} = 1, \ldots, T\}$ of T observations is defined for $(t\text{–}s)$, the time distance between the elements of each pair of observations as:

$$C(m,\varepsilon,T) = \#\{(t,s), // x(t,m) - x(s,m) // < \varepsilon\} / T^2 \tag{2}$$

where $x(t, m) = (x(t), \ldots, x(t - m + 1))$, $x(s, m) = (x(t), \ldots, x(s - m + 1))$, $//x(t, m) - x(s, m)// = max\ |x(t, m)_i - x(s, m)_i/, i = 1, \ldots, m\}$ for an *m*-dimensional vector and $\#\{.\}$ indicates the number of elements (Brock, 1990a, p. 432). In other words, for all possible *m*-histories $x(t, m)$ and $x(s, m)$, the correlation integral is that fraction of the pairs of data points (t, s) where the histories are closer than the radius ε. As a function of ε, it can also be considered as a joint cumulative distribution function. The measure of dimension of $\{x_t\}$ for the embedding value m that is used in the statistics is the elasticity of C with respect to ε:

$$d(\varepsilon,m,T) = dC(m,\varepsilon,T) / d\varepsilon\ \varepsilon / C(m,\varepsilon,T) \tag{3}$$

In other words, given the record of T observations, one forms all possible *m*-futures and counts the number of pairs of dates (t, s) for which $x(t, m)$ and $x(s, m)$ differ for less than ε. Fixing a particular *m*-history $x(t, m)$, the correlation dimension measures the percentage increase in neighbours in the neighbourhood of ε when ε is increased by 1 per cent. Brock and Dechert (1988) showed that if $\{\varepsilon\}$ is IID, then it is true that:

$$ln[C(m,\varepsilon)] = m\ ln[C(1,\varepsilon)] \tag{4}$$

This is the basis for the BDS statistic:

$$W(m,\varepsilon,T) = T^{1/2}[C(m,\varepsilon,T) - C(1,\varepsilon,T)m] / \sigma(m,\varepsilon,T) \tag{5}$$

where $\sigma(m, e, T)$ is the consistently estimated standard deviation. As the asymptotic distribution under the null of nonlinearity or chaos is not known, the chosen strategy was to fomulate the null that the series is generated by a linear system with IID innovations and, in that case, the authors proved that the distribution of W converges to $N(0,1)$ (Brock and Sayers, 1988, p. 80;

Scheinkman and LeBaron, 1989a, p. 216; Scheinkman, 1990, p. 111). Of course, if this is the case, $W = 0$. The test is powerful against chaotic and other complex or nonlinear structures, although it is unable to discriminate among them. Even for small samples the distribution is asymptotically approximated by the standard normal.

This is a general portmanteau test of the potentially forecastable structure, of non-stationarity or of hidden geometric patterns (Brock *et al.*, 1991, p. 3), which is presented as a nonlinear analogue of the Box-Pierce Q statistics used in ARIMA models (Brock *et al.*, 1996, p. 197). Although it is not a consistent test,[2] it provides relevant information about the system, and extensive Monte Carlo simulation work proved that it can reject the null for most cases of nonlinearity and chaos. Furthermore, compared with alternative tests, the BDS is presented as the only one robust to moment condition failure (Brock and De Lima, 1995, p. 23).

In common use, the researcher must first obtain a stationary representation of the series – typically, detrending and filtering it in order to avoid non-stationarity in mean and in variance – and then apply the test. It was proved that linear filtering preserves the same correlation dimension and the measure of the largest Lyapunov exponent, given the invariance of chaotic equations to linear transformations (see, for example, Brock, 1990a, p. 436; Lorenz, 1993, p. 223), although fitting a linear model to a time series introduces dependence in the residuals (Scheinkman and LeBaron, 1989b, p. 318), which is not considered to challenge the result.[3] In this case, the authors suggested the application of the test to the residuals, and then the use of a reshuffling diagnostics: in the case of chaos, the correlation dimension should be approximately the same for the series and for the residuals, but should increase dramatically if the residuals of the series were randomly resampled and the test applied again. In that case, the geometric ordered form would be destroyed and the computed dimension should approximate the infinite dimension of the white noise process.

The rejection of the null indicates the existence of hidden structures; that is, the presence of non-stationarity or of nonlinearity in the residuals of the estimated models. Of course, there is the case of findings of nonlinearity imposed by eventual non-covariance stationarity, or of structural changes over long periods;[4] it is in order to limit these departures from the standard conditions for the test that the series is linearly filtered in order to get stationarity.

Although there are some ambiguous and scarcely discussed claims, such as presenting the test as a 'nonlinear Granger causality test' (Brock, 1990b, pp. 233, 239), this test has been widely used in economics as well as in other fields in order to measure the correlation dimension and to test the null of IID. It proved to be a powerful diagnostics for model specification and it is still the single most widely used non-parametric method in nonlinear dynamics in economics.

NOTES

1. The lower bound indicates the number of variables necessary for an endogenous explanation of the series, not the correct model (Barnett and Choi, 1989, p. 151). Typically, the true dimension will be much greater: in the example of the Mackey–Glass equation, a ~1.95 correlation dimension is obtained, whereas the actual dimension of the state space is around 600.
2. There are known cases of undetected departures from nonlinearity (Brock and De Lima, 1995, p. 18).
3. The residual diagnostics may reject chaos [accept the null of IID] when in fact it prevails because the 'pre-whitening process' introduces lags and estimation noise. Computer experiments showed that this problem was not too serious if the number of lags was small, say 2 to 4' (Brock, 1990a, p. 436).
4. The authors here surveyed suggest that 'shifts in the unconditional variance could explain common findings of persistence in the conditional variance' (Brock and De Lima, 1995, p. 24). In the case of stock returns, which is a non-stationary process, one might ask if this is caused by discrete shifts in the unconditional variance, representing structural or institutional change, or by nonlinear complex processes. The current methods are unable to discriminate between these two hypotheses, as we shall see.

Commentary: measuring complexity – puzzles and tentative solutions

Steve Keen

Before chaos became part of the vernacular, Blatt argued that econometrics cannot possibly be meaningful. Economic time-series are clearly generated by complex, evolving non-linear processes, while standard econometric tests presume that the error terms in linear econometric models are random variables with zero means. This presumption cannot possibly be true in the light of the many specification errors which afflict such models (Blatt, 1983, pp. 340–44).

Louçã's chapter establishes that econometric methodology has still not evolved sufficiently to escape from the problems highlighted by Blatt. Though there are now econometric tests, such as the BDS statistic, which purport to test for the existence of chaos, they are still infected with the economic profession's predilection for linear models.

This economic obsession with linearity borders on a pathology. Since Lorenz's rediscovery of chaos in 1967, concepts of non-linearity and chaotic behaviour have permeated physics, all other physical sciences and even many social sciences. Yet, despite the existence of some enthusiastic proponents of non-linear economic analysis, and despite the previous history of economics adopting the dominant methodology in physics, mainstream economics and econometrics remain wedded to the linear perspective.

This is not the first time that economics has displayed resistance to a challenging new paradigm. Louçã identifies the 'implicit challenge of chaos on the postulate of rationality (and perfect information) and its implications on equilibrium' as a major reason for the resistance to chaos, and a similar explanation could be given to the resistance manifested six decades ago to dynamics. We are perhaps seeing a repeat of the discipline's shoddy treatment of dynamics in its modern treatment of chaos. Certainly, some of the sins committed in the 1930s and 1940s are being committed once more today.

Ignorance could excuse Hicks for his erroneous assertion that dynamic equilibria had to be unstable because 'A mathematically unstable system does not fluctuate; it just breaks down' (Hicks, 1949, p. 108). No such excuse is acceptable today, yet economists continue to cling to the notion of stable economic equilibria. Today, however, they appeal, not to mistaken mathematics, but to economic theory itself to justify the concept of hyperstable equilibria in economic data. Thus Jaditz and Sayers, in defending the methodology of the BDS statistic, comment that

> there are good theoretical arguments that many interesting economic series should have an important random component… based on the efficient markets hypothesis and the rational expectations hypothesis… In particular, they affect the economists' view of what the appropriate null hypothesis should be in statistical tests of chaos… the typical economist has a strong prior belief that economic phenomena in general and price series in particular ought to be modelled as stochastic processes, rather than as deterministic processes. (Jaditz and Sayers, 1993, p. 746)

This appeal to theory to justify a null of linearity could be superficially justified on the basis of the inconclusive history of tests for chaos in economic data. However, as Louçã (and also Jaditz and Sayers) documents, much of this inconclusiveness stems from disagreement over the suitability of short noisy economic data sets for analysis of chaos, the impact of exponential detrending and linear data-filtering techniques, and the appropriateness of a linear null hypothesis. The appeal to theory is also predictably blinkered. As Louçã points out, mainstream theories which at a simplistic level are linear 'lead to instability and chaos' after 'some minor adjustments not at odds with a realistic approach'. There are also extant many non-mainstream theories of the behaviour of economic and financial time-series which do not presume rational expectations or stochastic processes: Peters' Fractal Markets Hypothesis (Peters, 1991, 1994), Minsky's Financial Instability Hypothesis (Minsky, 1975, 1982), Kariya's Multivariate Time Series approach (Kariya, 1993) and behavioural models of finance (Haugen, 1999) all argue that, certainly in the case of financial data, the underlying processes are anything but stochastic.

The null hypothesis of the BDS statistic, that 'the data were generated by an independent and identically distributed stochastic process' (Dechert, 1996, p. 191) is therefore arbitrary, as is the requirement for linear filtering of the data.

Harrod argued for growth and cycle theory to be coextensive, in the belief that growth and cycle are interdependent, 'that the trend of growth may itself generate forces making for oscillation' (Harrod, 1939, p. 14). Instead we had the bifurcation of growth and cycle theory, with the former dominated by Solow/Swan equilibrium growth models and the latter the near-exclusive province of vacuous second-order difference equations.[1] Louçã shows that the same predilection to divide growth from cycle is alive and well in the BDS procedure. The stationarity required by the test is in part imposed on non-stationary series by exponential detrending. This 'assumes the existence of two completely separate and separable economic processes, the cycles and the trend, the latter being accounted for by a constant rate of growth' and, as Louçã comments, 'There is no justification whatsoever for these assumptions.'

The problems with the BDS statistic are not limited to its null hypothesis, as Louçã points out. The Grassberger–Procaccia test on which it is based presumes that the data lie on a single strange attractor. This presumption does not apply to known chaotic distributions such as the Lorenz model, in which there are three strange attractors; it is also challenged by structural change and bifurcations in the data.

Louçã notes instances of data massaging to remove structural breaks from time-series, as in the use of dummy variables to compensate for the Great Depression and World War II in Scheinkman and LeBaron (1989a), and comments that 'the smoothing out of periods of abrupt change may hide evidence of non-linearities'. While such a procedure is arguably justified for a war, it is nonsensical for the Great Depression unless it could be proved that the Great Depression was caused by non-economic forces. While some economists argue as much (blaming 'bad monetary policy'), Minsky's Financial Instability Hypothesis (Minsky, 1975) and Fisher's Debt Deflation Theory of Great Depressions (Fisher, 1933) argue that the Depression was caused by the accumulation of excessive debt during the euphoric 1920s. This proposition can be represented in non-linear models which generate an asymmetric process of debt accumulation in the context of a cyclical economy (Keen, 2000). It is feasible that data generated by an extended stochastic version of such models could fail the BDS test for chaos – because of the sharp break in the time series either side of the debt crisis – even though the basic model is clearly non-linear.

This weakness of the BDS statistic suggests another means to appraise the test's general relevance. The BDS statistic did quite well in Barnett *et al.*'s (1998) single-blind competition among tests for chaos, clearly identifying as chaotic data generated by a logistic map with the parameter set at Feigenbaum's constant. However, it could be that the test would not do so well with discretely sampled data from a Lorenz model – in which there are three strange attractors – or with data from a logistic map with the parameter varying over its chaotic range rather than being held constant, which would have bifurcations in the data set.

The general failure of the BDS statistic to find instances of chaos in economic data may therefore reflect the test's inability to cope with more general chaotic processes, and with processes generated by evolving systems, rather than an absence of non-linearity and chaos *per se* in economic data. Yet, as Louçã points out, the failure is being used to justify the conclusion that economic data are not generated by non-linear or chaotic processes, but by the stochastic linear processes of which economics is so enamoured.

Conceived as a means to test for chaos, the BDS statistic may in fact help inoculate neoclassical economics against the virus of complexity.

I am pessimistic about the possibility of convincing neoclassical economists of this interpretation. LeBaron's conclusion that 'The direct evidence for deterministic chaos in many economic series remains weak' (LeBaron, 1994, p. 397) appears to be shared by the majority of economists, if casual empiricism is any guide. If I had a dollar for every time I have heard an economist comment that 'not much seems to have come of chaos theory', I would not be a rich man – but I could afford many a fine meal.

Instead, I expect that economic and econometric research will display their own bifurcations. The vast majority of economists and econometricians will continue to build and test linear stochastic models. A minority will develop non-linear models, and attempt to develop appropriate statistical tests where both model and test can cope with bifurcations and structural change.

Interesting developments in this respect include Ozaki's local linearization technique for fitting continuous time non-linear stochastic differential equation models to data, and Smooth Transition Regression analysis, which generalizes Ozaki's technique to allow for smooth rather than abrupt structural shifts in data. Semmler and Koçkesen (1998) apply these techniques to estimating a two-dimensional non-linear model of financial and real variable interaction. The non-linear model gives better out-of-sample prediction than a linear alternative, and achieves something which is beyond the linear model: cycles continue in the non-linear model, whereas they rapidly peter out in the linear. Their findings on the superiority of the non-linear model as an out-of-sample predictor confirm the earlier results of Deutsch, Granger and Terasvirta (1994).

The innate superiority of nonlinear models over linear – in that they can endogenously generate the cyclical characteristics seen in economic data, whereas linear models cannot – is a useful guarantee that chaos and complexity analysis will not completely disappear from economics and econometrics. There are at least two other reasons why economics will not abandon complexity as completely as it once abandoned dynamics.

Firstly, an important difference between the modern era and economics' earlier flirtation with dynamics is that the shift to complexity and chaos has occurred across the sciences, whereas economics was isolated in its belated and manacled discovery of dynamics in the 1940s.

Secondly, while 'physics envy' has led economics astray in the past, it may be hoped that in the future it will inspire newcomers to economic analysis to at least dabble in the dangerous waters of complexity. One important irony here is that avid practitioners of non-linear analysis in economics will be relative outcasts within their own discipline, yet will enjoy comparative peer status with physicists. Equilibrium theorists, on the other hand, will hold the high ground within economics, but be derided by the hard sciences whose acknowledgment they crave.

As Louçã in part documents, the pervasiveness of complexity analysis everywhere but in economics is giving our discipline pariah status in the sciences. I expect that economics and econometrics will only escape from this diminished ranking in the chaotic aftermath of a decisive bifurcation in economic and financial data. Those who have accepted the 'pragmatic view' that 'probabilistic methods are for the time being the most appropriate technique for analysing economic time series data' (Liu *et al.*, 1992, S38) will be the last ones to see such a bifurcation coming.

NOTE

1. I say vacuous because it is easily shown that the archetypal Hicks–Hanson–Samuelson second-order difference equation is based on a fallacious definition of *ex post* investment, and an erroneous equating of *ex ante* investment to *ex post* savings (Keen, 2000).

REFERENCES

Barnett, W.A., A.R. Gallant, M.J. Hinich, J.A. Jungeilges, D.T. Kaplan and M. Jensen, (1998), 'A single-blind controlled competition among tests for nonlinearity and chaos', *Journal of Econometrics*, **82**, 157–92.

Blatt, J.M. (1983), *Dynamic Economic Systems*, Armonk: M.E. Sharpe.

Dechert, W.D. (1996), 'Testing Time Series for Nonlinearities: The BDS Approach', in W.A. Barnett, A.P. Kirman and M. Salmon (eds), *Nonlinear Dynamics and Economics: Proceedings of the Tenth International Symposium in Economic Theory and Econometrics*, New York: Cambridge University Press.

Deutsch, M., C.W.J. Granger and T. Terasvirta (1994), 'The combination of forecasts using changing weights', *International Journal of Forecasting*, **10**, 47–57.

Fisher, I. (1933), 'The debt deflation theory of great depressions', *Econometrica*, **1**, 337–57.

Harrod, R.F. (1939), 'An essay in dynamic theory', *Economic Journal*, **49**, 14–33.

Haugen, R.A. (1999), *The New Finance*, Upper Saddle River, NJ: Prentice-Hall.

Hicks, J. (1949), 'Mr Harrod's dynamic theory', *Economica*, **16**, 106–21.

Jaditz T. and C.L. Sayers (1993), 'Is chaos generic in economic data?', *International Journal of Bifurcation and Chaos*, **3**, 745–55.

Kariya, T. (1993), *Quantitative Methods for Portfolio Analysis*, Dordrecht: Kluwer .

Keen, S. (2000), *Finance and Economic Breakdown*, Cheltenham, UK and Lyme, US: Edward Elgar .

LeBaron, B. (1994), 'Chaos and nonlinear forestability in economics and finance', *Philosophical Transitions of the Royal Society of London*, Series (B), **348**, 397–404.

Liu, T., C.W.J. Granger and W.P. Heller (1992), 'Using the Correlation Exponent to decide whether an Economic Time Series is Chaotic', *Journal of Applied Econometrics*, **7** (Supplement), S25–39.

Minsky, H. (1975), *John Maynard Keynes*, Columbia: Columbia University Press.
Minsky, H. (1982), *Inflation, Recession and Economic Policy*, Armonk: M.E. Sharpe.
Peters, E.E. (1991), *Chaos and Order in the Capital Markets*, New York: John Wiley & Sons.
Peters, E.E. (1994), *Fractal Market Analysis*, New York: John Wiley & Sons.
Semmler, W. and L. Koçkesen (1998), 'The financial accelerator: a model and empirical estimations', unpublished manuscript.

10. Knowledge, ignorance and the evolution of complex systems

Peter M. Allen

INTRODUCTION: IS KNOWLEDGE AN ILLUSION?

On what basis can anyone or any organization 'know' what to do? How can they know what opportunities and uncertainties exist in the environment, and how they are changing? And, more importantly, how can possible future changes be anticipated, and how may we shape our strategies and decisions to better ensure our own survival and success? In traditional societies answers to these questions have been furnished by their mythologies, but in ours 'science' has become the dominant theory. But, as we shall see, this has been the 'science' of 'simple' systems, which in human affairs is wholly inadequate. The hope is therefore that we may get more useful answers from the theory of complex systems (Allen *et al.*, 1985).

Understanding 'reality', creating apparent 'knowledge', requires us to reduce the real complexity of any particular situation to a simpler, more understandable one, by making specific simplifying assumptions. When facing some situation the hope is that there exists a representation that, while being sufficiently simple to be understood, remains sufficiently 'realistic' to be useful. Of course, it is not at all certain that such a representation exists, but in our struggle to survive we cling to the hope that it does. Gaining knowledge is equivalent to knowing what simplifications can be made. This might be that we suppose that we are in a stable environment, and that we can rely on 'trial and error' to teach us practical heuristics. Ordinary wisdom will often be of this kind. However, if the world is changing, how can we gain knowledge to help decide what to do? What simplifications can we still make?

In order to clarify these ideas, let us consider the assumptions that must be made in order to represent a particular system as a mechanical object made up of coupled components, allowing prediction and optimization (see Figure 10.1). A mechanical model, such as a system dynamics model, appears to predict perfectly the future path of the system, but this seemingly solid piece of knowledge is only as good as the assumptions that underlie it. If these are compromised at any time, the 'knowledge' will be thoroughly misleading, since it will actually be making a false prediction. This may be worse than knowing that you 'don't know'. So 'knowledge' is really about being able to establish the veracity of the simplifying assumptions on which it relies.

But the problem of knowledge is deeper than this. If knowledge is to be of any use, it must affect the behaviour of those who possess it. But if they change their behaviour, the knowledge that they possessed may already be outdated, since it will now be operating in a 'different' system. So learning provides knowledge, but the use of that knowledge creates ignorance, or at any rate a 'decay' in the value and relevance of that knowledge. As soon as I know how to produce an improved product and I produce it, the market is changed as the knowledge affects my competitors, my customers' expectations and the prices of the relevant input materials and skills. The evolution and dynamics of knowledge and ignorance therefore becomes the fundamental currency of human systems, largely replacing that of physical strength, manual skill and dexterity. It is the capacity to continually create and 'use' relevant knowledge that is the key to success, and not the knowledge itself.

The Assumptions Used to Reduce Complexity to Simplicity

What are these assumptions?

1. That we can define a boundary between the part of the world that we want to 'understand' and the rest. In other words, we assume first that there is a 'system' and an 'environment', and that we can understand the workings of the system on the basis of its components, working in the context of the environment. For this to be useful we would also assume either that the environment was fixed or how it would change.
2. That we have rules for the classification of objects that lead to a relevant taxonomy for the system components, which will enable us to understand what is going on. This is often decided entirely intuitively. In fact we should always begin by performing some qualitative research to try to establish the main features that are important, and then keep returning to the question following the comparison of our understanding of a system with what is seen to happen in reality.
3. The third assumption concerns the level of description below that which we are trying to understand, and assumes that either all are identical to each other and to the average, or they have a diversity that is at all times distributed 'normally' around the average. With this assumption, changes in micro diversity are eliminated, as are the 'evolutionary' effects that this can have. We create a 'stereotype'-based simplification of reality,

whose 'typology' of functioning remains fixed and does not evolve. When we make this simplifying assumption, although we create a simpler representation, we lose the capacity for our model to 'represent' evolution and learning within the system.

4. That the overall behaviour of the variables can be described by the smooth average rates of individual interaction events. So, for example, the output rate for a group of employees in a business would be characterized by their average output rate. This assumption (which will never be entirely true) eliminates the effects of 'luck' and of randomness and noise that are really in the system.

The mathematical representation that results from making all four of these assumptions is that of a mechanical system that appears to 'predict' the future of the system perfectly. A fifth assumption that is often made in building models to deal with 'reality' is that of stability or equilibrium. It is assumed in classical and neoclassical economics, for example, that markets move

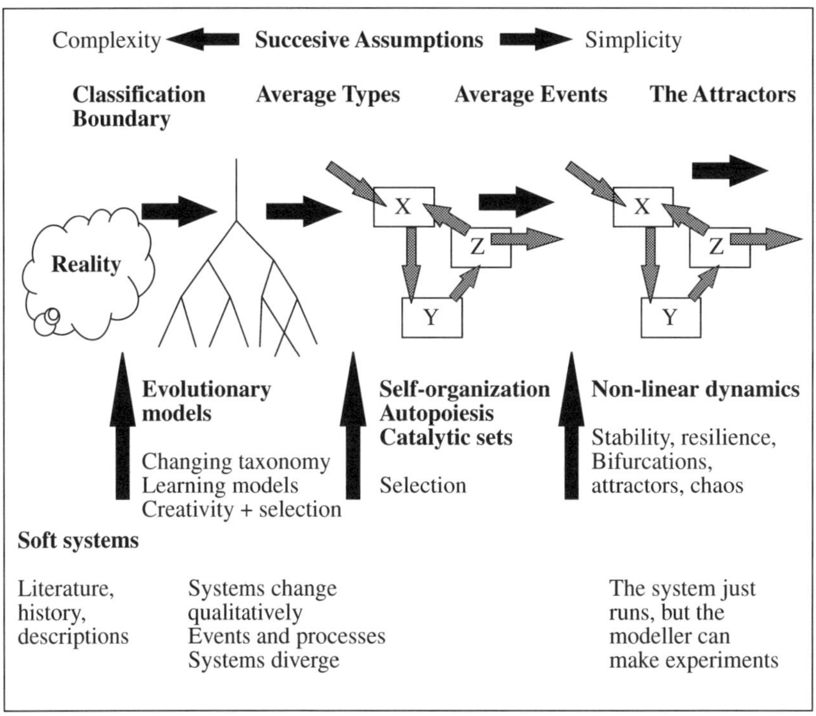

Figure 10.1 The assumptions made in trading off realism and complexity against simplification and hence ease of understanding

rapidly to equilibrium, so that fixed relationships can be assumed between the different variables of the system. The equations characterizing such systems are therefore 'simultaneous', where the value of each variable is expressed as a function of the values of the others. Traditionally, then, 'simple' equilibrium models like this have been used to try to describe economic markets. Although these can be useful at times, today we are attempting to model 'complex' systems, leaving their inherent complexity intact to some extent. This means that we may attempt to build and study models that do not make all of these simplifying assumptions.

THE MODELLING OUTCOMES OF DIFFERENT ASSUMPTIONS

The important point about the statement of assumptions is that we can now make explicit the kind of 'knowledge' that is generated providing that the 'necessary' assumptions can be made legitimately. Relating assumptions to outcomes in terms of types of model we have the following.

Equilibrium

Making all four assumptions plus equilibrium gives a static equilibrium model. Such models assume that the system is stationary, with a structure that is characterized by fixed relationships, simultaneous equations, between the different variables Of course, these relationships are characterized by particular parameters appearing in them, and these are often calibrated by using regression techniques on existing data. Obviously, the use of any such set of equations for an exploration of future changes under particular exogenous scenarios would suppose that these relationships between the variables remained unchanged. In neoclassical economics, much of spatial geography, and many models of transportation and land use, the models that are used operationally today are still based on equilibrium assumptions. Market structures, locations of jobs and residences, land values, traffic flows and so on are all assumed to reach their equilibrium configurations 'sufficiently rapidly' following some innovation, policy or planning action, so that there is an equilibrium 'before' and one 'after' the event or action, vastly simplifying the analysis. In order to justify the use of equilibrium assumptions, some more extreme practitioners invoke the theory of 'rational expectations' based on the claim that people can perfectly anticipate what everyone will do, thus taking the system to equilibrium even faster. Such an idea is clearly of a 'religious' nature and is probably not open to reasonable debate.

The advantage of the assumption of 'equilibrium' lies in the simplicity that results from having only to consider simultaneous and not dynamical equations. It also seems to offer the possibility of looking at a decision or policy in terms of stationary states 'before' and 'after' the decision. All cost–benefit analysis is based on this fundamentally flawed idea.

The disadvantage of such an approach, where an equilibrium state is simply assumed, is that it fails to follow what may happen along the way. It does not take into account the possibility of feedback processes where growth encourages growth, decline leads to further decline and so on (non-linear effects), which can occur on the way to equilibrium. In reality, it seems much more likely that people discover the consequences of their actions only after making them, and even then have little idea as to what would have happened if they had done something else. Because of this, inertia, heuristics, imitation and post rationalization play an enormous role in the behaviour of people in the real world. As a result there is a complex and changing relationship between latent and revealed preferences, as individuals experience the system and question their own assumptions and goals. By simply assuming 'equilibrium', and calibrating the parameters of the relationships on observation, one has in reality a purely descriptive approach to problems, following, in a kind of *post hoc* calibration process, the changes that have occurred. This is not going to be very useful in providing good advice on strategic matters, although economists appear to have more influence on governments than any other group of academics.

Non-linear Dynamics

Making all four assumptions leads to system dynamics, a mechanical representation of changes. Non-linear dynamics (system dynamics) are what results generally from a modelling exercise when assumptions (1) to (4) above are made, but equilibrium is not assumed. Of course some systems are linear or constant, but these are both exceptions, and also very boring. In the much more usual case of non-linear dynamics, the trajectory traced by such equations corresponds, not to the actual course of events in the real system, but, because of assumption 4, to the most probable trajectory of an ensemble of such systems. In other words, instead of the realistic picture with a somewhat fluctuating path for the system, the model produces a beautifully smooth trajectory. This illusion of determinism, of perfectly predictable behaviour, is created by assuming that the individual events underlying the mechanisms in the model can be represented by their average rates. The smoothness is only as true as this assumption is true. Systems dynamics models must not be used if this is not the case. Instead, some probabilistic model based on Markov processes might be needed, for example.

If we consider the long-term behaviour of non-linear dynamical systems then we find different possibilities.

1. Different possible stationary states: instead of a single, 'optimal' equilibrium, there may exist several possible equilibria, possibly with different spatial configurations, and the initial condition of the system will decide which it adopts.
2. Different possible cyclic solutions: these might be found to correspond to the business cycle, for example, or to long waves.
3. Chaotic motions of various kinds, spreading over the surface of a strange attractor.

An attractor 'basin' is the space of initial conditions that lead to a particular final state (which could be simple points, or cycles or the surface of a strange attractor) and so a given system may have several different possible final states, depending only on its initial condition. Such systems cannot by themselves cross a separatrix to a new basin of attraction, and therefore can only continue along trajectories that are within the attractor of their initial condition (see Figure 10.2). Compared to reality, then, such systems lack the 'vitality' to jump spontaneously to the regime of a different attractor basin. If the parameters of the system are changed, however, attractor basins may

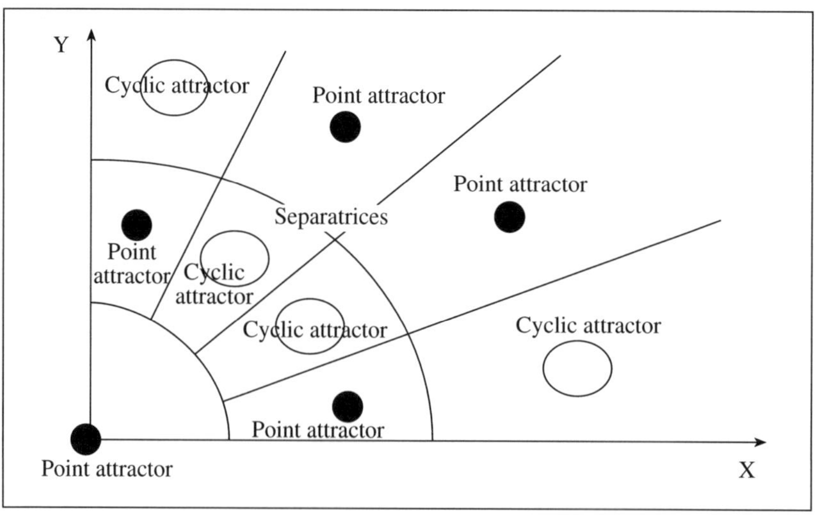

Figure 10.2 An example of the different attractors that might exist for a non-linear system These attractors are separated by 'separatrices'

appear or disappear, in a phenomenon known as bifurcation. Systems that are not precisely at a stationary point attractor can follow a complicated trajectory into a new attractor, with the possibility of symmetry breaking and, as a consequence, the emergence of new attributes and qualities.

Self-organizing Dynamics

Making assumptions (1) to (3) leads to self-organizing dynamic models, capable of reconfiguring their spatial or organizational structure. Provided that we accept that different outcomes may now occur, we may explore the possible gains obtained if the fourth assumption is not made.

In this case non-average fluctuations of the variables are retained in the description, and the ensemble captures all possible trajectories of our system, including the less probable. As we shall see, this richer, more general model allows for spontaneous clustering and reorganization of spatial configuration to occur as the system runs, and this has been termed 'self-organizing'. In the original work, Nicolis and Prigogine (1977) called the phenomenon 'Order by Fluctuation', and mathematically it corresponds to returning to the deeper, probabilistic dynamics of Markov processes (see, for example, Barucha-Reid, 1960) and leads to a dynamic equation that describes the evolution of the whole ensemble of systems. This equation is called the 'Master Equation' which, while retaining assumption (2), assumes that events of different probabilities can and do occur. So sequences of events that correspond to successive runs of good or bad 'luck' are included, with their relevant probabilities.

Each attractor is defined as being the domain in which the initial conditions all lead to the final. But, when we do not make assumption (4), we see that this space of attractors now has 'fuzzy' separatrices, since chance fluctuations can sometimes carry a system over a separatrix across to another attractor, and to a qualitatively different regime. As has been shown elsewhere (Allen, 1988), for systems with non-linear interactions between individuals, what this does is to destroy the idea of a trajectory, and give to the system a collective adaptive capacity corresponding to the spontaneous spatial reorganization of its structure. This can be imitated to some degree by simply adding 'noise' to the variables of the system. This probes the stability of any existing configuration and, when instability occurs, leads to the emergence of new structures. Such self-organization can be seen as a *collective adaptive response* to changing external conditions, and results from the addition of noise to the deterministic equations of system dynamics. Methods like 'simulated annealing' are related to these ideas.

Once again, it should be emphasized that self-organization is a natural property of real non-linear systems. It is only suppressed by making assumption (4) and replacing a fluctuating path with a smooth trajectory. The knowledge derived from self-organizing systems models is not simply of its future trajectory, but of the possible regimes of operation that it could adopt. Such models can therefore indicate the probability of various transitions and the range of qualitatively different possible configurations and outcomes.

Evolutionary Complex Systems

System components and subcomponents all coevolve in a non-mechanical mutual 'learning' process. These arise from a modelling exercise in which neither assumption (3) nor (4) is made. This allows us to clarify the distinction between 'self-organization' and 'evolution'. Here, it is assumption (3) that matters, namely that all individuals of a given type, say X, are either identical and equal to the average type or have a diversity that remains normally distributed around the average type. But, in reality, the diversity of behaviours among individuals in any particular part of the system is the result of local dynamics occurring in the system. But the definition of a 'behaviour' is closely related to the knowledge that that individual possesses. This in turn depends on the mechanisms by which knowledge, skills, techniques and heuristics are passed on to new individuals over time. Obviously, there is an underlying biological and cultural diversity due to genetics, and to family histories, and, because of these, and also because of the impossibility of transmitting information perfectly, there will necessarily be an 'exploration' of behaviour space. The mechanisms of our dynamical system contain terms that both increase and decrease the populations of different 'behavioural' or 'knowledge' types, and so this will act as a selection process, rewarding the more successful explorations with high pay-off and amplifying them, while suppressing the others. It is then possible to make the local micro diversity of individuals and their knowledge an endogenous function of the model, where new knowledge and behaviours are created and old ones destroyed. In this way we can move towards a genuine, evolutionary framework capable of exploring more fully the 'knowledge dynamics' of the system and the individuals that make it up.

Such a model must operate within some 'possibility' or 'character' space for behaviours that is larger than the one that is 'occupied' initially, offering possibilities that our evolving complex system can explore (see Figure 10.3). This space represents, for example, the range of different techniques and behaviours that could arise. Of course, this potential will itself depend on the channelling and constraints that result from the cultural models and vocabulary of potential players. In any case, it is a multidimensional space of which we would only be able to anticipate a few of the principal dimensions.

In biology, genetic mechanisms ensure that different possibilities are explored, and offspring, offspring of offspring, and so on, spread out in character

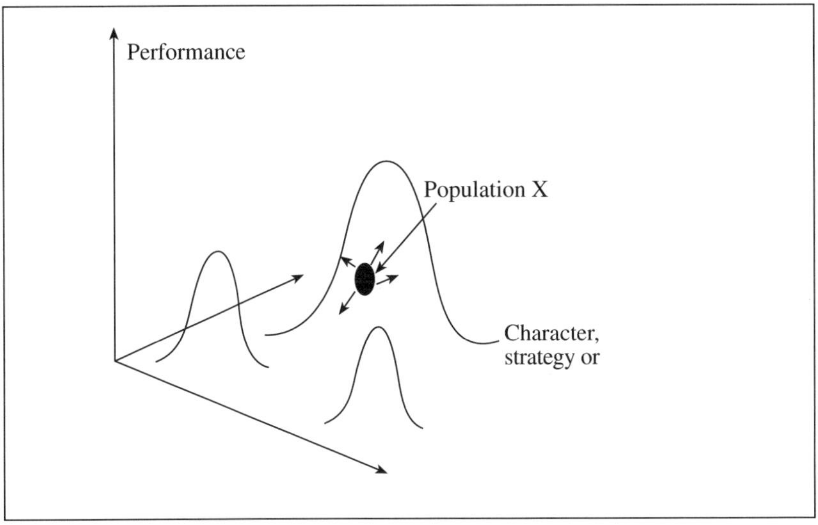

Figure 10.3 Explorations in 'possibility space' lead the population X to diffuse across the performance landscape, developing on the peaks. But the landscape is affected by the presence of the population X

space over time, from any pure condition. In human systems the imperfections and subjectivity of existence mean that techniques and behaviours are never passed on exactly, and therefore that exploration and innovation are always present as a result of the individuality and contextual nature of experience. Human curiosity and a desire to experiment also play a role. Some of these 'experimental' behaviours do better than others. As a result, imitation and growth lead to the relative increase of the more successful behaviours, and to the decline of the others. By considering dynamic equations in which there is an outward 'diffusion' in character space from any behaviour that is present, we can see how such a system would evolve. If there are types of behaviour with higher and lower pay-off, then the diffusion 'uphill' is gradually amplified, while that 'downhill' is suppressed, and the 'average' for the whole population moves higher up the slope. This is the mechanism by which adaptation takes place (see Figure 10.4). This demonstrates the vital part played by exploratory, non-average behaviour, and shows that, in the long term, evolution selects for populations with the ability to learn, rather than for populations with optimal, but fixed, behaviour.

In other words, adaptation and evolution result from the fact that knowledge, skills and routines are never transmitted perfectly between individuals

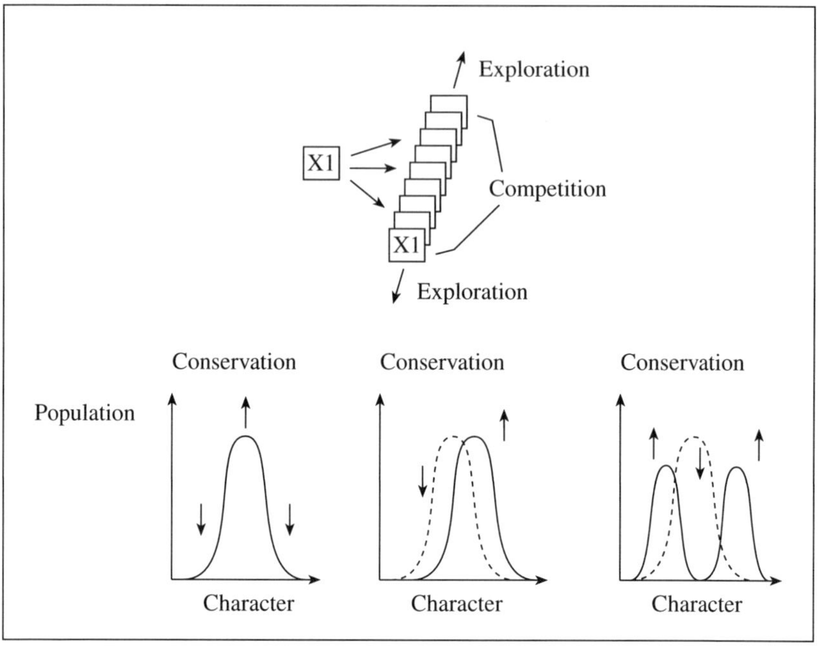

Figure 10.4 *If eccentric types are always suppressed, we have non-evolution. But, if not, then adaptation and speciation can occur*

and individuals already differ. However, there is always a short-term cost to such 'imperfection', in terms of unsuccessful explorations and, if only short-term considerations were taken into account, such imperfections would be reduced. But without this exploratory process, there will be no adaptive capacity and no long-term future in a changing world.

If we return to our modelling framework of Figure (10.1), where we depict the trade-off between realism and simplicity, we can say that a simple, apparently predictive system dynamics model is 'bought' at the price of assumptions (1) to (4). What is missing from this is the representation of the underlying, inner dynamic that is really running under the system dynamics (see Figure 10.5). However, if it can be shown that all 'eccentricity' is suppressed in the system, evolution will itself be suppressed, and the 'system dynamics' will then be a good representation of reality. This is the recipe for a mechanical system, and the ambition of many business managers and military men. However, if instead micro diversity is allowed and even encouraged, the system will contain an inherent capacity to adapt, change and evolve in response to whatever selective forces are placed upon it. Clearly, therefore,

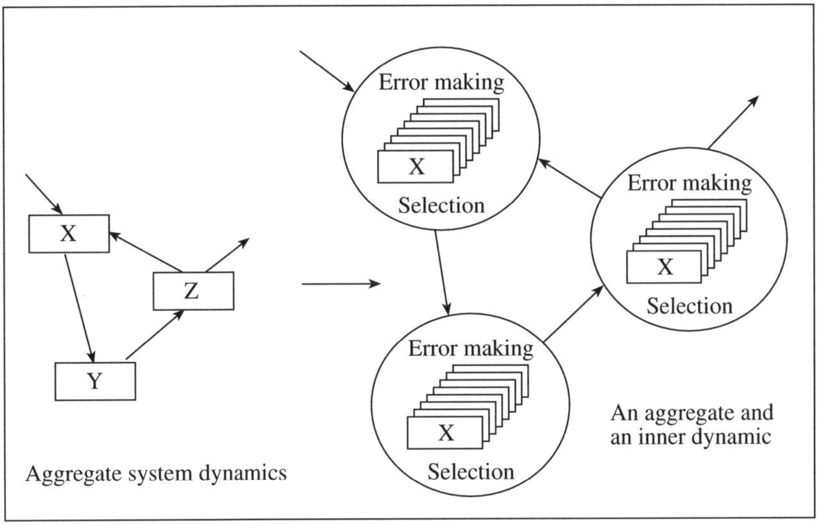

Figure 10.5 *Without assumption (3) we have an 'inner' dynamic within the macroscopic system dynamics. Micro diversity, in various possible dimensions, is differentially selected, leading to adaptation and emergence of new behaviours*

sustainability is much more related to micro diversity than to mechanical efficiency.

Let us now examine the consequences of not making assumptions (3) and (4). In the space of 'possibilities' closely similar behaviours are considered to be most in competition with each other, since they require similar resources, and must find a similar niche in the system. However, we assume that in this particular dimension there is some 'distance' in character space, some level of dissimilarity, at which two behaviours do not compete. In addition however, other interactions are possible. For example, two particular populations, *i* and *j*, may have some effect on each other (see Figure 10.6). This could be positive, in that side-effects of the activity of *j* might in fact provide conditions or effects that help *i*. Of course, the effect might equally well be antagonistic, or of course neutral. Similarly, *i* may have a positive, negative or neutral effect on *j*. If we therefore initially choose values randomly for all the possible interactions between all *i* and *j*, these effects will come into play if the populations concerned are in fact present. If they are not there, obviously, there can be no positive or negative effects experienced.

A typical evolution is shown in Figure (10.7). Although competition helps to 'drive' the exploration process, what is observed is that a system with

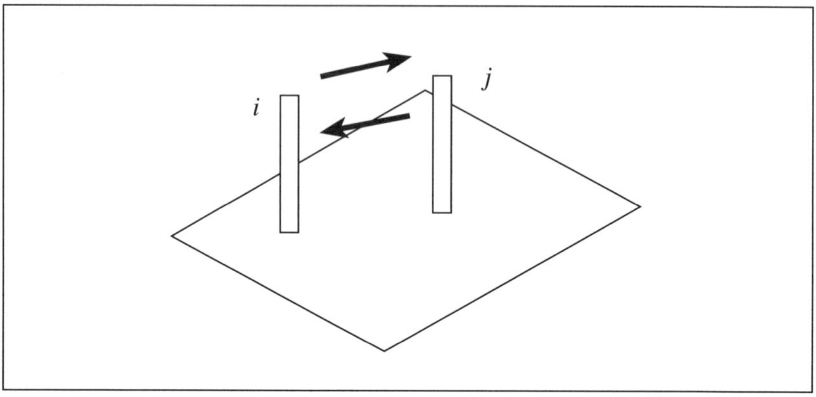

Figure 10.6 A population i may affect population j, and vice versa

'error making' in its behaviour evolves towards structures that express synergetic complementarities. In other words, evolution, although driven to explore by error making and competition, evolves cooperative structures. The synergy can be expressed either through 'self-symbiotic' terms, where the consequences of a behaviour in addition to consuming resources is favourable to itself, or through interactions involving pairs, triplets and so on. This corresponds to the emergence of 'hypercycles' (Eigen and Schuster, 1979), and of 'supply chains' in an economic system.

The lower right-hand picture in Figure (10.7) shows the evolution tree generated over time. We start off an experiment with a single behavioural type in an otherwise 'empty' resource space. The population initially forms a sharp spike, with eccentrics on the edge suppressed by their unsuccessful competition with the average type. However, any single behaviour can only grow until it reaches the limits set by its input requirements or, in the case of an economic activity, by the market limit for any particular product. After this, it is the 'eccentrics', the 'error makers' that grow more successfully than the 'average type', as they are less in competition with the others, and the population *identity* becomes unstable. The single sharply spiked distribution spreads, and splits into new behaviours that climb the evolutionary landscape that has been created, leading away from the ancestral type. The new behaviours move away from each other, and grow until in their turn they reach the limits of their new normality, whereupon they also split into new behaviours, gradually filling the resource spectrum.

While the 'error-making' and inventive capacity of the system in our simulation is a constant fraction of the activity present at any time, the system evolves in discontinuous steps of instability, separated by periods of taxo-

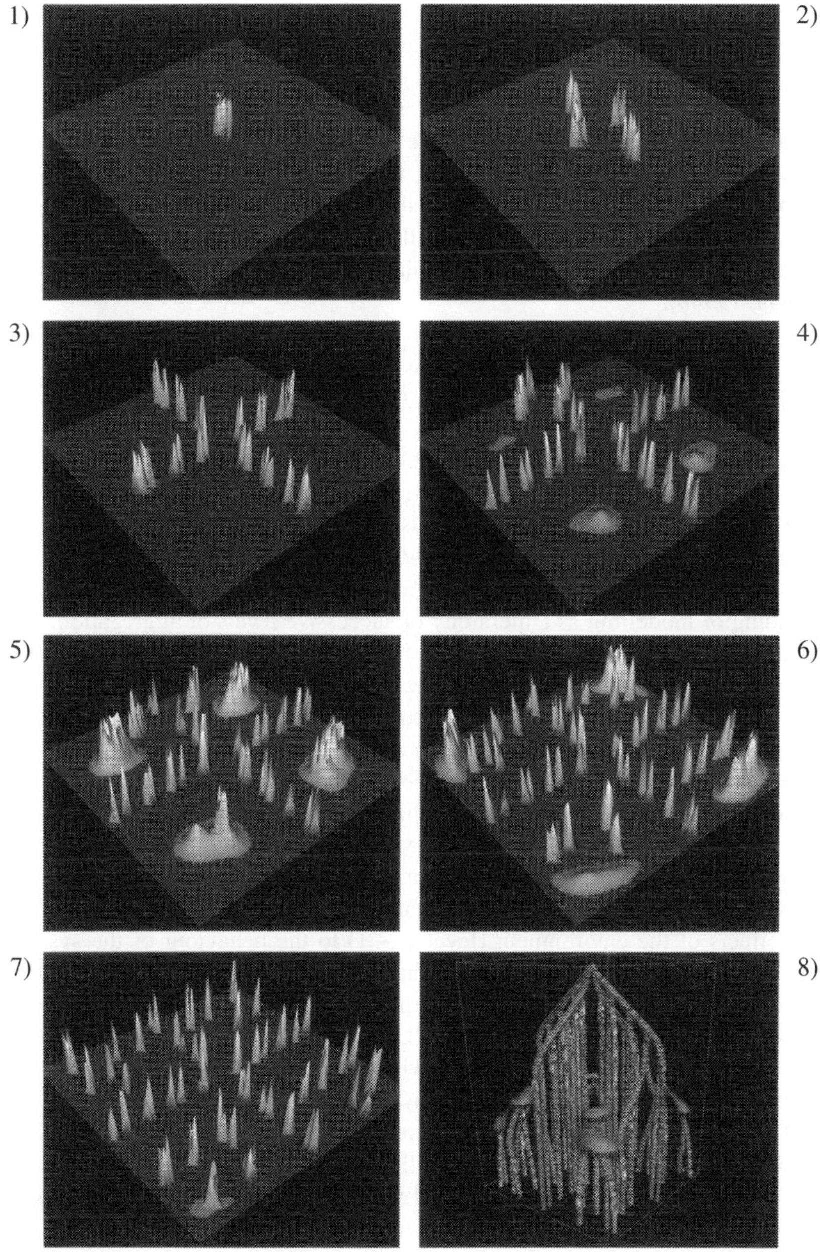

Figure 10.7 *A two-dimensional possibility is gradually filled by the error-making diffusion, coupled with mutual interaction. The final frame shows the evolutionary tree generated by the system*

nomic stability. In other words, there are times when the system structure can suppress the incipient instabilities caused by innovative exploration of its inhabitants, and there are other times when it cannot suppress them, and a new behaviour emerges. This illustrates that the 'pay-off' for any behaviour is dependent on the other players in the system. Success of an individual type comes from the way it fits the system, not from its own intrinsic nature. The important long-term effects introduced by considering the endogenous dynamics of micro diversity has been called 'evolutionary drive', and has been described elsewhere (Allen and McGlade, 1987a; Allen,1988, 1990, 1993, 1994a, 1994b).

THE GENERAL STRUCTURE OF MODELLING

Levels of Description and Coupling

We can summarize the different levels of model, from deterministic equations to full evolutionary models, as shown in Figure 10.8. Remembering the classification of parameters that was carried out earlier leads us to an understanding of modelling as a hierarchy of successive levels of aggregation. So, at any particular level, say a nation, there are exogenous effects such as world prices and climatic conditions that refer to the global level (L + 1). Then there are interactions and parameters that concern the interaction of different organizations and individuals within the nation, and spatial and organizational relationships which provide the functional structure of the system (level L). Below or inside this is the level within individuals and organizations that makes or allows them to behave as they do. This would include their internal structure, rules of functioning, codes of behaviour, knowledge and skills.

Now we can see that non-linear dynamics and self-organizing systems link the effects of the environment (level L + 1) to the behaviour of the system (level L), without allowing the individuals or internal organizations (level L – 1) to change or learn. But the evolutionary model allows both for an organizational response to the environment (L + 1) at the system level (L) and also for adaptivity and learning to occur within components at level L – 1. This couples the L + 1, L and L – 1 levels in a coevolutionary process.

This brings us to the use of different models for different purposes. If we wish to model a gearbox, and we are allowed to assume that its cogwheels do not break down, a fairly simple model will do. But a deeper description will be required in order to model the gearbox if we cannot assume that the cogwheels remain intact. In order to explore under what conditions such breakdown might occur, it would be necessary to consider the detailed metallurgy and local surface conditions in a much more sophisticated model.

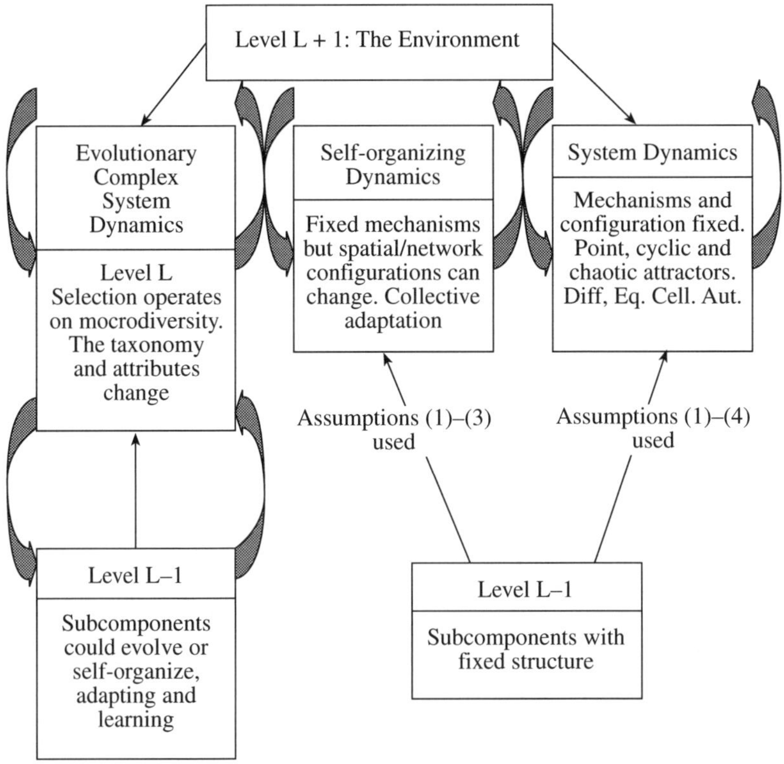

Figure 10.8 The hierarchy of modelling in which level L sits within L + 1, and is constituted by elements at level L – 1. Deterministic and Self-organising models link average L – 1 to L, but the evolutionary models relate the full, nested hierarchy, L – n, … L – 1, L, L + 1, …. L + n

In self-organizing models, it is assumed that the subcomponents have fixed internal structure, implying that they are not modified by their experiences. Nevertheless, such systems can respond to their environment through a collective change of spatial structure, which may lead to quite different system performance and to emergent properties. If the micro components have internal structure, and if, in addition, this can change through time, thus changing the behaviour of the individual elements, a complex evolution can take place as the emergent macrostructure affects the local circumstances experienced by individuals. This in turn leads to an adaptive response that in its turn changes the resulting system structure generated. Changes in the micro components affect system structure and its performance in the larger environment.

These changes in turn affect the experience of the system components, which in their turn affect the experiences of the micro components, and the factors to which they are adapting.

Complex systems modelling involving elements with internal structure that can change in response to their experiences leads naturally to a hierarchy of linked levels of description. If all the levels of description are 'satisfied' with their circumstances, the hierarchy will be stable. But when the behaviour and strategies of many individuals, at a given level, do not provide them with satisfactory pay-off in the macrostructure that exists, eccentric and deviant behaviour will be amplified, which may lead to a structural reorganization of the system. Stability, or at least quasi-stability, will occur when the micro structures of a given level are compatible with the macro structures they both create and inhabit, and vice versa.

Knowing the Limits to Knowledge

In seeking 'knowledge' we must derive a reduced description, which creates simplicity at the cost of making increasingly strong assumptions. The simplifications arise by taking averages, and writing in terms of *typical* elements of the system according to the classification scheme that has been chosen. Underneath the 'model' there will always be the greater particularity and diversity of reality, and its own endogenous dynamic. At the level of individuals, although many attributes will be shared, there will also be attributes that are not shared or common. These are 'dimensions' of description that are lost through averaging. Mechanical models clearly exclude these from their representation.

With self-organizing systems we may find that the system can spontaneously move from one type of behaviour to another as the 'noise' explores different attractor basins. The aim of the model then becomes to explore the different possible regimes of operation of the system, and the probabilities of moving towards these different attractors. However, we should remember that mechanical and self-organizing models are only of any significance *if the equations and the fixed mechanisms* within them *remain* a *good description* of the system. But, from our own experience we know that the taxonomy of the system, the representative variables and the mechanisms which link them, actually *change over time*. Because of this, any system of dynamical equations that we are running as a model of the system will only be a good description for as long as there is no evolutionary change and no new variables or mechanisms appear.

So what is 'knowledge'? A dynamic model will trace trajectories in time, and thereby give the impression that it can be used to predict the future. But this will only provide 'knowledge' if the model is correct, otherwise it will simply be misleading. On the other hand, it may create an 'illusion of knowledge' which may be sufficient to allow a decision to be made, and experience to be gained. The dynamic equations do not anticipate the *qualitative* changes that may occur when an evolutionary step takes place, and the taxonomy of the system changes, and therefore the 'stereotypes' included in the model become inadequate. While the taxonomy is stable and no new classes or types have appeared, the model may be fine, but a change in taxonomy will only be revealed when the model is shown to be incorrect, and in need of reformulation. So 'knowledge' is illusory if I do not know for sure that my assumptions hold. In physics and chemistry the predictive models which work so well rely on the fact that the individual elements that make up the system must obey fixed laws which govern their behaviour. The mechanisms are fixed, and simple molecules never learn. But people do. They change their beliefs, their aims, their skills, their roles, and they grow old, and are replaced by others. Actions and strategies are analysed, copied and tried in new circumstances, where clear conclusions cannot be drawn. Learning is necessarily imperfect, and so exploration and differential success continue to drive a changing background on which larger-scale systems operate.

Because of this uncertainty in the longer term, we cannot know what actions are best now. Even if individuals know exactly what they would like to achieve, because they cannot know with certainty how everyone else will respond, they can never calculate exactly what the outcome will be. They must 'take a gamble', and see what happens, being ready to take corrective actions if necessary. So, instead of 'knowledge' just being the output of a model, it is 'knowledge' to know that your model may break down and to monitor events continually with this in mind. Usually, however, the opposite attitude prevails and events that do not fit the 'expected' pattern are ignored or suppressed. From the complex systems approach we expect a system to run in a 'non-mechanical' way of constant adjustment and reappraisal.

So, if we are interested in gaining knowledge that is appropriate for making strategic decisions and planning, we must try to go beyond the 'mechanical' description with fixed structure and try to develop models which can describe structural change and emergent levels of description endogenously. In the next section we attempt to draw a firm conclusion concerning the message that evolutionary complex systems thinking has for us.

The Three Levels of Interaction

From Figure 10.8 we see that for complex systems there are three fundamentally different levels of description that are coupled together in a coevolutionary process. Gillies (1999), has called these levels the Three Pillars of Understanding, and shows them to be fundamental to an understanding of human organizations.

- *Environmental* factors are external to the network but in interaction with it. These will compose the forces of 'selection' acting on the network.
- *Interaction* factors relate to the internal structure of the system and the interactions between the agents in the system. This involves potential cooperation and competition in producing some 'composite' (emergent) product making use of the combined activities.
- *Performance* factors govern the individual agent's performance, due to internal characteristics, that can also reflect the performance and micro diversity of suppliers.

For each node of a network or supply chain, success and survival depend on the node being able to resolve successfully any differences between the selection coming from the environment which is imposing 'what is required' and the behavioural possibilities of the node with 'what it could do'.

Environmental pillar
The first set of factors concerns the environment that the model inhabits, and its changing dynamic nature. However, there are two important aspects to this. The first is that the 'environment' may in fact be rich and varied, so that a human system, such as a firm, could choose which environment it inhabited. Secondly, there is the issue of adapting to the choice of environment that actually is perceived, and whether this environment is changing slowly and steadily or, at the other extreme, unpredictably and potentially fast. Complex systems models will reflect both these aspects of choosing which part of the environment to aim for, yet also adapting to the changing environment. For any organization like a business or a public service, the most obvious environment is that of potential market demand, and of technical and organizational innovation. The important point about a complex systems model is that it is not about 'what is', but is about 'what could be'. For a firm it is about mapping the needs of potential customers, and the predictability of these, onto that of potential products, and trying to find the best 'match'.

Interaction pillar
The second set of factors relates to the cooperation, or competition, of the entities within the system, and captures the effects of resultant organizational structures. For any component of a system only contributes its own part to the overall success or failure of the system as a whole. The spatial configuration and the networks of communication can substantially change the overall

performance of the system, and the various system components can be characterized by strategies of cooperation or of competition. Again knowledge generation and sharing, trust and mistrust, social convention and so on can all play important roles in the functioning of the system as a whole.

Performance pillar
The third and final pillar of the model sets out factors that underlie the first two. What is the knowledge of individuals within the components of the system? How much diversity of knowledge exists? Are individuals, including mangers, operating on simple heuristics that they have learned by trial and error? Or does anyone within a business comprehend 'why' it is selling the number of goods that it is selling? And, if so, does anyone know 'why' they are using the production methods, organizational structure, job descriptions and responsibilities that they are? Obviously, in a changing environment, if heuristics are the basis for action, survival will be a matter of luck. Trial and error is the 'Darwinian' method of evolving adapted structures, but it is not necessarily a pleasant experience to participate in it. If 'knowledge' is the basis for action, what matters is the capacity to generate new knowledge as the old devalues. This requires, at the very least, an admission that 'present' knowledge must be continually questioned and that organizations should avoid locking present knowledge into their power structures. But it also implies the need for an exploratory, scanning activity within any organization, and for mechanisms that can evaluate the diverse information obtained. This, in turn, implies that we know the appropriate attribute space for such an evaluation.

These issues are all discussed at greater length elsewhere (Gillies, 1999).

SELF-ORGANIZATION OF ECONOMIC MARKETS

The Three-firms Model

The ideas developed in the sections above have been applied to a variety of systems, but here will be applied to the structuring of economic markets, as competition creates ecologies of firms producing goods in different market niches. The fundamental process can be explored initially using a simple model in which we consider the possible growth or decline of three firms that are attempting to produce and sell goods on the same market. The potential customers of course will see the different products according to their particular desires and needs, and, in the simple case examined here, we shall simply consider that customers are differentiated by their revenue, and therefore have different sensitivities to price.

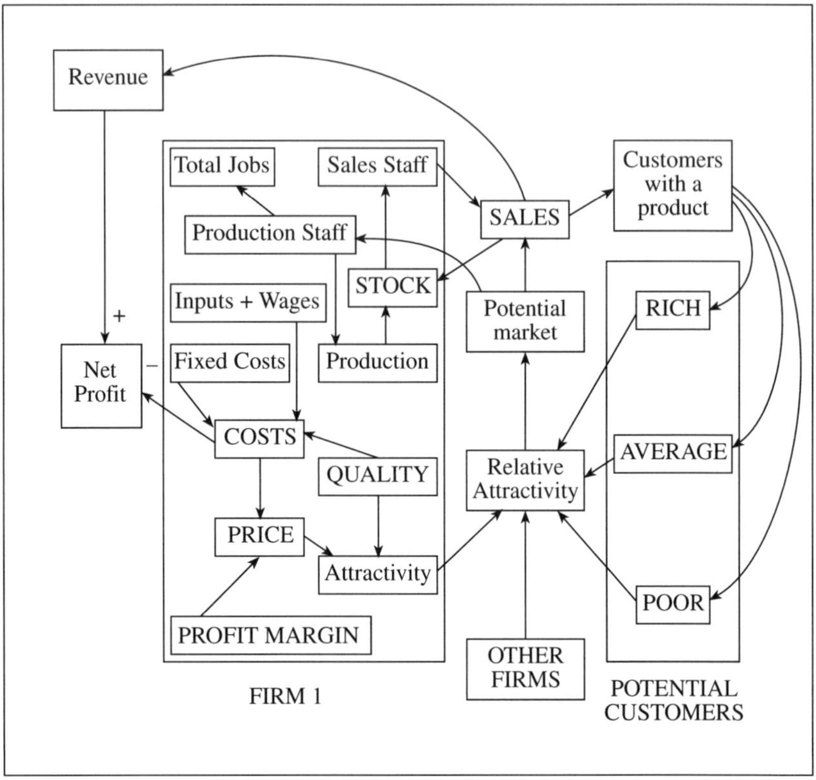

Figure 10.9 The three-firm model of the dynamic interaction of demand and supply in a market

The structure of each firm that is modelled is as shown in Figure (10.9). Inputs and labour are necessary for production, and the cost of these, added to the fixed and start-up costs, produce goods that are sold by sales staff who must 'interact' with potential customers in order to turn them into actual customers. The potential market for a product is related to its qualities and price, and although in this simple case we have assumed that customers all like the same qualities, they have a different response to the price charged. The price charged is made up of the cost of production (variable cost) to which is added a mark-up. The mark-up needs to be such that it will turn out to cover the fixed and start-up costs as well as the sales staff wages. Depending on the quality and price, therefore, there are different sized potential markets coming from the different customer segments.

When customers buy a product, they cease to be potential customers for a time that is related to the lifetime of the product. This may be longer for high-quality goods than for low-quality but, of course, many goods are bought in order to follow fashion and style rather than through absolute necessity. Indeed, different strategies would be required depending on whether or not this is the case, and so this is one of the many explorations that can be made with the model.

Let us briefly present an example of an exploration that the model permits. In the first run we play the role of Firm 3. We have a start-up size the same as the others, 1000 units. We choose to go 'up-market' and to make goods of quality 13 on the scale 1–20. In order to pay our fixed and start-up costs, we choose a high mark-up of 70 per cent.

The other players outcompete Firm 3, and it crashes after three years (see Figure 10.10). All firms generated dividends during this run, but, following market saturation, Firm 3 was squeezed and driven to bankruptcy. The financial

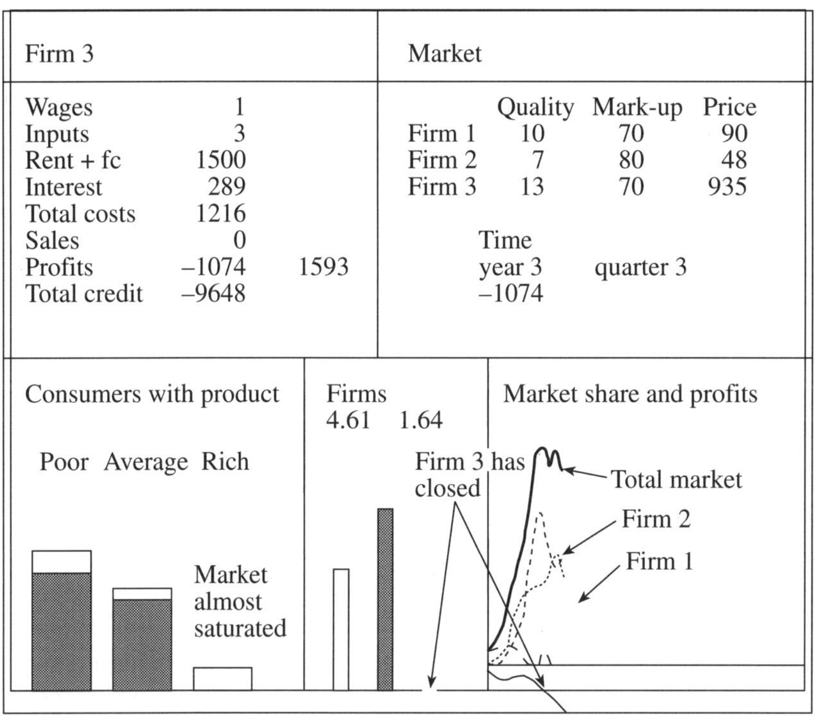

Figure 10.10 *An exploratory run, with Firm 1 and Firm 2 producing products at qualities 10 and 7 respectively, and mark-ups of 70% and 80%. Firm 3 with quality 13 and mark-up 70% fails after three years*

calculation allows for tax on profit and also for interest on the initial loans for start-up. Each firm has a 'credit limit', which it must not exceed. Strategies such as starting off with a very large initial size means borrowing a lot, and then having to pay back the extra interest. In this version all firms choose to start at the same size, 1000 units. Following the failure of Firm 3 with the choice of quality of 13 and mark-up and 70 per cent, reflection shows that perhaps it was overoptimistic to put such a high mark-up on the goods, and so the next strategy is with a mark-up of 40 per cent.

This is successful. Firm 3, the one we have chosen to play, stays in the game, and goes on to pay out dividends to its shareholders. Firm 2, however, manages to perform better, having a larger market of the 'poor' population and a high mark-up of 80 per cent. Firm 1, however, is eliminated (see Figure 10.11) and the obvious question is whether Firm 1 would have reacted 'in time' to its desperate situation. Perhaps it would have cut its mark-up in order to stay in play. In Figure 10.12 then, after some six years, Firm 1 responds to

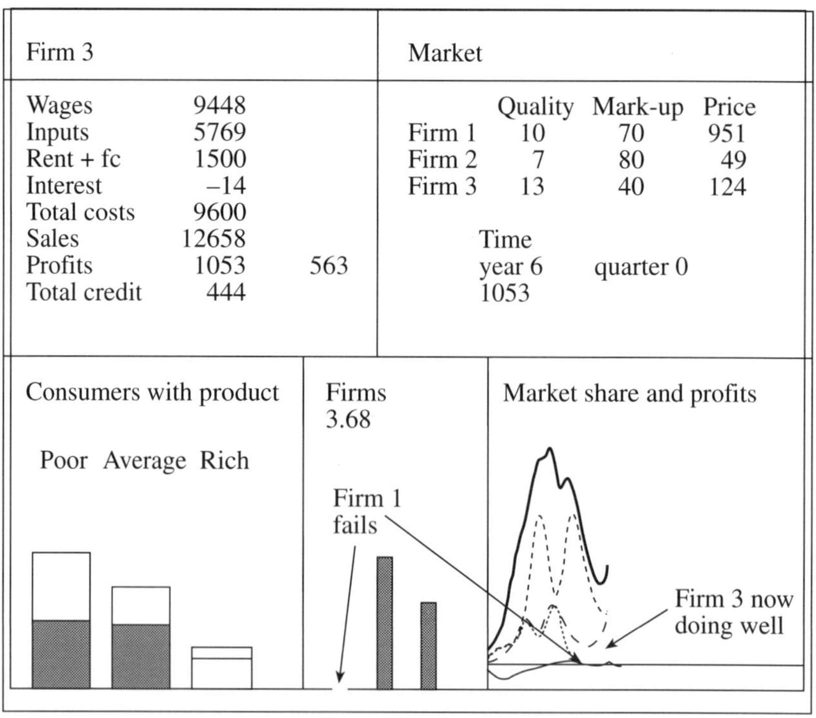

Figure 10.11 The only change here is that Firm 3 chooses a mark-up of 40% instead of 70%. It succeeds, and eliminates Firm 1

the pressure and cuts its profits from a 70 per cent mark-up to 50 per cent. The result is that it does not save itself.

However, if Firm 2 had cut its mark-up from 80 per cent to 40 per cent, then the result would have been different. Now it is Firm 2 that is eliminated, which then poses the question as to whether Firm 2 would have cut its profit margin in time to stop it being eliminated, and possibly put the pressure back on 3 or 1. Additionally, in all this, there is the question of the dividends paid out to shareholders. A strategy might lead to survival, but without a pay-off to its shareholders, it would not be sustainable through a lack of capital to counter depreciation. This illustrates the kind of strategic exploration that can be made.

In the model, interventions can be made at any time and different strategies can be tried out. Apart from the obvious ones concerning the quality and mark-up of the product, there is that of increasing the sales force, or having

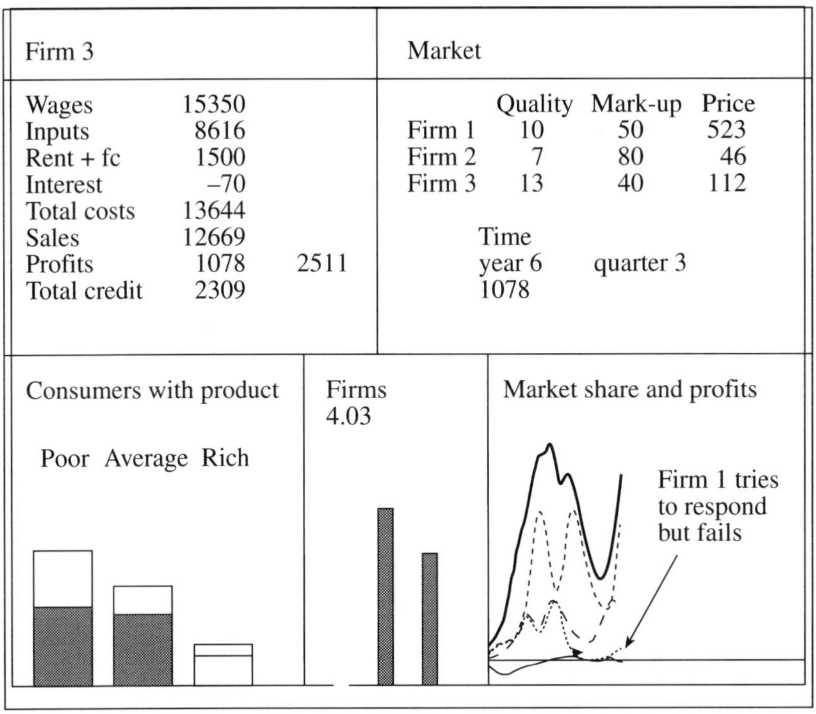

Figure 10.12 *When Firm 1 is about to be eliminated, after about six years operation, it changes its mark-up from 70% to 50%. This does not save it*

an advertising campaign. Also the model allows the exploration of the possible impacts of increased R&D. In addition, the model may be used to explore the strategies that might be relevant to changing external conditions, as the general level of wealth increases or the age pyramid of the population changes. Similarly, some aspects of technology assessment could be investigated, by examining the possible gains that could be obtained, and over what length of time, as the new technology changes the competitive relationship in the market and allows a larger market share to be tapped. But this extra market share would have to produce extra revenue over and above that involved in the investment and training required for the change. The model might therefore suggest where market densities were such that this was advantageous, and where it might not be.

A very important issue that arises in the modelling concerns the rationality of the manager of the firm in electing to adopt whatever strategy is chosen. In

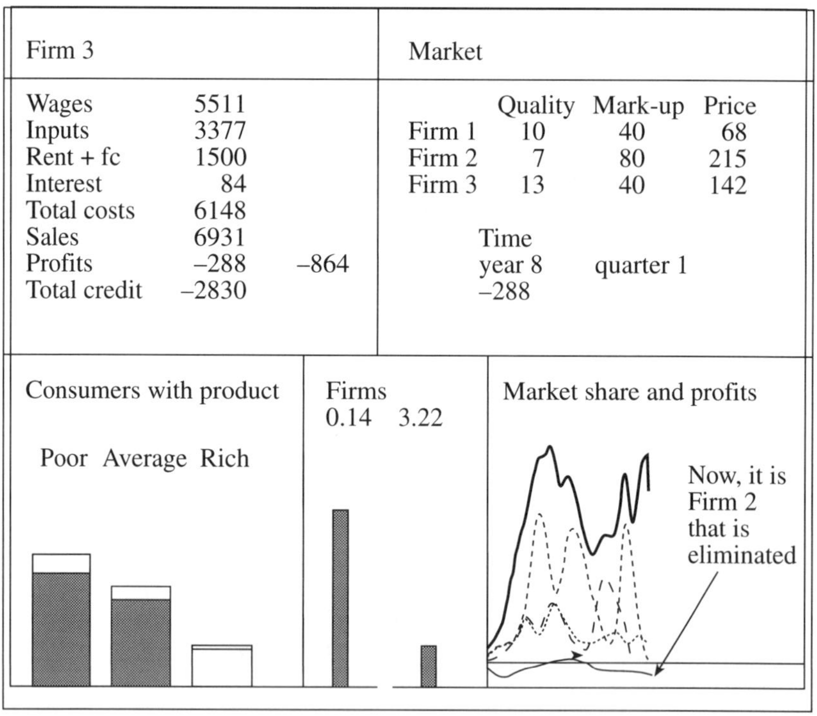

Figure 10.13 *If after about six years Firm 1 responds to the competition by decreasing its mark-up from 70% to 40%, then it succeeds in surviving, and eliminates Firm 2*

traditional economic theories firms are supposed to act, or to have acted, in such a way as to obtain maximum profit, but here we can see that, if we used the profit as the driving force for increased production, the system could not start. *Every new action must start with an investment.* That is with a negative profit. So, if firms do start production, and increase it, this cannot be modelled by linking the increase in production to the profit at that time. Instead, we might say that it is driven by the *expected profit over some future time.* But how does a manager form his expectations? Probably a model of the kind that is being described here is way beyond what is usually used and, in any case, there is a paradox. In order to build this model, in order perhaps for managers to formulate their expectations, the model requires a representation of managers' expectations. But this is only a paradox if we believe that the model is about *prediction.* Really, it is about exploration, the exploration of how we think a market works, and so it is a part of a learning process, which may indeed lead participants to behave differently from the way that was supposed initially. Such an outcome would already be a triumph.

Despite this paradox, and the difficulty in knowing what is going to happen beforehand, firms do start up, production is increased and economic sectors are populated with firms, even though there is this logical problem. Obviously it does not worry participants in reality. Since bankruptcies obviously also occur, we can be sure that the expectations that drive the investment process are not necessarily related to the real outcomes. In our model, therefore, we have simply assumed that managers want to expand to capture their potential markets, but are forced to cut production if sales fall. So they can make a loss for some time, providing that it is within their credit limit, but they much prefer to make a profit, and so attempt to increase sales, and to match production to this.

The picture that emerges from this study of a dynamically self-organizing market sector model is that of the emergence of product niches. It is the economies and diseconomies of production and distribution that will determine the number, size and scale of these niches, and they will depend on the initial history of the market sector in question as firms co-evolve. As new technology appears, or as the rest of society evolves, new attributes can come into play for the products. However, the effect and importance of these may be different when viewed by the producers as opposed to consumers.

Adaptive Learning in Economic Markets

The model pictured in Figure (10.9) can also be transformed into a 'learning' version by allowing the participating actors to explore strategy space using 'random numbers' to simulate their exploration. As a first step, the effectiveness of different learning rules can be tested on competitors that do not respond, but, more interestingly, they can be put in as rules applying to all competing firms. The results are complicated, and often counter-intuitive (whatever that means in such a complex system) because the rules adopted affect both the behaviour of one firm relative to the others and also the overall market size, and the rapidity with which potential customers are 'located' by salesmen. For example, in Figure 10.14, we investigate the following 'learning rules. 1) If profits for a firm are less than half the average in the sector, the firm tries out a lower mark-up, but if the profits of one firm are very large compared to the others, the profit margin is increased. 2) Also, if sales fall to a low value the sales force is increased. The size of the sales force is already part of the dynamical system, as the size of the stock of goods is maintained by changing the size of the sales force as the balance between production and sales changes. These rules are sufficient to turn the initial simulation of Figure (10.9), in which Firm 3 fails after three years, into a more long-term

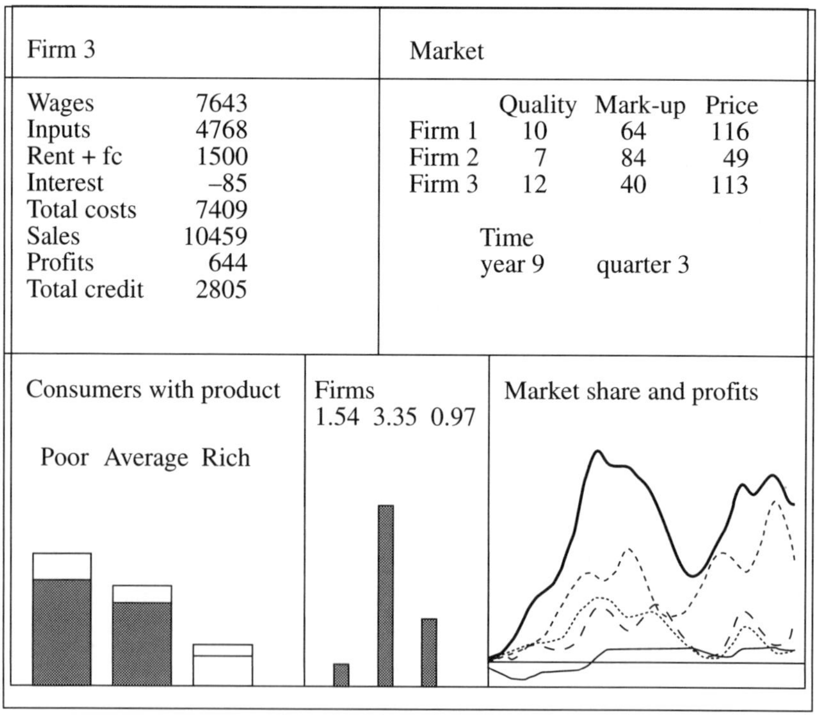

Figure 10.14 *The dynamics of three self-adapting firms. Instead of Firm 3 being eliminated after three years, all three are more resilient, with adaptive behavioural rules*

coevolution, where the three firms succeed in surviving for the ten years after the mutual adjustment of their parameters.

Despite the apparent success of this model, it turns out that on runs longer than this, in general, firms are still eliminated, and cannot get back into the system. This is because the response of lowering the profit margin when net profits have become low does not necessarily capture sufficient new customers to recapture market share scale of production, and lead to the recovery of the firm. Instead, it can spiral down to greater losses. In fact, it is difficult to imagine mechanical rules that can respond successfully to crises. And, in reality, adaptive responses are not 'mechanical': they are 'creative', and concern exploration and intuition rather than a fixed response. We need to move on to an evolutionary model of this complex learning process.

An Evolutionary Learning Economic Model

In reality, despite the fact that some firms will be eliminated, others will attempt to enter the market, and an evolutionary learning process will occur. We can also move a step further in building an 'evolutionary' model by considering a simulation as a 'learning system' which we can run in order to learn about the type of behavioural rules that provide resilience to a firm. Initially, we extend the three-firms model and give them these adaptive rules for their profit margins and sales force size. However, in addition we make the rule that, when one firm is eliminated, it is immediately 'relaunched' with some new parameters of profit mark-up and quality. It is also given a new initial loan and credit limit. The system then runs on in order to see whether the new firm can find a 'niche' for itself, possibly eliminating another player, or whether, instead, it fails in its new attempt.

By leaving the machine running for a long time, we can examine the evolution of the market, as the players attempt to find niches for their survival. These models are therefore used as ways of attempting to gain knowledge about possible market structures, and the consequences of different strategies. In the first run, the three different firms choose their quality and mark-up at random and, fairly soon, they discover how to produce and sell their products and almost saturate the market. In this particular case, both Firms 3 and 1 fail initially, and then, after about ten years, Firm 1 finds a quality and mark-up that allow survival. Firm 3 continues to struggle. The customers are more or less well served throughout, as the three firms spread across the quality axis.

For the second run, exactly the same system is used, but the initial conditions are different, and the random choices are also different. The outcome is totally different. The particular set of choices of quality and mark-up made by the firms turn out to be such that for a long period very few goods are sold.

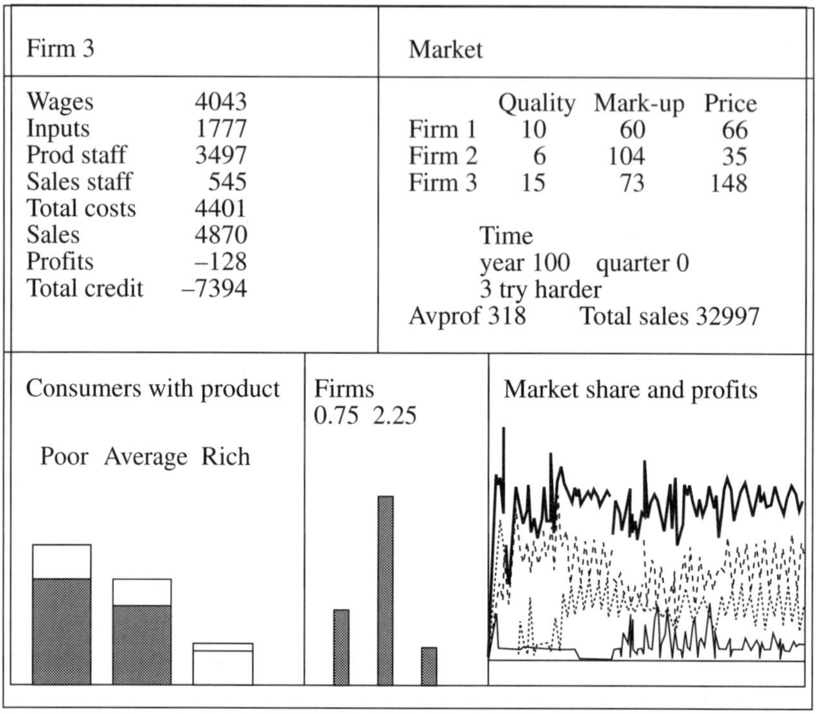

Figure 10.15 *Firm 2 dominates and the market reaches a fairly steady state, although Firm 3 is still searching for a stable niche after a long time*

Firm 1 actually fails and, through the whole simulation, attempts to find a set of viable values for the quality and mark-up of its product. However, the fact is that for nearly 40 'years' the firms have only succeeded in serving about half of the market. Their products are nearly all up-market and have high mark-ups, so although the rich and some middle-class consumers are customers, the poor are not. The high mark-ups mean that sales are low and, therefore, each firm believes (correctly) that a high mark-up is necessary to cover the fixed costs in such a limited market.

After about 50 'years' (in other words a long time), an instability occurs and Firm 3 experiments with a low mark-up, at the same time as Firms 1 and 2 move down market. Suddenly, the whole market practically doubles in size. After that, Firm 2 moves to quality 8 and forces Firm 3 into second position, with quality 14. However, both are now stable and the market is even larger. Firm 1 is still trying to find a niche at the lower end of the market.

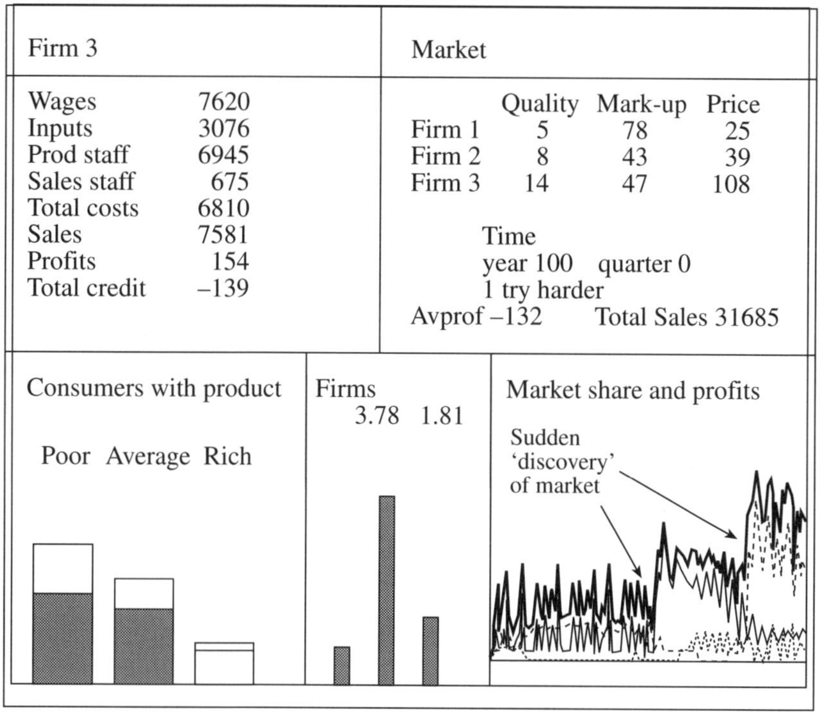

Figure 10.16 *Exactly the same equations, with a different initial condition and of random initiatives*

Other simulations using another random seed to define the initial values lead to other seemingly quite different types of outcome for the market evolution.

The models can be extended to consider any number of competing firms in the strategy space of 'mark-up' and 'quality'. A typical long-term simulation is shown in Figure 10.17. This shows the two-dimensional space of mark-up and quality, and the positions of the various firms. The rows at the top show the strategy, price, profit, present balance and sales of each firm, and the state of the market is shown in the lower left. The simulation shows us that using purely random searches of possible strategies does not necessarily lead to a very sensible distribution of the firms in the space of 'possibilities'. Our model needs to begin to represent the 'cognitive' processes of entrepreneurs, who for example, having failed (or seen others fail) with a particular kind of strategy (such as low quality, low mark-up) allow this to influence the parameters used for relaunch. Other possibilities could involve imitation.

These simple evolutionary models show us how resilient strategies will emerge from such systems and, in the case of particular market sectors, suggest how the rules of learning can also evolve. In other words, by testing firms with different rates and types of response mechanism, we can move towards understanding not only the emergent 'behavioural rules' for firms, but also the rules about 'how to learn' these rules. That is, how much to experiment, and with which parameters, and whether any new dimensions of attribute space can be invaded.

This is a key issue since real innovations concern new dimensions or attributes, and this can confer a temporary monopoly on a firm if it can move into some aspect of quality space that has hitherto been neglected. In this way an 'ecology' of products will eventually form, by taking up niches in a multidimensional attribute space. In time, a kind of 'ecology' will evolve, although there may still be occasional restructuring. Resilience, as a capability, will reside in the nature of the 'random exploration' factors that form part of the rules in relaunching a firm. In this model only the quality (two dimensional) and the mark-up are considered to be decision variables. However, we

Firm	Quality	Mark-up	Price	Profit	Balance	Sales	
1	2	0.39	0.07	–1038	–7629	59	____
2	11	0.62	0.75	4466	3000	34,153	____
3	10	1.30	1.01	334	–3527	5,436	____
4	11	1.06	1.02	1033	3000	7,398	____
5	12	1.27	1.35	1045	3000	5,404	____
6	6	1.16	0.39	727	3000	15,914	____

Avprof 2189
Total Sa 68365 Time 50
1
Try harder

£out 3.36 0.72 4.24 2.44 1.05
Maxpr 4,688
Firm 2

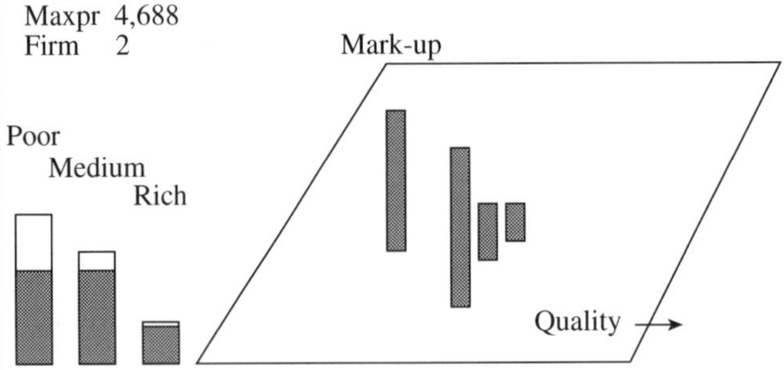

Figure 10.17 The situation of six competing firms after a long time. Firms have tried out various strategies. Whenever a firm fails it is relaunched with a new strategy picked at random

could also use other dimensions of quality space, the parameters of the equation governing the sales force, and also the 'research and development' parameter that can also lead to a change in the performance parameters of the firm.

The evolutionary model has a kind of 'Darwinian' evolutionary mechanism that allows entrepreneurs to explore the 'possibility space' for products of this kind. The pay-off achieved by any one firm or entrepreneur depends on the strategy (product quality and mark-up) used by the other entrepreneurs present. Clearly, this evolving picture should be compared to that of Figure 10.7, in which an initial population evolves into a simple ecology of interacting populations, in an evolutionary process that spreads out into the resource space.

The real evolutionary sense arises if we admit that no products have only a single dimension of 'quality'. There will always be such factors as performance, weight, efficiency, style, colour, noise, flexibility and so on, as well as simply price. Entrepreneurs would therefore explore different technologies,

Firm	Quality	Mark-up	Price	Profit	Balance	Sales
1	9	0.58	0.53	1587	3000	24,702
2	10	0.58	0.64	1375	3000	18,326
3	11	1.01	1.04	–677	–6749	1,400
4	11	0.94	0.96	867	3000	7,511
5	12	1.13	1.25	866	3000	5,256
6	6	1.01	0.37	359	1728	15,736

Avprof 1459
Total Sa 72922 Time 50
3
Try harder

£out 2.40 0.01 0.04 3.30 1.96 0.65
Maxpr 1,842
Firm 1

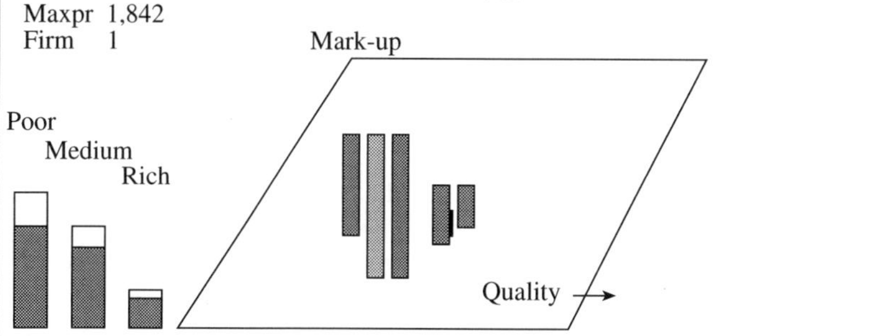

Figure 10.18 *This is an identical simulation over the same time period. Here, however, the only difference is that Firm 1 imitates the strategy of the most profitable company. This is clearly more successful than before*

organizational forms and production factors, as well as different types of product. This process would lead inevitably to a broader coexistence of different firms, since the multiple dimensions of attribute space produce a greater spread of consumer preferences, and less intense competition in general.

Evolution will result from the amplification of 'experimental' products that may well have different attributes from those already present. The presence of micro diversity (and not simply micro variety) in the 'ideas' and in the supply chain of an entrepreneur means that the new designs and products can span additional dimensions in attribute space, leading to a qualitative evolution in its fullest sense.

These simulations could be extended to consider the 'invasion' of hitherto empty attribute dimensions, so that a systematic approach could be made to the understanding of which new products would be successful, and where innovations should focus most effectively. The natural result of such an evolution would be for the attribute space initially 'occupied' to be expanded by the innovations that occur over the long term.

DISCUSSION

Knowledge and Assumptions

The fundamental points that have been made concern the scientific basis of knowledge, and its dialectic partner, ignorance. Successful performance can be achieved either by trial and error or through the capacity to generate appropriate knowledge. Knowledge of a situation at a given time is related to a trade-off between simplicity and realism. The whole question is whether or not a simple enough description can be found that is still sufficiently realistic to be useful. In the past, the desire for tractability has led to the use of very strong assumptions such as that of equilibrium. In microscopic studies this is often reflected in the assumption of a stationary probability distribution, while in macroscopic studies it assumes that there is a single equilibrium attractor – and that it is attained fast enough not to have to worry about any changes that may occur 'on the way'. This miraculous capacity to sweep the system rapidly to equilibrium is assumed by neoclassical economics to result 'naturally' from a rapid optimization process that is carried out by the individuals present. But, clearly, there is no serious demonstration of how precisely this might occur, and no practical reason to suppose that it does occur. It is the contention of this chapter that such an approach makes assumptions which are so strong that they are no longer relevant to most real situations. Despite this, these methods are widely used operationally.

Instead of this extraordinary assumption of equilibrium, the approach presented here states precisely the other assumptions made in the modelling exercise. It shows under what circumstances an equilibrium description would be valid, and when a deterministic ensemble average dynamic can be used. However, even in the latter case, the possibility of multiple equilibria, of limit cycles and of chaos emerge. As assumptions are relaxed, and more general models are derived, it is shown how this predicts self-organization and evolutionary and adaptive change. In other words, biological, social, technological and cultural evolution are the natural result of complex systems' behaviour, once the simplifying assumptions used to derive a simple, deterministic representation are relaxed, and micro diversity, local context and natural fluctuations are admitted explicitly. These new methods are not yet used operationally, or generally accepted.

However, mainstream economics was already challenged by the approach of Nelson and Winter (1983) which was that of 'evolutionary economics', describing the changes in a given market as being the result of competing firms with different characteristics. This work succeeded in attracting interest and support among economists, mainly related to studies of innovation, technological change and economic evolution. Models involving non-linear dynamics and innovation have been developed by Silverberg (1992), Saviotti and Mani (1993) and Brunner (1984). These ideas have also been explored by Dosi *et al.* (1988), Saviotti and Metcalfe (1991) and Leydesdorff and Van Den Besselaar (1994). Also Clark and Juma (1987) were led to the ideas of evolutionary economics, and these were further developed and described by Clark *et al.* in 1995.

Despite all this work, however, none of the models above really modelled evolution as the competition between firms or products, attempting to attract customers according to the comparative qualities of their products as perceived by their potential customers. Instead, they used essentially exogenous assumptions concerning the technological level and productivities of different firms leading to an evolution of the structure of the industry. However, the models presented here concern the competitive and cooperative evolution of the actual attributes of the different products, through a 'learning' dialogue between supply and demand.

The difference between the approach presented here and that of neoclassical economics concerns the assumptions that must be made. In neoclassical economics, an overall 'outcome' of actors' behaviour is assumed to occur, without a clear explanation of 'how' they could actually achieve this, and with no discussion of the trajectory of the system through time. If the behaviours of the actors are coupled, and if there are non-linear mechanisms in operation, this is difficult to justify, since there may be multiple equilibria, cycles, chaos or even evolutionary change. In the approach presented here, the behaviours of actors, and the mechanisms linking them, are shown to lead, under successively restrictive assumptions to:

- average dynamical equations, with possibly different attractor basins and regimes of operation, some of which may be point attractors, and may look like 'equilibria';
- a self-organizing system with changing structure and functionality;
- an evolving system of changing taxonomy.

However, the important difference is also in the idea of considering persistent non-equilibrium situations. In reality, focusing only on the 'attractor basins' of complex systems corresponds merely to a slightly generalized 'equilibrium' assumption. The idea of stable cycles, or even a stable chaotic attractor, is really not different in principle from that of an assumption of equilibrium. The real issue, therefore, is the acceptance of 'irreversibility', of the real passage of time and the reality of change (Dosi and Metcalfe, 1991). It is that of making models which accept that the systems we are interested in may be always 'on their way' to something, but never arrive, because their external environment and their internal components adapt and change as history unfolds. Instead of a fixed landscape of attractors, and of a system operating in one of them, we have a changing system, moving in a changing landscape of potential attractors. Creativity and noise (supposing that they are different) provide a constant exploration of 'other' possibilities. Some of these mark the system and alter the dimensions of its attributes, leading to new attractors, and new behaviours, towards which the system may begin to move, but at which it may never arrive, as new changes may occur 'on the way'. The real revolution is not therefore about neoclassical economics as opposed to non-linear dynamics having cyclic and chaotic attractors, but about the representation of the world either as having arrived at a stationary attractor, or as a non-stationary situation of permanent adaptation and change.

Emergent Coevolution

The macro structures that emerge spontaneously in complex systems constrain the choices of individuals and fashion their experience, so that, without the knowledge afforded by such models, there may not be any simple relation between the goals of actors and what really happens to them. Behaviours are being affected by 'knowledge' and this is driven by the learning experience of individuals. Each actor is coevolving with the structures resulting from the behaviour and knowledge/ignorance of all the others, and surprise and uncertainty are part of the result. The 'selection' process results from the success or failure of different behaviours and strategies in the competitive and cooperative dynamical game that is running.

What emerges are *ecologies* of behaviours, beliefs and strategies, clustered in a mutually consistent way, and characterized by a mixture of competition and symbiosis. This nested hierarchy of structure is the result of evolution, and is not necessarily 'optimal' in any simple way, because there are a multiplicity of subjectivities and intentions, fed by a web of imperfect information, and diverse interpretative frameworks. In human systems, at the microscopic level, decisions reflect the different expectations of individuals based on their past experience. The interaction of these decisions actually creates the future, and in so doing will often fail to fulfil the expectations of many of the actors. This may either lead them to modify their (mis)understanding of the world, or simply leave them perplexed. Evolution in human systems is therefore a continual, imperfect learning process, spurred by the difference between expectation and experience, but rarely providing enough information for a complete understanding.

But it is this very 'ignorance' or multiple misunderstandings that allows diversity, exploration and, hence, learning. In turn, the changes in behaviour that are the external sign of that 'learning' induce fresh uncertainties in the behaviour of the system, and therefore new ignorance. Knowledge, once acted upon, begins to lose its value. This offers a much more realistic picture of the complex game that is being played in the world, and one that our models can begin to quantify and explore.

The idea that evolution might lead to a community of interlocking behaviours is itself an important result. The history of a successful society within a region is largely a tale of increasing cooperation and complementarity, not competition. An economy is a 'complex' of different activities that to some extent 'fit together' and need each other. Competition for customers, space or natural resources is only one aspect of reality. Others are familiar suppliers and markets, local skill development and specialization, coevolution of activities to each other, networks of information flows and solidarities, that lead to a collective generation and shaping of exchanges and discourse within the system.

Evolving Knowledge, Beliefs and Ignorance

From the discussion above, evolution in human systems is seen to be less about 'population dynamics' of interacting stereotypes and more about the rapidly changing spectra of beliefs, of values and of methods of finding information. Clearly, this leads naturally to an acceptance of the importance of 'speculation' in such human systems. The important point is that the expected return on an investment is what drives investment, but this must depend on what people believe about the system. What people believe affects what happens, and what happens affects what people believe! This is a positive feedback loop that can be understood on the basis of the kind of models that we are developing. It severely affects the outcome of 'free markets', as we have seen repeatedly in commodity cycles, land speculation and the prices of almost anything of which there is a limited supply. Instead of market dynamics necessarily leading to a sensible and effective allocation of investment and resources, we will often find that it leads to massive misallocations of resources and much waste. As our simulations of evolving economic markets show, there is no clear way of differentiating 'speculation' from knowledge, and no clear definition of knowledge.

In a world of change, which is the reality of existence, what we need is knowledge about the process of learning. From evolutionary complex systems thinking, we find models that can help reveal the mechanisms of adaptation and learning, and that can also help imagine and explore possible avenues of adaptation and response. These models have a different aim from those used operationally in many domains. Instead of being detailed descriptions of existing systems, they are more concerned with exploring possible futures, and the qualitative nature of these. They are also more concerned with the mechanisms that provide such systems with the capacity to explore, to evaluate and to transform themselves over time. They address the 'what might be', rather than the 'what is'. It is the entry into the social sciences of the philosophical revolution that Prigogine (1980) wrote about in physics some twenty years ago. It is the transition in our thinking from 'being to becoming'. It is about moving from the study of existing physical objects, using repeatable objective experiments, to methods with which to imagine possible futures and with which to understand how possible futures can be imagined. It is about system transformation through multiple subjective experiences, and their accompanying diversity of interpretative, meaning-giving frameworks. Reality changes, and with it experiences change too. In addition, however, the interpretative frameworks or models people use also change, and what people learn from their changed experiences are also transformed. This creates new diversity and uncertainty concerning the future evolution of the system, and requires again the acquisition of new knowledge and the discarding of old, and these are important lessons for knowledge management in organizations.

ACKNOWLEDGEMENTS

The three-dimensional visualization (Figure 10.7) was made by Jack Corliss and M. Lesser at the Goddard Space Flight Center, NASA.

REFERENCES

Allen, P.M. (1985), *Towards a New Science of Complex Systems*, in 'The Science and Praxis of Complexity', Tokyo: United Nations University.

Allen, P.M. (1988), 'Evolution: Why the whole is greater than the sum of its parts', in Wolff, Soeder and Drepper (eds), *Ecodynamics*, Berlin: Springer Verlag.

Allen, P.M. (1990), 'Why the future is not what it was', *Futures*, July/August, 555–69.

Allen, P.M. (1993), 'Evolution: Persistent Ignorance from Continual Learning', in (ed.), *Nonlinear Dynamics & Evolutionary Economics*, Oxford: Oxford University Press, pp. 101–112.

Allen, P.M. (1994a), 'Evolutionary Complex Systems: Models of Technology Change', in L.Leydesdorff and P. Van den Besselaar (eds), *Chaos and Economic Theory*, London: Pinter.

Allen, P.M. (1994b), 'Coherence, chaos and evolution in the social context', *Futures*, **26**(6), 583–97.

Allen, P.M. and G. Engelen (1991), 'An integrated strategic planning and policy framework for Senegal', *Under Contract Article 8 946/89 for DG VII*I, Rue de la Loi, Brussels 1049, Belgium.

Allen, P.M. and M. Lesser (1991), *Evolutionary Human Systems: Learning, Ignorance and Subjectivity*, Chur, Switzerland: Harwood.

Allen, P.M. and J.M. McGlade (1986), 'Dynamics of discovery and exploitation: the Scotian shelf fisheries', *Canadian Journal of Fisheries and Aquatic Sciences*, **43**(6), 1187–1200.

Allen, P.M. and J.M. McGlade (1987a), 'Evolutionary drive: the effect of microscopic diversity, error making and noise', *Foundations of Physics*, **17**(7), 723–8.

Allen, P.M. and J.M. McGlade (1987b), 'Modelling complex human systems: a fisheries example', *European Journal of Operations Research*, **30**, 147–67.

Allen, P.M., G. Engelen and M. Sanglier (1983), 'Self-Organising Dynamic Models of Human Systems', in Frehland (ed.), *From Microscopic to Macroscopic Order*, Synergetics Series, :Springer Verlag.

Allen, P.M., M. Sanglier, G. Engelen and F. Boon (1985), 'Towards a New Synthesis in the Modelling of Evolving Complex Systems', *Environment and Planning B*, 'Planning and Design: Special Issue'.

Allen, P.M., G. Engelen and M. Sanglier (1986), 'Towards a General Dynamic Model of the Spatial Evolution of Urban and Regional Systems' in Hutchinson (ed.), *Advances in Urban Systems Modelling*, New York: Plenum Press.

Anderson, P.W., K.J. Arrow and D. Pines (eds) (1988), *The Economy as an Evolving Complex System*, Redwood City: Addison-Wesley.

Arthur, B. (1994), *Increasing Returns and Path Dependence in the Economy*, Ann Arbor: University of Michigan Press.

Barucha-Reid, A. (1997), 'Elements of the Theory of Markov Processes and their Applications', Dover Publications.

Brunner, H.P. (1984), 'Technological Diversity, Random Selection in a Population of Firms, and Technological Institutions of Government', in Loet Leydesdorff *et al.* (eds), 'Evolutionary Economics and Chaos Theory', London: Pinter.

Clark, N. and C. Juma (1987), *Long Run Economics – An Evolutionary Approach to Economic Change*, London: Pinter.

Clark, N., F. Perez-Trejo and P.M. Allen (1995), *Evolutionary Complex Systems*

Approach to Economic Development, Aldershot, UK and Brookfield US: Edward Elgar.
Dosi, G. and J.S. Metcalfe (1991), 'On Some Notions of Irreversibility in Economics', in P. Saviotti and J.S. Metcalfe (eds), *Evolutionary Theories of Economic and Technological Change*, Chur: Harwood.
Dosi, G., C. Freeman, R. Nelson, G. Silverberg and L. Soete (eds) (1988), *Technical Change and Economic Theory*, London and New York: Pinter.
Eigen, M. and P. Schuster (1979), *The Hypercycle*, Berlin: Springer.
Gillies, J.G. (2000), 'A Complex Systems Model of the Adaptability of Industrial Networks', PhD thesis, March, Cranfield University Library.
Glansdorff, P. and I. Prigogine (1971), *Structure, Stability and Fluctuations*, London: Wiley Interscience.
Haken, H. (1977), *Synergetics*, Heidelberg: Springer Verlag.
Leydesdorff, L. and P. Van Den Besselaar (1994), *Evolutionary Economics and Chaos Theory*, London and New York: Pinter.
Nelson, R. and S. Winter (1983), 'An Evolutionary Theory of Economic Change', Harvard University, Cambridge, MA: Belknap Press.
Nicolis, G. and I. Prigogine (1977), 'Self-Organisation in Non-Equilibrium Systems', New York: Wiley.
Prigogine, I. (1980), *From Being to Becoming*, New York: Freeman.
Prigogine, I. and I. Stengers (1987), *Order out of Chaos*, New York: Bantam Books.
Sanglier, M. and P.M. Allen (1989), 'Evolutionary models of urban systems: an application to the Belgian Provinces', *Environment and Planning A*, **21**, 477–498.
Saviotti, P.P. and G.S. Mani (1993), 'A Model of Technological Evolution Based on Replicator Dynamics', paper presentd at the workshop 'New Developments in Technological Studies: Evolutionary Economics and Chaos Theory', Amsterdam.
Saviotti, P. and S. Metcalfe (1991), 'Evolutionary Theories of Economic and Technical Change', Chur, Switzerland: Harwood.
Silverberg, G. (1992), 'On the Complex Dynamics of Technical Change and Economic Evolution', *Journal of Scientific and Industrial Research*, **51**(3), 151–6.

Commentary: knowledge, ignorance and the evolution of complex systems

Kevin Bryant[1]

INTRODUCTION

One advantage in responding to a contribution, rather than writing an original one, is that there is less obligation to aim for rigour, and more licence to engage in conjecture. The more complex the original contribution, the more justified is this standpoint – and a chapter on complex systems, by definition, is complex in itself. I will therefore take some opportunities to digress.

Peter Allen's chapter is a very valuable illustration of the problems in the 'standard' equilibrium model of neoclassical economics, and the potential that lies in an evolutionary systems approach. The chapter is important in three ways.

1. In order to choose an equilibrium model approach (or any other), particular assumptions and choices must be made. Allen spells out these different levels of assumption and divergent theoretical choices in a particularly useful way.
2. He illustrates his points with discussion of some relatively simple and easily understood models.
3. Perhaps most importantly, Allen concludes his discussion by drawing some particularly insightful generalizations.

ALLEN'S DESCRIPTION OF THE ASSUMPTIONS BEHIND DIFFERENT MODEL SYSTEMS

Allen's schematic assumptions or presuppositions can be quickly summarized as follows:

1. A boundary can be defined between the system and its environment.
2. We have a reasonable taxonomy for the components of the system.
3. Within any component subsystems, elements are either identical or have properties that are normally distributed about an average.

4. Overall (system) behaviours can be adequately described by the average of individual events or element (or subsystem) properties.

Allen points out that taking all four assumptions leads to a totally mechanical system where events are completely determined by the starting conditions. To make matters worse – to align this mechanical and deterministic system with 'reality' (more accurately, in order to simplify the mathematical tasks) – a further assumption is normally made:

5. The system will naturally move to an equilibrium position: thus we can describe the properties of the system by a set of readily solvable simultaneous equations.

The illustrative models discussed in Allen's chapter are based on the rejection of assumptions 3, 4 and 5. He is able to provide a graphic demonstration, given rather better choices on the 'trade-off[s] between simplicity and realism', as he describes it, that the neoclassical equilibrium model is quite misleading. Those of us who attended this workshop probably have little need to be convinced in this way, but the clarity and elegance of Allen's demonstration ought to present many others with much food for thought.

'REALISTIC' COMPLEX MODELS: HOW ELSE CAN WE EXTEND ALLEN'S ARGUMENT?

Given the useful way in which Allen has set out the schematic presuppositions for modelling, what further food for thought can we gain if we also look more closely at assumptions 1 and 2?

In fact, in the 'real world', what we see are not necessarily systems with sharp boundaries, but many systems with fuzzy and permeable boundaries as well. Moreover, the systems we perceive are not only hierarchical systems, but may also be overlapping ones: elements of one system may not only be subsystems with elements in their own right, but may simultaneously be elements of other systems. A taxonomy of the elements can be developed, but for any approximation to 'realism' this needs to be quite complex. And such a realistic model needs to include consideration of forces that operate along several non-financial dimensions, as Alison Wells and I have suggested elsewhere (Bryant and Wells, 1998, p. 90). As a generalization, I would conjecture that any broadly useful model of a complex economic system needs to be of this kind.

Figure 10A.1 presents an indicative sketch of a national economic system along 'realistic' lines as suggested above, with enough structure to give a

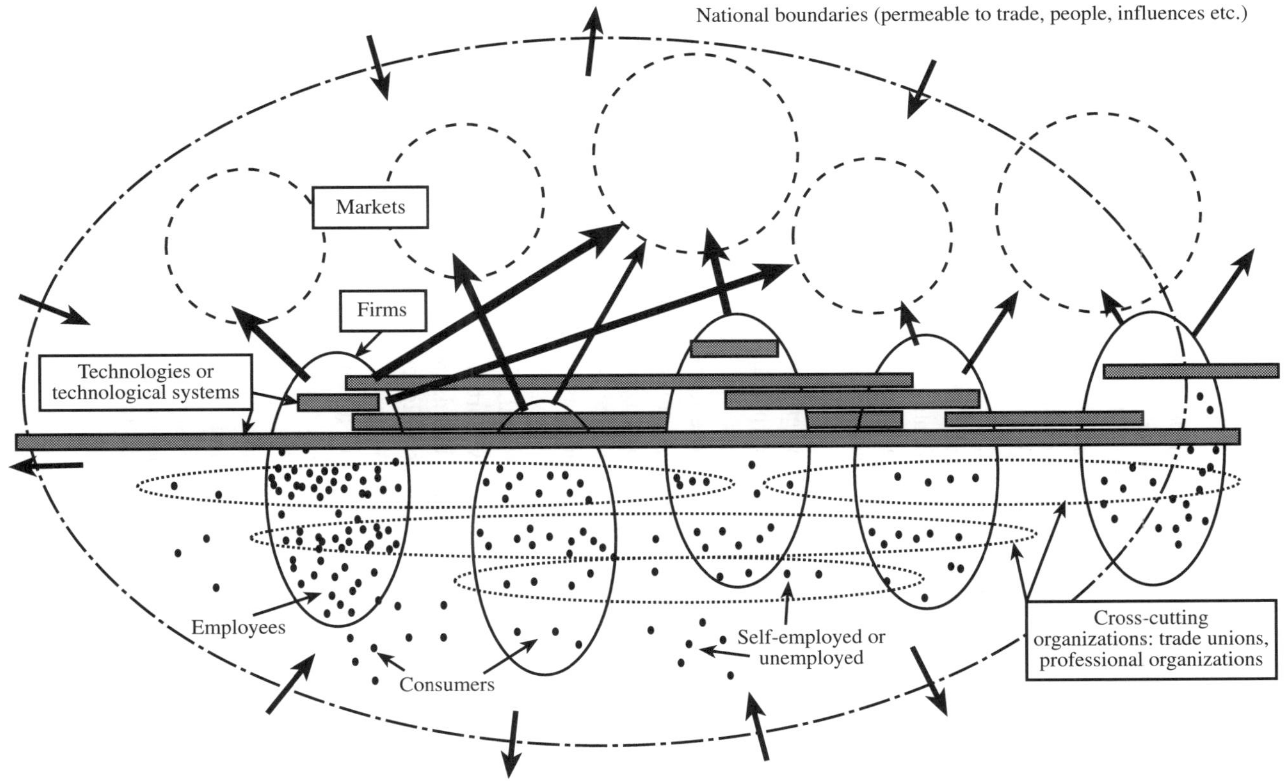

Figure 10A.1 *Indicative sketch of a national economic/innovation system*

flavour of complexity, but simplified enough to permit relatively clear representation. Here the components of the national economic system include several firms producing products (or services) that compete in a series of markets according to product type, which determines the characteristics of each market. And note that it is the *firms*, not the markets, that set the price of products (as Stan Metcalfe pointed out in this workshop).

In fact, there may also be several different kinds of components or elements to the national system. Firms are but one kind, the markets themselves are another. Individual people, the dots on the figure, are another element of the national system. But we know that, in reality, people have many different roles. In this simple representation, they are not only players in the national system overall, but may also be subcomponents (employees) of firms, and may simultaneously be subcomponents of other types of subsystems in the national system – professional organizations or trade unions, for example. People may also be agents (purchasers/consumers) in markets simultaneously with their role as employees and those outside the firms may be self-employed small business operators or unemployed. We may further suppose that there are a number of 'technologies' (perhaps better described as technological systems) common to several firms.

Within each firm, we may suppose that subcomponent elements interact and change according to 'routines', forms of organizational rules and behavioural patterns or habits along the lines suggested in the pioneering evolutionary model of Nelson and Winter (1982); see Bryant (1998, pp. 65–9) for a brief description. Other types of routine may govern elements within markets, trade unions and technological systems. And, more broadly, within the national system as a whole, there are legal, political and social institutions, the 'rules of the game', as described by North (1995), see Bryant (1998, pp. 72–7) for a discussion. 'Institutions' in this sense might also be described as 'systemic routines' and regarded as a higher level form of the organizational routines described by Nelson and Winter.

Now a fully functioning model of a national economic system may well require definition of other subsystem components and further elements, but the sketch provided in Figure 10A.1 and the description above should be sufficient for illustrative purposes. In two papers on 'artificial economies', Lane (1993a, 1993b) discussed models of this kind in some depth. More recently, Wolfson (1995) has sketched some outline specifications for building such models. Wolfson points out that some of the commercially popular computer simulations in the more sophisticated category of games (SimCity and Civilization II are well-known examples) are partly specified along such lines.

Of course, 'national' economic systems are themselves component elements of a global system, and some national systems are highly intermeshed with others (for example, the EU nations, Canada with the United States, and New Zealand with Australia).

Let me draw together some of the points that I have been aiming at. Firstly, markets are not *all* that is important in an economy. Markets are just one component of a national economic system – albeit a highly important one. Rather than maintaining a single-minded focus on markets alone, the work of Richardson (1990) and Loasby (1991) implies that it is more useful to regard the organization of economic activity as being the central task of economic analysis. (See the discussion in Bryant, 1998, pp. 75–6; a parallel point has also been made by Pelikan in the present volume.) The organization of markets, often taken as the be-all and end-all of economics, is simply a special instance of how economic activity might be organized. Whether markets should, or should not, be arranged to permit 'perfect' or near-perfect competition is another issue again. Studies of innovation and of business behaviour clearly indicate that firms have a key role in advanced economies, but it is often overlooked that business firms are for the most part centrally organized systems. And just as the form of organization of its component markets – their regulatory surrounds and the customary patterns of behaviour within – is important for an economy, so too are the corresponding organizational features of its component firms.

Secondly, it takes little elaboration on the simple model in Figure 10A.1 to see that non-financial considerations can be important. A realistic representation of Nelson and Winter's routines and their evolution over time will involve organizational and behavioural issues that will impinge on some technology and employee characteristics that may be non-financial. We could also readily define additional categories of people – management within firms, for example (not to mention governing boards and shareholders). This would bring in power relationships as a key non-financial issue in organizations. Further on this point, one might note that, within a model of this kind, just as firms can be considered as a key element of an economy, so too can the activities, behaviours, motivations and *raison d'être* for professional organizations and trade unions be accommodated. And for several analytical purposes it would be useful to do so. One reason for the difficulties that seem to exist in applying standard economic approaches to industrial relations may well be the inability of standard economic approaches to incorporate unions in their economic models. Indeed, some industrial economists have recommended actions that tend to remove unions from the real world, presumably so as to produce a better fit to their idealized models. This had its counterpart in the economies of the former Soviet bloc, where private business firms, among other institutions, were banned so that the real world faced by Soviet system planners would be in better accord with the idealized Marxist models of their economists.

Finally, a point that I want to draw particular attention to is that *the simulation methods available in modern information technology and software programming techniques can very readily handle quantitative computation in relation to 'realistic' complex systems* of the kind outlined above. To ask an interesting rhetorical question: why then do we not see a much larger share of the very substantial effort and financial resources that currently go into neoclassical economic modelling diverted into exploratory modelling of this kind? Stepping back in history behind this question: why did Solow's paper of 1957 (showing that an equilibrium model could reproduce a broad quantitative history of the US economy) so rapidly stimulate such a revolution in economic analysis, while Nelson and Winter's book of 1982 had such little immediate effect – even though Nelson and Winter clearly demonstrated that much more realistic ground assumptions than Solow's could equally well reproduce the past? In fact, the answer may be apparent from study of other technological/intellectual lock-ins, lessons from the diffusion of technology and ideas, 'first-mover advantage', the marketing problems that anything described as 'evolutionary' faces in the conservative religious climate of the United States, and the parallel development of computers alongside diffusion of Solow's ideas. For example, Solow's work (published in 1957) predated the widespread availability of mainframe computers, but given a relatively moderate investment of time and effort it was still feasible to use his approach to solve a sizeable set of simultaneous equations using electric calculators. Of course, as mainframe computers became available during the 1960s (roughly coinciding with the time needed for diffusion and absorption of Solow's ideas) the drudgery was removed from the calculations and it soon became feasible to solve ever larger sets of simultaneous equations. Thus, perhaps, was a particular form of computational economics born – and very firmly entrenched by the mid-1980s, when Nelson and Winter's work began to be diffused.

While this has strayed a little from Peter Allen's chapter *per se*, it is at least an illustration of the utility of his taxonomy of modelling assumptions and an example of the trains of thought that it can stimulate.

COMMENTS ON ALLEN'S DISCUSSION

I find it interesting that the literature on complex systems has been so spasmodic and slow to develop, often turgid in expression, disconnected to or ignorant of related work, and generally lacking in coherence. Or, at least, that is how much of it has appeared from my own limited reading of it. An earlier speaker in this workshop referred to Simon's seminal and clearly written paper on the nature of complexity (Simon, 1962). In the United States, this appeared to spark a good deal of thinking on complexity through the 1960s, with discussion of 'systems' of wide variety, as perceived across many disciplines (see, for example, Zwicky and Wilson, 1967; Whyte *et al.*, 1969). I suspect that these loosely connected studies were a major influence in the establishment of the Santa Fé school of complex system studies, which reached an early zenith by bringing together eminent 'systems' thinkers from a variety of disciplines. Notably, the Santa Fé Institute set up a valuable dialogue between economists, on the one hand, and physical scientists working on various natural systems, on the other (Anderson *et al.*, 1988).

Surprisingly, the economists among the Santa Fé discussants in 1988 did not draw what now seems the obvious connection with Nelson and Winter's 1982 study. In fact, this tradition of oversight seems to continue among many economists: Ormerod (1994, 1998) has recently produced two excellent studies discussing a 'realistic' economic modelling approach built on empirical studies of behaviour, but these too ignore the seminal contribution of the Nelson and Winter model and their various successors. (For a range of models subsequent to Nelson and Winter, see Silverberg and Verspagen, 1995, and the references provided in Allen's discussion.)

Over the same period, on the European side of the Atlantic, a separate school of complex system studies was established by Prigogine and a range of co-workers (beginning with studies of physicochemical thermodynamics, which happened to be the field which stimulated my own interest in systems and complexity). The Prigogine school has produced a number of very insightful studies of complexity (notably, Prigogine and Stengers, 1984). Of course, Peter Allen's own work has stemmed from this school and he provides the references in his chapter. I confess that much of the recent work I am not familiar with. But having considered that Clark and Juma (1987) was another unaccountably neglected work (the first, or one of the first substantial studies to appreciate the significance of the Nelson and Winter model), I now look forward to reading Clark *et al.* (1995), which I had not been aware of prior to reading Peter Allen's chapter.

Allen continues a tradition of the Prigogine school by making many perceptive comments on the nature and structure of systems:

- In a complex evolutionary system, 'Each actor is coevolving with the structures resulting from the behaviour and knowledge/ignorance of all the others, and surprise and uncertainty are part of the result.' *Co*evolution on many fronts is a key perception: Richard Nelson observed in the first session of this workshop that it is the coevolution of technology and legal and social institutions that is the driver of long-run economic growth.
- 'What emerges [in a complex evolving system] are ecologies of behaviours, beliefs and strategies, clustered in a mutually consistent way,

and characterized by a mixture of competition and symbiosis.' It is these interacting *ecologies* referred to by Allen that constitute the social institutions discussed by North (1995).

- 'The idea that evolution might lead to a community of interlocking behaviours is itself an important result. The history of a successful society within a region is largely a tale of increasing cooperation and complementarity, not competition.' This comment points to the importance of linkages and networking in evolving innovation systems – now strongly confirmed in a variety of recent empirical studies. For example, the recent major report resulting from the OECD's National Innovation System project discusses a broad range of supporting evidence (OECD, 1999, pp. 52–61, 79–89).

To digress by extending the last point, while competition and competitive pressures of various kinds undoubtedly play a major role in innovative systems, we need to ensure that this is not stressed to a degree that seriously inhibits simultaneous cooperation on other levels.[2] We might go even further, and also point to the importance of maintaining a diversity of activities. To me, it is probable that diversity, cooperation and competition are *all* key factors for the maintenance of an innovative economy. Historically, there seem to be examples of societies achieving innovation of various kinds even when just one of these factors was present (given other appropriate institutional factors). But I would conjecture that the most effective innovative economies need to maintain all three factors in some balance.

Returning to complexity in hierarchical systems, I would like to make another speculation, this time deriving from observation of the physical and biological world. In my original career as a physical chemist, one of the most interesting insights I was given was that, while the most powerful forces in a system determined structure at micro levels, it was actually the weakest forces that determined the macro structure. For example, strong atomic forces govern the structure of atomic nuclei; weaker electronic forces govern the structure of atoms and molecules; weaker-still intermolecular forces determine whether a large collection of molecules is constituted as a liquid, solid or gas; and the solar system's structure is determined by gravitational forces – weaker by many orders of magnitude than the other forces.

While it is not well acknowledged, the study of social and economic systems presents several intrinsic difficulties that are not faced in the study of physical or even biological systems. For example, social scientists are less often able to conduct controlled experiments; they do not often have the statistical certainty that huge aggregations of 'agents' provide;[3] and there is less uniformity among those agents. Nevertheless, by analogy with the physical and biological worlds, it is reasonable to conclude that less tangible and less measurable factors may have a substantial determining role in setting the broad characteristics of complex socioeconomic systems. An obvious example is the importance of *trust* as a key factor in any complex system involving human relationships – a point that has been made in various studies of innovation, as well as in other areas of the social sciences.

Finally, it would be remiss of me not to point to another highly important but less tangible factor in complex innovative economic systems: the *processes of learning* (see Bryant, 1998, pp. 62–4). But how much do we really know about these processes? As Peter Allen puts it: 'In a world of change, which is the reality of existence, what we need is knowledge about the process of learning.' Yes!

NOTES

1. The views expressed are personal views of the author, and are not necessarily those of ISR.
2. Brandenburger and Nalebuff (1996) have used the useful neologism 'co-opetition' to convey the need for simultaneous competition and cooperation.
3. The number of 'agents' in physico-chemical systems, for example, is typically in the order of 10^{20}, providing an extraordinary level of statistical certainty regarding behaviour of the system as predicted by the mathematics. Corresponding levels of certainty are not achieved in social and economic systems. Typical market systems in the real world may consist of 10 to 100 agents, yet, for a 'perfect' market', in strict mathematical terms, there should be an *infinite* number of agents if equilibrium is to be achievable.

REFERENCES

Anderson, P.W., K.J. Arrow, and D. Pines (eds) (1988), *The Economy as an Evolving Complex System*, Redwood City: Addison-Wesley.

Brandenburger, A.M. and B.J. Nalebuff (1996), *Co-opetition*, New York: Currency Doubleday.

Bryant, K. (1998), 'Evolutionary innovation systems: their origins and emergence as a new economic paradigm', in K. Bryant and A. Wells (eds), *A New Economic Paradigm? Innovation-based Evolutionary Systems*, Canberra: Department of Industry, Science and Resources (available from URL: *http://www.isr.gov.au/science/analysis*, as at July 2000).

Bryant, K. and A. Wells (1998), 'The consequences of complexity: implications of "systemic economics"', in K. Bryant K and A. Wells (eds), *A New Economic Paradigm? Innovation-based Evolutionary Systems*, Canberra: Department of Industry, Science and Resources (available from URL: *http://www.isr.gov.au/science/analysis*, as at July 2000).

Clark, N. and C. Juma (1987), *Long-run Economics: An Evolutionary Approach to Economic Growth*, London: Pinter.

Clark, N., F. Perez-Trejo and P.M. Allen (1995), *Evolutionary Complex Systems – An Approach to Economic Development*, Aldershot, UK and Brookfield, US: Edward Elgar.

Lane, D.A. (1993a). 'Artificial worlds and economics, Part I', *Journal of Evolutionary Economics*, **3,** 89–107.
Lane, D.A. (1993b), 'Artificial worlds and economics, Part II', *Journal of Evolutionary Economics*, **3,** 177–97.
Loasby, B.J. (1991), *Equilibrium and Evolution – an Exploration of Connecting Principles in Economics*, Manchester: Manchester University Press.
Nelson, R.R. and S.G. Winter (1982), *An Evolutionary Theory of Economic Change*, Cambridge MA: Harvard University Press.
North, D.C. (1995), 'Some fundamental puzzles in economic history/development', Washington University Economics Department Working Paper ewp-eh/9509001 (available from URL: *http://wueconb.wustl.edu/eprints/eh/papers/9509/9509001.abs*).
OECD (1999), *Managing National Innovation Systems*, Paris: OECD.
Ormerod, P. (1994), *The Death of Economics,* London: Faber & Faber.
Ormerod, P. (1998), *Butterfly Economics*, London: Faber & Faber.
Prigogine, I. and I. Stengers (1984), *Order Out of Chaos: Man's New Dialogue with Nature*, Boulder: Random House.
Richardson, G.B. (1990), *Information and Investment: A Study in the Working of the Competitive Economy*, 2nd edn, Oxford: Clarendon Press.
Silverberg, G. and B. Verspagen (1995), 'Evolutionary Theorizing on Economic Growth', in K. Dopfer (ed.), *The Evolutionary Principles of Economics*, Norwell, MA: Kluwer Academic Publishers (available from URL: *http://meritbbs.rulimburg.nl/Fun/Bart/verspagen.html* as at March 1998).
Simon, H.A. (1962), 'The architecture of complexity', *Proceedings of the American Philosophical Society*, **106,** 476–82.
Solow, R.M. (1957) 'Technical change and the aggregate production function', *Review of Economics and Statistics*, **39**, 312–20.
Whyte, L.L., A.G. Wilson and D. Wilson (eds) (1969), *Hierarchical Structures*, New York: American Elsevier.
Wolfson, M.C. (1995), 'XEcon: An experimental/evolutionary model of economic growth', Statistics Canada Research Paper No. 67 (available from URL: *http://www.statcan.ca/english/Vlib/Research/ana67.htm* as at March 1998).
Zwicky, F. and A.G. Wilson (eds) (1967), *New Methods of Thought and Procedure*, New York: Springer-Verlag.

11. Promoting innovation: an overview of the application of evolutionary economics and systems approaches to policy issues

Kevin Bryant[1]

POLICY AND A PRACTICAL ROLE FOR THE ECONOMIST

In summing up discussion at the 1996 Conference of the International Schumpeter Society, Robert Clower (1998, p. 411), drawing on an observation of Einstein's, remarked that, in a non-normative sense, economists could be regarded as the astronomers of the social sciences. However accurately this reflects the self-perception of economists, it does not reflect a common perception of economists by policy makers (who, in any event, are not always able to ignore the normative). In the real policy world, economists are more usually perceived as similar to plumbers.

Policy is about responding to issues – or, at least, to our perception of them. Policy makers might be faced with a major problem requiring immediate action, something akin to a burst water main. They might be dealing with an issue that is causing many angry complaints (something like a faulty sewerage system, perhaps). They might have a service in place – a policy tap from which funds are intended to flow for a particular purpose – but with serious leakages of various kinds that trickle or flood to unintended places and are financially wasteful.

In all the above cases, those with responsibility may seek a plumber–economist who can examine the issue with a policy toolbox in hand and suggest an appropriate course of action. The political pressures on policy makers to resolve issues or provide convenient and efficient services will usually mean that an astronomer–economist with an abstruse theoretical view of matters will frequently be unwelcome, especially where, in dealing with issues like a leaky funding tap, the suggested remedy is simply to remove the service completely.[2]

OUR CHANGING PERCEPTION OF ISSUES

Our perception of the nature of policy issues changes as our understanding evolves. The history of policy development since World War II can be simply viewed through observation of the changing policy labels that have been put in place over time.

In the 1950s–60s, countries generally put *science* policies in place in response to the Vannevar Bush linear view of the link between science and economic growth. Over the 1960s–70s, these came to be more usually described as science *and technology* policies, a response to the realization that technology did not equal science. From the late 1980s into the 1990s, there was a further name change to *innovation* policy as the linear model was largely abandoned (at least at the rhetorical level, if only to a small extent in mind-set and practice) and some awareness spread that innovation involved more than R&D alone. Currently, we are witnessing a further transition in nomenclature so that many countries now aim to have broad holistic or systemic policies for the *knowledge-based economy*.

These name changes are not merely window dressing (though for some, of course, they serve that purpose as well). Usually, they have involved real changes in older policies and new policies addressing issues that were previously unidentified. However indistinct and fuzzy the understanding of issues may remain, the changes do reflect an appreciation that earlier understandings were inadequate. To some degree at least, there has been a coevolution of policies that attempt to deal with innovation together with an improved understanding of its nature.

EMPIRICAL FINDINGS ON TECHNOLOGICAL CHANGE AND INNOVATION

Early views on the nature of innovation processes were substantially shaped by the historical experience of research and commercialization in the chemical and pharmaceutical industries. New chemical compounds were developed and investigated by an R&D effort and, if found to be useful, could then be commercialized through a relatively straightforward process of patenting and marketing. It was assumed that this step-wise process of research, development, patenting, marketing and subsequent diffusion – a 'linear model' of innovation and commercialization – was valid for all industries.

To a major extent, the more sophisticated understanding of innovation that has developed in recent years has derived from a substantial body of empirical studies over a broad group of manufacturing industries. A key finding is that small-scale and incremental innovation is of great benefit – that innovation is not solely concerned with radical R&D-stimulated change. Another is that extensive interactions and feedbacks are often necessary for innovation. Recognition of the importance of incremental change and communication has pointed towards issues of organization and management – and therefore the nature and role of business enterprises (firms), which are seen to have a central role as primary agents of change within an economy. These findings have been the starting point for the evolutionary and systemic approaches to innovation.

Kline and Rosenberg (1986) have argued that innovation processes 'must be viewed as a series of changes in a complete system not only of hardware, but also of market environment, production facilities and knowledge, and the social contexts of the innovation organization'. Although there are now more

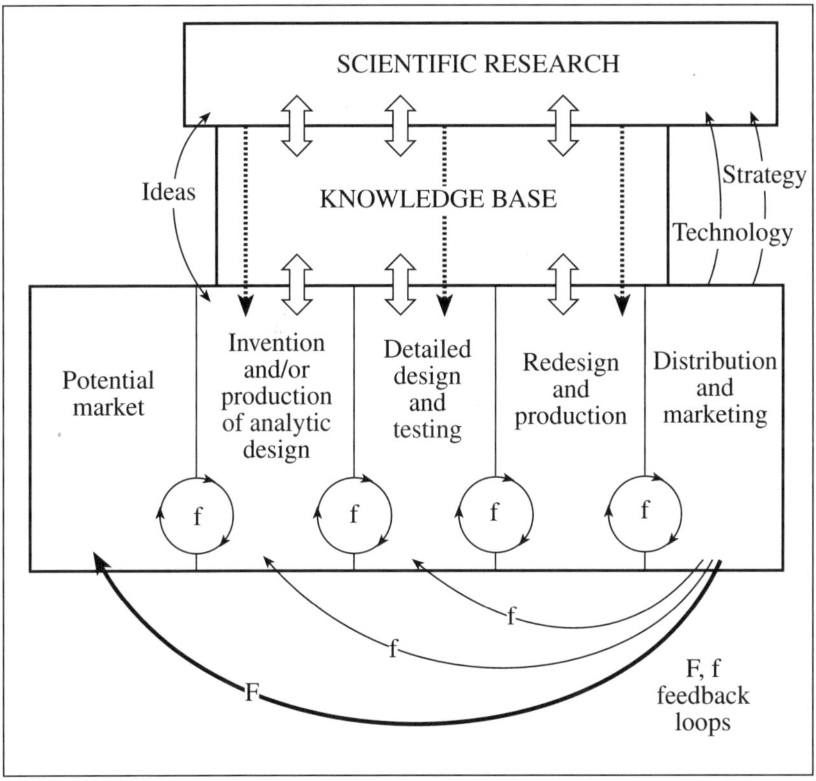

Source: Adapted from Kline and Rosenberg (1986, p. 290).

Figure 11.1 The Kline and Rosenbergs 'chain-link' model of commercial innovation

sophisticated models available, the 'chain-link' model of Kline and Rosenberg (1986) provides a useful and relatively simple illustration of the inter-activity involved in the processes of innovation (Figure 11.1).

The figure indicates that ideas flow in both directions, from science to technology and from technological effort to science. Technology may provide useful devices that enhance scientific research, and market signals may point to specific strategic directions where research is needed to back up commercially viable technology development. There are extensive feedback loops between all stages of the innovation and commercialization processes; these are the 'chain links' in the model.

The broad conclusions to be drawn from the empirical findings on technological change and innovation may be considered under five headings:[3]

- characteristics of technological change and diffusion;
- industry-dependent patterns of innovation;
- patterns in the behaviour of firms;
- issues of management and organization; and
- the social nature of innovation processes.

Characteristics of Technological Change and Diffusion

Several key observations have been made about the emergence, adoption and persistence of technologies. First, most new technologies keep changing incrementally as they diffuse. Not only are new technologies constantly modified as they diffuse and are adopted,[4] but older technologies react and compete by changing also. A prime example is the competition between sail and steam power over much of the nineteenth century. New technology will not always win this competition, sometimes the resulting improvement to old technology defeats it or at least substantially slows down the adoption of the new. Sometimes old and new technologies come to be used in combination.

Second, rather than being single 'complete' inventions, new technologies often emerge in continually changing *packages* that include expertise and experience (sometimes supported by substantial investment in supporting infrastructure). This is particularly true for a radically new technology. Successful implementation of a new technology may therefore involve adoption of a complex package or system of new developments. Since the implementation process may require much further work by innovators and substantial change and development of new competencies on the part of users, some of the subsidiary technologies may be slow in developing or in being adopted. This has been advanced as a large part of the explanation for the so-called 'productivity paradox' (see David, 1990).

Third, particular systems of technologies in a given sector can become excessively entrenched and self-reinforcing against radical change, so that they constrain the effective options open to firms. This phenomenon is described as 'lock-in'. On a larger scale, the development of associated infrastructure, services and powerful interests can lock in whole economies to particular forms of technology (Dosi, 1982).

Finally, there is sometimes a pronounced cultural aspect to particular technologies. When they are transferred to a different context, the adoption of new technology or methods may prove to be unsuccessful because of ingrained attitudes or expectations, or through the absence of particular modes of behaviour that were present in the place of origin.

Industry-dependent Patterns of Innovation

Studies by Pavitt (1984, 1994) have concluded that there are five broad groups of manufacturing industries that appear to have qualitatively different patterns of innovation.[5]

Supplier-dominated industries tend to involve process, organizational and incremental innovation, or innovative product design. Typically, these industries involve diffusion of capital goods and intermediate inputs of an innovative kind. Generally, these industries include traditional manufacturing industries such as textiles and clothing, paper and printing, wood products and simple metal products, as well as agriculture and housing. Firms tend to be small, but sometimes form networks for the purposes of marketing and distribution.

Scale-intensive industries involve both product and process innovation, and often large R&D laboratories. Firms are generally large, often vertically integrated, and are usually involved in high volume production, often involving complex products and production systems. Industries in this category include the major part of the automotive industry, electrical consumer goods, metal and non-metallic products and processed food.

Information-intensive industries are focused upon software and systems engineering associated with products (equipment and software) that constitute process innovation for their own or customer industries. Innovation in information-intensive industries often involves systems and software design, frequently of complex information-processing systems, and reverse engineering. Firms are generally large and the industries they are involved in may include finance, retailing, publishing and travel.

Science-based industries are generally based on radical innovation linked to scientific advances. Industries generally within this group include electronics, fine chemicals, pharmaceuticals and biotechnology. R&D is generally at high levels and undertaken within substantial laboratories. The generally discredited 'linear model' is sometimes a reasonable approximation for the pattern of scientific discovery and subsequent commercialization in these industries.[6] The innovative products are generally capital or intermediate inputs to other industries. Firms are normally large, but also include small high-technology 'start-up' firms.

Specialized suppliers are mainly involved in product innovations that are capital inputs to other industries. Firms in this group are sometimes small and the most successful are in close touch with their customers and user industries generally. Their specialization often means that innovation is highly firm specific and dependent on the cumulative skills and capabilities of key staff. Design is a key factor in this industry group. Australia's automotive supplier industry may fit into this category – so too do many specialized software companies.

Pavitt's valuable industry-based taxonomy illustrates the wide variety of innovation practice that exists across different industries. It demonstrates that there is no need for particular industries or particular firms to follow patterns of innovation that may not be appropriate to their circumstances. This taxonomy should not be regarded as a rigid classification system and some industries and firms will share the characteristics of more than one group. For example, Dosi (1988, p. 1149) points out that aerospace and some other defence-related industries have many of the characteristics of science-based industries, but also have much in common with scale-intensive industries. Pavitt's taxonomy is mostly confined to manufacturing. More empirical study is necessary to identify the characteristics of innovation in services and other non-manufacturing sectors.

Patterns in the Behaviour of Firms

Business studies have drawn some key conclusions on the characteristics and behaviour of commercial enterprises[7] in adopting and implementing new ideas. First, firms do not possess perfect knowledge of the technological options open to them. There is often a surprisingly large awareness gap in firms' information about new technology and it is the *perceived* characteristics of a new technology rather than its objective merits that affect decisions on whether to adopt it.

Second, undertaking R&D activity is now seen as a general means of enhancing a firm's capacity to make appropriate technological choices and absorb and make use of new knowledge of all kinds; the notion that R&D is merely a means of producing new technology is now viewed as a misunderstanding. This partly results from the observation that there is a very strong association between the existence of an in-house R&D effort within a firm and effective innovation in other respects. The high level of general capabilities and technological competencies required to undertake R&D, and the particular need for R&D staff to maintain awareness of new technological developments relevant to their firm's interests, provide a major resource of tacit knowledge in firms and therefore make a major contribution to their general processes of organizational learning.

Finally, there is substantial diversity in the competence, size and other characteristics of firms – even within the one industry. Therefore there are not necessarily any standard or 'best' solutions to innovation problems.

Management and Organization

Managerial capability and strategic direction[8] is of particular relevance for consistent innovation. Strategic issues include the competitive positioning of firms in relation to their intended markets; assessment of market trends; encouragement of searching and learning behaviours that seek to develop new ideas and collect, process and assimilate information; and firms' planning and coordination of finance, marketing, organisation and training. High-level management skills, good marketing and distribution channels, and customer-support capabilities all constitute good 'complementary assets' that allow firms to reap the benefit from innovations.

Technological choice and the implementation of technology beyond the point of adoption is difficult. Once new technology is adopted, building the technological competence to absorb and optimize it requires careful management. Good innovation practice involves management behaviour that fosters learning processes – in particular, the processes through which firms become better able to handle technological choices, negotiation and implementation.

Building the overall capabilities of an organization requires effective provision for learning: undertaking experimentation and searching, reflecting on experience and drawing the lessons from these processes. It is important for organizations to provide opportunities for reflection and conceptual consolidation that enable individuals within an organization to understand the relevance of what has been learned so that it can be integrated into, and serve as a foundation for, current and future activities. For this to occur, it is important that there are effective communication and channels for sharing information and experience – and for transmitting skills between and within organizations.

Social Nature of Innovation Processes

It is clear from the empirical findings outlined above that *innovation primarily involves social processes*; matters of technological hardware are a secondary aspect. Effective innovation is strongly associated with individuals' abilities to build awareness and learn – their abilities to absorb knowledge and develop the competence to put it into practice.

Effective innovation within organizations is strongly associated with their effectiveness in encouraging individuals in knowledge absorption and competence building, but they are unlikely to succeed in this process unless there are well-developed procedures and management practices that embed knowledge, competences and receptivity to new ideas across the organization as a whole. Becoming an effective 'learning organization' in this way is not easy, partly because much knowledge is tacit and not readily amenable to codification, but also because new habits of thinking (particularly receptivity) are difficult to inculcate. Tacit knowledge is embedded in the specialist skills, capabilities and expertise of individuals and/or across the organizations that employ them. Codified knowledge can be diffused relatively readily, but flows of tacit knowledge are subject to higher barriers since they require higher levels of communication (and therefore cooperative behaviour) and the development of deeper levels of understanding (and therefore more time).

Effective person-to-person interactions are crucial, both within and between organizations, if learning is to occur. Thus networking and linkages, both formal and informal, are central to innovation, a finding that has led to a systemic perspective. Communication and cooperation among firms, workers, regulators and public and university researchers is a valuable means of facilitating the flow of new ideas and thus the generation of novelty.

Customers in particular (and often suppliers) have been shown to be major sources of new ideas (von Hippel, 1988; Rothwell, 1992; Shaw, 1994). This implies that organizations need very effective linkages to customers and suppliers and openness to the absorption and development of new ideas from them.

The social nature of innovation means that *technological change within an organization always involves organizational change*.

A COHERENT VIEW OF INNOVATION ECONOMICS

The findings from empirical studies of the processes of technological change and innovation have been at the centre of the key theoretical developments that have led to the modern evolutionary approach to economics. Evolutionary economics now presents an innovation-centred and systemic perspective that has developed substantial coherence over the past decade. It clearly presents a challenge to mainstream neoclassical economic theory, and to its exogenous growth ('new growth theory') offspring. While mainstream economics has tended to focus its concerns on idealized concepts of markets, and issues of 'imperfections' that may cause a 'failure' in the market reaching an equilibrium state, the evolutionary and systemic approach suggests that it is often market imperfections – knowledge asymmetries and spill-overs, monopolies and conditions of disequilibrium – that fuel innovation and economic growth. By making *change* the central concern of economic theory, evolutionary economics reintroduces a basket of forces, agents and influences that are generally overwritten or explicitly excluded in standard economic formulations of the free market. Building on the empirical studies of innovation, ideas from several theorists have blended to constitute a new school of thought.

Firms have been accepted as central vehicles for innovation, technological diffusion and technological change on a broad scale. Therefore the importance of firms' capabilities or competencies has been recognized, as well as, crucially, the importance of the social and legal institutions, entrenched patterns of behaviour, and therefore historical circumstances[9] that may present them with opportunities and/or constrain both their external activities and their internal development of capabilities and competencies.

A radical approach to economic modelling developed by Nelson and Winter (1982) has proved catalytic in stimulating a research effort by several groups that is now culminating in a coherent evolutionary perspective. Nelson and Winter have instigated an approach where simulated economic systems evolve over time as firms adapt their internal behaviours and external strategies in response to competitive and other pressures along lines suggested by Schumpeter.[10]

A new synthesis of economic ideas has therefore emerged from research across a broad front. First and foremost, these ideas are based on empirical observation and on 'real-world' factors and behaviour, following a practical 'plumber–economist' mode rather than a loftier astronomical one. Some key perceptions arising from this new synthesis might be articulated along the following lines. The primary observation is that innovation is the driver of growth: technological and organizational innovation at the micro level of the firm, and broad-scale technological change and institutional innovation at national and global levels. Among other fundamental empirical observations are pervasive interactivity and interconnectedness between elements of systems, pointing to the importance of linkages (or the effects of their absence) within innovation systems (and broader socioeconomic systems).

Systems can be seen to operate at several largely self-organizing hierarchical levels: within firms, locally, within countries, transnationally and globally. They can be seen to operate within industry sectors and in relation to enabling technologies across sectors. And they operate within different spheres; for example, evidence points to the substantially separate existence of commercial innovation systems (consisting of firms) and science systems (consisting of universities and other public research organizations). But in none of these examples are systems fully isolated; there are important intersections and interactivity in all cases.[11]

As the point above indicates, '*national* innovation systems' are only one perspective on system issues. ('Clusters' at the local level are another.) Nevertheless, there are many national specificities and, since national governments (and many institutions) exert most of their influence at national levels, this is a perspective that deserves a primary focus.

For the majority of issues, the realities of turbulent dynamic change and the presence of influential forces that are not wholly financial in character point to there being no universal optimums. Thus 'imperfections', gaps, inefficiencies or poor linkages within systems are mostly relative and cannot be assessed in any absolute sense. Empirical comparison and careful comparative analysis is therefore needed to identify inefficiencies or points of weakness in systems.

Markets and their cost–price forces are certainly recognized as key factors within real-world systems, but imperfections in markets are observed as omnipresent in practice, and more often than not are large in magnitude and multiple in character. Thus seeking to frame consideration of economic issues in ways that revolve around neoclassical market failure as a central point of reference is frequently of limited value. In particular, to attempt discussion of technological change and innovation issues in this manner is to beg for the application of Ockham's razor.

The formal algebraic models of static equilibria at the core of neoclassical theory are replaced by an alternative approach, broader in conception but equally quantitative, that relies on computational algorithms which seek to simulate dynamic non-equilibrium systems with interacting and evolving elements. The nature of the simulation models created through this approach should permit the intellectual realm of economics to invade and exploit fertile border areas of sociology and human and organizational behaviour. Thus, within useful simulation models, there is the potential to place key non-financial forces on a comparable footing with purely financial considerations.[12]

Among substantial contributions from the work of North (1981, 1990, 1995) on the importance of social and legal institutions have been the perceptions (a) that transaction costs (both financial and non-financial) and uncertainty are major problems for players within systems, of comparable magnitude to issues of cost and price within neoclassical markets, and (b) that the social and human need to optimize both these factors constitutes the major driver for institutional change at macro levels and (we may reasonably conclude) organizational change at the micro level.

The perceptions above point to the importance of high levels of trust both at organizational levels and in macro-level systems. Trust lowers transaction costs and increases certainty. In organizations, trust therefore facilitates teamwork (and hence productivity, innovation and growth) and reduces the need for expensive monitoring. Correspondingly, high levels of trust between players in higher-level systems will reduce the need for regulatory effort and the imposition of sanctions; productive cooperation and beneficial change will be facilitated.

At the micro level of the firm, technological change is *always* accompanied by organizational change, whether planned or not. Failure to plan and take the need for organizational change into account will produce many tensions and will increase the chances of an unfavourable result for the firm. Correspondingly, we can reasonably conclude that *if broad technological changes at the macro level of an economy are not accompanied by appropriate institutional changes then tensions of one kind or another are likely to develop.*[13]

AN EVOLUTIONARY AND SYSTEMIC APPROACH TO INNOVATION POLICY

What starting points or axiomatic assumptions for policy, conceived in the conceptual framework discussed above, should be drawn from empirical studies and observation? At a fundamental level, such studies recognize that so-called 'market imperfections', for example transaction costs, imperfect knowledge, 'bounded' rationality and the inclusion of non-financial considerations in decision making; the existence of different, and continually changing products within single 'markets'; substantial variation in power and competence among economic agents; and situations where groups of agents make arrangements to act in concert, are all a pervasive and significant characteristic of economic systems, especially in the current global economy. In summary, *'market imperfections' are universal – and are necessary to drive change.*

However, beyond that 'zeroth' level, the following might be a tentative list of policy axioms.

1. There is the general observation at the macro level that long-run economic growth depends on innovation, involving both favourable technological change and favourable change in social and legal institutions.
2. Effective linkages (and thus low-cost transactions), through appropriate legal and social institutional arrangements, formal arrangements between organizations, and through the informal customary behaviour of individuals, are crucial to the effective operation of systems.
3. Among the various players in economic systems, the activities of commercial organizations (firms) are of more direct significance to economic growth than the commercial activities of private individuals, whose contribution is substantially indirect.

4. At the micro level, the continuing success of firms – their commercial competitiveness – is highly dependent on both technological and organizational innovativeness.[14]
5. The importance of innovativeness to growth and the central role of firms in innovation are by themselves sufficient to justify government interventions that seek to maintain or achieve appropriate levels of commercial innovation within the national system.[15] Thus, in general terms, a '*variety of government actions ... have to be directed towards a single end: increasing the population of innovative firms in the economy*' (OECD, 1996, p. 212, italics added).

Keith Smith has examined the rationales for government intervention that appear to follow from a systems approach to innovation and technological change (Smith, 1998, pp. 41–4). He points to four areas of possible 'systemic failure' – areas where the possibility of improving systemic efficiency may justify government actions:

- *infrastructure failure*: failures resulting from inadequacies in infrastructure, either with respect to physical infrastructure or with respect to knowledge bases;
- *transition failure*: failures in transition between technological paradigms, when skills and capabilities in groups of firms are overtaken by sudden and unexpected changes in technology that swamp firms' capacities to respond adaptively;
- *lock-in failure*: failures at a system-wide level, when a complex of technologies and their associated physical, skills and social infrastructures is dominant to such an extent that it effectively prevents the adoption of alternatives (i.e., the system 'locks-in' as in a traffic gridlock);
- *institutional failure*: failures in social or legal institutions, particularly when broad-level technological changes are not matched by appropriate institutional changes.

Hofer and Polt (1998, pp. 12–13) have put forward a number of principles on which to base innovation policy. We can summarize and further develop these as follows. Diversity, competition and cooperation should all be maintained, the first to provide novelty and allow for uncertainties,[16] the second as an incentive to innovate, and the third to build essential linkages,[17] noting that all three factors interact in a 'tense relationship' and that some balance should therefore be struck between them. In any event, maintaining a variety of activities implies that the neoclassical doctrine of 'comparative advantage' is not an appropriate basis for policy action.

Policy should particularly support and encourage experimental behaviour, for example by focusing attention on innovation and knowledge as the bases of competencies (and therefore competitiveness) and by tolerating and learning from the 'mistakes' that may result.

Policy should be process-oriented focusing on system design and the improvement of social and legal institutions, with the aims of encouraging linkages that (a) lower transaction costs (including non-financial, as well as financial costs), and (b) facilitate access to skills and knowledge bases so as to enhance diffusion and promote 'learning organizations'.

Policies should seek to influence expectations, as this can assist in building social consensus and in disseminating new technologies.

The rationales for policy intervention in the evolutionary and systemic approach to economics appear to represent a significant expansion on those suggested by neoclassical theory. In some respects the rationales are different in kind. From a neoclassical perspective, interventions based on systems approaches could be faced in some instances with charges of unfairness in that public interventions could result in private benefits that might arguably outweigh public 'spill-over' benefits by a significant margin. That is, in addition to blanket incentives involving 'indiscriminate' market mechanisms, it seems conceivable that activities aimed at increasing the overall number of innovative firms, or preserving their numbers if they are under threat, or maintaining or increasing variety in terms of technologies or industry sectors, might sometimes include direct intervention and support to improve the competitive position (or continued existence) of particular firms or groups of firms.[18]

But is this fair? The answer to the charge of unfairness may be that within the global economy the prospect of achieving even an approximation to a perfect market is highly unlikely on several fronts, and that in the face of pervasive market imperfections blanket interventions are not necessarily effective for all firms. Furthermore, provided the assisting instrument is well-designed,[19] private benefits will only accrue to assisted firms where those firms actually succeed in becoming successful innovators. In this sense, the private benefit translates to a public benefit, in that higher levels of innovation produce more competitive industries, increased general wealth through increased amounts of taxes paid by the firms concerned, and higher per capita growth. In some instances, 'transition failure', in Smith's sense, might be a justification for assistance of this kind.

A further answer lies in an important point made by Lipsey and Carlaw (1998, pp. 49–50). Evolutionary approaches suggest that there are substantially more types of spill-over benefits than are readily identified in neoclassical theory. Lipsey and Carlaw identify four types of spill-overs that create opportunities for useful policy interventions, and pitfalls for policies that ignore them. For example, improvements to the efficiency of one technology may thereby increase the effectiveness of many other technologies in ways that cannot be appropriated by the initiators. Changes to technology can also have spill-over effects on surrounding structures, for example where new technologies alter the value of elements such as existing capital, firms, skills, locations and existing technologies. Similarly, changes in one element of the structure, for example physical capital, may require changes in elements like human capital, location, organization and so on, representing a series of spill-overs within the structure. Finally, experience in the use of new and imperfect technologies generates non-appropriable new knowledge which benefits producers and future users by assisting in product improvement.

It is clear from the above that there will be few universals in terms of specific policies. Smith (1998, p. 49) makes the point that 'the details of policy must vary widely to suit particular national, regional, and local needs'. Both Smith and Hofer and Polt each stress that the complexity that becomes necessary in this approach to innovation policy requires the policy process itself to become information-intensive. Therefore, they suggest that particular attention should be given to competence-building among policy makers. Further, in Hofer and Polt's terms (1998: 12), innovation policy itself must become experimental – it must be prepared to keep trying new policy tools and to reorganise itself according to changing circumstances.

MAPPING ISSUES IN THE INNOVATION POLICY TERRAIN

Early in this discussion, the point was made that policy frequently involves the clarification and better understanding of issues, and that this often involved clarification and development at a conceptual level. Given that, informed by the empirical findings and theoretical work outlined above, how might governments assess gaps in innovation systems or seek to improve their interconnections, or otherwise make them more effective or efficient? One approach is to map and monitor the major issues demanding a policy response in relation to the overall innovation system. By identifying the system's weak points, governments can consider intervening to ensure that innovativeness is encouraged. Figure 11.2 is an attempt to construct a map of this kind.[20]

In a situation where we face a complex system (or, if a more fine-grained view is taken, a set of overlapping and intersecting systems), seeking a relatively simple taxonomy of issues, of the kind presented in Figure 11.2, might well be the best that we can do. In essence, the map attempts to represent some of the broad perceptions discussed above in terms that might provide an organized checklist of possible innovation policy issues or useful points of leverage for government actions.

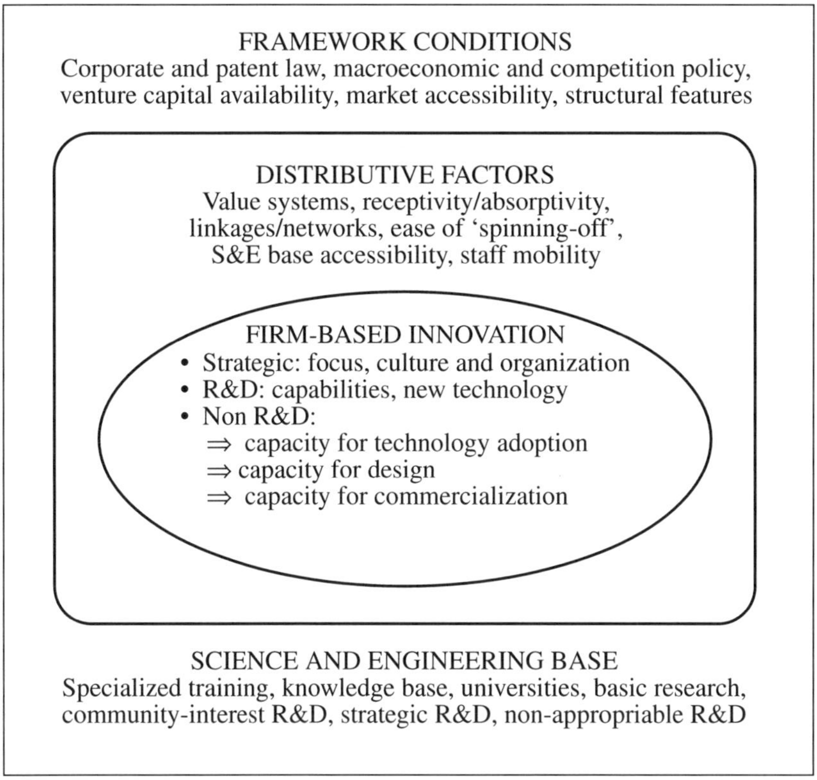

Figure 11.2 Systemic issues in innovation policy

Firm-based innovation covers the dynamic internal factors that directly influence firms' innovative capacities:

- strategic issues of focus, firm culture, management, organization and business planning,
- capacities for undertaking R&D in-house,
- competence in technology absorption (that is, receptivity),
- competence in design,
- competence in new product commercialization,
- capacities for staff and organizations as a whole to learn effectively and maintain practices of continuous incremental improvement.

The central location of this domain within the map is intended to reflect the central role that commercial enterprises play in technological innovation and the separateness of the commercial innovation system from the science system, as established in the work of Dasgupta and David (1994, p. 487), discussed in Bryant (1998, p. 74).

Distributive factors are those mainly social institutions that influence organizations' access to external information and capabilities, together with the capacity for the system to generate new innovative firms and distribute new ideas and developments rapidly and effectively:

- ready access to skilled personnel, research providers and new technology sources,
- strategic linkages between organizations with complementary skills and competencies,
- attitudes and customs that encourage innovative 'spin-offs' and entrepreneurs,
- business and social ethics that value trust and openness,
  high levels of knowledge codification (to facilitate transfer).

David and Foray (1996, p. 26), discussed in Bryant (1998, pp. 70–71), have drawn attention to further factors (largely ones that fall into the category of social institutions) that influence what they describe as the 'distributive power' of an innovation system.

The science and engineering (S&E) base covers organizations and arrangements that provide training, skilled personnel and research outputs, including new ideas and developments that may be distributed through the innovation system:

- specialist education, including the encouragement of creativity and entrepreneurship,
- excellent basic and applied research infrastructure,
- high-quality research effort directed towards 'community good' purposes, and support for non-appropriable innovation activities,
- outputs that are accessible to firms.

As referred to above under 'firm-based innovation', the work of Dasgupta and David (1994, p. 487) indicates that the science and engineering base is best considered as a distinct component of innovation systems in the broad sense. The difference between science as the development of understanding and technology as the development of practical devices also needs to be appreciated (see Bryant, 1998, p. 54; Brooks, 1994).

Framework conditions cover the broader legal and political institutions and the structural framework within which firms exist and carry out their business, and which set the rules for access to markets and (domestically) for their operation – infrastructure, policies, financial, legal and other institutional arrangements:

- communications and industrial infrastructure – suppliers in complementary industries,
- competitive sources of venture capital,
- appropriate competition policies balanced by encouragement for cooperative innovation,
- an effective intellectual property system,
- access to markets,
- a well-educated workforce and community,
- appropriate macroeconomic settings.

These are the better-recognized group of legal and social institutions – the ones that are more tangible in an everyday sense than those listed above as distributive factors.

TOOLS FOR SYSTEM DIAGNOSTICS

A 'benchmarking' approach is often suggested as a useful means of comparing innovation systems. Where a broad range of quantitative indicators and qualitatitive assessments are utilized – relating to a range of the issues highlighted in Figure 11.2, for example – this may prove valuable, particularly where disparities are used as the basis for asking further questions and undertaking more intensive or specific case studies. However, an excessive reliance on purely quantitative measures can be undesirable, given that there is often more doubt on the precision of measures than is acknowledged, and even more doubt in cases where data are fed into algorithms whose validity or applicability is not questioned.

In addition, there is often little appreciation of the differences in 'benchmarking' complex systems as opposed to simple systems. For example, we could readily compare electric power generation installations (simple systems) in different cities – Brisbane and Stockholm, for example. Both inputs and outputs could be clearly identified, measured and costed for each installation and the relative efficiency of each readily compared. But what if we wished to compare the cities of Brisbane and Stockholm? Each city is a highly complex system and it is not easy to define or identify 'inputs' and 'outputs' in a comprehensive or useful way: these concepts have largely dissolved. The implication is that, as we move from simple to complex systems, we cannot necessarily apply the same set of indicators or similar 'benchmarking' techniques to derive a reliable measure of relative costs and

Table 11.1 Illustrative analyses of systemic failure or weakness using Keith Smith's taxonomy

Macro-level system (national)	Micro-level system (firm or other organization)
<u>*Infrastructure failure*</u> *in knowledge base*: for example, insufficient engineers or tacit scientific or other knowledge within an economy means that firms are disadvantaged against foreign competitors in easy recruitment or access to skills or knowledge base	<u>*Infrastructure failure*</u> *in readily accessible skills*: for example, lack of professional, design or trade skills leads to shoddy, unappealing or faulty products; or lack of R&D or informed searching/learning behaviours leads to inability to improve products or make good choices on new technology or strategic direction
in physical infrastructure: for example, inadequate or faulty communications network or electricity supply	*in equipment*: for example, outdated, inappropriate or faulty production equipment; too few phone lines, poor office facilities
<u>*Transition failure*</u> *Casualties when wide-ranging technological or institutional paradigms are challenged*: for example, world market domination of Swiss (mechanical) watch-making industry rapidly eliminated by Japanese electronic companies, causing problems for highly skilled craftsmen and firms with no knowledge base in electronics; unforeseen effects such as widespread firm difficulty or unemployment from policy/regulatory changes that lack transition planning, such as the major overnight reduction in Australian manufacturing tariffs in 1974	<u>*Transition failure*</u> *Unforeseen difficulties after a radical change in equipment, technology or managerial or organizational arrangements*: for example, inadequate training of equipment operators or lack of appreciation that equipment needs hard-to-access skills of a new kind; organizational economies that unwittingly deskill, or inhibit essential long-term processes such as adequate record keeping
<u>*Lock-in failure*</u> For example, global domination of very large oil companies and automobiles/internal combustion engines, coupled with magnitude of petrol distribution infrastructure, strongly inhibits electric-powered transport; tight bureaucratic control of further technological innovation, coupled with sanctions on outside contact, leads to stagnation in technological advancement (as in old China)	<u>*Lock-in failure*</u> For example, eventual failure of large nineteenth-century sailing ship firms (staff highly trained in sailing technology unable to adapt to steam technology)
<u>*Institutional failure*</u> For example, no patent protection means little incentive to innovate; excessive patent protection inhibits technological diffusion; overzealous competition policy inhibits fruitful cooperation	<u>*Organizational failure*</u> For example, over-zealous commitment to particular technology; inadequate financial procedures or record keeping; low-trust workplace

benefits. Of course, innovation systems are not as complex as cities; probably, 'inputs' can be reasonably defined for innovation, but 'outputs' are certainly a subject for considerable debate.

'Market failure' analysis is sometimes ventured as a diagnostic tool by those attempting to apply mainstream neoclassical economics to innovation policy. Keith Smith's (1998) taxonomy of 'systemic failures', outlined in table 11.1, offers a valuable alternative.

Table 11.1 serves to illustrate that Smith's taxonomy might be applied as a rapid checklist in diagnosing the health of a system at any level. In conjunction with Figure 11.2, it could provide a useful adjunct to the toolbox carried by the 'plumber–economist'.

CONCLUSION

Studies of innovation have revealed a complex phenomenon involving multiple actors and influences within dynamic systems. The picture that has unfolded has been difficult to integrate within the prevailing neoclassical economic theory. Instead, stimulated by a diverse range of thought from outside the current mainstream, a new school of economic theory has emerged. This perspective acknowledges the reality of technological change and the key role played by institutional innovation. Further, it acknowledges the incompleteness of information, rationality that is shaped and constrained by social institutions, the importance of searching and learning behaviours, knowledge as a form of capital, the centrality of 'the firm' as a vehicle for innovation and the coexistence of cooperative connections together with competition in the market. This new economic paradigm points to innovative activities being organized and fostered within systems that operate and interact at many levels – global, transnational, national, local sectoral and firm level, for example. As a consequence of this new thinking for firms, it seems clear that there will rarely be a single 'best' way of managing innovation processes. And, as a crucial consequence for governments, policy interventions to promote innovation can now be supported by rationales that are richer and more extensive than those suggested by neoclassical economics.

NOTES

1. The views expressed are personal views of the author, and are not necessarily those of ISR. This work draws on earlier papers (Bryant, 1998; Bryant and Wells, 1998a, 1998b). I am grateful to Alison Wells for her contributions to those papers and for her suggestions on this chapter.
2. One might describe the perfect cosmological market of the neoclassical astronomer–

economist's standard model as a universe in which a few issues can be readily addressed by visualizing sun- moon- and star-like agents in circular orbit around the earth, with the great advantage that simply solvable mathematical equations can be applied. But the dynamics associated with planet- or comet-like matters, technological change and innovation, for example, cannot be readily taken into account. At least in recent years, 'new growth theory' has explicitly recognized some of these problems and, as Ptolemy did with ancient astronomical models, has attempted to correct for the deficiencies by adding on some elegant mathematical extensions, albeit of a somewhat *ad hoc* nature. Nevertheless, for most economists in the mainstream of the profession, nothing akin to the post-Ptolemaic Copernican revolution has occurred. There has been little recognition of the challenge that technological change and innovation present to economic theory.

3. The empirical work is summarized in more detail in Bryant (1998, pp. 54–64), drawing significantly on Dodgson and Bessant (1996, pp. 41–4), which provide more detailed referencing to original studies. Extensive reviews and summaries of empirical findings are available in Dodgson and Rothwell (1994) and Freeman (1994).
4. Usually, the original innovators or their competitors keep modifying product innovations to assist their acceptability. With process innovation, it is often the customer who will make the changes.
5. See also the useful summary provided by Dosi (1988, pp. 1148–9).
6. It was the chemical industry in nineteenth-century Germany that introduced the large R&D laboratory, a major organizational innovation in itself. Because chemical compounds have highly specific structures, newly developed ones can be readily specified for patenting purposes. Chemical reactions and processes can also be readily specified. In addition, chemical-based product innovations are not usually subject to incremental change as they diffuse, nor are they generally associated with a substantial number of supporting technological developments. This is why the processes of commercialization and diffusion are generally simpler in the case of the chemical and pharmaceutical industries. This will also hold in the emerging biotechnology industry.
7. Empirical studies have generally accepted the 'competence perspective' on the nature of firms and their strategic management. These important views on firms and their role within economies have recently been well articulated in a series of major publications – see Foss and Knudsen (1996), Foss (1997) and Foss and Loasby (1998), together with the related contributions of Richardson (1990) and Loasby (1991) – but can be traced back largely to Penrose (1959).
8. See, for example, Loasby (1998) and Langlois (1998).
9. See, for example, David (1994), Freeman (1995) and North (1981, 1990, 1995).
10. Silverberg and Verspagen (1995) have provided a useful summary of subsequently developed models, while Dosi and Nelson (1994) provide a broader review of later work.
11. In a commentary on Peter Allen's contribution in Chapter 10 of this volume, I have outlined some approaches that might be taken to modelling such systems.
12. It also seems feasible to expand the utility of evolutionary economics well beyond consideration of innovation. In outline, Phillimore (1998) has already made a number of suggestions along these lines.
13. It may well be the case that there are insufficient institutional mechanisms (in legal and social terms) for broadly distributing the benefits of technological change. In that case, to the extent that technological change causes dislocations through displacing employment, tensions will certainly develop if no actions are taken to encourage appropriate institutional innovation. See the discussion below in relation to Keith Smith's (1998) categorization of systemic 'institutional failure'.
14. Given that a firm can be considered as a 'system' in its own right, this might be seen as a micro-level restatement of the first point.
15. What level may be considered 'appropriate' should be assessed through comparative analysis, remembering that there are few 'absolutes'.
16. In the face of change and uncertainty, maintenance of diversity is a key strategy. It also promotes cross-fertilization where novelty may result from transfer of ideas between different spheres.

17. In relation to the present, efforts to maintain diversity, openness to competition and cooperative links may appear inefficient, but in the long term they are likely to prove essential for economic survival.
18. Clear sets of guidelines laid down in advance, including tests based on comparative assessment, and high levels of transparency would be needed to cover such instances and avoid providing easy routes towards 'pork-barrelling'.
19. This, together with the requirements in notes 15 and 18 above, is a complex and demanding brief for policy makers.
20. This map builds slightly on earlier efforts in Bryant *et al.* (1996, pp. xv, 3–9) and OECD (1997, pp. 31–8).

REFERENCES

Brooks, H. (1994), 'The relationship between science and technology', *Research Policy*, **23**, 477–86.

Bryant, K. (1998), 'Evolutionary innovation systems: their origins and emergence as a new economic paradigm', in K. Bryant and A. Wells (eds), *A New Economic Paradigm? Innovation-based Evolutionary Systems: Discussions of Science and Innovation 4*, Canberra: Department of Industry, Science and Resources (available from URL: *http://www.isr.gov.au/science/analysis*, as at July 2000).

Bryant, K. and A. Wells (1998a), 'A new school of thought', in K. Bryant and A. Wells (eds), *A New Economic Paradigm? Innovation-based Evolutionary Systems: Discussions of Science and Innovation 4*, Canberra: Department of Industry, Science and Resources (available from URL: *http://www.isr.gov.au/science/analysis*, as at July 2000).

Bryant, K. and A. Wells (1998b), 'The consequences of complexity: implications of "systemic economics"', in K. Bryant and A. Wells (eds), *A New Economic Paradigm? Innovation-based Evolutionary Systems: Discussions of Science and Innovation 4*, Canberra: Department of Industry, Science and Resources (available from URL: *http://www.isr.gov.au/science/analysis*, as at July 2000).

Bryant, K., L. Lombardo, M. Healy, L. Bopage and S. Hartshorn (1996), *Australian Business Innovation – A Strategic Analysis: Measures of Science and Innovation 5*, Department of Science and Technology, Canberra: Australian Government Publishing Service.

Clower, R.W. (1998), 'New Microfoundations for the Theory of Economic Growth?' in G. Eliason and C. Green (eds), *Microfoundations of Economic Growth – A Schumpeterian Perspective*, Ann Arbor, The University of Michigan Press.

Dasgupta, P. and P.A. David (1994), 'Towards a new economics of science', *Research Policy*, **23**, 487–521.

David, P.A. (1990), 'The dynamo and the computer: an historical perspective on the modern productivity paradox', *American Economic Review*, **80**(2), 355–61.

David, P.A. (1994), 'Why are institutions the "carriers of history"?: Path dependence and the evolution of conventions, organizations and institutions', *Structural Change and Economic Dynamics*, **5**, 205–20.

David, P.A. and D. Foray (1996), 'Accessing and expanding the science and technology knowledge base', *STI Review*, **16**, 13–68.

Dodgson, M. and J. Bessant (1996), *Effective Innovation Policy: A New Approach*, London: International Thomson Publishing Company.

Dodgson, M. and R. Rothwell (eds) (1994), *The Handbook of Industrial Innovation*, Aldershot, UK and Brookfield, US: Edward Elgar.
Dosi, G. (1982), 'Technological paradigms and technological trajectories', *Research Policy*, **11**, 147–62.
Dosi, G. (1988), 'Sources, procedures and microeconomic effects of innovation', *Journal of Economic Literature*, **26**, 1120–71.
Dosi, G. and R.R. Nelson. (1994), 'An introduction to evolutionary theories in economics', *Journal of Evolutionary Economics*, **4**, 153–72.
Foss, N.J. (1997), *Resources, Firms and Strategies: A Reader in the Resource-based Perspective*, Oxford: Oxford University Press.
Foss, N.J. and C. Knudsen (1996), *Towards a Competence Theory of the Firm*, London: Routledge.
Foss, N.J. and B.J. Loasby (eds) (1998), *Economic Organization, Capabilities and Co-ordination: Essays in Honour of G.B. Richardson*, London: Routledge.
Freeman, C. (1994), 'The economics of technical change', *Cambridge Journal of Economics*, **18**, 463–514.
Freeman, C. (1995), 'The "national system of innovation" in historical perspective', *Cambridge Journal of Economics*, **19**, 5–24.
Hofer, R. and W. Polt (1998), 'Evolutionary innovation theory and innovation policy: an overview', in K. Bryant and A. Wells (eds), *A New Economic Paradigm? Innovation-based Evolutionary Systems: Discussions of Science and Innovation 4*, Canberra: Department of Industry, Science and Resources (available from URL: *http://www.isr.gov.au/science/analysis*, as at July 2000).
Kline, S. and N. Rosenberg (1986), 'An overview of innovation' in R. Landau and N. Rosenberg (eds), *The Positive Sum Strategy: Harnessing Technology for Economic Growth*, Washington: National Academy Press.
Langlois, R.N. (1998), 'Capabilities and the theory of the firm' in N.J. Foss and B.J. Loasby (eds), *Economic Organization*, London: Routledge.
Lipsey, R.G. and K. Carlaw (1998), 'Technology policies in neoclassical and structuralist–evolutionary models', *STI Review*, **22**, 31–73.
Loasby, B.J. (1991), *Equilibrium and Evolution – An Exploration of Connecting Principles in Economics*, Manchester: Manchester University Press.
Loasby, B.J. (1998), 'The concept of capabilities' in N.J. Foss and B.J. Loasby (eds), *Economic Organization*, London: Routledge.
Nelson, R.R. and S.G. Winter (1982), *An Evolutionary Theory of Economic Change*, Cambridge MA: Harvard University Press.
North, D.C. (1981), *Structure and Change in Economic History*, New York: Norton.
North, D.C. (1990), *Institutions, Institutional Change and Economic Performance*, Cambridge: Cambridge University Press.
North, D.C. (1995), 'Some fundamental puzzles in economic history/development', Washington University Economics Department Working Paper ewp-eh/9509001 (available from URL: *http://wueconb.wustl.edu/eprints/eh/papers/9509/9509001.abs* as at March 1998).
OECD (1996), *The OECD Jobs Strategy: Technology, Productivity and Job Creation*, **2**, Paris: OECD.
OECD (1997), *Proposed Guidelines for Collecting and Interpreting Technological Innovation Data: 'Oslo Manual'*, 2nd edn, Paris: OECD/Eurostat.
Pavitt, K. (1984), 'Sectoral patterns of technical change: towards a taxonomy and a theory', *Research Policy*, **13**, 343–73.

Pavitt, K. (1994), 'Key characteristics of large innovating firms' in M. Dodgson and R. Rothwell (eds), *The Handbook of Industrial Innovation*, Aldershot, UK and Brookfield, US: Edward Elgar.

Penrose, E.T. (1959), *The Theory of the Growth of the Firm*, Oxford: Basil Blackwell.

Phillimore, J. (1998), 'Neo-Schumpeterian economics: political possibilities and problems', *Journal of Australian Political Economy*, **42**, 48–74.

Richardson, G.B. (1990), *Information and Investment: A Study in the Working of the Competitive Economy*, 2nd edn, Oxford: Clarendon Press.

Rosser, J.B. (1991), *From Catastrophe to Chaos: A General Theory of Economic Discontinuities*, Boston: Kluwer.

Rothwell, R. (1992), 'Successful industrial innovation: Critical factors for the 1990s', *R&D Management*, **22**, 221–39.

Shaw, B. (1994), 'User/supplier links and innovation' in M. Dodgson and R. Rothwell (eds), *The Handbook of Industrial Innovation*, Aldershot, UK and Brookfield, US: Edward Elgar.

Silverberg, G. and B. Verspagen (1995), 'Evolutionary Theorizing on Economic Growth' in K. Dopfer (ed.), *The Evolutionary Principles of Economics*, Norwell, MA: Kluwer Academic Publishers (available from URL: *http://meritbbs.rulimburg.nl/Fun/Bart/verspagen.html* as at March 1998).

Smith, K. (1998), 'Innovation as a systemic phenomenon: rethinking the role of policy' in K. Bryant and A. Wells (eds), *A New Economic Paradigm? Innovation-based Evolutionary Systems: Discussions of Science and Innovation 4*, Canberra: Department of Industry, Science and Resources (available from URL: *http://www.isr.gov.au/science/analysis*, as at July 2000).

von Hippel, E. (1988), *The Sources of Innovation*, London: Oxford University Press.

Index